Empire of Silver

Empire of Silver

Silver

A New Monetary History of China

JIN XU

（徐 瑾）

Translated by

STACY MOSHER

Yale UNIVERSITY PRESS/NEW HAVEN & LONDON

Yale University Press books may be purchased in quantity for
educational, business, or promotional use. For information,
please e-mail sales.press@yale.edu (U.S. office) or
sales@yaleup.co.uk (U.K. office).

Set in Minion type by IDS Infotech Ltd.
Printed in the United States of America.

Library of Congress Control Number: 2020942590
ISBN 978-0-300-25004-6 (hardcover : alk. paper)

A catalogue record for this book is available from the British
Library.

This paper meets the requirements of ANSI/NISO Z39.48–1992
(Permanence of Paper).

10 9 8 7 6 5 4 3 2 1

Money is people.
Ancient Greek proverb

Money has no smell.
English proverb

There is no subtler, no surer means of overturning the existing basis of society than to debauch the currency. The process engages all the hidden forces of economic law on the side of destruction, and it does it in a manner which not one man in a million is able to diagnose.
Macroeconomist John Maynard Keynes (1883–1946)

Monetary history is part of history in general, and one aim of studying it is to aid the understanding of history in general.
Chinese monetary historian Peng Xinwei (1908–1967)

I knew where I was going from the day I decided to become an economist. I set out to understand what made economies rich or poor because I viewed that objective as being the essential prerequisite to improving their performance . . . My objective as a graduate student was to find out what made economies work the way they did or fail to work. Economic history appeared to be the best field for that objective.
Douglass C. North (1920–2015), 1993 Nobel Laureate in economics

Contents

Empire of Silver

Introduction

The Curse of Silver

> How much better to acquire wisdom rather than gold, and to acquire
> understanding is more desirable than silver.
>
> *The Holy Bible, Proverbs 16:16*

> The nations with which economic historians are chiefly concerned organize
> their economic activities under the form of making and spending money . . .
> Cannot economic history be organized most effectively around
> the evolution of pecuniary institutions?
>
> *American economist Wesley C. Mitchell (1874–1948)*

"Silver, i.e. white gold." So says the second-century Chinese dictionary *An Explication of Written Characters*. Silver is a precious metal, second only to gold in value.

While the West is obsessed with gold, Chinese seem to have always been preoccupied with silver. Throughout Chinese history, from ancient times to the present, the love of silver seems to have deepened over time, and the arduous process of silver becoming China's base currency conceals the secret threads of China's momentous historical changes. Silver haunts China's remote antiquity. From an archaeological perspective, the Shang (Yin) dynasty (c. 1600–1000 B.C.E.) used silver, cowries, and other such materials: "The roads for trade with farmers and artisans were open, and tortoiseshell, cowries, gold, coins, knives and cloth were widely used as currency. These date as far back as the rule of Gaoxin Shi, before the Shang,[1] but no records survive. . . . The currency under Yu of Xia[2] included three metals, yellow, white and red, as well as coins, cloth, knives, tortoiseshell and cowrie."[3] Here "white" refers to silver. During the Spring and Autumn and Warring States periods,[4] silver already possessed some of the functions of currency, and various silver cowries and other currency from that time have been unearthed. Even so, prior to the Five Dynasties (907–960),[5] silver was mostly used for ornamentation and reward, and it did not serve as a major medium of exchange from the Qin to the Han dynasties: "Under Qin rule there were two grades of currency: gold as the higher currency, and bronze cash, of the same material as the Zhou currency, called the Banliang. Pearls, jade, tortoiseshell, cowrie, silver and tin were classified as instruments, decoration and treasure, not as currency."[6] Silver's course from "not currency" to monetization as legal tender has not been without complications.

During China's Warring States, Qin, and Han periods, gold and bronze cash were most widely used. The Six Dynasties (222–589) and Sui and Tang dynasties used both bronze coins and silk. During the Song, Jin, Yuan, and early Ming dynasties, paper currency called cash notes (qianchao) circulated. Only from the Five Dynasties onward did silver gradually become a medium of payment. From the Northern and Southern Song dynasties onward, silver came into common use along with bronze cash, and it was officially monetized in China in the mid- and late Ming dynasty. Over the next 500 years, up until the 1830s, China retained silver as its currency through wars large and small and countless catastrophes, with both tael silver and silver dollars in common use.

Compared with the monetary history of the West, China's monetary system displayed different characteristics from the outset. In ancient times, the West had a multitude of small kingdoms and international trade flourished. Although a king could designate a currency and its worth within his country, these stipulations could not be applied in the domains of other countries. From earliest times, coins minted from precious metal were locked in as acceptable materials of commerce in the international market. As early as the seventh century B.C.E., the kingdom of Lydia in Asia Minor began minting coins from an alloy of gold and silver (electrum) with set weights and denominated value (China did not begin minting silver coins until the last years of the Qing dynasty). This paved the way for the predominance of precious metal coins in the monetary history of the West.

In comparison, for most of the time before the mid-Ming dynasty, various base-metal coins (bronze, iron) constituted the main forms of Chinese currency, interspersed with some precocious legends of monetary history such as China's ultimately failed experiment with paper currency, which lasted more than 400 years, from the Northern Song to the early Ming dynasties. Looking back at China's monetary history, the overlap of inflation and deflation frequently lured the government into large-scale plunder of private wealth by issuing large-denomination currencies with no reserve value, or by minting inferior coins. Defying draconian laws and harsh bans, ordinary citizens fought back by boycotting bad money and privately minting currency. At the end of the day, even if the emperor was willing and needed to accept market testing, the fate of China's various currencies—from the bronze half-ouncer (*banliang*) and five-grainer (*wuzhu*) coins to the Kaiyuan coins and on to the Song dynasty's bronze and iron coins and paper currency—was basically inseparable from the rise and fall of dynasties.

Even after silver was monetized from the mid-Ming onward, silver was used as a metage (weighted) currency in China, and not in the minted form that had long been customary in the West. Before the Sui and Tang dynasties, tael (*liang*) silver in the form of ingots (*yinting* or *yinding*), silver cakes (*yinbing*), or tablets (*yinhu*) can be traced back to the Han dynasty. Ancient ingots (*ting*) were interchangeable with sycee (*ding*), and beginning with the Song dynasty they were typically called silver ingots or silver sycee, while sycee began being called *yuanbao* in the Yuan dynasty. It is said that in the third year of the Yuan dynasty (1266), the term *yuanbao*, meaning "Yuan dynasty treasure,"[7] was applied to silver cast into fifty-tael sycee at balancing standard (assay) bureaus (*pingzhunku*). At the outset, "*yuanbao*" appeared on bronze coins as well as on silver sycee, but eventually it became a generic term for silver sycee. Generally speaking, from the

Han to the Ming dynasty, silver sycee gradually developed from a round cake form into an elongated form, and then contracted in the middle for the *yuanbao* form.[8] In numismatic terms, this development made the currency more attractive, but in practical use it was an inconvenient and a retrograde step. As for the silver dollar, before China minted its own silver dollars (*yuan*), silver dollars predominantly came from overseas and were called foreign (*waiyang*) dollars.

Silver as a metage currency required not only inspection of its purity and quality, but also a multitude of exchange methods in different places, making it inconvenient to use. It was not until the Republican era that the silver dollar officially replaced the silver tael, and silver was able to circulate as China's standard currency. Furthermore, although China's monetary history has included a number of financial organs such as pawnshops, silver shops, and local private banks, it took a long time for China to develop a modern banking system. This was a major impediment to the expansion of China's credit system, and even to its transformation into a modern state.

A detailed study of China's monetary history shows that its shifting forms and systemic development are inseparable from specific historical changes, and that changes in currency correspond to the advance and retreat of dynasties. Silver is a continuous but concealed thread in history's dense fabric. Gaining a fresh understanding of China's monetary history and grasping the critical progress of silver in China's monetization require integrated study of economic history, political history, financial history, military history, and other disciplines, and a reexamination of Chinese history from a broader perspective. In other words, understanding currency additionally requires new clarity regarding the main arteries and veins of Chinese history.

For traditional Central Plains dynasties, defending imperial rule meant responding to challenges from within and outside of the country. External challenges are typically overlooked in traditional narratives, but in fact, ethnic minorities were not a transient presence in Chinese history. Over the centuries, nomadic peoples from the northern steppes were likely to cast covetous gazes southward at any juncture, and up to a million soldiers maintained combat readiness on either side of the Great Wall. Peace, whether won or temporary, put heavy demands on the military capacity and access to resources of the Central Plains dynasties. Even more crucially, the military forces that required such enormous material support tended to be more loyal to the generals who led them than to the remote imperial court, and emperors often had difficulty deciding between the loyalty and the combat readiness of their armies. This constituted a thorny domestic challenge.

Power is addictive, but how is it to be preserved? The empire's internal power struggles implied an impetus for systemic change. The Western Zhou dynasty (1045–771 B.C.E.) put faith in the power of bloodlines and clans and ruled the country under feudalism, but ended up united with the Qin and Han through annex warfare. From the Qin and Han through the Tang dynasties, imperial courts experimented with various ways of using military power to maintain control over the intransigent resistance of the local nobility and latent forces of rebellion among separatist warlords, their lamentable failure reaching a climax in the rebellion of An Lushan and Shi Siming.[9] Correspondingly, the military system oscillated between a conscription system (such as the local militia [*fubing*] system) and a mercenary system. The conscription method was simple and amazingly effective but hard to sustain without relying on the innate valor of the grasslands peoples, while the mercenary system entailed enormous expenditure and posed challenges in terms of maintaining the loyalty of the troops.

Under attack from without and within, the ability of dynasties to draw on resources was constantly tested. When a dynasty first came to power, the large amounts of unclaimed territory allowed smooth implementation of various kinds of land equalization systems, as well as various finance and taxation methods, mainly tax paid in kind. With the passage of time, however, the annexation of land and special privileges enjoyed by influential clans made it difficult for the imperial court to maintain its financial resources, necessitating various kinds of monetizing tax revenue reform plans. Reforms by Yang Yan, Wang Anshi, Zhang Juzheng, and Emperor Yongzheng emerged over the course of nearly 1,000 years. Their essence was the desire to sustain the imperial government through tax revenues.

Entering modern times, the erosive power of the global influx and outflow of silver had a profound effect on China's economy, and even its domestic affairs, from the fall of the Ming dynasty to the Opium Wars, as well as the numerous political battles, unrest, and economic crises that followed. Ironically, after the beleaguered Republic of China bade farewell to silver and entered the era of paper currency, it immediately fell into hyperinflation, replicating the paper currency episodes of the Southern Song centuries before and nearly wiping out a millennium of progress in Chinese currency in one fell stroke.

In the process of silverization, the Celestial Empire also experienced fading imperial glory, not only losing its leading ranking in GDP to the West, but even lagging behind its Asian neighbor, Japan. Back when silver was monetized in the late Ming and early Qing, many enlightened thinkers forcefully condemned silver's baneful influence. Huang Zongxi said, "Today silver alone is permitted to be used in paying taxes and in market transactions, and it has become the greatest evil in the land."[10] Wang Fuzhi likewise stated, "Hunger with nothing to eat, cold with nothing to wear, leading the nation to death, that is silver!" Blaming silver for regime change and the empire's sagging stature was not limited to the Ming; in the late Qing, Kang Youwei[11] also held, "Is it not ludicrous that an ancient nation with 5,000 years of civilization and 400 million people could perish merely because of silver declining and gold rising?" This interpretation remains part of the great debate over how China fell into backwardness.

Do silver and backwardness have an accidental and coincidental or a causal relationship? Was silver a root cause of China's backwardness? Sorting through the centuries-long history of silver, we see that the fate of silver accompanies an ancient empire's struggles and entanglements, and that behind silver's metamorphosis is not only dynastic change but the rise and fall of civilizations. Fastening our gaze on silver gives us a glimpse of China's path to modernization.

This book is divided into three parts. In the remainder of this Introduction, I will lay out the book's arguments and its observational framework. The five chapters that make up the main body of the book will focus on historical fact. Chapter 1 summarizes the divergent fate of silver in Asia and the West, Chapter 2 details the paper currency experiments of the Song and Yuan dynasties, Chapter 3 analyzes the Ming dynasty's silver standard and its interaction with globalization, Chapter 4 explores how the nominal silver standard devolved into chaos and collapse in the late Qing, and the final chapter is a monetary history of the Republic of China, beginning with silver and ending with its fiat currency (*fabi*). The final part of the book consists of an Afterword, a Chronology of monetary and financial events in the East and West, and other such material.

Before extensively using silver, Chinese largely used paper currency, an innovation that transcended the times.

Ancient Greek philosophy had a theory of "gold, silver, bronze, and iron": All human beings were born of earth and were meant to be brothers and sisters, but the gods mixed certain metals into their souls to create three types. The first type of human had gold mixed in, and therefore was the most precious and capable of ruling; the second had silver mixed in and comprised the auxiliaries or soldiers; and the last was bronze or iron, for farmers and other craftsmen.[12]

Myths are metaphors for reality. Corresponding to the gold, silver, and bronze ages in Western mythology, ancient China also had a formulation of gold, silver, and bronze (as well as using cloth, knives, tortoise shell, and cowries). The monetary history of the East and the West developed in different stages. In the West the stages can be roughly divided into the commodity standard, gold–silver bimetallism to the gold standard, and then the paper currency standard (perhaps we should add a new stage, the digital age that we are now welcoming in). The evolving forms of currency were meant to adapt to the economy's constant monetization. At the dawn of civilization, currency probably originated as gifts, then entered the commodity era, during which items from seashells to pepper served as currency, with gold and silver occupying an important position among them. East and West both experienced eras in which gold and silver were used along with various kinds of metal coins. In the eighteenth and nineteenth centuries, Europe gradually transitioned from gold–silver bimetallism to the gold standard, and with the development of the modern banking system and the flourishing of the bond market, the West ultimately transitioned to a paper currency standard in the twentieth century.

Paper currency can be considered the highest stage in humanity's development of currency and is not on the same plane as metal currency.

Successful paper currency, especially legal tender, relies on a credit agreement between the market and the state. In contrast, China's large-scale experiments with paper currency back in the Song, Yuan, and Ming dynasties, and the failures at that stage, constitute a crucial link in silver's ultimate triumph in China.

Before the Five Dynasties, silver was used in China mainly in the decorative arts and was seldom seen once gold became used as a medium of payment after the Han dynasty; the Tang dynasty monetary system used a combination of bronze coins and silk. By the Song dynasty, the use of silver migrated from upper-class society to the general populace and gradually took on the status of a medium of payment. References to silver became much more numerous in various literary sketches and commodity price records. Even more noteworthy is that China produced the world's first paper currency at that time. While gold–silver bimetallism was still in use during the Middle Ages in the West, China's experiment with paper currency began on a significant scale in the Northern Song.[13]

The Northern Song's *jiaozi* (exchange note) was issued as far back as the early eleventh century, during the first year of the Northern Song's Tiansheng era (1023), and circulated for nearly eighty years, emerging 600 or 700 years earlier than the first paper currency in Western countries. In retrospect, the Song dynasty can be considered truly distinctive. The emergence of paper currency in the Northern Song reflected the flourishing Song economy, arguably the historical zenith of the Chinese economy, during which it surpassed that of the West. On the other hand, the expense and financial pressure of that empire's expeditionary wars created the historical conditions for widespread use of paper currency. The first Song emperor, Zhao Kuangyin (917–975), rose to power amid the chaos of war in the Five Dynasties and Ten Kingdoms period (902–979) and established a civilian-controlled mercenary army of as many as 1.2 million soldiers at the outset of the dynasty. Frontier disturbances were constant during the Song, and the Liao and Jin kingdoms and Mongolia all had powerful armies that the Song confronted for hundreds of years. In order to sustain its enormous military expenses, the Song broke with common practice and vigorously developed a commodity economy, not only making it the leading economic power among

China's premodern dynasties, but also causing rapid advancement in the economy's monetization; currency in various forms made up 80 percent of its fiscal revenue (compared with no more than 20 percent during the most flourishing period of the Tang dynasty). Weighed down by its immense military outlay, however, the Song remained under tremendous financial pressure, and this also created the historical opportunity for paper currency. Unfortunately, because the paper currency first and foremost served the needs of the imperial court's wartime finance, as the military situation became critical, the currency collapsed under excessive issue.

At that time, it wasn't only the Song dynasty's *jiaozi, huizi* (account note), and other financial innovations that anticipated the world trend. The paper currency of the Song's longtime nemesis, the Jin dynasty, also achieved considerable success until Mongolia's armored cavalry emerged from the desert and swept across the land. Yet the story of paper currency doesn't end here. The subsequent Yuan and Ming dynasties followed in the Song's footsteps and magnified its abuses by issuing all kinds of paper money. This paper money gradually moved toward nonconvertibility, and some had the quality of fiat currency. As in the Song dynasty, excess issuance of this currency inevitably produced bad results.

With the rise of paper currency, silver initially had no legitimate status; at one point the Yuan dynasty restricted the use of silver, and the early Ming dynasty banned it. The ban failed to stem its use in private transactions, and as silver gradually became monetized, the Ming had no alternative but to lift the silver ban in its middle and late periods. In the first year of the Longqing era (1567) it stipulated, "For the purchase of goods valued at one silver coin or above, either silver or bronze coins can be used; for under one silver coin, only bronze coins can be used." Silver attained legal authorization as a currency, and during the Jiajing era, the government formally stipulated the exchange ratio between silver and bronze coins. The status of silver reached its height from then on and held it until the early 1930s.

When paper currency suffered defeat, silver was able to shine as a currency during the Ming dynasty. With the passage of time, the harshness of the early Ming Hongwu regime finally succumbed to the vitality of economic development, just as major geographical discoveries brought massive quantities of New World silver flowing into China and turned the Ming dynasty economy from stagnant ripples into a mighty torrent. The classical Chinese novel *The Golden Lotus* vividly describes the flourishing late Ming commodity economy, for which the inflow of foreign silver and its monetization were the most critical driving force.

The failed experiment with paper currency over three dynasties wrought silver's ultimate victory in China. For premodern empires, metal currency was hard to control, while bank notes were the most convenient form of currency; furthermore, the inadequate supply of precious metals in ancient times made economic problems a common occurrence. If paper currency had been issued in appropriate amounts, this would have benefited the government's finances and brought enormous dividends in boosting the economy. In other words, paper currency in itself can be considered an "upgrade" from metal currency to fiduciary currency, and if utilized properly can greatly benefit an economy, the typical case being the British pound sterling's decisive role in England's rise.

Under the dominance of China's war logic and imperial mindset, however, the innovation of paper currency didn't bring prosperity but rather excessive issue. During the Song, Yuan, and Ming dynasties, China attempted to skip the silver standard and proceed straight to the paper currency standard, but lack of restraint defeated the premature advent of paper currency. In competing with paper currency in the private sector, silver was better for preserving value against inflation and for hoarding, and most crucially, silver was a currency immune from being rashly plundered by those in power, since the imperial court had no way of "printing" silver. For this reason, silver became the market's natural choice. Under the latent but formidable power of market selection, the paper currency experiment, from the tragedy of the *huizi* in the Song dynasty to the failure of the *baochao* (treasure note) in the Great Ming, inevitably ended in failure.

China's paper currency was another cultural flower of ancient empire fated to bloom prematurely, all of the intelligence and shrewdness behind it self-destructing under lack of restraint and boundaries. Looking back at the 1,000-year story of silver, its competition had an enormous effect on paper currency, beginning with the *jiaozi*, which can be considered the prelude to the monetization of silver, and ending with the *fabi*, which marked the end result of silver's monetization.

How could a country with little silver production maintain a silver standard for 500 years? The answer lay in foreign silver.

China was a silver-deficient country. A glimpse of the amount of silver it produced can be gained from records of silver revenues (that is, silver tax) in the *Ming Shilu* (official history of the Ming dynasty). In terms of average annual silver revenues, the period from the twenty-third to the twenty-sixth year of the Hongwu period produced the least, an average of 25,070 taels per year, or a total of 75,070 taels for all three years. After that it leaped to more than 200,000 taels, but then dropped again. In terms of total revenue, in the 130 years from the twenty-third year of the Hongwu period to the fifteenth year of the Zhengde period, the total was more than 1.13 million taels.[14] This means that silver tax revenues during the Ming dynasty averaged 100,000 taels per year. The silver tax rates on silver production in the Ming dynasty were higher than in the Song and Yuan dynasties, and also higher than in Spain at that time (it is generally believed that Spain's gold tax was 1/20, and its silver tax was 1/10). The Ming dynasty silver tax is generally believed to have been around 30 percent of the silver production quota.[15] Calculated in this way, Ming dynasty silver production was not very high, averaging a little more than 300,000 taels per year (see Table 0-1).

This meager silver production was naturally unequal to the historic task of the Ming dynasty's economic monetization. In fact, this burden was mainly borne by the large-scale influx of foreign silver. Foreign silver mainly came from two sources. Traditionally it was Japanese silver; silver frequently appears among articles of tribute to the imperial court during the Tang dynasty, and it was also common for various kinds of coins to be among the items taken back to Japan. Even more significant was silver from the American continents, which entered China through various trade channels. The process of China's transition to a silver economy was inextricably tied to the first globalization initiated by major geographical discoveries.

The sixteenth century was a watershed. After Christopher Columbus drew European attention to the New World in 1492, an American

Table 0-1. Average Silver Tax or Silver and Gold Tax per
Year in the Ming Dynasty

Reign period	Average silver or silver and gold tax (taels)
Taizu (1390–1393)	25,070 (+)
Chengzu (1402–1423)	224,313 (+)
Renzong (1424–1425)	106,432
Xuanzong (1426–1434)	256,450 (+)
Yingzong (1435–1463)	46,541 (+)
Xianzong (1464–1486)	61,913 (+)
Xiaozong (1487–1504)	54,628 (+) (gold and silver)
Wuzong (1505–1520)	32,920 (gold and silver)

Source: Quan Hansheng, 1966, "The Ming Dynasty's Silver Classifications and Silver Production Quotas"

Indian named Diego Gualpa discovered an enormous silver deposit in the Andes uplands in 1545. This silver mountain, called Cerro Rico (Hill of Riches) by the delighted Spaniards, became a symbolic event in the exploration of the Americas. With the discovery of the mercury needed to refine silver in Peru in 1563, New World silver mining burgeoned. Financial historian Charles Kindleberger calculated that at its peak, production of silver in all of the Americas reached 300 tons a year.[16]

New World silver mines satisfied the European mania for precious metals. Europeans had initially gone to the New World in search of gold; in Engels's words, "*Gold* was the magic word that drove the Spanish across the Atlantic Ocean to America; *gold* was the first thing the white man asked about when he set foot on newly discovered soil."[17] With the discovery of the Potosi silver mine in Peru, silver became an object of even greater interest than gold in the West from 1560 onward. In Asia, this coincided with the Ming dynasty's desperate thirst for silver, as a result of which American silver poured into China and took on a new role in the histories of Asia and the West.

Arbitrage between the gold–silver exchange ratios in China and Europe was a major impetus in the great transcontinental flow of silver. China's gold–silver exchange ratio was always higher than Europe's; in the early years it was 1:3 or even lower, and in the early Ming it was around 1:6 to 1:5, and then 1:8 to 1:7; right up until the Qing dynasty it was still higher than in Europe. In the Middle Ages in Europe the ratio was generally 1:14 to 1:10 or even higher (according to the figures of American economic historian Earl Hamilton in 1934, from 1643 to 1650 the gold–silver exchange ratio was 1:15.45).[18] American gold and silver mines were a major driver of change in worldwide precious metal prices. The sixteenth-century discoveries caused European gold and silver prices to plunge to nearly one-third of their original levels, and the relative value of silver to gold dropped even further.[19] Adam Smith, living in the eighteenth century, observed that prior to the discovery of American gold and silver mines, European mints stipulated an exchange ratio between pure gold and pure silver of 1:12 to 1:10, but then in the seventeenth century it became 1:15 to 1:14. The reason was that although gold and silver mines were discovered in the Americas at almost the same time, the silver mines were even richer than the gold mines. In comparison, the ratio in China was 1:10 or 1:12, and in Japan it was 1:8. The large-scale production of silver in the Americas led to an even greater discrepancy between the gold–silver exchange ratios in Asia and the West, while also inevitably creating immense room for international arbitrage in precious metals.

The major geographical discoveries ignited a surge of globalization. The Philippine archipelago became a transfer station for American silver to enter Asia, and what linked everything together was trade. In the words of Chinese economic historian Yan Zhongping, "Silk flowed into the Philippines and silver flowed into China."[20] Apart from silk, other Chinese textiles were also very popular; Chinese cotton had already elbowed out Spanish cotton in the Mexican market by the end of the sixteenth century. Scholar Quan Hansheng calculates that between 1565 and 1765, silver with a total value of 200 million pesos was shipped from the Americas to the Philippines. (The peso was a monetary unit widely used in the former Spanish colonies, generally believed to have converted into Chinese treasury [*kuping*] silver at a rate of 0.72 treasury ounces [taels].) According to scholar De Comyn's calculation,[21] between 1571 and 1821, silver with a total value of 400,000 pesos was shipped from the Americas to Manila, of which one-fourth to one-half flowed into China. Quan Hansheng, however, holds that the exchange ratio was higher than 1:2, and, adding in the 400 million dollars brought to Guangzhou by trade with European countries, he estimates that about 600 million dollars' worth of American silver was imported to China between 1700 and 1830, converting to approximately 430 million taels.[22]

The German-born economist Andre Gunder Frank's research on silver has attracted considerable notice in the public sphere. His theoretical system couples Asia's status at that time with its ability to absorb silver. His estimates of silver inflow, higher than those of Quan Hansheng and other experts, are quite controversial. He holds that from 1493 to 1800, 85 percent of the world's silver and 70 percent of its gold came from the Americas.[23] More than 80 percent of the silver was shipped to Europe, and Europe shipped 40 percent of that amount to Asia; 20 percent of the silver remaining in the Americas was also shipped to Asia.[24] The conclusion is that worldwide silver production totaled 120,000 tons starting in 1600 (or 137,000 tons starting in 1545), and half of that production went to Asia. During this time a total of 60,000 tons was imported to China, or approximately 1.920 billion taels.[25] This figure is quite possibly too high, but it indicates the enormous intake of silver in the Ming dynasty.

Even if the amount of silver stock from China's previous dynasties is added in, the amount of imported foreign silver is still much greater than the domestic stock during the same period. Scholar Liu Guanglin believes that the Song dynasty's silver stock did not exceed 150 million taels, and under the influence of the Yuan dynasty's ban on the circulation of silver, as well as loss to Central Asian countries, hoarding, burial with the dead, and other factors, the amount of silver left behind from previous dynasties during the Ming dynasty was no more than 30 million taels. Adding in the Ming dynasty's silver production of 20 million taels, the total amount of silver stock in the early sixteenth-century Ming dynasty was 50–60 million taels, while from the mid-sixteenth century onward, the amount of imported foreign silver was around 200 million taels. There are fairly large discrepancies among these various calculations. The

American scholar Richard von Glahn estimates 192–197 million taels; Chinese scholar Wu Chengming estimates 86–111 million taels; while Kamiki Tetsuo, Yamamura Kozo, and others estimate 232–289 million taels, around four times the amount of local silver stores.[26] In spite of inconsistencies among the figures calculated by various scholars, the indisputable consensus is that China became the world's "hoarder" of silver from the Ming and Qing dynasties onward. Here I should emphasize that there has been a great deal of research on silver in the Ming and Qing dynasties, and the objective of many scholars is to provide benchmarks that can be passed down as a frame of reference in this sphere. My ambitions are focused elsewhere, however; I simply hope to provide different perspectives for readers' reference, but also, through the sorting and analysis of fragmentary historical facts, to present a more coherent logic of money. Apart from similarities and differences in silver data, we should look at larger patterns, that is, the logical derivatives and historical contexts beyond the figures.

Economic calculations from antiquity are not easy; even the GDP calculations of a heavyweight economist such as Angus Maddison, although considered the most authoritative, are still very controversial. Chinese silver in particular involves not only various units of measurement but also scattered and singular source material. For this reason, readers should be skeptical of the various data on silver imports and exports and focus more on changing trends. As Harvard historian and economist David S. Landes has said, in speculative calculations, "the numbers deserve credence only if they accord with their historical context," and "the leverage of even a small mistake extended over two hundred years is enormous."[27] I've always maintained that economics should ideally be a combination of data, logic, and history, and that economic historical research should, under the premise of understanding the context of the data, always allow for doubt.

The inflow of silver not only nullified the energetic efforts of dynasties from the Yuan onward to ban silver, but also caused the Chinese economy to more rapidly monetize and inadvertently join in the mix of globalization. The difference is that Europe's Age of Discovery increased the impetus for Europe to embark on its Industrial Revolution, and from then on its main economic entities adopted the gold standard and even began using paper currency. The Asian empires, however, quietly held fast to silver and became entangled in outflows or inadequate inflows of silver.

After the Ming dynasty, as China entered the Qing dynasty, the inflow of silver continued as before. The Qing dynasty monetary system basically continued the Ming's system of "using silver for large sums and copper cash for small sums." Lessons from the paper currency of the previous dynasty led the Qing to avoid similar experiments. Silver linked China's economy to the world even more during the Ming and Qing dynasties. As foreign silver became ingrained in the Chinese economy, the Chinese government was no longer able to control its flow rate, and this had a significant impact right into the Republican era. In the 1930s, someone asserted, "The price of silver was the core issue of China's modern financial economy."[28] In the most classic example, before the Opium Wars broke out, the "silver leakage" caused by opium became the main topic of memorials submitted to the Daoguang Emperor by his top ministers. In this book I've especially featured the research of Taiwanese scholar Lin Man-houng, which shows that the outflow of silver did not reach its peak during the Opium Wars, as most people think. From the altitude of history we can see that the essential focal point of the Opium Wars was not a silver war, but a trade war against the backdrop of unavoidable conflict and collision between two civilizations.

Apart from politics, the Chinese economy was also disrupted by foreign silver. When silver inflow increased, the monetization of China's economy gained traction, as evidenced in the novel *The Golden Lotus,* in which everyone is engaged in commerce, as well as in the rich landscape of southern China in the Qing dynasty. Exports increased, people lived and worked in peace and contentment, silver was increasingly traded in the marketplace, and the economy flourished. When the inflow of silver decreased, China suffered severe deflation, exports decreased, people became conservative, silver began to be withdrawn from circulation, silver hoarding increased, the fiscal administration became increasingly atrophied, and ultimately even war and rebellion resulted. This transpired in both the late Ming and the late Qing. During flourishing times, silver was the icing on the cake, but in times of decline, silver became the last straw.

As currency and financial expert Frederic S. Mishkin has said, the financial system is the brain of the economy.[29] The endless flow of silver was the white blood of China's economy, and changes to its dynamics affected the nerve center of the Chinese economy, creating overstimulation, convulsions, and even disorders. Even when in possession of substantial amounts of silver, empires still declined. In other words, silver was very important, but possessing silver was not the same as prosperity, and in fact the inflow of silver could be seen as the result rather than the cause of the monetization of China's economy. The inflow and outflow of silver drove periodic convulsions in the Chinese economy, but the core factor that determined the success or failure of an empire was, as always, the intrinsic flaws of the imperial system. Did the inflow of silver decide the fate of empires, or did the direction of the empire influence the flow of silver? Actual history is the result of countless individual interactions, including that between the fate of silver and the rise and fall of empires.

The Opium Wars hastened China's modernization, but the late-arriving modern financial intermediaries had difficulty advancing amid competition with overseas rivals. Although silver emerged triumphant in the market's spontaneous choice, China's monetary system was in fact always in a passive state; for many years, the empire's most critical fiscal and taxation power fell to customs, and an effective monetary system was not established even in the Republican era.

When overseas study in Japan was a popular trend in the early twentieth century, a twenty-six-year-old Chinese student completed his studies in economics in Kyoto and went to say goodbye to his teachers before leaving. One of the Japanese teachers told him: "The name China can only be considered a geographical name, not a country. The Beijing government's decrees do not apply beyond the capital, and the provinces and regions are fighting among each other, each doing things their own way and each issuing bank notes and minting bronze coins. Which region are you planning to go to now? I think that if you go back, you may have no way out."

Standing at the same point in time, the two people's experience and perspectives were different, so their views toward China were naturally different. This student was offended by his teacher's remark, and he later recalled losing his temper. He returned to China without hesitation and subsequently became a leading authority in the Chinese banking world.

This man was Zi Yaohua, who personally witnessed silver's gradual withdrawal from the Republic's currency system. His Japanese teacher can also not be written off; he was the prominent sinologist Naitō Toro-jiro (a.k.a. Naitō Konan), the first person to propose the "theory of Tang-Song transition."[30] Naitō Konan's observations at that time were in fact quite accurate; the monetary chaos explained the torpor of China's political economy, a situation that could be traced back to the Ming and Qing eras, or even earlier.

After the Ming and Qing dynasties, China had a nominal silver standard, but it was highly problematic. Silver had never been coined, and in practice, uncoined silver, silver fragments, and silver dollars were used simultaneously. Added to that, given differences in weight and purity standards, conversion rates included not only "physical silver taels" of varying weights and purity, but also "virtual silver taels" that differed in value according to region and use—more than 100 types in all.

The varied measurement units for silver created unprecedented chaos in China's monetary system, and the chaotic monetary system in turn resulted in an atrophied and backward economy and financial system. Coupled with a frail and divided nation, the use of silver became a symbol of backwardness and was even considered a kind of "white curse." Even now, many observers still emphasize that China's use of silver and loss of sovereignty over its currency are what led to its lagging behind in the Great Divergence between East and West during the Ming and Qing dynasties. If we accept, according to this viewpoint, that the fall of the Great Ming Empire was caused in part by the rebellion of Li Zicheng, and that this was related to the reduced inflow of foreign silver, and also that changes in the inflow of silver triggered economic crises and even war in the late Qing and Republican eras, rather than pursuing the question of whether or not silver should have been used, we should focus on why China used silver. Why did the system behind silver never change? Why did the European continent, which also used silver for a long time, not replicate China's disastrous policies, but instead gradually nurture a modern paper currency and banking system?

Silver continued to circulate in China as late as the Republican era. The Beiyang government was weak and grossly incompetent apart from Yuan Shikai's small contribution to unifying the currency system, and even then there were many instances of excessive issue of currency, as during the "Beijing bank note panic." During the Beiyang era, central authority declined, but the power of the private sector burgeoned. China's new-style banks began to rise, and a modern financial system materialized out of nowhere. After the Republic of China's government was established, centralized power increased, and China was finally able to eliminate the tael and convert to the dollar. The Kuomintang (Nationalist) government originally planned a transition from the silver standard to the gold standard, but because of the worldwide economic crisis and the United States' Silver Purchase Act, China once again "upgraded" by skipping over the gold standard and going directly into the legal tender (*fabi*) stage. Legal tender notes were meant to be an upgrade to China's currency system and an achievement in unifying the currency, but under conditions of domestic turmoil and foreign invasion, finance was once again reduced to an appendage of politics, with undesirable results. The excessive issuance of *fabi* could not be contained, and the excessive issue of the *jinyuanquan* (gold dollar certificates) that replaced the legal tender notes was absolutely unprecedented. Consequently, paper currency was responsible for the worst case of runaway inflation in modern Chinese history, the severity of which exceeded all expectations. As in the past, this experiment with paper currency led to the fall of a government. And after paper currency was abandoned, silver was quietly resurrected in private circulation.

The chess game between silver and paper currency was in fact a trial of strength between conservatism and greed. This chess game can have different results if played with checks and balances on power, and in this sense, paper currency was a systemic bonus that eluded China's grasp. The British pound sterling was issued only after the Bank of England was established in 1694, a good 600 to 700 years after China's *jiaozi*. The pound was originally a bank note of the Bank of England, which was only a private bank when it was first established. Even so, after the pound came into being, it maintained a stable value for more than 200 years. The British pound's strength established a powerful foundation for England to vault from being a country on the frontier of Europe to an empire on which the sun never set.

In my book *The Money Printers*, I explore the success of the British pound, and at the same time ponder China's failure with the *fabi* and *jinyuanjuan*. Comparing the currency systems of the two countries can be seen as a comparison of positive and negative feedback. China's paper currency cycle was often the prelude to the dynastic cycle. Increasing military spending resulted in financial deficit, and financial deficit led to the immoderate printing of currency. Under hyperinflation, good money continued to exist, while bad money collapsed, and the Republic even reverted to metal money and a barter economy. During the legal-tender reforms of the 1930s, the government ordered silver withdrawn from circulation, but with the failure of the *fabi* and routing of the *jinyuanjuan*, silver in fact never really left the Republic's economic life.

In theory, the central bank should be the crucial and ultimate defense against inflation. In ancient times there was no independent central bank or restraints on the government, so experiments with paper currency were doomed to fail. Although a central bank emerged in the Republican era, it did not in fact meet the qualifications of a central bank in the modern sense, but was only a countinghouse cashier controlled by the government. Not surprisingly, the Chinese economic historian Du Xuncheng refers to it as "a freak of nature."

The great flaw of Chinese politics is in the malpractice of personal rule in which China has been tangled for millennia. The Japanese-American political scientist Francis Fukuyama in recent years constructed a theory that orderly societies require a combination of three factors: the state, the rule of law, and accountable government, in a stable balance.[31] This apparently simple "political sandwich" is not easy to attain, however, and the Republican government, facing division within and the circling of antagonistic powers without, was ultimately unable to extricate itself from printing currency.

To sum up Fukuyama's theory, China has always had to face the problem of bad emperors. This implies that China's top-down power structure is in fact very hard to effectively restrain, in the financial sphere as well. The financial system typically developed because of the financial needs of the state, which determined the short stave of the financial system. This was even more the case with currency; experiments with paper currency were a chess game between the government and the market. Finance is essentially trust, and precisely because of that, metal currency has incomparable advantages for the general populace in an autocratic era, while experiments with paper currency can only succeed in political systems that can constrain government greed. This method continues to arise in modern times but remains imperfect.

In the 1,000-year struggle between silver and paper currency, from the time that paper currency was invented in the eleventh century until the end of the *jinyuanjuan* reforms that took over from physical gold and silver in the twentieth century, silver's victory was the government's defeat, and silver's defeat was also the government's defeat—it was human greed, and even more a major systemic failure.

Finance and taxation occupy an intermediate zone between currency and imperial power. From ancient times to the present, taxation has been a crucial force in historical change. The strong have the power to collect taxes from the weak, and the weak use their payment of taxes as a counter in their chess game with the powerful. In other words, tax revenue is the main gaming platform for political power and economic power, and attitudes toward and engagement with taxation constitute the principal content of relations between the state and the market; finance is the offspring of this interaction. In tandem with China's economic development and monetization, China's tax system evolved from payment in kind to payment in currency. The use of silver to pay the equivalent value of grain tax emerged in the Tang dynasty and became mainstream practice from the mid-Ming onward, at around the same time that paper currency was receding from use.

In the Song, Jin, Yuan, and Ming dynasties, it was financial predicaments that led empires to repeatedly resort to the excessive issuance of paper currency. Finance and taxation form the basis of an empire's operations, and the income of Chinese empires always relied primarily on agriculture. Under these circumstances, the attitude toward commerce was basically one of constraint, as the government was unable to depart from traditional patterns of fiscal administration. Per capita income also sank into a low-level equilibrium, and, adding in the inefficiency of the

taxation system, this further consolidated the empire's organizational ossification. By way of contrast, European royal courts traditionally drew
their revenue from land leases, judicial fees and fines, and so on, and as
the countries of Western Europe increasingly moved toward mercantilism during the Age of Discovery, customs duty and other taxes and levies
became increasingly important, constituting more than half of the royal
family's income in England. While relying on merchants to obtain financial revenue, regents transferred their governing power, and ultimately
constitutional government and fiscal administration brought about systemic leaps.

The crux of the straitened circumstances of Chinese imperial taxation was the limited ability to collect taxes. After the Tang dynasty, the
prime minister's power shrank, and the office of prime minister didn't
even exist after the Ming dynasty. The tradition of the emperor needing
to consult with the prime minister no longer existed, which meant that
monarchical power was concentrated to an unprecedented degree, accompanied by a decline in managerial efficiency. Centralized imperial
authority meant that the emperor had to decide on all matters, great and
small, and while the public finance system looked solid, it was actually
very inefficient.[32] The public finance sphere lacked a professional organizational agent; the minister of works was ostensibly in charge of fiscal
administration but in reality functioned only as an accountant, and it
was hard for him to do anything without the emperor's support. Under
most circumstances, therefore, from the Yuan, Ming, and Qing, and even
into the Republican era, the government's financial resources were only
at sustenance levels, and deficit spending occurred with every natural
disaster or war. Government decline routinely led to the excessive issue
of currency, which would ultimately collapse, while silver continued to
circulate among the general populace, and the more the government issued currency, the more the currency declined, until it finally died out;
this can be considered the Chinese-style currency printing cycle.

Taking the watershed era of the Ming and Qing Empires as an example, the two empires can generally be seen as a single unit in terms of
the nature of their systems. During the Ming and Qing, China was severely tested by nomadic peoples; the empire began moving toward in-
troversion, and the power structure became even more despotic, revolving

around the emperor. With the elimination of the position of prime minister, the relationship between sovereign and subjects became even more hierarchical, and the civil official clique united in resistance against the rise of imperial authority. The Qing Empire, although ruled by an external ethnic group, relied on the Ming dynasty's system sustained by generations of capable emperors, with the result that the Qing Empire resembled a fortified version of the Ming. Yet, as Chinese-American historian Ray Huang has said, compared with the volatile character of the Second Empire, composed of the Sui, Tang, and Song, the Third Empire, composed of the Ming and Qing, was immobile.[33] The empire's systemic involution led to organizational ossification that prevented it from changing along with world trends. When the West embarked on the Industrial Revolution, the Ming and Qing Empires contented themselves with the continued inflow of American silver and did not make any substantial amendments to the imperial system.

Ming and Qing taxation was not as harsh as might be imagined, maintaining a rate of around 10 percent. The Chinese government is thought of as a traditional "night watchman" government; apart from the traditional thinking of not seeking gain at the people's expense, an even more important reason is the fettering of the empire's capacities. China's traditional government can be considered "small government," epitomized by the late Qing, when the population swelled, but this kind of "small government" actually originates from weak fiscal administration. On the one hand, financial and taxation capacity is limited, and on the other hand, the government is also limited in the amount of public services it can shoulder. Limited public services coupled with the monopolization of power make improvement of the finance and taxation system even more difficult. The resulting excessively cumbersome system has the sole objective of sustaining dictatorship. Feeble fiscal administration made the government redundant and inefficient, its administrative proficiency lower than that of its foreign counterparts. Consequently, in an era of competition between nations, China naturally came in last.

It is worth mentioning that the Ming and Qing taxation system was unique in that its formal tax revenue was set to maintain the total budget of the fiscal administration at the outset of each reign. This led to fiscal arrangements that typically combined formal taxes with hidden fees. On the one hand, the imperial government's tax-levying capacity was low, and the abundance of silver resulted in a decrease in silver's purchasing power, which in turn caused steady shrinkage of the purchasing power of nominal tax revenue; on the other hand, China's centralized system was never able to overcome the problem of much of the population being beyond the reach of the government. Since local fiscal administration was weak, when the government's formal revenue quotas could not satisfy demand, all kinds of levies would emerge.

The strength or weakness of fiscal administration affected the imperial political system, and invisible taxation became a shadow of nominal finance. As the sundry levies added to nominal taxes continued to grow, the empire's corruption steadily worsened, creating a new cycle. To confront this model, the central government attempted to use a "Single Whip tax system"—supplementary salaries and other methods to channel various covert finances into the formal fiscal system—but new taxation items cropped up again and again, and the empire was never able to escape the "Huang Zongxi rule."[34] It is because of this that the Japanese scholar Iwai Shigeki describes the Ming and Qing fiscal mechanism as "original-amount fiscalism," that is, repeatedly enlarging the scope of assessed finance but without eradicating or even reducing covert finance, ultimately forcing the empire into financial crisis and eventual decline.[35] The root causes of the cycle of disorderly fiscal administration leading to political chaos were, first, the lack of effective bottom-up supervision, and second, the failure to get to the bottom of corruption—or, using the language of economics, incentive incompatibility. This shows that the emperor or the empirical system proxy was ostensibly battling corrupt officials, but in fact it was a quixotic struggle, that is, resistance against powerful systemic inertia.

Comparatively speaking, various European countries had different routes to success or failure in modern finance and taxation. Modern England got a relatively late start and was unable to obtain American silver, but by selling off its rights and interests, Great Britain gained the support of merchants, which led to England's taxation rates being higher than the Ming dynasty's over the long term, and also higher than those of continental European countries at that time. One previous viewpoint held that the West developed by plundering other countries, but in fact colonial empires also had different pedigrees: Spain's immense colonies gave it access to gold and silver, but while Great Britain, France, and Holland obtained very few precious metal resources from their colonies, their subsequent development was better than Spain's. These countries initially also hoped to discover gold and silver in their colonies, and explorers promised to pay one-fifth of any gold and silver to the monarch in exchange for permission for their voyages. Adam Smith early on noticed that the North American colonies were developing better than other places, and he also observed, "The colony of a civilised nation which takes possession either of a waste country, or of one so thinly inhabited that the natives easily give place to the new settlers, advances more rapidly to wealth and greatness than any other human society." The colonizers bring with them "the habit of subordination, some notion of the regular government which takes place in their own country, of the system of laws which support it, and of a regular administration of justice."[36]

The conclusion of these historical observations has more recently been verified by granular economic research. Research by economists Daron Acemoglu and James A. Robinson finds that as the British government began expanding its scope from 1688 onward, its outlay rapidly reached around 10 percent of national revenue. This expansion originated from the support of tax revenue.[37] This phase was also the era when England's power increased, and the reason was the establishment of Parliament, which controlled the king's power to levy taxes; once Parliament was able to control the government, the king repeatedly delegated power, and this made the British government great and powerful. The British government was able to take on more services, giving England an advantage in competition, and establishing a foundation for its overseas voyages and world domination.[38] As for the Spanish government, although it possessed enormous amounts of silver, its inability to establish a state system like England's doomed it to economic stagnation and government bankruptcy.

Finance's influence on history is enormous, far-reaching, and profound, yet finance alone is not enough, and currency is merely one kind of power; what matters is how other powers, such as imperial power and government power, are demarcated, managed, and tamed. Historian Niall Ferguson has concluded that England's success is inseparable from finance, and this success is founded on systemic checks and balances, that is, a "square of power" consisting of a tax-gathering bureaucracy, a central bank, a national debt market, and a parliamentary institution.[39] In my book *The Money Printers,* I borrow the research framework of Ferguson, Douglass North, and others to expound in detail on the relationship of mutual promotion and constraint between England's rise and the financial system of the Bank of England.[40]

A superficial observation comparing the Chinese and Western financial systems easily identifies one missing link from China's financial history: The Chinese government didn't have the ability to take on debt, so there was no way for a bond market to emerge and for its corresponding system to be constructed. But this viewpoint is not without its limitations; from the late Qing onward, China in fact attempted various forms of domestic and foreign debt. The Qing dynasty's fiscal administration is generally acknowledged to have had absolutely no problem sustaining a balanced budget before the Xianfeng period (1851–1861), but once the Taiping Rebellion and other wars broke out, financial pressures increased exponentially, and the government was compelled to draw support from its duty on provincial transit. As hostilities increased, foreign powers came swarming in, bringing with them a new financial tool—government bonds.

As early as 1867, under the rationale of "urgent military payroll demands," the westward march of the Chinese army under the late Qing statesman Zuo Zongtang (General Tso) was financed by taking on external debt, using customs duty receipts as collateral. The Hangzhou merchant Hu Xueyan acted as intermediary to borrow 1.2 million taels of silver from foreign merchants in Shanghai, establishing a precedent for Zuo Zongtang himself to take on foreign debt six times. This is considered one of the original instances of the Chinese government taking on foreign debt (another version states that foreign debt originated in the fourth year of the Tongzhi period [1866]). From 1894 onward, foreign debt increasingly became the main blood transfusion machine for the financially hard-pressed Great Qing Empire, and quite a lot of funding for the Westernization Movement[41] also came from foreign debt.

From 1900 onward, the amount of money to be repaid every year also redoubled to upwards of 40 million taels.

This burgeoning debt relationship was rooted in dual fiscal and military failure, which reduced China's financial resources, and even its territory, to collateral without bringing any fundamental change to China's financial system. In terms of financial institutions, those with the most plentiful and stable profits were mainly distributed among the foreign banks; the foreign bank buildings that rose one after another in Hong Kong and along the Shanghai Bund are crystallizations of this segment of history. The sphere of influence of foreign banks in China was often decided by their sovereign states, the classic case being the British-owned Hongkong and Shanghai Banking Corporation (HSBC). According to Yang Duanliu's *Historical Sketch of Qing Dynasty Currency and Finance,* the Qing government borrowed money nine times from foreign governments from 1895 to 1911; HSBC alone shouldered these loans three times, on two occasions cooperating with the Deutsch-Asiatische Bank, and the other loans were also carried out with the cooperation of multinational banks.

As to China's domestic commercial institutions, they were basically unable to compete with their foreign counterparts in terms of funding power or entry thresholds, and when domestic banks finally had the opportunity to take part in issuing bonds, they still faced the possibility of the government reneging on its debt without having the power to indirectly control or even directly extort repayment. All of this can be glimpsed in Hu Xueyan's ultimate bankruptcy and the collapse of the Republic's government bonds, not to mention how the Bank of China was subsequently forced to increase its government-owned shareholdings.

Essentially, national debt is a derivative financial product under capitalist logic (Marx said that public debt is one of the most powerful levers of primitive accumulation).[42] As Engels said, in order to maintain public power, the state needs citizens to pay tax: "With advancing civilization, even taxes are not sufficient; the state draws drafts on the future, contracts loans, state debts."[43] Under commercial civilization, the parties involved in both borrowing and lending need to have corresponding restraints. Compared with British historian Niall Ferguson's "square of power," China did not in fact lack the motivation or even the ability to take on debt, but it always lacked a parliament to restrain the emperor—that was the case even after it launched a modern financial market.

The kind of mechanism that emerged in Great Britain has its unique, or at least very rare, qualities. This kind of mechanism soon spread throughout the world, and Britain's political system spread with it. The Chinese Empire had neither a competent tax-collecting system nor a powerful parliament restraining imperial authority; what it had was an unwieldy government and a cowed populace. As a result, many exploratory government bonds were reduced to disguised distribution.

This shows that technological change did occur in China, whether in the form of the Northern Song paper currency or the financed government bonds from the late Qing onward; their ultimate failure makes it clear that under the old power rules before the social system completed its transition to modernity, it was difficult to fundamentally change the fate of finance in service to politics, and self-defeat was ultimately also hard to avoid. Any innovation that is beneficial to society intrinsically depends on a benign overall systemic structure, but the financial innovations that occurred in Chinese history, the so-called late Ming sprouts of capitalism, were breakthroughs prioritized only in some regions or departments, and there was no way to smash what French historian Fernand Braudel calls "history's bell jar."[44] This inertia in government and business remained just as formidable in the Republican era, and continued even today: The abilities of capital and entrepreneurs were limited to a very small area, the benefits of systemic rent-seeking exceeding the benefits of technical innovation, and private capital, ever at a disadvantage vis-à-vis the state, could never be marshaled into a powerful epochal current.

Comparing the routes of historical development in China and the West, it is the lack of fetters on centralized power that made well-intentioned systemic designs become counterproductive. In terms of the Chinese and Western fiscal systems, many scholars emphasize that China's traditional early finance and taxation differentiated between the imperial court's fiscal administration (internal) and the state's fiscal administration (external). This was once regarded as China's advantage, but in practice it was probably not optimal.

The difference between internal fiscal administration in the East and West is no less than the difference between the Chinese and Western feudal systems. China's pre-Qin era originally also had feudal lords, but after the Qin and Han, feudal lords lost their ruling power, and China gradually moved from a feudalism with nobility, property, and heredity to a feudalism lacking fiefdom and heredity; land was gradually separated from its associated powers, and fiscal power also gradually became concentrated under the management of the central government. This also required clarifying the sources and uses of the fiscal system. In Chinese history, the eras during which internal and external fiscal administration were clearly distinguished were the Qin and Han, especially the Han. During this time the minister of revenue managed the state's fiscal administration,[45] and the main income came from land tax, corvee, and so on; while the minister steward (*shaofu*) managed the imperial family's finances, of which the main income came from mining royalties, tribute, and so on. This differentiation gradually blurred after the Han dynasty, and became obscure by the Tang and Song dynasties. But there were also situations when the imperial treasury supplemented the state treasury; the first Song emperor once stated that the imperial treasury was for emergencies and not for personal enjoyment: "It is necessary to prepare for military actions and famines and not react on the spur of the moment. Therefore this treasury is in place." The second Song emperor, Taizong, installed a state treasury to store the tribute and taxes from the prefectures. He told his ministers that he was concerned that the officials in charge of these assets might not handle them properly, and that they might be wasted, which would put pressure on the people. For this reason, the emperor did not treat the tribute and taxes from the people as personal property to use as he pleased.[46]

While the Song dynasty imperial treasury had a tradition of replenishing the state treasury, its existence was an implicit allocation to the state coffers, and even increased the centralization of the Song dynasty's fiscal administration. The Song dynasty's imperial treasury gradually became dominated by the imperial court, and the three ministers originally empowered with keeping track of the palace treasury gradually lost their power to be informed, while the emperor became more directly involved in allocating and encroaching on property rights. The difference between internal and external was even more pro forma by the Ming dynasty; the Board of Revenue had no power to intervene, and quite a few emperors even drew from the state coffers to replenish the imperial household's storehouse. The relationship between the internal treasury and the Board of Revenue became even more blended during the Qing dynasty, and the expansion of imperial power caused the internal treasury to grow exponentially. Those below imitated those above, creating collective chaos in the bureaucracy and the burgeoning of "surplus fees" and other such covert taxation imposed by various grades of officials in addition to statutory taxes.

Therefore, while systems such as the internal treasury and original-amount fiscalism ostensibly benefited the state's financial management, the lack of systemic restraints ultimately caused them to deviate from the original intentions and even led to contrary results, becoming a link in the major failure of empires.

In comparison, kings in the West were feudal lords in the true sense, and fiscal revenues came largely from the monarch's personal land income or seigniorage income, so that monarchs generally lived by their own means. Taxes were for the most part levied to meet the costs of war, resulting in the emergence of public finance. This is the historical reason for the British Parliament directing fiscal administration.[47]

Due to the lack of overall systemic change, the Chinese Empire's fiscal administration, in spite of undergoing quite a few reforms under capable high-level officials, was never able to break through its limitations, and this trapped the empire in a continuous cycle of inefficiency from the Ming and Qing dynasties onward. Even with the arrival of the modern Nationalist regime, Thomas Rawski estimates that its 1931 financial expenditures were lower than under Japan's Meiji government in 1880.[48] A corresponding organized mobilization was also never able to deeply penetrate the Chinese interior, especially the rural regions, and this enormous vacuum allowed the Communist base areas to separate and encircle the cities. Ultimately the cities lost their economic and military superiority; the Nationalist government can be seen as doomed from the start by its fragile fiscal administration system.

A genuine market economy implies the expansion of human cooperation and order. The reason that Chinese antiquity was unable to derive extensive cooperation and order from its vast territory, abundant resources, and industrious people was that the shift from a closed-off economic situation to an open economic situation requires systemic guarantees of property rights and other rights. As Peruvian economist Hernando de Soto notes, the main effects of property rights include features such as fixing the economic potential of assets, integrating dispersed information into one system, making people accountable, making assets fungible, networking people, and protecting transactions.[49]

"Big government" or "small government" is not the measure of whether a government is good or bad; only governments with formidable financial resources can succeed in a competitive age. Simplified libertarianism advocates "small government," but in fact, a government's accountability is more important than its scale. Historical cases are too numerous to mention, but comparing Spain and England, Spain possessed silver while England possessed a system and ultimately won. Under a "small government" administration, the property rights system is absent, and it is difficult for a market economy to take shape. The fate of the Ming dynasty's Shen Wansan and the Qing dynasty's bankrupt salt merchants proves that while imperial power can endow commercial privileges for a time, it can also strip away those privileges in an instant. That's why even though China early on produced private local banks (qianzhuang), money-exchange shops, and other such organizations that in their technical details were not unlike Western banks, ultimate protection of property rights was always difficult to obtain, expanding the scale of property rights was impossible, and a monetary system and financial system in the modern sense were unable to take shape.

The monetary system also makes it possible to compare China's and Japan's different historical paths. Quite a few Japanese economic historians point out that Japan didn't begin trying to mint coins until the seventh century, and these had limited circulation, with a return to bartering in the eleventh century; it was not until Japan began trading with China in the twelfth century that it drew in large amounts of coins from the Song dynasty. Song dynasty bronze coins had an enormous effect on Japan, and Song dynasty exports of bronze coins could bring a tenfold profit.[50]

By the Ming dynasty, Japan was still dependent on Chinese bronze coins while at the same time exporting silver to China. With the inflow of American silver into China, Japanese silver began to be used domestically instead, and during the Shogunate Period gold, silver, and bronze existed concurrently. Mining commenced at the Iwami Ginzan silver mine in 1526, and the adoption of the Korean soot-blowing smelting method led to a significant increase in silver production. The Edo shogunate took more direct jurisdiction over silver mining and began paying attention to the outflow of precious metals. Producing its own silver made Japan more independent in terms of its monetary policy, but even though it enjoyed monetary sovereignty based on its own silver, Shogunate-era Japan remained more backward than China. It wasn't until the seventeenth century that Japan began minting its own currency, and it took an entire century for these coins to gradually replace the Chinese coins that had been flowing into Japan since the Middle Ages.

In 1853 the American naval commodore Matthew Perry commanded his fleet to enter Edo Bay, forcing the shogunate government to sign the Kanagawa Treaty (in Japanese, the "Japan and U.S. Treaty of Peace and Amity") the next year. Perry's expedition not only changed Japanese history, but also indirectly changed the narrative of China and the world. Disadvantaged by the arrival of the Americans, Japan chose to engage in reform and spared no effort in revamping its financial system during the Meiji Restoration. This greatly facilitated Japan's ability to stand out in modernized competition. After defeating China in the Sino-Japanese War of 1894–1895, Japan used Qing reparations to adopt the gold standard and became a rising imperial power, a narrative that provides much food for thought. We should note that it was systemic reform, and not merely precious metal or even monetary sovereignty, that led to Japan's rise.

As the first country to use coins, China has a monetary history that spans thousands of years; there were metal specie during the Warring States period, and Song China invented the world's first paper currency. Regrettably, the traditional financial system's inability to produce a banking system meant that paper currency was not properly utilized after its invention. China was compelled to revert to the silver standard, and for a long time silver was a weighed currency, slowing the advancement of the finance system for hundreds of years.

Finance and banking are of major significance to the industrialization of developing countries. Japan and Germany are prime examples of how only a powerful fiscal system can sustain a budget oriented toward economic development and then generate the positive feedback of economic development needed to sustain the government. In other words, without fiscal strength, it is impossible to support the modernization of a governmental system. China was never able to create this positive cycle from the Ming and Qing onward; even the Republican government was unable to accomplish the modernization of its finance and taxation, and the government never gained adequate support from tax revenue.

The financial predicaments of the Song, Yuan, Ming, and Qing dynasties and the Republic are not foreign to today's context. On the institutional economics level, tax is essentially an institutional rent; through tax relations we can examine institutional relations, with currency as a link between the two. As economist Mancur Olson says, roving bandits become stationary bandits because the income of stationary bandits is higher and more stable than that of roving bandits, and when stationary bandits evolve into a government adept at collecting taxes from the general populace, it is more effective than a government that only knows how to pillage and plunder.[51]

The American economic historian Bradford DeLong once said that the history of the twentieth century was overwhelmingly economic history.[52] In fact, the history of all eras is economic history, with the flesh and blood of economics concealed under a political and military epidermis, and finance as a blood vessel that never stops pulsing.

Yet, financial history, especially monetary history, is often relegated to the ignominy of willful exaggeration and distortion in popular literature, and to being more or less ignored by mainstream scholars; even the question of whether money matters is still argued endlessly in macroeconomics. Kindleberger points out that economic history often lacks focus. He cites a fellow economist affirming the importance of finance and money in history: "The nations with which economic historians are chiefly concerned organize their economic activities under the form of making and spending money . . . Cannot economic history be organized most effectively around the evolution of pecuniary institutions?"[53]

Why did the East fall behind the West in modern times? This question has evoked countless responses as a variant of the famous Needham Question,[54] the Holy Grail of economic history. Historians tangle with momentous events such as the Industrial Revolution, while economists grope around for the details of the handicraft industry. It is worth noting that the dimension of monetary finance is seldom mentioned. In fact, Europe had a financial revolution before its Industrial Revolution, and this financial revolution was the reason why capitalism was able to take off. So Chinese history's insoluble enigma is not necessarily attributable to (the use of) silver, but the fate of silver can provide possible explanations and answers.

Let's shift the scene back to 1262, when the two poles of world civilization, Venice in the West and the Southern Song in the East, both faced the specter of war, and funding for these wars hung by a thread. Almost simultaneously, the authorities of both places came up with plans to deal with their emergencies, both involving the most advanced financial innovations of that time. The Southern Song's Jia Sidao raised military funding by using the steadily devaluing *huizi* to buy up public land and strip the populace of wealth. Venice took a different road: Its parliament authorized the government to mortgage its tax revenue, and when a fiscal deficit developed, the administration issued government bonds paying interest of 5 percent. In retrospect, Venice's financial innovation summoned the magic power of public debt as capital and effectively led Europe into an era of financial revolution. As for China, the excessively issued *huizi* did not regain the favor of the market; rather, public discontent and unrest threw open the door for invasion by the Mongolians. The collapse of its currency ultimately led China onto the road of a silver economy, and the financial watershed of the thirteenth century virtually decided the different fates of the East and West.

Even if history has no hypotheticals, it is tempting to consider what Jia Sidao might have done if the *huizi* hadn't been devalued. If the Public Land Law had succeeded, the Southern Song wouldn't have crumbled. When the young Marco Polo arrived in Hangzhou at the end of the thirteenth century, he probably would still have considered it the most beautiful and noble city in the world, but he might not have, in accordance with Yuan dynasty convention, referred to the genteel Jiangnan region as a barbarous province.

Returning to history in progress, we witness China taking the lead on finance and currency, but in the wrong direction. China at a very early stage had "flying money" (*feiqian*) for remitting funds, as well as pawnshops, silver shops, and other such establishments for credit transfer; the Song dynasty's paper currency originated in private institutions; and private local banks (*qianzhuang*) and money-exchange shops (*piaohao*) experienced extraordinary growth in the Ming and Qing dynasties. So why didn't China produce a modern banking industry? The crux of the problem was China's failure to develop a banking system. This created a closed loop in which the lack of banks prevented the development of a modern state, and the lack of a modern state made it difficult to develop a banking system in the genuine sense.

In a long-range review, this can be seen as the great economic divergence between East and West. Scholars typically believe that China didn't fall behind the West until the sixteenth century, or even the eighteenth century, but I believe that before this great economic divergence, there was already a great financial divergence, and although hidden, this divergence is the secret key that opens the bell jar of economic development. Many economic historians have revealed that the frontrunners after the seventeenth century, from Holland to England to the United States, first carried out financial reforms; even Japan, Russia, and other countries that only began Westernizing at the end of the nineteenth century all experienced varying degrees of financial revolution as their countries modernized, and newly emergent financial intermediaries played a critical role in financing industrial takeoff. In contrast, China retreated after the Song dynasty's failed radical advance, and its monetary and financial institutions remained premodern.

Whether using paper currency or silver, one of the cruxes of China's premodern monetary system was its failure to achieve "bankification." The unbankability of China's currency led to the failure of China's paper currency system and forced it to take the silver route. Without banks, and without the coinage of silver, progressing from bank notes to paper currency was out of the question. Currency could only exist in the form of confusing and outmoded metage currency. Without banks,

China's savings couldn't be capitalized, because only sectors such as credit institutions make it possible to remove constraints on capital and create more complex credit transactions. Without banks, China's commercial institutions were unable to become companies, or to expand or emerge from the confines of interpersonal relationships. And without banks, the issuance of currency could not be centralized, and nothing like a central bank could emerge.

The lack of banks became the crucial factor that prevented China's economy from breaking through its closed loop. In contrast, banking institutions were a major boon to industry during Japan's decades of reforms in the nineteenth century. Japanese banks steadily advanced through trial and error, initially referencing the American model and then the British and German models, with the result that in the Meiji era, Japan's banks emerged in three main forms: First were the superbanks that circulated funds for tycoons; next were the policy banks established by the government; and then came more than 1,000 small banks that serviced local markets. This mutual alliance among industrialists, bankers, and the government hurled Japan into modernization with typhoon force.

The difficulty of banks taking root in China and silver's corresponding struggle constitute the hidden financial thread in China's economic history, and also conceal the constant chess game between state power and market forces. The Ming and Qing eras coincided with immense change in the outside world. Was silver the reason for China's falling behind? In a sense, silver was a symbol of China's financial backwardness. If China, like Western Europe, had established new-style banking institutions, silver would gradually have been withdrawn from circulation and become reserves. But China's traditional financial institutions were unable to support the vigorous growth of industry and commerce or even social progress, so silver was always the mainstream choice. In a certain sense, any country infiltrated by a precious metal like silver bears a kind of "resource curse"; not only China was that way, but even the Spanish crown, which possessed a steady stream of New World silver but declared bankruptcy more than ten times in the sixteenth and seventeenth centuries.[55]

Going a step further, what constrained China's traditional financial system? The financial industry is an appendage of commerce—it can be considered the superstructure of the superstructure—while historically commerce in China has always existed as an appendage to politics, which makes the financial industry an appendage to an appendage. This meant that even though China's financial industry on the technical level had *jiaozi*, private banks, money-exchange shops, and other piecemeal innovations, it was a low achiever on the institutional and systemic level. While China's Ming dynasty was still experimenting with royal treasury notes, Europe's most successful banking family, the Medici, had already emerged. Regarded as riffraff in the early fourteenth century, this family controlled Florence for three centuries and produced three popes, two French royal consorts, and multiple princes and dukes, as well as bankrolling brilliant artists such as Raphael, Da Vinci, and Michelangelo. Their biggest clients were monarchs and popes, expanding their influence into the political sphere in a way that Chinese merchants could not easily replicate. At a time when, without protection of property rights or personal safety to speak of, direct plundering of wealth by those in power was the most convenient method, why bother with the more circuitous banking model? The Spring and Autumn Period still had the merchant king-maker Lü Buwei, but the Ming only had Shen Wansan, whose family was exterminated and his property confiscated.

By the late Qing, having witnessed the power of Europe and America and even Japan, officials advocating Westernization finally recognized the power of finance, apart from gunboats and cannons. Zheng Guanying said during the Guangxu period (1875–1908): "Self-strengthening requires commerce, and commerce has its basis in banks. Western countries all establish banks to support commerce and serve as a resource hub for all the trades, as well as a source of funds to maintain the general situation."

Zheng Guanying had a clear understanding of the benefits of banks, listing ten main advantages:

> This is a summary of how they benefit the people and the country: In the rise and fall of banks are hidden the fundamental principles of administering the country, requiring communication from above and below, near and far. The first benefit is gathering the country's wealth and profit and

preparing it for use when needed; the second is planning major national economic projects such as railways and shipbuilding; the third is providing short-term credit in war or natural disaster; the fourth is relieving the financial burdens on government caused by raising loans from foreign banks with heavy interest; the fifth is more flexibly accepting securities as collateral rather than the strict requirements of foreign banks; the sixth is that if the country's thriving silver shops and local private banks run short of cash, the bank can transfer funds so that the market is not undermined and business can be strengthened; the seventh is treating it like a treasury that pays annual interest, rather than subjecting it to the dark calculations of those who grasp for profit; the eighth is making no distinction between deposits by the government and by the private sector; the ninth is reducing reliance on foreign banks for foreign exchange; and the tenth is circulating bills of exchange in case of cash shortfalls on the market.[56]

In contrast to Zheng Guanying's knowledge, the first student to study overseas in the Republican era, Yung Wing,[57] put practical effort into establishing a national bank. Yung Wing was already talking about a national bank when he went to the Taiping Heavenly Kingdom in 1860 to see his friend Hong Renxuan,[58] and in 1896 he submitted a memorial to the Qing government requesting the establishment of such an institution. His "Request to Establish Banking Regulations," "Draft Bank Articles Continued," and other documents focused on setting up banks, launching paper currency, strengthening industrial entities, and monitoring mortgaged assets, and he emphasized that the business model of banks must be Westernized: "Banks should imitate Western countries such as Britain and France; with repeated reform they improve with each change, American banks most of all. Japanese banks are also of great interest. This draft references American banking regulations, first establishing a headquarters in the capital, and then establishing banks in each provincial capital and trading port. Total banking capital should be 10 million *yuan*, under unified allocation by the Board of Revenue."[59]

During the self-strengthening movement following the Sino-Japanese War of 1894–1895, the idea of a national bank enjoyed considerable support for a time, and the minister of works, Weng Tong, commended Yung Wing's long residence in the United States as "essential for discussing banking." This proposal had already gotten the nod, but it offended quite a few vested interests, and tycoon Sheng Xuanhuai's suspicion, jealousy, and obstruction prevented it from being carried out. The frustration that Yung Wing experienced was the common fate of Western-educated intellectuals in China, and it reflects the difficulty of China's financial launch. Ultimately the delays prevented China's banking industry from transforming itself amid domestic unrest and foreign harassment, even while sparing no effort to catch up during the Republican era.

In comparison, money-exchange shops flourished for a time during the late Qing, but they faced business challenges in the early twentieth century. At one point they attempted to transform into new-style banks, but their scale was too small; even their combined capital was less than that of the newly established Board of Revenue (*Hubu*) Bank (see Table 0-2). Significant differences in terms of management, services, and

Table 0-2. Capitalization of Credit Bureaus (*Zhangju*), Money Exchange Shops, and Hubu Bank at the End of the Qing Dynasty

Type of bank	Year	Branches	Total capitalization (silver taels)	Maximum (silver taels)	Minimum (silver taels)	Branch average (silver taels)
Credit bureau	1910	52	1,138,600	70,000	3,200	21,897
Money exchange shops	1911	23	5,589,000	500,000	60,000	242,870
Hubu Bank	1908	1	10,000,000			10,000,000

Source: Huang Jianhui, 2002, *History of Shanxi Money-Exchange Shops*

scale prevented money-exchange shops from turning into modern banks, not to mention gaining the same level of political recognition.

Regarding the financial practices of premodern China, including *jiaozi* currency, local private banks, silver shops (*yinpu*), and money-exchange shops, even when similar to their overseas counterparts in their technical details, they never developed into complete and powerful financial institutions, and their scale was never large enough; the essential reason was that credit never extended far beyond interpersonal relationships. Taking it a step further, finance in premodern times typically assisted the government's fiscal administration, the backwardness of which hampered the industry's development. That is why China's flourishing commerce could give rise to a traditional money trade, but could not foster a banking system in the modern sense.

Finance is essentially credit, and social credit in turn decides the capabilities and scope of the financial system. At the same time, this credit must rely on the joint protection and sustenance of state and market forces. The development of finance also implies intertemporal and transindividual transfer of credit, and this trading relationship depends on safeguarding the rights of the individual.

The triumph of silver was the market's choice, and the emperor was obliged to reluctantly accept it. On the other hand, although it was the market's choice, silver's victory was ultimately Pyrrhic, constituting a "lose-lose" situation for both the government and the people—China was never able to shake off the fetters of systemic inertia, and the silver system was never able to evolve into a banking system. This prevented currency and finance from bringing greater room for growth and becoming the primary driving force for the economy. The intermediate forces between politics and capital and between rule of man and rule of law were always disadvantaged and even deficient. Capital was either unable to obtain political protection and was annihilated, or anxiously sought political protection and smothered itself. Commercial failure and success are usually bound by common cause to politics, and this is especially the case with finance.

Silver was admired and desired and also cursed and criticized, and rapid changes in the inflow of silver changed the fates of Chinese dynasties. Even now, some commentators grumble that China's use of silver caused a loss of monetary sovereignty, but viewed another way, silver's failure in China was in fact just one aspect of empire's great failure. Finance could hardly experience substantive breakthrough before systemic transformation. It was the trend of empire's political economy that determined the features of China's financial history, as well as silver's persistent influence and even its enormous demand. China wallowed in silver, was content with silver and deluded by silver; the constraints of power made the sense of security that silver provided irresistible. As a result, time and time again China was out of sync with world trends, and capitalists and entrepreneurs were mentally incapable of escaping Braudel's "bell jar."

History is endless recollection, and finance is endless innovation; the interaction between the two constitutes a dynamic process of creative destruction.[60] Finance is not a blank piece of paper, and the history of finance is not only about the secret of money, but is a unique perspective and indistinct main thread of rise and fall, beginning and end. Looking back at the history of silver, apart from seeing abruptness and inevitability in the fate of silver, we see the rise and fall of empire. The only way out for a route-locked civilization is to escape historical inertia and systemic suppression. Regret is not enough; we need to compare yesterday's successes and failures with the present.

The Divergent Fate of Silver in the East and the West

With that the goddess swept into the cavern's shadowed vault, searching for
hiding-places far inside its depth while Odysseus hauled his treasures closer
up, the gold, durable bronze and finespun robes, the Phaeacians' parting gifts.

Homer (9th to 8th centuries B.C.E.), The Odyssey, Book 13

Yellow gold is called *dang,* its beauty is referred to as *liu;* white gold is
called silver (*yin*), its beauty is called *liao.*

Erya: Interpretation of Implements

The crucible is for silver, and the furnace is for gold, and the Lord tests hearts.

The Holy Bible, Proverbs 17:3

PORTIA: (*to servant*) Go draw aside the curtains and discover
The several caskets to this noble prince.—
A curtain is drawn showing a gold, silver, and lead casket.
(*to MOROCCO*) Now make your choice.

MOROCCO: The first, of gold, who this inscription bears:
"Who chooseth me shall gain what many men desire."
The second, silver, which this promise carries:

"Who chooseth me shall get as much as he deserves."

This third, dull lead, with warning all as blunt:

"Who chooseth me must give and hazard all he hath."

How shall I know if I do choose the right?

PORTIA: The one of them contains my picture, Prince.

If you choose that, then I am yours withal.

William Shakespeare (1564–1616), The Merchant of Venice

The Origins of Money

Even love has not turned more men into fools than

has meditation upon the nature of money.

William Ewart Gladstone (1809–1898)[1]

What exactly is money?
This question continues to captivate people; economist John Kenneth Galbraith once mockingly said that answers to this question are "invariably incoherent."[2] Money concerns both the rich and the poor, and affects not only the fate of individuals but also the future of sovereign states. Money is a man-made deity, as well as the invisible blood vessels of the world; the essence of finance lies in the flow of money, and cultural heritage relies on going with the flow. Anthropology increasingly reveals that the earliest economies were all related to religion, and market economy may have been nurtured in a planned economy under religious guidance: "It has long been known that the first markets were sacred markets, the first banks were temples, the first to issue money were priests or priest-kings."[3] Humanity's love of money is a primitive drive and collective subconscious, especially toward precious metals such as gold and silver. This predilection has carried over into modern society, even if in concealed form, for example in the mania for the gold standard or physical currency.

"Light comes from the East" applies to civilization as well as religion, and also to money. At a time when humanity had just learned to write, the progenitors of Mesopotamian civilization, the Sumerians, used silver as a currency to record debts, and pollen, spices, and wheat also emerged as currency. Ancient Chinese early on recognized the importance of money in the national economy. As stated in *The Book of Han: Food and Commodities*: "Of the eight aspects of governance in *The Book of Documents*, the first speaks of food and the second speaks of commodities. Food is what we call farm-produced grains for eating; commodities is what we call cloth and silk for clothing as well as gold, knives, turtle shells and cowries, and it is through the possession or lack of these things that wealth and profit are determined. The two are the foundation of the people's livelihood." The writings of past generations are full of statements such as "The foundation of wealth is in food and commodities," and "From earliest times, food and commodities came first in the survival of the people."[4]

With the economic and financial development resulting from more than thirty years of reform and opening, the aspiration and drive for money have become an important link in the China story. The Chinese public's ignorance of and thirst for economic knowledge are also reflected in a collective preoccupation with money, resulting in a plethora of books of widely varying quality in recent years. A documentary film entitled *Money,* one of the better national productions, opens with the artfully expressed statement: "She is clay tablets on the Mesopotamian Plain, she is seashells used for trade by the ancient civilizations of the Yellow River, she is the gold of Asia Minor's kingdom of Lydia, she is the insignia of the medieval banking guilds of Florence, Italy. She is a vehicle of desire, a tool of exchange, most familiar and also most unknown to us—she is money."

Yap Island, one of the Caroline Islands in the Pacific Ocean, with a population of around 5,000 to 6,000, had no metal, and its only natural resource was rocks. In their trading activities, the islanders used large stone discs called *fei* as a form of currency. These discs were transported to the island by boat from a limestone quarry more than 400 miles away. If a transaction involved a *fei* too large to be conveniently moved, it was left in place, sometimes without so much as a mark to indicate the exchange. A certain family once tried transporting a *fei* of mammoth proportions and outstanding quality, but it sank to the bottom of the sea. Even so, local people acknowledged the family's ownership of that *fei*, making the family the wealthiest on the island. After Germany bought Yap Island in 1899, the American explorer William Henry Furness III visited that mysterious place and produced a detailed record of this practice two months later.

When this case study was published in 1910, it attracted little public attention. The first to take notice of it was the famous economist John Maynard Keynes, while serving with the British Treasury in 1915. He commended the logic and wisdom of the Yap Islanders, observing, "Modern practice in regard to gold reserves has a good deal to learn from the more logical practices of the island of Yap."[5]

An even more celebrated citation of the Yap Island case came from the great monetarist Milton Friedman in explaining what money is. While acknowledging that many people in the modern world may consider the Yap Islanders silly and illogical, Friedman observed: "For a century and more, the 'civilized' world regarded as a concrete manifestation of its wealth metal dug from deep in the ground, refined at great labor, and transported great distances to be buried again in elaborate vaults deep in the ground. Is the one practice really more rational than the other?"[6]

Keynes and Friedman, separated by decades and representing widely disparate economic viewpoints, each paid tribute to the monetary concepts of the Yap Islanders; this historical coincidence highlights the distinctiveness of the Yap Island case in understanding that the essence of money is credit. The eighteenth-century Scottish philosopher, economist, and historian David Hume once said that because humanity had endowed gold and silver with imagined value, in an even broader sense, the value of money is based on a mental evaluation, and the essence of money is in everyone accepting it as a medium of trade based on trust.

Similar arrangements were often seen in ancient societies. In 3,000 B.C.E., Mesopotamia used clay tokens to record treaties; fist-sized clay enclosures called "bullae" have been uncovered in large numbers in archaeological sites. Inside the hollow part of the bullae are symbols representing numbers and goods involving various loans, contracts, and records of account. Many scholars believe that this information specifically represents

various goods and services, from cotton cloth, honey, and sheep to working days, and that some symbols indicate a loan contract that the creditor
could transfer to a third party. This shows that human beings were making financial arrangements 5,000 years ago, and even more that the value
of money was based on a community's acknowledgment of credit. Communities can be large or small, and the foundation of one society's monetary system may seem completely bogus to another society. What is vast
wealth to A may be pilferage or even rubbish to B; people pay with what
they are mutually willing to believe in.

Understanding that the essence of money is credit, we need to re-
vise classical theories about the origins of money.

When the great historian Qian Mu (1895–1990) spoke of China's
ancient economy, he devoted a section to money, emphasizing its importance in ancient Chinese society: "Connecting the cities with the
countryside, and allowing dealings between agriculture commerce, was
a major issue in which currency played an important role. China's early
money was gold and bronze cash, which remained popular right up
through the Qing dynasty."[7] In fact, gold rarely circulated in the marketplace. The economist Qian Jiaju believes that what is now known as currency (*huobi*) was in fact two different things in ancient times. The *Rites
of Zhou* mentioned nine items of payment, with *huo* referring to pearls
and cowries and *bi* referring to skins and silks; these items were commonly used as currency at various times.[8] The old form of the Chinese
character *huo* combines the characters for "converting" and "cowrie." It
symbolizes the fact that in many cultures, cowries were the progenitor
of currency. *Shuowen Jiezi*[9] states: "Money [*huo*], that is, conversion. A
thing to facilitate exchange."

Both the creation of words in ancient China and the deductions of
later generations to a greater or lesser degree imply a general understanding that money came into being for the purpose of exchange. This
is similar to the view of the progenitor of economics, Adam Smith, who
apparently saw money as a simplified form of bartering, especially precious metals such as gold and silver: "If . . . instead of sheep or oxen, he
had metals to give in exchange for [salt], he could easily proportion the
quantity of the metal to the precise quantity of the commodity which
he had immediate occasion for."[10]

How were the metals differentiated? Adam Smith further explained the relationship between metals and economic standards: "Different metals have been made use of by different nations for this purpose. Iron was the common instrument of commerce among the ancient Spartans; copper among the ancient Romans; and gold and silver among all rich and commercial nations. Those metals seem originally to have been made use of for this purpose in rude bars, without any stamp or coinage." Smith also cited the view of the ancient historian Timaeus: ". . . till the time of Servius Tullius, the Romans had no coined money, but made use of unstamped bars of copper, to purchase whatever they had occasion for. These bars, therefore, performed at this time the function of money."[11]

As intelligent as Adam Smith was, his inference was not necessarily entirely accurate; after all, Greeks and Romans began using gold and silver specie at a very early date. Even more noteworthy is that Smith started the traditional view among economists that money originated for the exchange of goods. Many economists authoritatively assert that once trading activity began, the emergence of money was inevitable. This apparently orthodox viewpoint has also sparked controversy. The problem is in how trading activity emerged among human beings. Was it in the form of barter right from the outset?

Records of barter occur very early in China, even to the era of Shennong (the Divine Husbandman), the legendary father of Chinese agriculture (some 5,000 years ago). The *Zhouyi* records: "The market opens at noon, and people gather from various places, assembling goods from various places. After trading, each leaves with the items he wanted." But was this an exchange or a kind of gift? And how much of a role did money play? Writings on economics typically define money as having three functions: as a medium of exchange, a measure of worth, and a means of storing value. Historically, however, a great deal of anthropological evidence reveals money as a kind of gift. The Cambridge University anthropologist Caroline Humphrey concludes, "No example of a barter economy, pure and simple, has ever been described, let alone the emergence from it of money. All available ethnography suggests that there never has been such a thing."[12] The American anthropologist David Graeber endorses this conclusion. In attempting to redefine money and the nature of debt, he believes that the economic theory of barter origi-nating from self-interest is a myth.[13]

In these various discussions regarding money, it can be hard to judge who is right or wrong; this explores the boundaries of human knowledge and intelligence, so it's no wonder that meditating on the nature of money has "turned more people into fools" than love has done. As David Hume (who died in 1776, the year that *The Wealth of Nations* was published, and who is said to have greatly influenced Adam Smith) wrote in "Of Commerce" (1752), "When a man deliberates concerning his conduct in any particular affair, and forms schemes in politics, trade, economy, or any business in life, he never ought to draw his arguments too fine," but when reasoning upon general subjects, "the difference be-tween a common man and a man of genius is chiefly seen in the shal-lowness or depth of the principles upon which they proceed." This is even more true in the case of money; any individual's understanding is truly limited, but the basis of their reasoning is very important. That is why we need to maintain an open mind when striving to view history through the perspective of money.

From the anthropological perspective, David Graeber's vision looks broader; he has clearly been influenced by the French anthropolo-gist Marcel Mauss's research on primitive barter and gift-giving.[14] What is the value of this kind of research? It generates another explanation for the origins of money; the narrow definition that economics previously provided is clearly not imaginative enough. In this anthropological ex-planation, people didn't barter but rather exchanged gifts, sometimes in the form of tribute, sometimes with a present given in return at some later time, and sometimes purely as a gift. In environments where every-one is acquainted, the medium of mutual gift-giving is credit, and mon-ey came into being in the course of this kind of gift-giving activity, which when taken a step further can result in IOUs. In other words, money can be seen as a credit contract arrangement.

"Money originated from IOUs." This statement sounds fantastical, but there are faint hints of it in modern culture. In the American drama series *666 Park Avenue*, the specific amount of money that each person owes the protagonist is sometimes displayed as a brand on the skin of the debtor. This is like an ancient cycle and dubious metaphor: The

symbol on currency implies how much is owed to someone else, revealing how the human monetary system is established on credit.

Silver's Fate in the East and the West

Discussing money requires talking about gold and silver. As a revolutionary theorist, Marx was especially passionate about monetary
theory. One of his famous sayings is, "Gold and silver are not by nature
money, but money consists by its nature of gold and silver."[15] This saying
has been borne out by the natural properties of gold and silver being
well suited to taking on the attributes of money. The history of finance
shows that it was customary in the past for people to cast precious metals into coins for use in trade, and the names of our currencies today are
typically derived from that time, indicating that this currency contains a
certain weight of precious metal in the form of pence, pound, or mark;
even China's silver tael was a measure of weight.

Silver is so important that it repeatedly turns up in religion and
history. "Render to Caesar the things that are Caesar's, and to God the
things that are God's."[16] Everyone knows that this famous quote by Jesus
is related to silver coins. According to the New Testament, while Jesus
was teaching, the Pharisees tried to trick him into saying something
wrong, so they asked Jesus, "Is it lawful to pay taxes to Caesar, or not?"
Here Caesar referred not to the great emperor, but rather to the Roman
Empire. But Jesus perceived their ill intentions and told them to take out
a silver coin to look at. The Pharisees took out a denarius (a Roman silver coin roughly equivalent to a day's wages for a worker, and commonly used to pay taxes), which bore the image of Tiberius Caesar. Jesus
cleverly pointed to the image and asked who it was, and when the others
said it was Caesar, Jesus replied, "Render to Caesar the things that are
Caesar's, and to God the things that are God's." Jesus linked the question
to reality and left his opponents speechless.

In this story, Caesar signified or represented a silver coin, and also
the secular regime behind the portrait on the coin. This shows that very
early on, silver currency was tied to ruling power. It's no wonder that
British Museum curators explain, "Silver was a highly valued substance
with strong symbolic associations with royalty, wealth and power."[17]

Even today, some scholars assert, "The wheels of this global market were oiled by the worldwide flow of silver."[18] Ancient Chinese spoke of silver as "white gold." Gold and silver invariably appear together in ancient writings. *Erya: Interpretation of Implements* states: "Yellow gold is called *dang*, its beauty is referred to as *liu*; white gold is called silver (*yin*), its beauty is called *liao*." There are further clues in the Chinese character for silver, which is made up of the component symbols for gold and *gen*, meaning "boundary." The original meaning of "silver" is supposedly "a metal with a value second only to gold."

From the historical standpoint, the use of silver in the West began very early and even played a crucial role in history. Everyone knows that the traitor Judas betrayed Jesus for thirty pieces of silver. This naturally triggered people's indignation and led to Judas being cursed as a traitor for the next 2,000 years. One reason for the indignation was the paltry reward for the betrayal; silver coins were worth less than gold coins, and how much were thirty pieces of silver actually worth? Since no one can agree on the specific silver coin referred to, it's hard to determine the value. Some say it was the aforementioned denarius, while others say it was a different coin called the shekel. Later generations record that Judas used this money to buy a plot of land, but he fell to his death, so the land was known as a "blood field."

In the later years of the Roman Empire, various barbarian tribes rose up. The Franks were the most successful branch of the Germanic peoples. Their leader, Charlemagne, revived the Roman Empire in the eighth century, in one stroke expanding the Frankish kingdom and single-handedly unifying Western Europe. After Charlemagne died, his empire was divided into Germany, France, and Italy, and to this day he is still called "the father of Europe"; some say he is the King of Hearts on French playing cards. Charlemagne's status can likewise not be underestimated in the history of money. In the year 781 he reformed the currency of his empire, and the new currency was all made of silver because his empire possessed the largest amounts of this precious metal. It was he who stipulated that one pound of silver equaled 240 deniers, and that each denier contained around two grams of silver, while one pound of silver was also equivalent to 20 sous, the gold coin at that time. This meant that gold and silver had an exchange ratio of 12:1. The exchange ratio between gold and silver currency in the West basically fluctuated around this level for the next 1,000 years.

Shakespeare wrote his play *The Merchant of Venice* during the reign of the British Empire's Elizabeth I. At that time, trade and commerce were already going strong, giving silver an even more important role. *The Merchant of Venice* was written during the reign of China's Wanli Emperor during the Ming dynasty. This play is not only about love and friendship, but also about money and the secrets of capitalism, and contains abundant descriptions of the relationship between gold and silver.

The Jewish moneylender Shylock is obsessed with "my silver" and "money," and he compares gold and silver coins bearing interest to ewes giving birth to lambs [Act 1, Scene 3]. The protagonist Portia's father arranges for her suitors to choose among chests of gold, silver, and lead, and the one who chooses correctly will be allowed to marry her, but in fact it is the lead chest, worth the least, that is the correct choice. Someone chooses the gold chest because the value of gold is greatest: "Or shall I think in silver she's immured, / Being ten times undervalued to tried gold? / O sinful thought! Never so rich a gem / Was set in worse than gold. They have in England / A coin that bears the figure of an angel / Stamped in gold, but that's insculped upon; but here an angel in a golden bed / Lies all within" [Act 2, Scene 7].

The man Portia favors chooses the lead chest, denouncing how gold and silver, especially silver, have been used. "Therefore then, thou gaudy gold, / Hard food for Midas, I will none of thee. / Nor none of thee, thou pale and common drudge / 'Tween man and man" [Act 3, Scene 2].

Leaving aside a literary analysis of Shakespeare's classic, from the perspective of the history of finance, the exchange ratio between gold and silver back then was not as high as in subsequent generations, and silver was clearly much more commonly used than gold in the West at that time. Indeed, silver was more widely used in both Asia and the Western world for the great majority of the time because its value was lower.

Silver, discovered more than 5,000 years ago, has a shorter history than gold, and its fate has always been inextricably tied with that of gold.

The value of the two has not always been consistent in the West, and at one point silver was more valuable than gold. Marx wrote: "Production of silver requires mining and in general a relatively high level of technical development. The value of silver is therefore originally higher than that of gold, although it is absolutely less scarce."[19] Advancements in smelting and the discovery of silver mines in the Americas resulted in an endless stream of New World silver into Europe and Asia, and subverted the existing order in both regions. It is worth again emphasizing that even in the 200 years under the gold standard from the seventeenth century onward, silver didn't completely withdraw from the historical stage or everyday transactions. In the West, gold's superiority to silver was in fact slowly and progressively established, and finally set at the end of the nineteenth century. This shows that while both gold and silver are precious metals, the monetization of gold and silver didn't begin to diverge until the eighteenth century.

Silver was not used very much in China at the outset. When the Qin Emperor unified China's currency, silver was not listed among the three grades of currency that he stipulated should be used throughout the country. "In the Qin, the currency of China was unified as three grades. Gold was the superior coin called *yi*; bronze was known as the 'half-tael,' its weight inscribed, and was the secondary currency; and pearls, jade, tortoise shell, cowrie, silver and tin were categorized as vessels, ornamentation and treasure, not as currency."[20] Even in the Han dynasty, when Sima Qian was writing, "silver" during the reign of Han Wudi (187–140 B.C.E.) was an amalgam of silver and tin, in which silver was the main component, while silver during the reign of Wang Mang (33 B.C.E.–23 C.E.) was genuine silver.

When Wang Mang reformed the social system,[21] the currency system was an important piece, and because it concerned the national economy, it had an enormous effect. Wang Mang reformed the currency four times, and the weight of his "large-spring 50" coin was 2.5 times that of the Western Han five-grainer,[22] but its value was set at 50 times that of the latter, sparking a financial crisis. He cracked down harshly on the private minting of coins and even banned the private possession of copper and coal, but even when he made illegal minting a capital offense, he was unable to completely end the practice. Qian Mu believes that the complicated and chaotic currency system confused ordinary people, and the rejection of his currency became Wang Mang's greatest administrative failure. "So many people violated the law that they were locked up in carts and delivered to the *Zhongguan* (the official in charge of minting coins) in Chang'an.[23] Six or seven out of ten died of anxiety on the way, which shows how oppressive Wang Mang's currency system was."[24] This shows why the law needs to take human considerations into account; with the crackdown on private minting so unpopular, it couldn't be effectively implemented and only oppressed countless people. "There was unemployment in farming and commerce, foodstuffs and commodities went to waste, and the people wailed in the streets." The failure of Wang Mang's reforms led to the spread of "commodity currency." As recorded in *Book of the Later Han: Annals of the Guangwu Emperor*, Part II: "After the chaos under Wang Mang, cloth, silk, gold and grain were used for money. Five-grainer coins began circulating at that time." Here the word "gold" is usually understood as referring to both gold and silver. The circulation of gold and silver as currency from this time onward can be regarded as a legacy of Wang Mang's currency reforms.[25]

From the Wei-Jin period (220–420 C.E.) onward, the influence of Buddhism and other external cultures made gold and silver popular. Besides religious usages such as the casting of Buddhist images and decoration of Buddhist temples, gold was also used for reward and ornamentation, and it was naturally also used as minted currency. The widespread use of gold during the Wei-Jin Northern and Southern dynasties period (420–589 C.E.) created shortages, so gold was supplemented with silver, and the use of silver gradually increased from then on.[26] External influences on the popularization of gold and silver cannot be overlooked. One was the use of gold in Buddhist structures, and the second was international trade: "Since some countries on the Silk Road, such as the Greater Yuezhi, Arsacid, Daqin, Nantianzhu [Medieval India] and Funan, preferred using gold and silver, they all used gold and silver to trade with China's Jiao-Guang region."[27] In the Tang dynasty, gold and silver were used more by the upper classes, and more as a commodity. After the

Northern and Southern Song, gold was mainly for stored value and for paying large sums, while silver was used by ordinary people along with bronze coins; this was even more the case after the Jin and Yuan dynasties. The use of silver in China gradually increased, and ultimately made China the world's largest silver kingdom.

As mentioned before, this was an evolving process. Silver's eventual transformation into a measure of value in China in fact originated under Mongol rule in the Yuan dynasty. Scholar Pang Xinwei has hypothesized that the Mongols may have been influenced by neighboring ethnic groups such as the Khwarazm.[28] Even so, paper currency was still mainly used in the early years of Mongol rule—the so-called certificates (*chao*)—and the circulation of gold and silver was prohibited, but it was hard to curtail their use among the general public. After the Ming dynasty was established, bank notes withdrew from history, and China ultimately adopted the silver standard.

In the past, the Western world used a mixture of gold, silver, and bronze coins to settle international accounts, corresponding to the almost simultaneous practice in China's Ming and Qing dynasties of "using silver for large sums and copper coins for small sums"; the two practices in fact shared some similarities. Scholars generally agree that the international monetary system, a major product of the international financial system, emerged in the latter half of the nineteenth century, especially from the 1870s onward. From then on gold existed as the fundamental international currency. This also occurred almost simultaneously with China's currency reforms and adoption of the silver standard at the end of the Qing dynasty. At this point China and the West moved in diametrically different directions, toward the gold standard on one side and the silver standard on the other. Many scholars believe that the widespread use of silver in the Ming and Qing dynasties was the "focal point" of China's connection with the world market,[29] and silver even became a symbol of the modern world's "erosion" or "invasion" of the ancient empire. At the same time that silver declined in the West, its role was strengthened in the East. Why did silver take two different roads in the East and the West? And did this decide the different trends in these two worlds? In any case, following the hidden vein of silver may allow us to pick up reverberations and echoes from the depths of history.

The Gold and Silver Chess Game

In retrospect, the more widespread use of gold always seemed tied to rising productivity levels. The Lydians are credited with producing the earliest metal specie in the seventh century B.C.E. Historian Herodotus considered them the earliest minters and users of metal currency, and the earliest retail traders.[30] The coins of the Lydians were made of electrum, an alloy of silver and gold known as "white gold." One of their most famous early coins was called the "lion," composed of a little more than half gold and more than 40 percent silver. Very soon, the total weight of the electrum coin was set at 14.15 grams, and it was denominated as a "stater."[31]

After that, the fountainheads of Western civilization, the Greeks and Romans, started using gold coins. In most cases, the standard medieval currencies were silver, with gold returning to circulation in Italy, a harbinger in this respect. In 1252, Genoa molded the Christian world's first gold coin, after which gold was used for large transactions in fourteenth-century continental Europe, while silver continued to dominate everyday trade.

Gold was not commonly used early on, apparently because of its excessively high value per weight unit. "Silver was the dominant money throughout medieval times and into the modern era. Other metals were too heavy (such as copper) or too light (gold) when cast into coins of a value convenient for transactions."[32] The insufficient production of gold was another reason for the popularity of silver in Europe. Before the great geographical discoveries in the New World, European silver mainly came from Central Europe. The constant flow of silver into Europe up until the seventeenth century made gold–silver bimetallism increasingly problematic. The stability of the gold standard became increasingly apparent, and it gradually stood out among the various competing currency systems to become the mainstream choice. This era has often been referred to as the classic gold standard period. In fact, the gold standard was not altogether consistent; numerous gold standard types and definitions have caused major headaches for experts.

Over the next two centuries, even in England, where the gold standard was strongest, when Newton appraised the value of the British pound in 1717,[33] the British were mainly using silver as before; even after England established its gold standard in 1816, silver retreated only gradually rather than all at once. The status of gold in Europe was not established until the end of the nineteenth century. In the early twentieth century it became the cornerstone of the international monetary system, and the British pound sterling, with its value firmly linked to gold, became the most common currency for international remittances at that time.

The triumph of the gold standard was not without its fortuitous factors; England's insistence on a gold standard and its national power served as a major impetus. Historical economic data show that the world entered a period of rapid globalization of trade from the mid-nineteenth century onward, and England, as the first industrialized country, took up one-third of total world trade in 1870.

Under these circumstances, England was bound to have an influence on anyone who wanted to do business with it. England set the trends in the nineteenth century, and its central banking system and monetary standards were emulated. At the same time, repeated wars tested the stability of Britain's currency. After the Franco-Prussian War, Germany dumped silver, afflicting many countries with "imported inflation." Modern banking and international trade caused the once-overvalued gold to become functional and reliable, and European countries that had once favored gold–silver bimetallism rushed to adopt the gold standard. The gold standard soon became the main economic option. When Europeans look back at the years prior to World War I, they often refer nostalgically to the "gold era."

The widespread adoption of the gold standard in the nineteenth century was essentially a market choice. If currency is seen as a product with a very strong "network externality," as suggested by economist Barry Eichengreen, a country's monetary policies are not created independent of other countries. Put simply, "the source of their interdependence was the *network externalities* that characterize international monetary arrangements," just as people use the Microsoft Windows operating system, not because it is the most efficient, but because the majority of people use this system, which gives it an even greater superiority, leading to a steady increase in the number of users.[34] Likewise with the international monetary system, once England took the lead and became the world's greatest trading nation after the Industrial Revolution, emulating its monetary system became a pragmatic and feasible choice for any country that wanted to do business or develop trade with England, as happened with Germany and Portugal.

The Failure of Bimetallism

The historical chess game between gold and silver ended with the triumph of the gold standard. Apart from the apparently fortuitous factor of England leading the way by adopting the gold standard, another key factor was the excessively troublesome aspects of the gold–silver bimetallism once popular in Europe. One of the main problems with bimetallism was establishing an exchange ratio between gold and silver, which fluctuated as a result of production and other external factors.

Bimetallism was once the mainstream choice in Europe. Although Genoa adopted the gold standard in the mid-fifteenth century, up until the early nineteenth century, the major nations apart from England, including Germany, the Austro-Hungarian Empire, Russia, and countries of the Far East, all implemented silver standards, and bimetallist countries "formed a connecting bridge between the gold and silver currency blocs."

Why did so many countries prefer bimetallism? A key reason was that gold production was limited and its currency value was stable, making it suitable for international remittances, but the gold value scale was too high for everyday transactions. People who opposed the gold standard joked that "the rich treat gold coins like pocket money." Historically, European countries typically adopted bimetallism, and even after England switched to the gold standard, it maintained silver as legal tender for a number of years. Silver was not demonetized until 1774, and was not abolished as legal tender for small transactions until 1821. The essence of bimetallism was to ensure that gold and silver could circulate together in the market.

It looked as if bimetallism was a two-pronged approach that most European countries sincerely believed could regulate the proportion of gold and silver. Under ideal conditions, the market would automatically adjust itself according to the gold and silver exchange ratio, and thereby achieve stability; in actuality, it more often fluctuated according to the flow of capital. For example, in the seventeenth century, Brazilian gold was transported to Great Britain, and this kind of exogenous effect would lure people into carrying out arbitrage on the various gold–silver exchange ratios, which then increased the inequivalence in the exchange ratio, and so on, effectively crippling bimetallism and even making it less convenient than a single metal standard. Table 1-1 shows fluctuations in the gold–silver exchange ratio over time.

Table 1-1. Exchange Ratios in China and Overseas from the Sixteenth to Eighteenth Centuries

Year	China	Japan	India	Great Britain	Spain
1534	1:6.363	—	—	1:11.50	1:12.00
1568	1:6.00	—	—	1:11.50	1:12.12
1571	—	1:7.37	—	1:11.50	1:12.12
1572	1:8.00	—	—	1:11.50	1:12.12
1575	—	1:10.34	—	1:11.50	1:12.12
1580	1:5.50	—	—	1:11.70	1:12.12
1588	—	1:9.15	—	1:11.70	1:12.12
1589	—	1:11.06	—	1:11.70	1:12.12
1592	1:7.00–1:5.50	1:10.00	1:9.00	1:11.80	1:12.12
1596	1:7.50	—	—	1:11.90	1:12.12
1604	1:7.00–1:6.60	1:10.99	—	1:11.90	1:12.12
1609	—	1:12.19	—	1:12.00	1:13.13
1615	—	1:11.38	—	1:12.00	1:13.13
1620	1:8.00	1:13.05	—	1:12.50	1:13.13
1622	1:8.00	1:14.00	—	1:12.50	1:13.13
1635	1:10.00	—	—	1:13.00	1:13.13
1637–1640	1:13.00	—	—	1:13.50	1:15.45–1:13.13
1660–1669	1:10.00+	—	1:16.16	1:14.50	—

1671	1:10.00+	—	1:16.025	1:15.19	—
1675	1:10.00+	—	1:17.224	1:15.557	—
1677	1:9.00	—	1:14.131	1:15.36	—
1700	1:10.00+	—	1:14.46	1:14.674	—
1709	1:10.00+	—	1:15.157	1:14.617	—
1714	1:10.00+	—	1:13.184	1:15.15	—
1719	1:10.00+	—	1:12.759	1:15.40	—
1721–1730	1:10.50	—	—	1:15.50	—
1731–1740	1:10.90	—	—	1:15.10	—
1741–1750	1:12.50– 1:11.77	—	—	1:14.93	—
1751–1760	1:14.90	—	—	1:14.55	—
1761–1770	1:15.00	—	—	1:14.81	—
1771–1780	1:15.47	—	—	1:14.64	—
1781–1790	1:15.23	—	—	1:14.76	—
1791–1800	1:15.40	—	—	1:15.42	—

Source: Qian Jiang, 1988, *A Survey of International Silver Flow and Import to China from the Sixteenth to Eighteenth Centuries*

This situation gave rise to the famous Gresham's Law, the so-called rule that "bad money drives out good." The classic manifestation of this law under bimetallism was that when the market exchange ratio for silver and gold coins differed from the statutory exchange ratio, currency that had a higher market exchange ratio than the statutory exchange ratio ("good money") would gradually decrease, and currency that had a lower market exchange ratio than the statutory exchange ratio ("bad money") would gradually increase. For that reason, the differing official prices among various countries triggered international capital flow. For example, in the fourteenth century, France set the exchange ratio between gold and silver at 11.11, while Great Britain's was slightly higher at 11.75. This meant that silver was undervalued in Great Britain and gold was overvalued, and the inevitable result was that silver flowed into France and gold flowed into England. Even when kings used draconian laws to obstruct the outflow of precious metals, they were unable to disarm the free will of the market.

Countless similar examples throughout the centuries suggest that bimetallism became a source of trouble. Fluctuations in the gold–silver exchange ratio typically led to recoinage, which in turn triggered price imbalances. After setting its gold–silver exchange ratio in the eighteenth century, England had little choice but to gradually move toward a gold standard. This move is closely associated with the famous physicist Isaac Newton. In the customary narrative, scientist Newton is dismissively described as becoming obsessed with theology in the latter half of his life. In fact, Newton served as warden of the Royal Mint for twenty-eight years (1699–1727), almost as long as his thirty years as a physicist, and his competence in this role led to his being knighted by the king.

Although his appraisal by subsequent generations is not unanimous, Newton truly left his mark on history as a financier. His term in office corresponded with the crucial period when England transitioned to the gold standard. As England experienced an outflow of silver and was inundated with recoinage, Newton in 1717 set the price of gold at 3 pounds 17 shillings 10.5 pence per troy ounce.[35] It has not been ascertained how Newton arrived at this valuation, but in terms of the history of British finance, the significance of this move is almost as great as his inquiries into why an apple fell on his head.

This gold–silver exchange ratio was imperfect and even mistaken; still excessively high, it created a chain effect and gave rise to surprising consequences that developed in England's favor: Due to this price fixed by Newton, silver continued to flow out of England, which then fully embraced the gold standard. A century later, in 1816, England legally declared itself a gold standard nation, and this system and exchange ratio were miraculously preserved up to modern times. Even the most censorious financial historians are forced to admit that Newton's perhaps dauntlessly ignorant move established the gold standard in 1717. In any case, history records that the value of the pound sterling was set in 1717 "at a gold price which lasted, with lapses from 1797 to 1819 and from 1914 to 1925, until 1931."[36]

Other countries followed England's example during the nineteenth century, and the gold standard ultimately prevailed over confusing bimetallism. The former currency confusion caused by arbitrage and recoinage was also alleviated with the invention of bank notes, and the British model based on the gold standard became the mainstream model at the beginning of the twentieth century.

Even so, silver was still used as currency and was not demonetized in major countries until the nineteenth century. In the early twentieth century, the majority of countries adopted the gold standard and issued currency "anchored" to gold, implying that the value of the fiat currency of the various countries was pegged to a set weight of gold. The British pound sterling deservedly continued benefiting from being the first currency pegged to gold.

At this point, rather than asking why these countries collectively transitioned to the gold standard at the end of the nineteenth century, it would be better to ask why bimetallism was sustained in these countries for several centuries. This was due to systemic inertia. Bimetallism gave states the power to set the gold–silver exchange ratio, which further ensured their seigniorage; additionally, technological advancements such as introducing the steam engine to the minting process made cutting and striking gold coins even more convenient.

Bimetalism Is Not Utopia

The Chinese say that enough money can make the devil push a grindstone, and Westerners are even more enamored of bullion. Columbus idolized gold even more, mentioning it sixty-five times in his diary for a journey lasting less than 100 days.[37] In a letter from Jamaica in 1503, Columbus wrote: "Gold is most excellent; gold is treasure, and he who possesses it does all he wishes to in this world, and succeeds in helping souls into paradise."[38]

Marx quoted Columbus while rather mockingly comparing the sixteenth and seventeenth centuries to the infancy of bourgeois society: "Nations and princes were driven by a general desire for money to embark on crusades to distant lands in quest of the golden grail."[39] Whether we acknowledge it or not, history illuminates the present, and gold holds a fatal attraction for humanity. What makes gold (or the gold standard) so attractive even in the present day, and why does everyone from economists to conspiracy theorists do their utmost to play it up?

The crux of the matter is people's profound fear of inflation. Indeed, painful memories of repeated hyperinflation in the twentieth century are almost all related to a government's profligate issuance of paper currency, which is also the story of the demise of the gold standard. The worship of gold has been constantly reinforced, from primitive memory to history lectures, so it's no wonder, to the bemusement of financial historians, that even up to the present, the gold standard implies the stability of a currency's actual value even more than a sovereign paper currency such as the U.S. dollar.

Disastrous hyperinflation typically emerged through paper currency, from the Weimar Republic's mark to the Republic of China's *jinyuanquan,* which was worth less than the paper it was printed on, to Zimbabwe's banknotes, which set a world record for the largest number of zeros on a currency. Comparatively speaking, people are inclined to believe that bona fide commodity money such as gold and silver brings a sense of security over stable currency values, and even exemption from government control. "If money consisted wholly of a physical commodity of this type, there would be, in principle, no need for control by the government at all. The amount of money in society would depend on the cost of producing the monetary commodity rather than other things. Changes in the amount of money would depend on changes in the technical conditions of producing the monetary commodity and on changes in the demand for money. This is an ideal that animates many believers in an automatic gold standard."[40]

The lessons of the past resurface, reigniting worries over inflation, and quantitative easing along with China's "currency overshooting" have made "gold die-hards"[41] as ubiquitous as ever. People in the paper currency era are attempting to return to the warm embrace of the gold standard, and with recurring reports of housewives buying gold, the regression to commodity currency seems to have become a rallying cry.

Ideals are beautiful, but reality is much bumpier. Imagination, however beautiful, is no match for true logic. The truth is that gold is not capable of beating back inflation; as to the gold standard, not only is there no going back, but the old times were not as beautiful as imagined, not to mention that we are equally unwilling to accept the pain of deflation. Some people grumble: "The fallacy contained in the phrase 'gold standard' is one of the most widespread fallacies that has duped the world. Believing that there is one specific gold standard is a fallacy. This illusion masks what is actually a huge discrepancy in the currency standards under the name of the gold standard, which has pushed the world to the brink of disaster."

Although the gold standard sounds classy, it is itself a commodity standard, and the problem with commodity standards is reflected in the gold standard. Macroeconomist John Maynard Keynes trenchantly denounced the fanaticism for gold as a "barbarous relic"—barbarism looks derogatory, but it also denotes the strong attraction gold holds for people, given that instinct lies behind barbarism. The gold standard survived less than one hundred years, until gold was demonetized in the 1970s, so a complete understanding of gold still requires returning to history.

Monetarist Milton Friedman was also no fan of the gold standard: "It should be noted that despite the great amount of talk by many people in favor of the gold standard, almost no one today literally desires an honest-to-goodness, full gold standard. People who say they want a gold standard are almost invariably talking about the present kind of standard, or the kind of standard that was maintained in the 1930s; a gold standard managed by a central bank or other government bureau."[42] He also felt it would be unrealistic to return to commodity standards such as the gold standard: "An automatic commodity standard is neither a feasible nor a desirable solution to the problem of establishing monetary arrangements for a free society. It is not desirable because it would involve a large cost in the form of resources used to produce the monetary commodity. It is not feasible because the mythology and beliefs required to make it effective do not exist."[43] Friedman concludes that actual commodity standards have deviated too far from a simple pattern that requires no governmental intervention: "Historically, a commodity standard—such as a gold standard or a silver standard—has been accompanied by the development of fiduciary money of one kind or another, ostensibly convertible into the monetary commodity on fixed terms. There was a very good reason for this development."[44]

Historically, the monetization of gold was a gradual, centuries-long process, and a certain amount of time was also required for people to accept its withdrawal from a currency role; at the very least it required a psychological reconstruction. This was also the case for other commodity standards, from the familiar gold standard to the once popular silver standard and gold–silver bimetallism, as well as primitive cowries and so on, which all qualify as commodity standards. The commodity standard was once pervasive in human society. As Milton Friedman says, commodity standards are also normal behavior throughout human history: "Historically, the device that has evolved most frequently in many different places and over the course of centuries is a commodity standard; i.e., the use as money of some physical commodity such as gold or silver, brass or tin, cigarettes or cognac, or various other goods."[45] A recent study found that with the decline in quality and quantity of food available in American prisons, instant noodles have replaced tobacco as the new prison currency, and that two packages costing US$0.59 each can be exchanged for clothing and other items worth nearly US$11.[46]

The gold standard is in fact a relatively primitive form of currency, and not the effective weapon against inflation that so many people imagine it to be. After all, decreasing the precious metal content of metal currency has been a favorite method of rulers, and paring, cutting, and grinding metal currency were common methods in the past. Economist Steven Ng-Sheong Cheung admits that the existence of money can to a great extent reduce transaction costs, but he emphasizes the conflict of interest behind it: "Those who issue or control currency will have great power, especially if that organization is a privileged or monopolistic government. Power can be abused. Because saving on transaction costs brings enormous profit, fraudulent behavior easily emerges."[47]

Counting on a return to the gold standard or even a commodity standard to evade governmental authority is unrealistic and inconsistent with the laws of historical evolution. One key reason is that commodity currency is not economical, and the commodity standard was a primitive method of taking up resources. "The fundamental defect of a commodity standard, from the point of view of the society as a whole, is that it requires the use of real resources to add to the stock of money. People must work hard to dig gold out of the ground in South Africa in order to rebury it in Fort Knox or some similar place. The necessity of using real resources for the operation of a commodity standard establishes a strong incentive for people to find ways to achieve the same result without employing these resources. If people will accept as money pieces of paper on which is printed 'I promise to pay units of the commodity standard,' these pieces of paper can perform the same function as the physical pieces of gold or silver, and they require very much less in resources to produce."[48]

The commodity standard has other problems as well: For example, because production is constrained by natural resources, commodity goods usually lead to a credit-deficient money famine.

Although the commodity standard is much more advanced than barter, it is not without its own obstructions. Commodity currency was a chaotic hodgepodge of various specifications and compositions, and even precious metals such as gold and silver routinely faced the possibility of counterfeiting. The Spartans were reportedly defrauded by counterfeit gold coins, and a fanaticism for alchemy in the Middle Ages has left a deep impression. A multitude of currencies increases transaction costs, with Europe and China no exceptions. I will explain this in detail later in the book while describing the Qing dynasty's chaotic currency values.

Confusion inevitably brings inconvenience to trading, especially where international trading flourishes. Adam Smith pointed out that currency in Genoa and Hamburg very seldom consisted purely of the coins of the realm: "Such a state, therefore, by reforming its coin, will not always be able to reform its currency. If foreign bills of exchange are paid in this currency, the uncertain value of any sum, of what is in its own nature so uncertain, must render the exchange always very much against such a state, its currency being, in all foreign states, necessarily valued even below what it is worth." This disadvantageous exchange inevitably caused traders to suffer a loss in the payment of foreign bills of exchange.[49] Inconvenient liquidity clearly increases transaction costs and causes the proliferation of all kinds of privately minted coins and even counterfeit money—I should add here that in ancient times the power to mint coins was derogated to the private sector and was not a matter of free choice, as some scholars believe. In the past, official currency was often poorly produced, and privately produced forgeries were difficult to eradicate, to the point where good money was sometimes chased out by bad money. Under these circumstances, even reminting failed to address the chaotic situation. "Before 1609 the great quantity of clipt and worn foreign coin, which the extensive trade of Amsterdam brought from all parts of Europe, reduced the value of its currency about nine per cent below that of good money fresh from the mint. Such money no sooner appeared than it was melted down or carried away, as it always is in such circumstances."[50]

Under these circumstances, it was difficult to determine the percentage of precious metal content, or even if the coin was genuine or counterfeit, and calls for professional organizations emerged in the market. In order to maintain the market's normal operations and deal with the problem of good and bad money, these regions developed the forerunners of modern banks. In 1609, Amsterdam established a bank (the Wisselbank, which was the most important bank in the seventeenth century and after many twists and turns became ABN Amro) in order to "remedy these inconveniences." Its strategy was to accept two kinds of currency and grant appropriate value to the worn coin of the realm. "This bank received both foreign coin, and the light and worn coin of the country at its real intrinsic value in the good standard money of the country, deducting only so much as was necessary for defraying the expense of coinage, and the other necessary expense of management. For the value which remained, after this small deduction was made, it gave a credit in its books. This credit was called bank money, which, as it represented money exactly according to the standard of the mint, was always of the same real value, and intrinsically worth more than current money."[51]

This was a historical opportunity. That the world's first public bank came into being in the prosperous commercial city of Amsterdam was no coincidence. Its objective from the outset was to screen the value of multitudes of currencies and establish currency standards. This systemic plan brought an end to the problems of the commodity standard and led to transactions gradually casting off the constraints of metal, and Europe transitioned into an era of emergence and reform of the banking system. Of course, the final separation from the gold standard didn't occur until the Great Depression in the twentieth century. It was the painful lessons of the Great Depression that led the financial community to recognize the contradiction between the functions of the gold standard and of "liquidity's lender of last resort."

As for China, a financial revolution in paper currency unfolded prematurely, and the fate of this empire-dominated reform was completely different from that in Europe.

The Song and Yuan Dynasties
Experimenting with Paper Currency

The urban money *mo,* for official use [equals] seventy-seven [cash];
in the street market, seventy-five; for buying fish, meat or vegetables, seventy-
two; for gold and silver, seventy-four; for pearls, hiring a slave girl, or
buying insect and ant [poison], sixty-eight; for written material, fifty-six.
Its value in the market varies.

Meng Yuanlao (Song dynasty), The Eastern Capital: A Dream of Splendor

Penniless while eating at an inn, I usually seek a friendly host;
instead I encounter an actual businessman, and must rely on
alms to escape.

Shen Meng (Song dynasty), Quotations of Zen Master Ji Diandao

CAI: How can you say that? Wait for me to go home and prepare
some cash certificates to thank you.

DONKEY ZHANG: Do you dare resist and try to cheat me with
cash certificates? Sai Luyi's rope is still here; I can still strangle
you to death.

Guan Hanqing (Yuan dynasty), Injustice to Dou E

Within the mountain stands a great old man, who keeps his back

turned toward Damietta and gazes on Rome as on his mirror; his

head is fashioned of fine gold, his breast and arms are pure silver,

then to the fork he is of brass, and from there down all of choice

iron except that the right foot is baked clay, and he rests more on

this than on the other. Every part except the gold is cleft by a fissure

that drips with tears, which gather and force their way down

through the cavern there, then take their course from rock to rock

into this depth.

Dante Alighieri[1] (1265–1321), The Divine Comedy

Paper Currency During the Tang–Song Transition

Chinese tend to look back at the Song dynasty in silent criticism. Everyone knows that "reading Song history is a tearful process"; the Song is regarded as a dynasty during which China became enfeebled. The master of moderation, Qian Mu, commends the Song economy as marking the beginning of the modern economy: "Before the Tang dynasty, China could be called a premodern society, but from the Song dynasty to the present it can be called a modern society." At the same time, Qian holds that among the Han, Tang, Song, Ming, and Qing dynasties, "the Song was the poorest and the weakest link. In terms of its political system, it also contributed the least."[2]

In fact, under different evaluation criteria, the Song had its strengths; in terms of per capita economic standards and cultural life, it can be considered an era of exceptional refinement and prosperity among China's dynasties. Chen Yinke once stated: "The culture of the Chinese race evolved over thousands of years and reached its zenith in the Southern Song." The achievements of the Song are appraised highly overseas; the freedom of its cities, its commercial life, and its flourishing culture and education combined to form the "dawning era" of China's modernization.

Japanese historian Naitō Konan came up with the concept of "Tang–Song transition" (or "reformation"), pointing out that the Tang marked the end of the Middle Ages and the Song launched the modern era. This notion has triggered wide-ranging discussion and in-depth study from the time it was proposed in 1910. In Qian Mu's words:

> In discussing the shift from China's premodern to modern society, the crux is the Song dynasty. The period before the Song can generally be referred to as premodern China, and the period after the Song is later China. Before the Qin, China was still a feudal aristocracy. The landed gentry emerged from the Eastern Han onward. The Wei-Jin, Northern and Southern dynasties, Sui and Tang were all ranked societies, an alternative form of the ancient aristocracy. From the Song onward, China became a society composed purely of common people. Apart from the incursion of Mongolian and Manchu rulers as a privileged class, those who joined the political elite were all talented scholars selected from among the commoners, and there were no remnants of ancient feudal aristocracy or traditional ranks. The Song dynasty therefore marked a complete change from the past, from politics and economy to society and daily life.[3]

China's Spring and Autumn period was a classic feudal society. By feudal I mean that states were built on fiefdoms. After King Zhou of Shang established his rule, feudal lords of shared and different surnames dispersed throughout the vast region. At that time, the territory was sparsely inhabited, with an extensive distribution of "savages," and Zhou feudalism was in fact a kind of "armed colonization" under which the emperor conferred ownership not only of land but also of the people— that is, the savages—on the land. According to *The Rites of Zhou,* feudal lords "controlled the imperial domains enclosed within their boundaries," that is, the area encircling a city, called a "state"; the Zhou nobility (or feudal clans with different surnames) occupied the center of the state and gradually conquered the aboriginal peoples (the "savages") and lands outside of the city. The conquered "savages" were organized according to the principles of the well-field system, paying tribute in the form of taxes and levies in kind and forced labor, or corvee, while "countrymen" consisted of soldiers, artisans, traders, and so on, who engaged in warfare, the production of bronze implements and other goods, the offering of sacrifices, and other such activities. Countrymen lived in groups under the patriarchal clan system, with the entire society organized under the emperor, feudal nobility, and the feudal classes of senior official, soldier, and so on. Like the European kings of the feudal era, the Zhou Emperor possessed the greatest military strength but did not directly manage the internal affairs of the feudal nobility, and was also constrained by the clans and aristocracy.

The feudal system undoubtedly had its advantages as the simplest and easiest organizational method for ruling a country as vast as China. In the early days, the great power of consanguineous patriarchal clans and the Zhou Emperor's military superiority enabled the feudal system to cope with its challenges. Over time, however, both factors gradually declined, and Western Zhou feudalism gradually evolved into wars for supremacy during the Spring and Autumn period and the mergers of the Warring States. As for the feudal nobility, expansion is dynamically inevitable, but once wars of annexation began, there was no turning back, and the cruel logic of warfare constantly strengthened competition for reform among the various feudal states. That's why the well-field system was inevitably scrapped in favor of agricultural production and the organization of resources. Salt and iron, irrigation works, fisheries and herding, transport, and artisanal industries entered the popular domain, and iron implements proliferated. Lord Shang Yang's reforms (c. 350 B.C.E.) replaced the consanguineous nobility with an administrative bureaucratic apparatus, and the status and interests of the populace were no longer based on kinship but rather on military enterprises, using reason rather than tradition to enhance organizational capacity for warfare in a way that ultimately united the country.

On careful examination, the Qin regime's success was not attributable solely to the achievements of legalist tyranny. Scrapping the well-field system was a reform toward privatization that conformed to historic trends, and it resulted in a great increase in agricultural production. The Qin Emperor's focus on development, especially roadways and irrigation works, was also beneficial. Financial support was available for military organization, and the conscription army system was advantageously integrated with the mercenary system: Serving in the army was obligatory but generously rewarded, producing a dauntless and powerful military force. Apart from state-owned industry, the Qin Emperor also encouraged private industry and commerce. The unification of money, the written language, the road system, and weights and measures were all examples of good governance. Before China was united under the Qin, each state had its own currency with its own characteristics and range of circulation, mainly for use in local trading within that state and region; long-distance trading, however, required exchanging gold or coins. This to some extent shows that the circulation of base metal coins required the backing of political authority, and that specific, discernible forms endorsed by the government were accepted by the public as currency. After the Qin united China, the government went a step further by monopolizing the minting of money.

The fall of the Qin was certainly due to the excessive labor imposed on the populace. As successor to the Qin, the Han learned this lesson and allowed the population to rest, but its fiscal system had its strengths and weaknesses. Land rent was light, but corvee was burdensome, sustaining the conscription system that the Western Han enacted in prefectures and counties. Under this system, the powerful central army and frontier forces relied on the support of the central fiscal administration. The minister of revenue was in charge of state finances, which drew income from farmland and the population, while the imperial treasurer managed the emperor's private finances, which drew income from nonagricultural sources such as "mountains and marshes," that is, iron and salt. The development of a commodity economy increased government revenue in modest increments while dramatically increasing the revenues of the privy purse. Han Wudi (reigned 141–87 B.C.E.) treated the latter as his private property and used it to sustain his expeditions against the Xiongnu, and when local strongmen declined to make "voluntary" contributions, monopolies were established in salt and iron, coinage and minting, and transport. Pitting the interests of ordinary people against those of the emperor, these measures bankrupted privately run industry and commerce. Since the Han dynasty had not developed a specialized capacity and system for levying commercial taxes, it resorted to prosecuting people for hoarding strings of cash, and encouraged people to inform on local strongmen and others who were unwilling to declare their taxes.

Han Wudi won his war against the Xiongnu, but at the cost of impoverishing society and the economy, and in his later years he issued an imperial decree shouldering the blame: "Since ascending the throne, I have been arrogant and unreasonable, causing distress to the country, for which I repent. I will henceforth cease all actions that harm the citizenry and waste the country's resources." When the Eastern Han was established, it changed to a voluntary mercenary system. Emperor Guangwu established armed forces in vulnerable areas and put an end to armies in prefectures and counties, but the strength of the central army was inadequate; when in need of soldiers, the emperor was obliged to allow recruitment of local armies, laying the groundwork for warlords to carve up the country.

In fact, the political structure of the Former and Later Han dynasties always suffered from the inability of the central authorities to directly administer the prefectures and counties. Han prefectural magistrates were situated between Zhou feudal lords and Qing governors; their power within their localities was considerable, and they controlled military, financial, and judicial matters, as well as the selection of local officials. Prefectural magistrates were naturally happy to form alliances with rich and powerful local clans, which reduced their reliance on the central government. This greatly expanded the power of the rich and powerful clans, and the period up until the Tang can be referred to as "gentry society." The Western and Eastern Jin dynasties (265–420) and the Northern and Southern dynasties (420–589) were eras when the power and influence of the gentry were overwhelming. Even in the Tang dynasty, when officials began to be enlisted through the civil service exam system, political power was still controlled by the clans. Whether in the central Shaanxi plain or in the northeast, the imperial court's political power and influence relied on the support of the clans.

The political status of the clans corresponded to the rise of the manor economy. Military units and farming households that found the government's oppressive exploitation unendurable aligned with the manors; this led to a steady growth in the actual power of the manors while the central government's revenue sources steadily shrank, and it increased the central government's reliance on the clan structure. Later generations credit the second Tang emperor, Li Shimin, with being open to advice, but this may actually have been a matter of necessity: Li rose through the ranks of the Guanlong Group,[4] founded by one of the great generals of the Western Wei (535–557). He ascended the throne supported by military nobility such as the Guanlong Group, as well as by prominent aristocratic clans in Shandong and elsewhere, so even as emperor he had to demonstrate his appreciation of the powerful clans. Compared with the subsequent Qing emperors, this was similar to the situation of kings under the Western European feudal system.

The Tang dynasty began experimenting with an imperial civil service examination system, which turned out to be an essential step in establishing a central administrative system. Even so, many scholars received honorary titles rather than entering the ranks through the examination system, so the emperor was surrounded by clan influence as before. The Tang emperor Xuanzong tried to gain greater power by depending on the northern tribes, but this planted the seeds for the rebellion of An Lushan and Shi Siming in 755.

The rebellion of An Lushan and Shi Siming is generally regarded as a watershed. During this time, most of China's powerful clans collapsed and scattered, and the north lost its status as an economic hub. Politically, China began moving toward a bureaucratic system, while socially it began moving toward a society for ordinary people; in economic terms, the manor model was bankrupted, and financially the country began monetizing taxes, while militarily it began moving toward a recruitment system. This transformation ultimately led to the grand experiment of the Song dynasty, which boasted the greatest economic accomplishments of China's imperial dynasties and created an economic environment in which experimentation with paper currency could be carried out. This is the story of paper currency that will be narrated in the next section.

The Northern Song's Jiaozi and the Emergence of Paper Currency

Before the Song and Yuan dynasties, China and other countries used commodity money. China used base metal coins, while the West used precious metal coins. With the emergence of paper currency in the

Song and Yuan, money began taking clearly divergent paths in the East and the West.

The function of silver was much stronger in the Song dynasty than in the Tang; silver appeared with increasing frequency in both official records and literary journals. Silver became much more widely used in society at large, with numerous records referring to silver drinking vessels. Research by the Japanese scholar Kato Shigeshi on gold and silver in the Tang and Song finds that this was a key period in the development of China's gold and silver currency. His research indicates that during the Tang and Song, gold and silver already had the function of money, but were mainly used by the government and in the upper levels of society. During the Song dynasty, silver was used not only in government outlays such as military emoluments and awards and the purchase of foodstuffs for frontier defense, but also in the private sector for gambling, donations, gifts, and so on. As the status of silver money improved, ordinary citizens made increasing use of it.

Yet, the use of silver in the Northern and Southern Song remained limited. During the Northern Song, silver was typically used for commercial purposes. Shen Kuo,[5] a participant in Wang Anshi's reforms during the Northern Song period, observed: "Gold and silver, currently regarded as valuable throughout the land, are only for use as implements and not as currency." But during the Southern Song, silver actually served a number of pricing functions, as recorded in books such as *Random Jottings at Yunlu* by Zhao Yanwei. An examination of the historical record indicates that silver's comprehensive monetization began in the Song, and gold also made up a substantial amount of currency. The time was not yet ripe for the more widespread use of silver, however, and at this juncture it was paper money that played a key role in the currency experiment. The Song dynasty's immense and extended experiment with paper money constituted a turning point in China's financial history, and ultimately established the foundation for the silverization of Chinese currency.

The Northern Song *jiaozi* (exchange note) and the Yuan *baochao* (treasure note) both reflected the backstage competition between paper and metal currencies, especially silver, and even more the chess game between imperial authority and will and the private marketplace. In fact, paper currency's entanglement in Chinese history lasted for centuries and through several dynasties, as recorded in vignettes that still come to life when read today. The failure of the paper currency experiments of the Song, Yuan, and Ming dynasties ultimately affirmed the value of silver; from a different angle, the emergence and obliteration of paper currency in China actually paved the way for the ultimate monetization of silver.

At a time when the West was wavering between gold and silver and even transitioning to the gold standard, the Chinese had still not abandoned the use of "coin" in daily life. Scholars often see this as evidence of lack of development in a country's industry and commerce. This phenomenon is surprising, given that China's productivity in the Tang and Song dynasties was by no means inferior to that of the outside world. Even more shocking is that China issued the world's first paper currency, the *jiaozi,* at this time. This seems inconsistent with typical monetary patterns, because the issuing of paper money is usually considered a higher stage of currency, emerging after gold–silver bimetallism.

So how did the story of paper money begin in China, and how did it end? Why did paper money emerge in China hundreds of years ago?

The birth of paper money, that is, the legendary *jiaozi,* was to a great extent related to economic prosperity, the providential cause and effect of a great era and a small territory. It is a story of money's spontaneous evolution, transcending era theory. The story of China's *jiaozi* reveals the cultural splendor of this ancient empire (paper money in fact appeared in the year 1000, and economists of later generations have joked that the Chinese became used to the sight of paper money, and did not share the amazement of foreign countries). It is also a case study in the patterns of currency, and the tragedies that can result when the economic environment and systemic framework are inadequate to sustain a form of money such as paper currency.

The Song is considered the world's first maritime empire.[6] Its glorious civilization resulted from a combination of revolutionary developments in commerce, transportation, agriculture, and urban living. Population and per capita income increased dramatically; during the reign of Song Huizong (1100–1126), the population reached 100 million, more than a 200 percent increase over the Han and Tang. "In the Yuanfeng years of the reign of Emperor Shenzong of the Northern Song, there were more than forty prefectures with more than 100,000 households, and during the

Chongning years of the reign of Emperor Huizong of Song there were more than fifty, while during the Tang dynasty there were only a dozen or so."[7] The urban structure of the Song dynasty also gradually surpassed the limits of commercial and residential districts, shifting from the Tang dynasty's "enclosed streets and markets" to "merged streets and markets." The lifting of the ban on night markets led to a rapid flourishing of urban life and unprecedented freedom. The Song dynasty's economic prosperity not only exceeded that of the Tang dynasty, which is customarily regarded as a flourishing age, but was a time in Chinese history when per capita income briefly surpassed that of Europe. It is worth mentioning that the Song dynasty separated commercial tax from agricultural tax and developed what came to be regarded as an integrated commercial tax system. This means that the policy of inhibiting commerce began shifting toward a policy to tax commerce, and the levying of commercial tax became more systematized. "Local governments periodically announced commercial tax rules and changes in them, and each prefecture, county, and town established taxation organs. This means that the collection of commercial tax first became systemized in its own right during the Song dynasty."[8]

The Song dynasty may represent the apex of prosperity of the Chinese empire. During the Northern Song, trade flourished to an astonishing degree, and with technical developments such as shipbuilding, the "maritime Silk Road" that began linking China to the world through its ports during the Han dynasty reached its pinnacle during the Song. Song China developed trade with dozens of countries, and trade in Guangzhou, Quanzhou, Ningbo, and other port cities flourished to an extent that is hard to imagine now. In addition, apart from the frontier trading that continued through centuries of war and peace in the Song, Liao, Jin, and Western Xia periods at government-established border trading posts (markets), there were also all kinds of private trading as well as smuggling. The scale of this trading was amazing; just taking the example of the relatively widespread trade in commodity sheep, the Song dynasty imperial household kitchen used tens of thousands of sheep per year, and public and private purchases of Khitan sheep along the river totaled more than 400,000 *min*[9] per year.[10]

The Song dynasty taxation system also had an unprecedented abundance of commercial tax categories. Prior to the Song, commerce was controlled more than taxed, and although the Tang dynasty did its utmost to levy commercial tax, it was not systematic, while the Song dynasty systematized all kinds of commercial tax revenue. The tax rate during the Northern Song is conservatively estimated to have reached 10 percent. A contemporary record states: "Goods and food from everywhere arrive at the capital; endless convoys of ships bring goods for public and private trading."[11] The emphasis on commerce and the development of the civil service helped Song civilization evolve to an unprecedented degree; it attained balance and expansion in the spheres of statism and privately owned economy, and pursued a defensive policy in external relations, but it was fairly radical in the commercial aspects of the economic sphere, especially in places such as Sichuan, Fujian Jiangsu, and Zhejiang. The emergence of paper money can be considered a result and symbol of Chinese civilization reaching its pinnacle in competition with the West.[12]

At the same time, the Song took quite a lenient attitude toward the wealthy; compared with today's "antiwealth" rhetoric, it could be considered "pro-wealth." During the Northern Song period, Emperor Taizong said: "The wealthy clans help me defend the country. Money is needed to deal with robbers and with unrest at the borders. Taxes need not be raised, so the people don't cry out in protest. Soldiers and farmers have enough to live on, and local garrisons protect the people."[13] Other officials apart from the emperor were also quite tolerant and affirming toward the wealthy. For example, during the Northern Song, Su Che[14] stated that the emergence of wealthy households was a rational development, and that the peaceful coexistence of the poor with the wealthy was the foundation of stability:

> Prefectural counties large and small have wealthy residents;
> this is an inevitable and rational development. As it is said, "It
> is natural for the quality of things to be unequal." Prefectural
> counties rely on [the wealthy] for strength, the state depends
> on them for security. It is not a matter of concern nor should
> it be rejected. It makes the wealthy content with their wealth
> and not overbearing, and the poor content with their poverty
> and not lacking. Sustaining the dependence of the poor and
> wealthy on each other keeps the kingdom stable.[15]

Going a step further, the Southern Song's Ye Shi[16] recognized the role of the propertied class in stabilizing society. He said that the wealthy served as a pivot holding together society's upper and lower classes, and he even criticized the notion of attacking the rich to aid the poor: "The wealthy are the foundation of the prefectures and counties, on whom those above and below rely. The wealthy nurture the common people for the emperor as well as contributing upward. Although the rich accumulate gain for themselves, it is due to their diligence and therefore proper."[17]

History is filled with tragedies of civilization's decay, and the history books inevitably ascribe virtue to the victor. The Song dynasty's greatest failing was its military, but if the Song really had such a weak military, how was it able to rise from the chaos of the Five Dynasties and Ten Kingdoms, and then hold out for centuries against the world-class military regimes of the Liao, Jin, and Mongols? In the hundreds of years from its founding to its extinction, the Song dynasty was either in a state of war or preparation for war, and had no choice but to pursue a long-term policy of "defending the interior and vacating the exterior" (that is, posting most of the imperial guards to defend the capital, with only a minority garrisoned on the periphery), struggling to gain time for the country to develop. In fact, the Song's military strength should not be regarded with contempt; its conventional forces at one point numbered 1.2 million, more than those of many other dynasties, and its military expenditure was enormous. Using logistics as an example, the Song installed warehouses in every locality, which required military supplies such as grain stores and armories. In addition, the supervising officials were tasked with managing the trading of salt, tea, and liquor at a profit and levying taxes on them to achieve adequate development.[18] An empire capable of sustaining such enormous military outlay must have had systemic management and economic strength, and an economic mindset permeated the Song's everyday operations; paper currency emerged amid this competition.

The earliest paper money emerged in Sichuan, and apart from the general background of the Song dynasty, Sichuan's particularities also came into play. Sichuan was a special case during the Song. Having avoided the chaotic wars of the Sui and Tang, Sichuan enjoyed a relatively independent economy and flourishing trade. Lacking copper, it

relied on iron coins, but the drawbacks of such coins in terms of porta-
bility became increasingly apparent. Historical records abound on this
point, typically regarding the amount of iron coins housewives had to
carry to market to buy salt: "Ten strings [*guan*] of small coins typically
weighed sixty-five catties,[19] while one string of large coins weighed
twelve catties; market transactions of three to five strings were hard to
hold and carry" (in the Song dynasty, a string equaled 770 coins). In
another example: "In Sichuan one often sees iron coins so light that
they're carried by mule-pack in amounts of 20,000." Records of this sort
are ubiquitous. The exchange ratio between iron coins and copper coins
was ten to one, and one can visualize the inconvenience of carrying
them. "In Jiangnan,[20] iron cash has long been used, with ten equivalent
to one copper coin; with the surge in the price of goods, the people are
inconvenienced," and "Sichuan and Shaanxi use copper and iron coins,
each copper coin the equivalent of ten iron coins."

The development of trade in tea leaves and horses, and the cumbersome nature of iron coins, ultimately resulted in the *jiaozi* emerging
in the relatively independent and exceptional Sichuan: "The people of
Sichuan, finding iron coins heavy, privately exchange notes called *jiaozi*
to facilitate trade, overseen by sixteen wealthy households."[21] At the outset *jiaozi* were issued by sixteen wealthy merchants as receipts in private
transactions in place of precious metals, silk, and other forms of currency. The *jiaozi* can be seen as an early type of money order. *History of
the Song: Food and Commodities* says, "The *jiaozi* method took over from
the Tang flying money [*fei*]."

One very interesting fact in the emergence of paper money is the
time-lag in terms of the physical attributes of metal currency and the
promotion of innovation at the finance level; in Sichuan it was iron,
while in the West it was copper. Centuries later, Europe's earliest experiment with paper money occurred in Sweden in the sixteenth century.
One reason was that Sweden possessed the largest number of copper
mines in Europe at that time, so the currency of that country was mainly copper; the value of copper at that time was 1 percent that of silver.

The government eventually took notice of the privately issued
jiaozi, and prodding by local officials ultimately led to the emergence of
an official *jiaozi.* Beginning in the second Tiansheng year of the Song's

Renzong reign (1024), the Song government officially issued *jiaozi* paper currency in the amount of 1,880,000 strings, its style "consistent with that issued by the people in its width and size."[22] Counterfeiting or privately printing *jiaozi* currency became a serious crime, and over the next two years a quota of 1,256,340 strings was issued. Subsequent circulation limits of *jiaozi* were divided into terms typically lasting three years, and when the term finished there was a transition during which the new currency was exchanged for the old. Originally the issuance of *jiaozi* was set at a quota of 1.5 million strings per term against reserves of 360,000 strings of iron coins. The convenience of the *jiaozi* triggered a steady decrease in the amount of iron coins in circulation from 500,000 strings in the early years of the Northern Song; the dwindling circulation of iron coins indicates that the *jiaozi* was welcome.[23]

With the intervention of the state, the *jiaozi* achieved even greater success. It not only resolved the problem of trust in privately issued *jiaozi*, but was also welcomed by Sichuan tea merchants engaged in transregional and transnational trading. This led to the *jiaozi* trading at higher than its nominal value. Su Che records: "The Sichuanese profit from the convenience of *jiaozi*, with one string selling at a premium of 10 percent."

The *jiaozi*'s commercial success made it a key component in state finance, and as the Song sought solutions to its steadily increasing military expenses, all sorts of financial innovations continued to ferment. In order to ensure military provisioning and encourage merchants to transport goods to the frontier regions, the Song authorities invented a kind of promissory note, payable upon presentation, to offset merchants' transportation costs. At that time tea and salt were the most popular commodities of trade, but eventually they were overtaken by military supplies. These negotiable instruments could be redeemed for iron cash or *jiaozi*, making them easy to use. Eventually they were centrally issued in the capital, Kaifeng.

Wang Anshi's radical new policies and the vast expense of the border wars caused inflation in the amount of currency in circulation. Wang Anshi's reforms have not been uniformly praised, but there is no denying that they greatly enhanced the monetization of the Northern Song economy, and thereby increased the demand for currency. At the same time, war with the Tangut of the Western Xia on the northwestern frontier continued unabated, and military costs were often calculated in the tens of millions of strings. The minting of copper coins in the Southern Song tripled in the period from 1073 to 1084 alone, at a rate of more than 5 million strings per year. Statistics indicate that the Northern Song minted 260 million strings of copper coins, more than the amount of coins minted by all of the other dynasties put together. This reflects the flourishing state of the Song's commodity economy. The invention and circulation of paper currency at one point effectively compensated for the shortage of copper coins.

Unfortunately, the calm could not last, and war threw the Song economy's rhythms into confusion, followed by excessive issuance of *jiaozi*. The amount of official *jiaozi* issued and in circulation steadily climbed, until the Zhezong Shaosheng years (1094–1097), when the war in Shaanxi injected confusion into the term and the issuance of the *jiaozi*. "The term and amount increased in order to purchase grain and recruit soldiers at the Shaanxi border, to at least hundreds of thousands of *min* and up to millions of *min*. Short of money, Chengdu printed it without stipulating the term or number."[24] Furthermore, the currency needed to be propped up by commerce, and in response to fiscal pressure, tea leaves gradually shifted from private trading to a state monopoly in the Song dynasty. This led to a drop in demand for the *jiaozi*. The imbalance in supply and demand, combined with public expectation of a devaluation of the *jiaozi*, led to further devaluation, with new *jiaozi* trading for old at a ratio of one to four or even one to five—only one-fifth of its face value. Ultimately the *jiaozi* was abandoned by both the government and the market.

During the reign of Song Huizong and the war with the Western Xia, there was no choice but to convert the *jiaozi* into another paper currency called the *qianyin* (coin voucher), and the "*jiaozi* authority" (*jiaoziwu*) became the "*qianyin* authority." Prior to this, the *qianyin* had been a popular negotiable instrument in Shaanxi and other places for a considerable length of time. The *qianyin* was issued in an even more disorderly fashion than the *jiaozi*: "It was issued at a rate more than twenty times that under Tiansheng,[25] and the value steadily decreased." With no reserve funds, the devaluation was appalling; the *min,* supposedly equivalent to a string of 1,000 bronze coins, was devalued to one-tenth of that amount. It is worth noting that the *qianyin* still existed in the Southern Song, and after Emperor Gaozong moved the capital south of the Yangtze, he prepared reserves of 700,000 strings of bronze coins to issue more than 30 million strings' worth of *qianyin*. "In seven years in the Shaoxing reign, [*qianyin*] were issued three times at a total value of more than 37.8 million strings. In the last years, this increased to more than 41,470,000 strings, while the total iron cash reserves reached only 700,000 strings."[26]

The Southern Song Currency Famine and the Profligate Huizi

Before the story of the Northern Song's *jiaozi* completely ended, it had a sequel in the Southern Song.

The Southern Song generally carried on the system of the Northern Song, but as the Southern Song contented itself with ruling only part of China, and as its economic hub moved farther south, its economic system expanded relative to the Northern Song and gave rise to quite a few financial innovations. At one point, in fact, the Southern Song's survival depended on the salt certificate (*yanyin*) system.

Salt certificates were vouchers that the government sold to merchants under the salt monopoly. The salt certificates were equivalent to negotiable securities and financial instruments. After the pared-down Southern Song imperial court was established, the Jin army made frequent forays south and there was instability on all fronts, to the point where Emperor Gaozong (Zhao Gou) even fled by ship. During an interval of more than ten years from the time that Zhao Gou ascended the throne in Shangbing, Henan, to the formal designation of Hangzhou as the capital, the easily transportable salt certificates were very helpful in raising money for military and other expenses; there was even a saying that "the move south to establish the state relied on salt notes," referring to Emperor Gaozong's move south and salt certificates. Before ascending the throne, Gaozong had served as his army's commander-in-chief, and in an effort to raise money for military costs to rescue the throne in the Jingkang Incident,[27] he issued salt certificates, through which he soon obtained 500,000 *min* in coins. Even Gaozong's southern sojourn to found his state in exile bears the imprint of merchants buying salt certificates.

The addition of salt profits to government revenue is recorded as early as the Spring and Autumn period, in 700 B.C.E. Guang Zhong in the state of Qi took advantage of the coastal geography to benefit from salt and iron, the beginning of the so-called salt laws. From then on, the salt industry alternated between government and private hands. The Tang dynasty had salt and iron commissioners from the time it was founded, and eventually these positions were merged into a new government finance department, the State Finance Commission (*Sansi*). During the Song dynasty, the status of the State Finance Commission was on the same level as that of the prime minister, and salt profits were exploited to the nth degree with an even more comprehensive salt law that initiated the use of salt certificates and other systemic innovations. During the Huizong era, under the economic reforms of the powerful prime minister Cai Jing,[28] the use of salt certificates became even more prevalent and extensive, and this system continued through subsequent generations. *History of the Song Dynasty: Food and Money* records that the salt law was reformed during the reign of Emperor Suzong of Tang, and the famous salt commissioner Liu Yan vigorously reorganized the system. Total salt profits for the entire country reached 400,000 *min* per year, and by the last years of the Tang, they made up half of the government's tax revenues. During the Zhezong period of the Northern Song, income from the Huai region and Shandong's Xiechi Lake alone reached 4 million *min*, composing two-thirds of the government's tax revenues. By the Gaozong period of the Southern Song, income from one salt production site in the Hailing district of Taizhou, Jiangsu Province, converted into 6–7 million *min*; the income from that single prefecture exceeded the Tang dynasty's entire national income.

Although the use of salt certificates expanded, they were not genuine currency, but were more like debentures. In terms of paper currency, the Southern Song's best-known currency was the *huizi* (account note). It could even be said that it was not until the Southern Song that paper currency circulated widely in China as fiat currency. The government first began issuing *huizi* during the thirtieth year of the Southern Song's

Gaozong Shaoxing period (1160), and the next year it installed a *huizi* authority (*huiziwu*) in imitation of the Sichuan *jiaoziwu*, and set the denominations and reserve funds: "Its operations referenced the Sichuan money laws. The southeastern regional circuit [*lu*] taxed for military needs and designated the money in three denominations of 1,000, 2,000 and 3,000. The Deputy Minister of Revenue, Qian Duanli, oversaw it and granted the state treasury 100,000 *min* in coin as reserves."[29] The *huizi* circulated in different regions as Southeastern *huizi*, Hubei *huizi*, Huainan *huizi*, and so on. Compared to the similarly regional iron coin-backed *jiaozi* originating in Sichuan, the *huizi* had a much more extensive circulation, and its reserves were mainly in copper coins or even silver. The Southern Song general Wu Jie issued a *huizi* backed by silver reserves in Hechi[30] that is considered China's earliest use of the silver standard. It also shows the expanded function of silver as currency; at that time, *huizi* and silver values had an inverse relationship: "When the *huizi* was of lesser value, silver was of higher value, and when the *huizi* was valued higher, silver was valued lower."[31]

Paper currency emerged during the Northern Song and reached its heyday during the Yuan, but the role it played in the intervening Southern Song cannot be written off. If it can be said that the spread of paper currency in the Northern Song was only a localized phenomenon, the paper currency of the Southern Song had a nationwide circulation. Paper currency's emergence in the Song dynasty was a natural result of the flourishing monetary economy, but also an innovation compelled by military pressures.

The spread of the *huizi* originated in the financial exhaustion of the Southern Song government. The territory controlled by the Southern Song was only half the size of that of the Northern Song, but the rich and populous southern territory where the government relocated had extensive economic resources; apart from expanding overseas trade, the government continued charging additional types of taxes besides the land tax, such as a capitation levy (*jingzhiqian*), silk-conversion levy (*zheboqian*), liquor levy (*tianjiuqian*), and so on. Compared with the standards of the Northern Song and subsequent empires, the Southern Song, in spite of its small territory and population of only 60 million concentrated mainly in eastern and western Zhejiang and Sichuan, had higher revenues than the Northern Song, an indication of the Southern Song's economic prosperity and the fiscal acumen of its officials. During the last years of the Southern Song's Xiaozong reign, government revenues were more than 65.3 million *min,* compared with only around 50 million *min* during the Zhezong reign of the Northern Song.[32] But while the Southern Song's fiscal administration ably expanded sources of income, the pressure of various kinds of military expenditure and foreign reparations forced it to draw on funds months or even half a year in advance.

The second reason for the *huizi* was the increasing frequency of currency famines. Currency famines were recorded during the Sui and Tang dynasties, but by the Song dynasty they were even more frequent. This was due to the shortage of copper. Before the Sui and Tang, commerce was not developed enough, and official policies prohibited the private minting of bronze coins. Later, trade gradually increased, but with private minting banned, the price of copper rose, making the minting of coins profitless; neither the government nor the private sector was motivated to mint coins. With copper prices rising, the general public was even more inclined toward recasting bronze currency into implements at a profit of 500 percent to as high as 1,500 percent. For example, it is recorded that during the Tang dynasty, 1,000 bronze cash could yield six catties of bronze, each catty selling for more than 600 cash, nearly four times the original face value. The markup was even higher during the Song dynasty. A record from the Gaozong period states: "Melting 10 cash yielded one tael of copper, which when recast as an implement could sell for 150 cash."[33]

Beginning in the Tang dynasty, government policies shifted from banning the private minting of coins to banning the removal of coins from the country and the melting of coins for casting into implements, which indicates that currency famines had become prevalent. By the Song dynasty, the shortage of copper coins caused the outflow of coins to become a hot issue, as much as the subsequent outflow of silver or today's outflow of *renminbi.* At that time the phrase "taken across the border in heavy carts, brought back in packed ocean vessels" was used to describe the outflow of copper coins to bordering countries and even overseas. The Song dynasty, continuing former policies, issued prohibitions against the outflow of copper coins by land and sea, while the Jin, Western Xia, and other countries used various means to obtain copper coins through smuggling, cross-border copper mining, and utilization of the short-string system.[34] Korea, Japan, and Southeast Asia swarmed after copper coins at that time, often selling commodities at one-tenth of their value in order to obtain them. Although a small number of Chinese coins flowed into Japan during the Ming dynasty, the inflow of Song coins was far greater, and the effect much more extensive and protracted.

Wang Anshi launched his reforms during the Xining period of Emperor Shenzong's reign. One of Wang's policies was to scrap the prohibition on coin production and take in privately held wealth to recoup the government's military costs. Once the ban was eliminated, the outflow of Song coins to foreign countries accelerated, and the currency famine became even more serious. There are ubiquitous records of this—for example, a record from the Shenzong reign: "Year after year, eastern and western Zhejiang have experienced severe shortages of currency, which people call a money famine." During a currency famine, money became expensive and goods became cheap. The Song government minted coins on a large scale and seized privately held coins through the service exemption act (mianyi fa).[35] The government coffers rapidly filled, while private trade withered, and many people became refugees because they could not afford to pay their taxes.

The shortage of copper caused corner-cutting in the minting of copper coins in comparison with previous dynasties. In the third Jingyou year of Emperor Renzong's reign (1036), 2.81 million guan of copper coins were minted with the content debased by a total of more than 878,000 catties; the leftover copper was used to mint another 169,000 guan of copper coins. This led the Song dynasty populace to favor the currency of previous dynasties—for example, the Tang dynasty's kaiyuan coin.[36] The outcry against the "high cost of goods and scarcity of money" became even more pronounced during the Southern Song. When the huizi emerged in the thirtieth year of the Shaoxing era, the objective was to mint 500,000 strings of copper coins, but ultimately only 100,000 strings were minted.[37] Was there really a lack of money during the Song dynasty? The Song actually minted a considerable number of copper coins. Scholar Gao Congming calculates that during the entire Northern Song period some 262 million strings of copper coins were minted, not counting existing coins, while Peng Xinwei estimates the total amount of currency in circulation at that time at 240–250 million strings. The Japanese scholar of Song history Miyazawa Tomoyuki believes that most of the copper coins in circulation flowed back into the state coffers as tax revenue, with a total of more than 70 million strings in a single year, and that is why fewer copper coins were circulating in the market.[38] But Wan Zhiying points out that this argument ignores the fact that the imperial court spent the money in the state treasury almost as fast as it took it in, and that the amount of copper coinage in circulation was therefore as enormous as ever. On the other hand, Gao Congming estimates that by the end of the eleventh century, the total value of commodities in circulation was 150 million strings. Based on that figure, the Song dynasty's copper coins supply was by no means inadequate for the amount of trade at that time.[39]

Yet, the currency famine was not simply a shortage of copper coins. As scholar Zhu Jiaming has noted, China experienced currency famines repeatedly from the Han dynasty onward. The core issue was that "the demand for the form of currency made up chiefly of copper coins was greater than the supply; in other words, the supply of currency lagged behind demand and was not able to satisfy the market economy's demand for money."[40]

This contradiction was very evident in the Song dynasty. On the one hand, a large number of copper coins were being hoarded or exported to foreign countries and were effectively not circulating in China; on the other hand, with the Song dynasty's development of a commodity economy while lacking a fiduciary money-creating mechanism like our modern banks, the amount of copper cash available could not properly meet the demands of trade; the Song dynasty currency famine was in itself an expression of economic demand. The Japanese scholar Shiba Yoshinobu accurately distinguishes the Song dynasty's commercial trade from that of previous dynasties in its extensive and simultaneous development of regional markets, provincial markets, long-distance trade, and international trade. Copper cash alone was inadequate to sustain this booming trade, so large numbers of iron, bronze, paper, and silver currencies soon emerged and circulated in various localities.[41] In fact, with the development of a private economy as well as domestic and international trade, the increasing amount and scope of trading required a simpler, more convenient, and higher-face-value currency; in this respect, both the initial paper currency and subsequently silver currency were superior to copper cash. I have already discussed the defining quality of money, which is that any form of currency that gains the public's trust can circulate as money, and those with greater prestige can even trade at a premium. This was fully reflected in the currency practices of the Northern Song.

Building on the foundation of public confidence, if a government becomes involved in the appropriate management of currency, so-called fiat currency may emerge. Taking the Northern Song *jiaozi* as an example, the paper currency issued by the state immediately qualified as fiat currency, its credit based on the state's acknowledgment of its value. A metal-standard paper currency implies that the paper currency is directly linked to the value of a commodity currency, ensuring its credit: The *huizi* was initially directly convertible into copper cash and could be used in transactions with the government to buy salt vouchers, tea vouchers, and other valuable vouchers, and to pay taxes. Miyazawa Tomoyuki believes that the Song dynasty fiscal and monetary system had a decisive significance in terms of vertical flow between the private sector and the government, and it molded the environment in which money was extensively used in Song dynasty economic life. Gao Congming, however, believes that this vertical flow was based on the wide-ranging horizontal flow of currency in private trade.[42] The actual practice of Song dynasty paper currency indicates that the Song government respected private-sector rules in following the trend of economic monetization and pushing forward a fiat currency, and that was crucial to the *huizi*'s success.

Eventually the *huizi* developed to the point of being unconvertible. The government hoped to use *huizi* as much as possible in paying official salaries, military expenses, and so on, and to accept *huizi* as little as possible in its revenue, therefore stipulating that taxes should be paid in the form of "nine parts cash and one part *huizi*." The unintended negative consequence was an acceleration of the *huizi*'s withdrawal from circulation. In transactions with the government such as the purchase of tea vouchers and salt vouchers, people used *huizi* rather than copper cash, the Southern Song version of "bad money driving out good money."

The pragmatic Southern Song government eventually realized that it could lead people to accept the *huizi* only by treating it the same as copper cash. For that reason, it implemented a "half cash and half *huizi* system," that is, with copper cash and *huizi* each making up half of its finances. This meant that *huizi* and coins had equal status, and the *huizi* was issued the next year under the stipulation that half of the currency would be in *huizi* and half in cash: "The newly issued *huizi* was negotiable for civilian and military use in the Huai River region, Zhejiang, Hubei, and regional circuits west of the capital. Apart from salt producers being paid entirely in cash, military pay and provisions in circuits without water transport should be paid entirely in *huizi*, while military pay and provisions near waterways should be paid half in cash and half in *huizi*. Other forms of military pay should be defrayed in *huizi* according to rank."[43] The system of using half coin and half *huizi* was repeated, but throughout the Southern Song, the basic principle was that decreasing the amount of *huizi* issued made it more popular.

It is worth mentioning the Southern Song's Xiaozong period. Emperor Xiaozong was the second ruler of the Southern Song and is considered a person of considerable achievement. The posthumous rehabilitation of Yue Fei[44] earned him a great deal of political capital. As the seventh-generation descendant of the first Song emperor, Xiaozong's ascent returned the throne from the lineage of the second Song emperor to that of the first. His nearly thirty-year reign, from 1162 until 1189, revived the Southern Song. In the Chunxi era of his reign (1174–1189), the *huizi* was basically equivalent to coin, and there are records of "traveling merchants vying to use the *huizi* in trading" and "soldiers and civilians preferring *huizi* to coins," and even the statement that "mulberry notes were weightier than gold."[45] So-called mulberry notes, or bank notes, referred to paper currency, because paper, especially currency, was often made of mulberry bark. Referring to the situation of the *huizi*, the Southern Song poet Xin Qiji wrote during the Chunxi era that using half coin and half *huizi* effectively made the *huizi* valuable.

> In the past, coins were regarded as more valuable than *huizi* in receiving payment; when the government supported distribution, coins were seen less than *huizi*. Therefore, people

consistently exchanged the *huizi* at 610 or 620 [cash], and soldiers and civilians decried its declining value in the thoroughfares. In recent years, people have paid using half *huizi* and half coin, which has made the *huizi* more valuable than before, exchanging for 700 [cash] or so (in the Jiangyin military district it is exchanged for 740 cash, and in Jiankang prefecture for 710 cash). For this reason it is valued more.[46]

The use of the *huizi* was inseparable from the flourishing of commerce. Merchants preferred the *huizi,* not only for convenience and as a hedge against inflation, but also because a certain amount of tax was levied on gold and silver. Emperor Xiaozong himself said the *huizi* made him "sleepless for nearly ten years" and that "in most cases, using *huizi* less makes it more valuable, and using it more makes it less valuable"; in other words, he understood the relationship between the value of the *huizi* and the amount in circulation. This shows that the Southern Song economy's capacity for fine-tuned regulation and control had attained a reasonable standard after being tested and adjusted in practice.

In terms of monetary theory, the Song dynasty applied the traditional Chinese theory of "mutual balance between mother and child" (*muzi xiangquan*).[47] This theory expressing the relationship between large and small currency was stated as early as the Spring and Autumn period. A historian of the Eastern Zhou's state of Lu, Zuo Qiuming (fifth century B.C.E.), wrote in *Guoyu: Zhouyu:* "The weightier and larger currency is the mother, and the lighter and smaller currency is the child. When currency is less valuable than goods, promote the heavy currency for expensive goods on the market; this is called the mother's power over the child. When currency is worth more than goods, promote the light currency for cheap goods on the market rather than wasting the heavy currency; this is called the son's power over the mother." The meaning of this quote is that the currency's weight and value should match the circulation of commodities and the standard of goods, with heavy currency used for expensive goods and light currency used for cheap goods, striking a balance between mother and child. With the emergence and proliferation of paper currency during the Song dynasty, "mutual balance between mother and child" gradually became the relationship between copper coin and paper currency (especially the *huizi*). The Southern Song's Yang Wanli noted, "Concerning money and *huizi*, the ancients bequeathed the mutual balance between mother and child. In today's money there are two mothers: copper coins south of the Yangtze, and iron coins north of the Huai river. There are also two children: the *huizi* is the child of the copper coin, and the new *huizi* is the child of the iron coin. Mother and child cannot be separated; hence the money will be used together."[48] This theory was eventually extended to the relationship between silver and copper coins, and had quite a profound effect on China's monetary history; generally speaking, it was reflected in the control and management of the amount of currency.

The system of using half coin and half *huizi* established the *huizi*'s legal status, but in practice the *huizi* was limited by the quantities in which it was issued. Like the *jiaozi,* the *huizi* was eventually issued in set terms. Originally, one term was three years, and the value quota was set at around 10 million strings. When the term expired, the old *huizi* would be reclaimed and replaced. In retrospect, the secret of the *huizi*'s success was maintaining appropriate reserve funds, along with controlling the amount of *huizi* and encouraging the equivalent value of the *huizi* and copper coins. The late Ming philosopher Huang Zongxi admiringly appraised the accomplishments of the *huizi*:

> The reason why the Sung could do this lay in its having a limit on each issue, which was backed by a reserve of 360,000 strings of cash and also supported by other items such as salt and liquor. When the people wanted paper money, cash was paid into the Treasury. If they wanted cash, paper money was paid into the Treasury. If they wanted salt or liquor, paper money was paid into the monopoly administration. Therefore, having paper money in one's hand was the same as having cash. One reason why it was essential to place a limit on each issue was so that the actual cash reserve of the issuing authority would correspond to the amount of paper money issued. If there were no limit, successive printings would be uncontrolled. Another reason was so that after each issue of so much paper money, so much could be withdrawn from

circulation with the next issue. Thus counterfeits could be easily detected. Without limited issues, the amount withdrawn or issued could not be tracked. Such was the Currency Stabilization System of the Sung dynasty.[49]

The good times didn't last long for the *huizi*, however. Even guided by the theory of "mutual balance between mother and child," the *huizi* ultimately perished as a result of excessive issue. Once again, warfare threw everything into confusion. In the second year of the Southern Song's Kaixi period (1206), Temüjin rose to power, took the name Genghis Khan, and established the Mongol Empire. In the same year, the Southern Song's hawkish faction temporarily prevailed, and Emperor Ningzong issued his imperial edict for the "Kaixi Northern Expedition" against the Jin dynasty. During the Xiaozong Longxing era, there were only around 4 million *guan* of *huizi*, but as finances became critical, especially from 1206 onward, the issuing of *huizi* increased dramatically and multiple issues of *huizi* were mixed together. In the first Kaixi year, before the war (1205), the thirteenth issue of *huizi* was 55.48 million with a term of nine years. In the second Jiading year, after war was declared (1209), the fourteenth issue of *huizi* was 112.63 million, with the term changed to twenty-two years.[50]

This destroyed the public confidence the *huizi* had enjoyed during Emperor Xiaozong's reign. Paper currency became the last refuge for rescuing the country, as well as a money-management technique that continued to be widely adopted by emperors, generals, and ministers: "At the imperial court, among government officials, no strategy was heard except to add a *liaozhiju*[51] to create wealth; all effort went toward printing mulberry notes as a wealth management technique. The greater the amount of mulberry [paper currency], the less its value."[52] If paper currency was issued without a corresponding commodity in reserve, it would ultimately have value only on paper. The redoubled production of *huizi* also implied its accelerating devaluation. Scholar Qi Xia's analysis based on rice prices indicates a steady increase in commodity prices during the Southern Song dynasty. In the Gaozong era (1141), the price of rice at one point was 100 cash (*wen*) per *dou*,[53] but during that period it inflated from 300 cash to 500 cash and ultimately soared to 3,400 cash

100 years later, in the Lizong era of the later Song (1240). This trend intensified under war conditions. In the eighteenth issue of 650 million strings' worth of *huizi* in 1246, the 200 string domination of *huizi*, with a face value of 200,000 cash, was not enough to buy a pair of straw sandals: "The eighteenth issue's 200 was not enough to trade for a straw sandal or to meet a soldier's needs for one day . . . Living in hunger, cold and hardship, they could not be expected to fight to the death."[54]

As the *huizi* steadily devalued, the rule of "bad money chasing out good" once again came into play. Copper coins gradually withdrew from circulation in the market, and the half-*huizi*, half-cash system became difficult to sustain in either revenue or expenditure. Originally introduced to alleviate the coin famine, the *huizi* ended up making the situation worse, and the increasing frequency of money famines crippled the economy. Toward the end of the Southern Song, someone lamented, "The scarcity of money and high cost of goods has reached an extreme in recent years. People feel uncertain and the marketplace is desolate." The Song's competitiveness was not in military matters; it had always been the economy that sustained the lifeblood of the Song court, and the economy's ultimate collapse likewise decided its fate.

In the fourth year of the Jingding era (1263), the Southern Song printed an additional 150,000 strings of *huizi*. At the end of the Song, as the Yuan army loomed, Prime Minister Jia Sidao continued issuing currency in excessive amounts. New *guanzi* (communicating medium) were also issued with the intention of replacing the *huizi*, but that only caused further devaluation of the *huizi* so that it was hardly worth one cash.[55] After that, the Yuan main forces went south to Lin'an and converted the Yuan's *zhongtong* notes into *huizi* at an exchange rate of 1:50, and the *huizi* withdrew from the historical stage. At that time the *huizi*'s devaluation was intense, while the *zhongtong* note was quite firm. The Southern Song had not yet formally collapsed, but this price did not buy popular support or stabilize popular opinion.

From the *jiaozi* to the *huizi*, the result was always devaluation due to financial crisis. The currency famine brought about by the tight supply of copper coins led to paper currency being issued in larger amounts, and the increasing amount of paper currency issued led to its devaluation because of inadequate reserves. This vicious circle was due to the fact that the Song dynasty's collateralized financial resources were continuously eroded by warfare, leading it onto the road of profligate issuance and devaluation. The *jiaozi* and *huizi* were both initially issued privately, which inevitably created confusion. For example, the wealthy merchants who first issued private *jiaozi* ran into money problems and suffered runs on their currency, so the government stepped in to issue *jiaozi* and enhance public trust in the currency, squeezing the privately issued *jiaozi* out of the market. This implies that at the very outset, government-issued paper currency enjoyed greater public trust than privately issued paper currency, and even traded at a premium. However, once the state abused this trust by issuing excessive amounts of currency, the inevitable result was devaluation and abandonment by the market. Ultimately, the Song dynasty's demise also became inevitable: "The Song state became parasitic and was deserted by its own citizens."[56]

The Chinese took pride in the Song dynasty's paper currency, but war took them back to zero. We have witnessed the creativity of Song civil society and the nimble economic administrative abilities of the bureaucracy, but setbacks in war led to a loss of control over finances. Runaway fiscal policies inevitably led to runaway monetary policies, and the *jiaozi* was ultimately no match for the unfolding financial and monetary tragedy. The *jiaozi, huizi,* and other currencies ultimately succumbed to inflation, depriving Song rulers of the dividends of reform. Song dynasty paper currencies withdrew from the stage, but greed and stupidity endured. Especially as a dynasty approached collapse, it indulged in ever more desperate attempts to plunder private wealth by issuing paper currency. It was the same for the Song and the Jin, and the Yuan was also unable to avoid it, while the Ming completed paper currency's last act in premodern China.

The Decline of Paper Money and Marco Polo's Limitations

The Song dynasty's currency famine also plagued its adversaries. Officials in neighboring states racked their brains to prevent the outflow of copper coins, which the use of fiat currency failed to address. As a rival of the Southern Song, the Jin dynasty did little better in terms of the fate of its fiat currency.

Influenced by the Song, the Jin dynasty early on established a bureau to issue paper currency. The Jin's exchange certificates (*jiaochao*) had a seven-year circulation term, but in the chaos of war, they were also issued in excessive amounts. Although the Jin dynasty attempted to set commodity prices, it ran out of options, and by the time the Jin fell in 1222, "the official price of silver had increased by a multiple of more than 400,000, and the market price by more than 10 million. One hundred *min* in *jiaochao* could only buy a bowl of noodles, and 10,000 strings was required to buy a cake."[57] Economists have found the speed of devaluation and the intensity of commodity pricing measures comparable only to the *jinyuanquan* of a much later era.[58] It is worth mentioning that the Jin was even more copper-deprived than the Southern Song, and therefore encouraged the use of paper money that much more, and coupled with the hoarding of copper coins by members of the public, this led to increasing use of silver. Many documents from the last years of the Jin dynasty record rice being priced in silver, and its excessive use in private trade even led to grave-robbing to dig up silver.[59] It was because of this, the Japanese scholar Kato Shigeshi believes, that the use of silver as currency began with the Jin,[60] and not, as many people believe, with the Ming. In any case, silver began to stand out during the Song and Yuan dynasties because of the shortage of coin and the decline of paper currency.

The Mongolian nobility who exterminated the Jin dynasty also adopted the methods of the Jin (and in fact also of the Southern Song) by issuing paper currency that was denominated in silk or silver. The Yuan dynasty epitomized the issuance of paper currency in premodern times, and scholars of monetary history credit it with occupying a niche in the history of currency. A Japanese scholar has even referred to it as "an unprecedented and unreplicated monetary policy." The Yuan dynasty not only created a dedicated distribution system for paper currency, but also established the precedent of unlimited legal tender, a precursor to the fiat currency used by various countries in subsequent generations. By way of comparison, the bank certificate of the Bank of England that was the precursor to the British pound did not make its debut until the seventeenth century.

After the Yuan dynasty took over the territory ruled by the Southern Song, it began banning the use of copper coins and used its currency, *zhongtong* notes, to buy up *huizi*. In the last years of the Southern Song, the first treatise on China in a European language mentions paper currency: "The common money of Cathay is a paper of cotton, in length and breadth a palm, and on it they stamp lines like those on the seal of Mangu."[61] The author was William of Rubruck (1220–1293), a Flemish Franciscan missionary and explorer who traveled to Mongolia and recorded the conditions there.[62] It appears that the Yuan dynasty absorbed the lesson of the Southern Song and Jin dynasties; their currency was initially backed by reserves that preserved the stability of the *zhong-tongchao* and other currencies for many years. The Yuan currency system was described in detail by the Italian explorer Marco Polo. Although Marco Polo's account is full of fantastical tales and is considered "a combination of verifiable fact, random information posing as statistics, exaggeration, make-believe, gullible acceptance of unsubstantiated stories, and a certain amount of outright fabrication," Jonathan Spence points out that Marco Polo was the first Westerner to claim to have observed China from the inside, and his descriptions have imprinted themselves in Western minds to the present day.[63] Many of the vivid details in his book can be confirmed by standard historical accounts, especially the portion on paper currency. It is even possible to ask, given the timing of Marco Polo's book, whether the embryonic forms of paper currency that subsequently appeared in Europe might have been modeled on China's experience.

Marco Polo provided detailed descriptions of the paper currency, from its creation to its use, and even roughly calculated and compared the value of paper currencies:

> The emperor's mint then is in this same city of Cambaluc, and the way it [money] is wrought is such that you might say he has the secret of alchemy in perfection, and you would be right. For he makes his money after this fashion. He makes them take of the bark of a certain tree, in fact of the mulberry tree, the leaves of which are the food of the silk-worms, these trees being so numerous that whole districts are full of them. What they take is a certain fine white bast or skin which lies between the wood of the tree and the thick

outer bark, and this they make into something resembling
sheets of paper, but black. When these sheets have been prepared [by soaking the bast in water, then pounding it into a
pulp and making it into paper that is no different from cotton
paper except that it is black], they are cut up into pieces of
different sizes.[64]

The face value of this paper currency was equivalent to various amounts
of silver coin, or even gold coins.

Apart from value ratios, Marco Polo's journal also recorded the
mandatory use of paper currency:

With these pieces of paper, made as I have described, he
causes all payments on his own account to be made; and he
makes them to pass current universally over all his kingdoms
and provinces and territories, and whithersoever his power
and sovereignty extends. And nobody, however important he
may think himself, dares to refuse them on pain of death.
And indeed everybody takes them readily, for wheresoever a
person may go throughout the Great Kaan's dominions he
shall find these pieces of paper current, and shall be able to
transact all sales and purchase of goods by means of them
just as well as if they were coins of pure gold. And all the
while they are so light that ten bezants' worth does not weigh
one golden bezant.[65]

Paper currency relied on the prestige of the monarch, and also brought
convenience to the monarch, who became the largest printer of money
and extended and defended the statutory value of paper currency in
various domains. "The chief officer deputed by the Kaan smears the Seal
entrusted to him with vermilion, and impresses it on the paper . . . And
the Kaan causes every year to be made such a vast quantity of this money, which costs him nothing, that it must equal in amount all the treasure
in the world."[66] The Yuan paper currency was not only used to cover
military expenses, but was also welcomed by merchants, and worn-out
old money could be exchanged for new money.

When any of those pieces of paper are spoilt—not that they are so very flimsy neither—the owner carries them to the Mint, and by paying three percent of the value he gets new pieces in exchange. And if any Baron, or anyone else soever, hath need of gold or silver or gems or pearls, in order to make plate, or girdles, or the like, he goes to the Mint and buys as much as he list, paying in this paper-money . . .

. . . Furthermore all merchants arriving from India or other countries, and bringing with them gold or silver or gems and pearls, are prohibited from selling to any one but the Emperor. He has twelve experts chosen for this business, men of shrewdness and experience in such affairs; these appraise the articles, and the Emperor then pays a liberal price for them in those pieces of paper. The merchants accept his price readily, for in the first place they would not get so good a one from anybody else, and secondly they are paid without any delay. And with this paper-money they can buy what they like anywhere over the Empire, whilst it is also vastly lighter to carry about on their journeys.[67]

Marco Polo noted that this currency was also used for the military payroll, and that its value was the same as gold and silver.

In order to compel and encourage use of the currency, the Yuan put considerable effort into manufacturing and promoting it:

All these pieces of paper are issued with as much solemnity and authority as if they were of pure gold or silver; and on every piece a variety of officials, whose duty it is, have to write their names, and to put their seals. And when all is prepared duly, the chief officer deputed by the Kaan smears the Seal entrusted to him with vermilion, and impresses it on the paper, so that the form of the seal remains printed upon it in red; the Money is then authentic. Anyone forging it would be punished with death.[68]

The greatest beneficiary was clearly the monarch:

> He buys such a quantity of those precious things every year
> that his treasure is endless, whilst all the time the money he
> pays away costs him nothing at all. Moreover, several times in
> the year proclamation is made through the city that anyone
> who may have gold or silver or gems or pearls, by taking
> them to the Mint shall get a handsome price for them. And
> the owners are glad to do this, because they would find no
> other purchaser give so large a price. Thus the quantity they
> bring in is marvelous, though these who do not choose to do
> so may let it alone. Still, in this way, nearly all the valuables in
> the country come into the Kaan's possession ... Now you
> have heard the ways and means whereby the Great Kaan may
> have, and in fact has, more treasure than all the Kings in the
> World; and you know all about it and the reason why.[69]

When the economy flourished, currency was issued; when the economy
continued to flourish, currency was excessively issued and began to de-
preciate in value; currency continued to be excessively issued, the economy declined, the dynasty fell, and the currency was withdrawn. This
was by and large the Chinese cycle of issuing currency. The prosperous
scenario described by Marco Polo likewise inevitably became obsolete.
With expansion overseas and extravagant spending domestically, the
late Ming and early Qing philosopher Gu Yanwu once exclaimed that
the amount of gold and silver awarded by the Yuan dynasty was the largest in history (the amount of silver exceeded the amount of gold).[70] The
happy scenario for the Yuan dynasty's bank notes didn't last long. At
the outset currency values were stable, and various localities even established exchange bureaus called *pingjunku,* with reserve funds of gold,
silver, silk, and so on to back the currency, which was convertible. As the
political situation became chaotic in the mid- and late Yuan, the currency reserves were centralized in the capital and it was impossible to
convert currency in the private sector. A trend developed of issuing
bank notes with no reserve backing, and excessive issuance became inevitable. The profligate issue of paper currency resulted in commodity

prices increasing by multiples. A situation emerged in which a 10 *ding* bank note (at that time one *ding* [ingot] was equivalent to 50 strings, and one string was equivalent to one tael of silver) could not be exchanged for one *dou* of rice, and people reverted to barter until inflation ultimately made state revenues impossible to sustain:

> The price of goods soared by more than ten times. With domestic turmoil, military provisioning, rewards of food and drink, countless amounts of money were printed every day. Vessels and carts were loaded for transport, convoys of ships delivered goods to distribute among the people everywhere. Once worn out it was no longer used. In the country's capital ten *ding* could not buy one *dou* of grain. Eventually trade was carried out by barter in all prefectures and counties, and paper currency in government or private hands became unusable. People regarded it as bad money, and its use by the state thereby faltered.[71]

Bank notes were a major theme of the Yuan dynasty; although many awards were in gold and silver, official salaries were paid in bank notes and rice, and silver made up only a tiny portion of tax revenues. However, Mongolia and its subjugated Central Asian territories such as Khwarazm had traditionally used silver, and with the devaluation of bank notes, silver began to flourish in China. Most bank notes used silver as their face-value denominations, the monetary standard was mostly coupled with gold or silver, and silver was widely used among the general population. For example, the works of the great Yuan playwright Guan Hanqing mention banknotes, but also contain numerous mentions of silver. The Prologue to *Injustice to Dou E* states: "The young protagonist is utterly penniless, wandering destitute in Chuzhou. Here one Granny Cai has money, and the young protagonist, lacking travel money, borrowed 20 taels of silver from her. By now he owes her 40 taels."

Yuan dynasty paper currency went through the stages of the *zhongtong* notes, *zhiyuan* notes, and *zhizheng* notes, from being fully backed by gold reserves to being issued in excess, but paper currency basically always served as legal tender, and the inconvertibility of paper currency anticipated the world trend. It has even been said that the Yuan dynasty's paper currency influenced the emergence of paper currency in Europe. Economist Gordon Tullock, regarded as the originator of rent-seeking theory, was also fascinated by Chinese paper currency. His research quotes Marco Polo's account of Yuan dynasty paper currency at great length, while at the same time regretfully pointing out Marco Polo's limitations—that is, his belief that paper currency was an effective means for the government to obtain money, while being unaware of the consequences of constantly reissuing currency, such as the decline in its value.[72]

In fact, the chaotic situation of paper currency not only led to a reversion to commodity economy, but also bolstered faith in precious-metal currencies such as silver. In order to encourage the use of paper currencies such as the *zhongtong* notes and *zhida* notes, Kublai Khan's Yuan court prohibited the use of copper coins in market transactions. Subsequent dynasties imitated this method, but it was doomed to failure; the market's trading rules ultimately prevailed over the will of the emperor. The Yuan dynasty authorities finally stopped issuing the *zhida* notes and copper coins in the fourteenth century, and lifted the ban on gold and silver.

The Lessons of Inflation and the Rise of Silver

The history of paper currency in China may be called a history of messy clever fixes. Qian Mu put it succinctly: "The Song and Yuan dynasties used paper money, but both indulged in the malpractice of excessive issuance." Notably, overseas scholars acknowledge that in the thirteenth century China advanced a premodern monetary theory that demonstrated a standard higher than that of Europeans in the same time period. So why did paper currencies repeatedly collapse, and what lessons can we learn from it?

The crux of the matter is the boundaries of sovereign credit. The circulation of fiat currency implies the enhancement of national credit, and the behavior of a strong government decides the direction and effectiveness of monetary policies. As the saying goes, "Rulers manage the economy by controlling the currency." The problem is in who supervises the supervisors. History shows that when a government takes control of private paper currency, it is initially able to use the advantages of paper currency to alleviate deflation to the benefit of the economy. Unfortunately, this excellent start has never continued through to the end, and the temptation to overissue currency always prevails when no constraints are imposed.

The hard-learned lesson is that if the government is entrusted with too much power over money, it cannot always be adequately monitored and restrained. Milton Friedman believes that the potency of money is expressed in Lenin's famous dictum "The most effective way to destroy a society is to destroy its currency." The trick is to establish institutional arrangements that "enable government to exercise responsibility for money, yet at the same time limit the power thereby given to government and prevent this power from being used in ways that will tend to weaken rather than strengthen a free society."[73]

The rise and fall of the *jiaozi* and its successors to a great extent reflect the divergence between East and West regarding money. From the time of ancient Greece, intrinsic value has been an essential condition of money in the West; the law is not adequate to endow a currency (and even less a paper currency) with value: "The value of substances used as money derived from their exchange values as commodities."[74] Indeed, most of the time people were able to freely mint currency; as long as they paid a seigniorage (coin) tax, anyone could go to the mint to exchange gold and silver for currency.

Taken a step further, this was facilitated by the divisions and competition among large numbers of feudal lords in the West, and the lack of a centralized government monopolizing the issuance of currency. Conversely, Asian emperors historically made currency serve politics. Monetary theories and policies always emphasized the ruler's role in creating currency; that is, "It is the ruler's stamp, not the intrinsic value of the monetary medium, that confers value."[75]

According to this logic, the focus of monetary policy was usually how to make it better serve the state or the rulers; economic considerations were usually not the primary factor, and political factors became the crux of the matter. Rulers seemed always to have great confidence in their own abilities to manage macroeconomics. One scholar appraises the concepts of China's premodern rulers regarding money in this way: "Chinese monetary thought and policy was predicated on enabling the ruler to overcome the vicissitudes of dearth and plenty and to provide for the material needs of his subjects. The ruler could accomplish this goal by tightly controlling the supply of money to ensure stable prices and ample supplies of goods."[76]

The patterns of economic performance were completely different in premodern society from what they are today. The systemic arrangements that the great monetarist Milton Friedman calls for, such as making the government responsible for money and limiting the government's power, would have been an incredible luxury in premodern China. The scarcity of gold, silver, and other precious metals naturally imposed powerful constraints on rulers' impulse to excessively issue currency, and the economy often suffered from deflation, that is, so-called money famines. Conversely, as opposed to standard currency, in the West coins were the main source of seigniorage tax, because they were usually low-cost, easy to obtain, and convenient to reissue.

For China, bronze or copper coins had always been the main fractional currency circulating among the general public. This was the case even after a silver standard was established. China's emperors were consequently often vexed by copper shortages, and frequently dealt with the problem by producing low-grade coins, imposing draconian restrictions on the export of copper, and other such methods.

In the familiar example of the Tang dynasty, its economic development capabilities were already constrained by currency. The Tang continued the Sui dynasty's system, in which coins, silk, and occasionally gold were the main currencies. The Tang dynasty's coin-and-silk system has attracted considerable discussion; nowadays the use of bolts of silk fabric in trading sounds like something out of the *Arabian Nights,* and some people have exaggerated the role of silk. In fact, coins were always the main form of currency. Silk was used slightly more in private transactions, and official salaries were mostly calculated in the form of rice and other commodities, with a small portion paid in coins. It is worth noting that it was usually when inflation surged that the coin-and-silk system prevailed. In fact, when cash became devalued, the commodity economy automatically flourished. This not unique to the Tang, but was a continuation from the Northern and Southern dynasties, and the shortcomings of commodity currencies were also very evident, in particular the inability to standardize them. As stated in *The Book of Jin: Biography of Zhang Gui:* "When cash was not used, bolts of silk were cut into pieces and spoiled. This caused problems with exchange in the market. Women's handiwork was ruined, and the loss of the cloth for making into clothing was a great evil."

The Tang dynasty was often hit by deflation, and at a later stage, Buddhist images were destroyed so their metal could be minted into coins. Under these circumstances, the possibility of supplementing the currency with a certain amount of coins or even paper money could be considered a good thing for both the rulers and the general populace. The monetary historian Peng Xinwei observes: "If paper currency was not issued in excessive amounts, people were certain to enjoy stable commodity prices."

If kept within a certain range, excessive issue of currency and devaluation could be considered expedient, but ultimately, wealth cannot be created out of thin air, and history has shown time and time again that when inflation reaches a certain level, it inevitably triggers the collapse of the monetary system, the financial system, or even the government. As for what makes the general public abandon paper currency and return to commodity bartering, economists believe that bartering is extremely inefficient, but currency devaluation can make the bartering option attractive, leading to the emergence of various currency substitutes throughout history: "The use of cigarettes in postwar Germany harks back to the use of tobacco in colonial Virginia."[77] Ultimately, gold and silver are the most important commodity currencies.

The paper currency farce basically ended in the Ming dynasty, and the Qing dynasty's extreme caution in using paper currency, apart from temporarily issuing it during the era of the Taiping Heavenly Kingdom, shows the deep impression left by the paper currency inflation of the Yuan and Ming. It is worth pointing out that China's failed experiment with paper money was not just a matter of national character; it obeyed the universal law of economics. Inflation resulting from the excessive issue of currency remains a worldwide problem even today. From another perspective, would privately issued paper currency enjoy better credit than that issued by the state? Based on the early experience of China's *jiaozi,* privately issued currency is also not reliable, but by automatic clearing in the market within a limited scope, it is unlikely to give rise to the extreme situation that arises when a state abuses its credit. On the other hand, given the fluctuating nature of modern economies, a stable central bank that can serve as the "lender of last resort" in a credit collapse is in fact essential; this is the harsh lesson humanity has learned after countless financial crises.

This is not a flight of fancy, but rather history's progressive evolution. In the eighteenth century, the Bank of England was a private bank that was still exploring whether it should take on certain responsibilities of a central bank. In the West, so-called paper currency was in fact a special kind of bank note. Back then, more than 200 banks issued bank notes, with the 1797 restriction on cash payouts being an exceptional case. An economist of that era, David Hume, clearly perceived the pros and cons of the state becoming involved in the credit of paper money; he believed that the credit of a national currency was generally better than that of a private currency, but it required ensuring that this advantage would not be abused:

> If the public provide not a bank, private bankers will take advantage of this circumstance; as the goldsmiths formerly did in LONDON, or as the bankers do at present in DUBLIN: And therefore it is better, it may be thought, that a public company should enjoy the benefit of that paper-credit, which always will have place in every opulent kingdom. But to endeavor artificially to encrease such a credit, can never be the interest of any trading nation; but must lay them under disadvantages, by encreasing money beyond its natural proportion to labour and commodities, and thereby heightening their price to the merchant and manufacturer.[78]

The intervention of state credit implies squeezing out private credit, and if handled properly, this can help the overall situation by reducing transaction costs. But power also means responsibility, and Hume acknowledges that a public bank will greatly reduce business transactions by private banks and currency brokers. The state is therefore obliged to take on a corresponding responsibility: "So large a sum, lying ready at command, would be a convenience in times of great public danger and distress; and what part of it was used might be replaced at leisure, when peace and tranquility was restored to the nation."[79]

A deeper point of discussion is therefore how to avoid abuse of power, or in other words, the excessive issue of paper currency. Whether or not it is under a commodity standard, paper currency is a credit arrangement, and it may be difficult to completely avoid government intervention even if there is a strong and independent central bank serving as the monetary institution. As Milton Friedman has argued:

> Once fiduciary elements have been introduced, it has proved difficult to avoid governmental control over them, even when they were initially issued by private individuals. The reason is basically the difficulty of preventing counterfeiting or its economic equivalent. Fiduciary money is a contract to pay standard money. It so happens that there tends to be a long interval between the making of such a contract and its realization. This enhances the difficulty of enforcing the contract and hence also the temptation to issue fraudulent contracts. In addition, once fiduciary elements have been introduced, the temptation for government itself to issue fiduciary money is almost irresistible. In practice, therefore, commodity standards have tended to become mixed standards involving extensive intervention by the state.[80]

Human tragedy lies in greed always prevailing over reason, and the convenience of paper currency often takes a turn toward disaster. Whenever war erupts, states rely on printing money or reducing currency values, and this exacts an enormous price from both the victor and the defeated. For example, in the war during the Song dynasty's Kaixi period (1205–1207), the Jin dynasty emerged victorious, but its domestic paper currency increased by ten times in subsequent decades.

Ancient warfare tested the mobilization of resources, and the fact that many of China's premodern emperors relied on the excessive issue of currency and not a more modern financial plan is no coincidence but rather the result of systemic inertia. This might suggest to us that the financial differences between China and Western Europe in the thirteenth century were not only in their paper currency, but even more in the relationship between the government and the public in reacting to the sudden financial needs triggered by war. The divergence between Chinese and Western finance can be most distinctly illustrated by the way war was financed in Lin'an in the East and Venice in the West in 1262. In the East, the Southern Song government directly provided credit and issued paper currency in the form of fiat currency, ultimately progressing toward its excessive issue. At almost the same time in the West, when Venice, Genoa, and other Italian city-states faced the financing demands of war, they issued public bonds, and trading in bonds and debentures developed from that. This comparison shows that when the state controls finances, it is strong but in fact also fragile, because this implies that the state doesn't need market forces, and also that it will ultimately lose public support due to lack of restraint.

However, if we hold that history knocks at the door only once or twice, we should not underestimate human obstinance and the lure of and resistance to printing currency that runs through the history of money. For China, paper currency returned under the centralized currency system of the Nationalist government in the 1930s, and the packaging of modern fiat currency could not gloss over the innate abuse of economic logic, resulting in the historical cycle of malign inflation. The subsequently rushed introduction of the *jinyuanquan* in 1948 was likewise a declining regime's attempt to pillage private assets through paper, and the crisis in 1949 also originated in part from the complete loss of public support brought on by inflation. Crossing centuries of history, the dimwittedness and stubbornness of rulers were replicated to such an extent that there seemed to have been no progress whatsoever. The paper-currency experiments of the Song, Jin, and Yuan all ended in inflation, not only leading to the withdrawal of copper coins as good money from the market, but also causing silver to be increasingly used as a replacement. When it was impossible to trust paper currency, even the government's explicit ban could not prevent silver from remaining part of normal life and gradually flourishing as the mainstream currency.

1262: Jia Sidao's Purchase of Public Fields, and Selling Bonds in Venice

In the first year of the Southern Song's Duanping period (1234), the united Song and Mongol forces destroyed the Jin dynasty, and the Southern Song became the only opponent to the Mongols on Chinese soil. The Mongol invasion of the south in 1258 caused enormous loss to the Southern Song, and even greater financial debt. In the later stage of Emperor Lizong's reign, the Southern Song government was forced to rely even more on the "harmonious purchase" or *hedi* system, that is, procuring grain from its subjects at low cost. By then the state's provisioning of its frontier armies relied entirely on the *hedi* system.[81] In order to sustain the *hedi* system, the imperial court could only continue issuing paper currency, exacerbating inflation and creating a vicious circle. These circumstances made the "public lands law" the logical next step. The public lands law allowed the state to alleviate the problems of the *hedi* system by buying privately owned land (especially land owned by officials) that surpassed a certain quota. In 1262, toward the end of Emperor Lizong's reign, Jia Sidao submitted a petition recommending the public lands law and enumerating five benefits: stabilizing the price of goods, restraining the issue of paper currency, controlling wealth, replacing the *hedi* system, and provisioning the army.

> The frontier armies cannot defend the country without enough to eat; if everything relies on *hedi,* paper currency is necessary. Feeding the army requires extensive *hedi;* since *hedi* is required, the production of bank notes cannot be reduced. The present plan will benefit the country and the people, provide the army with food, increase the value of currency, and not infringe on ancestral land. Based on the grade of officials and their landholdings in the *hedi* areas . . . buy one-third of the land of official households exceeding the limit and make it public land. Ten million *mu* of land can produce 6 to 7 million piculs[82] of rice per year, more than is needed to supply the army. It will make *hedi* unnecessary,

provision the army, reduce the creation of bank notes, stabilize prices, and equalize wealth—five benefits in one.

If the public lands law was so good, why hadn't it been done before? This was mainly related to the Song dynasty's land system. During
the Tang dynasty, the government didn't allow the buying and selling of
land, although the "land equalization policy" (*juntianzhi*) existed in
name only by the end of the Tang. Compared with the Tang, the Song
dynasty had a larger population and less land, and from the outset "did
not establish a land system" and "did not restrict annexing." In other
words, the Song dynasty land system adopted a laissez-faire approach
and placed few requirements on the status of either buyer or seller. This
was due to the rise of civic culture and signified progress in terms of
private property rights. Traditionally, this system was believed to encourage the annexing of property, and the Song court was always critical
of merging property, but even under the land equalization policy,
the rights and interests of farmers had not enjoyed substantially better
protection; they were still at the mercy of rich and powerful clans, and
concentrated landholdings were unavoidable. The Song's land policies
facilitated the free flow of capital and economic production and undermined the concept of family status; they essentially endowed ordinary
people with the power to buy and sell land, and farmers who lost their
land at that time had employment opportunities in industry and commerce, not unlike today's urbanization of farming communities.

However, over time, the powerful and moneyed social strata seized
the opportunity to annex more land while using their official status to
minimize their payment of taxes to the state. The Northern Song began
issuing decrees limiting landholdings and stipulating the maximum
amount of land that could be owned by different grades of officials. This
wasn't targeting land mergers, but only required paying tax on land exceeding the tax-exempt quotas. These regulations had a certain economic rationality and were similar to today's declaration of assets for taxation.

This sounds like a good policy, but it infringed on too many interests, and Emperor Lizong was initially very hesitant. Jia Sidao "indig-
nantly went to argue his case," and the public lands law was presented to
the public in 1263. Jia Sidao's method was to abolish the *hedi* system and

at the same time buy one-third of all land exceeding the landholding quota of 200 *mu*. After selling their land, wealthy households would be exempted from *hedi*. The plan was initially implemented in six relatively wealthy and populous prefectures in the Jiangnan region south of the Yangtze River. Continuing for twelve years until Jia Sidao fell from power, it had an enormous impact on Chinese history.

In spite of ongoing resistance, the public lands law initially showed positive results. Jia Sidao started off with his own family property of 10,000 *mu*, and after half a year more than 2 million *mu* had been purchased, collecting enough rent to finance central and peripheral outlay. The thinking behind the public lands law wasn't bad, but in practice it paid for good land with devalued *huizi*, while the purchase price paid for the land was already considerably lower than the market value. The plan was additionally compromised by the honor system for declaring assets and the difficulty of reselling a tax-exemption certificate (*dudie*). "For land above 5,000 *mu*, paid in a half-part silver, five parts official appointment letter [*guangao*], two parts tax-exemption certificate, and two and a half parts *huizi*; below 5,000 *mu*, paid in a half-part silver, three parts official appointment letter, two parts tax-exemption certificate, and three and a half parts *huizi*; below 1,000 *mu*, paid half in tax-exemption certificate and half in *huizi*; 500 *mu* to 300 *mu*, paid fully in *huizi*." The small share paid in silver was really a disguised form of plunder, especially since items such as official appointment letters and tax-exemption certificates could not easily be transferred in private hands. "The six prefectures were agitated."[83]

Jia Sidao intended the public lands law to rescue the *huizi*: "Rescuing the paper currency requires no longer printing paper currency; no longer printing paper currency requires eliminating *hedi*; eliminating *hedi* requires buying land exceeding the limit." In other words, his plan was for the government to buy up private land at low prices; with enough land, the government would no longer need to rely on *hedi*; and without using *hedi* to pay expenses, the issue of *huizi* could be reduced. But in actual practice, this plan exacerbated the vicious circle of inflation caused by inadequate finances: The *huizi* was not strong enough to buy adequate grain, so more *huizi* had to be printed to buy the fields of wealthy households; the greater availability of *huizi* caused its devaluation and reduced its purchasing power, so the problem was not solved.

If the prices paid had been fair, the public lands law would not have been so bad, but under the Southern Song's straitened financial circumstances, the system was essentially aimed at addressing financial deficit by seizing wealth from the rich. Although this method looked as if it would help finances and in the short term did accumulate a large amount of land, the use of state power to violate private property rights ultimately created public resentment. With Jia Sidao's eventual fall from power, it became a mere formality, and financial crisis became inevitable.

In 1274, Kublai Khan issued an imperial edict to attack the Southern Song, and the next year Jia Sidao led 130,000 soldiers to meet the enemy attack. After being defeated at Dingjiazhou, Jia was demoted and his policies were scrapped with him. Jia was burdened with a bad reputation, and the next emperor absolved the previous emperor of responsibility for the land purchases and returned the land to its previous owners: "The public land [law] is most injurious to the people, and the resentment it caused has courted disaster for more than ten years. As of today, the land will be returned to its owners and tenants are ordered to become soldiers."[84] It was too late, however. In 1276 the Southern Song capital, Lin'an, fell into enemy hands. Most of the public land reverted to the Yuan court and was given out as rewards.

Zhao Yun, Emperor Lizong, was the fifth monarch of the Southern Song and reigned nearly forty years, from 1225 to 1264. From his early protracted struggle with the powerful minister Shi Miyuan to the dejection of his last years, his "occupation of Luoyang in the Duanping year" and the public lands law drew the most censure. In the first year of the Duanping era (1234), the united Song and Mongol forces destroyed the Jin dynasty, and the Southern Song tried to recover the Northern Song's original territory in Luoyang and Kaifeng. Due to inadequate army provisions, however, the Southern Song suffered a bitter defeat, and the Mongols accused it of "betraying the alliance," causing the outbreak of war between the Song and the Mongols that battered the Song power structure, destroyed its state finances, and undermined public support; it could be considered the straw that broke the camel's back for the Southern Song court. *History of the Song* gives the following appraisal:

> Lizong reigned long, like Renzong . . . [85] Greedy for land, he forsook the alliance. The troops occupied Luo[yang], conflict followed, the country was torn by war, and the border territories were pressed. Hao Jing[86] was sent as an envoy, but [Jia] Sidao rejected the peace offerings. The Mongols, feeling deceived and rejected, laid siege, and [Luoyang] self-destructed. What a pity! Self-indulgent in his middle years, [Lizong] was indolent in governance and given over to drink, devolving his power to treacherous court officials. Wishing him long life would be empty talk and of no benefit.

Emperor Lizong didn't enjoy tranquility after death either. During the reign of the Yuan's Toghon Temür, the Western Xia's Yang Lianzhenjia served as supervisor of Buddhist teachings in Jiangnan, putting him in charge of Buddhist affairs south of the Yangtze. He and a monk from the west excavated the Southern Song's imperial mausoleum, looting its treasure and discarding the human remains. They built a white stupa over the remains of the Southern Song emperors, called Zhennan, "Suppressing the Southerners."[87] Emperor Lizong's corpse had been soaked in mercury to preserve it, and when his tomb was looted he still hadn't decayed. The tomb raiders hung the corpse in a forest to drain off the mercury, and the skull was cut off to use as a drinking vessel, after which the torso was incinerated. It is said that after the Ming dynasty was founded and the first Ming emperor, Zhu Yuanzhang, heard of this matter, he lamented it for a long time. Lizong's skull was found in the Yuan's Dadu palace after having passed through many hands. The emperor ordered it laid to rest in the original Yongmu Mausoleum in Shaoxing.

This incident has often been cited as evidence of the brutality of the Yuan rulers, but Zhu Yuanzhang's subordinates were not much better. In the middle period of the Yuan, Zhu Yuanzhang's general, Hu Dahai, attacked Shaoqing and looted and desecrated corpses in the Song mausoleum. His actions were recorded in *Record of Protection of Yue* (*Bao Yue Lu*): "The enemy troops excavated graves, from Lizong and

Lady Cixian down to the tombs of numerous officials without exception; gold, jade and treasure were bundled and carried away. The faces of the corpses were all as if alive, perhaps due to mercury, but they were hacked and defiled to the greatest extent possible." Reading this record, Zhou Zuoren felt dismayed, even if it came from the enemy side: "Hu Dahai was no different from Yang Lianzhenjia."[88]

As for the "creator of bad precedent" of the public lands law, Jia Sidao, he was posthumously listed in *History of the Song: Biographies of Treacherous Officials,* and his policies were vilified because of his moral flaws and image of having harmed the country. Apart from personal cultivation and character, Jia Sidao and Wang Anshi were somewhat alike; both were prime ministers who combined political and financial power and were supported by their emperors. Their overwhelming power was actually an infringement on the political system; although they did not violate the taboos of those times, both attempted to do so. That is why even though Jia Sidao is included in the *Biographies of Treacherous Officials,* the first Yuan emperor, Kublai Khan, did not have a low opinion of him, and after the Song was vanquished he praised him openly: "A single scholar Jia defended the city. With 100,000 troops you could not prevail, and after months of killing you could not withdraw; how could that be the scholar's crime?"[89]

This was not necessarily because Jia Sidao was so capable, but because the nation's fortunes depended on a single person. One of the problems of the Song dynasty's fiscal administration was that the outlay was enormous, and managing finances became a strategic issue for all prime ministers. Wang Anshi transferred control of tea leaves, horses, and so on from the hands of merchants to the state, and Jia Sidao turned low-cost, privately held grain fields into a public financial resource; both methods aroused public dissent and discord and intensified divisions within the imperial court.

In retrospect, were there alternatives? Around the same time that Jia Sidao hatched his land-purchase plan, a similar situation arose in Europe. In March 1262, Venice faced a serious military challenge. Its opponent was the powerful Byzantine emperor and his ally, Genoa. Seeking to protect itself under financial pressure and the fog of war, Venice's highest organ of power, the Grand Council, issued a decree that permitted the government to spend up to 3,000 lire per month for its routine needs. Spending beyond that amount had to be used to pay the government's creditors 5 percent interest. The decree also authorized the government to collect tax revenues to service public debt. This decree came to be regarded as the greatest financial innovation of the thirteenth century and anticipated the Italian city-state Monti bond system.[90]

On another occasion, when war made the government desperate for funding, budget deficits pushed the government to engage in systemic rejuvenation and created demand for trade, and government bonds became an asset that could be traded and transferred. This pioneering undertaking should not be underestimated; today's U.S. Treasury bonds and eurodebt are in fact based on the transfer of debt and revolving payments.

Setting aside the moral question, we should ask, why does Jia Sidao or China's kleptocracy invariably deal with financing problems by plundering the populace? Jia Sidao's tragedy seemed to lie in promoting unequal commercial transactions in a society that lacked a sufficient commercial environment. His public lands law can be considered a failed experiment in the agrarian civilization of that time. Although the Southern Song was China's most commercially developed era at that point, the entrenched power structure and rules of the game left Jia with few options in terms of financial instruments or economic alternatives.

By way of contrast, when European banks first emerged, their biggest clients were monarchs, and bankers won a place for themselves at the negotiation table. The Medici banking family ruled Florence for three centuries, and the Rothschild family (famous European financiers) had dealings with God's spokesmen and money-borrowing nobility. As for China's emperors, even when they were operating in deficit mode or living from hand to mouth, they were never able to obtain the help of banks. There was no conduit for dialogue or trading between commerce and power, or between the people and imperial authority.

Economists focus on per capita earnings, and political scientists focus on divergences between political systems. Comparing the economic lifeblood of China and Europe, the bankification of money may be the greatest reason for the vast difference between their respective financial paths. Modern economics is credit economics, and the core of

credit economics is debt, which means that money is constantly capitalized and loans are increasingly monetized; the deepening interaction
between the two constitutes the big picture for finance today.

That's why looking back at the thirteenth century may be revealing.
Thirteenth-century China experienced the collapse of the *huizi* and the
jiaochao, followed by the fall of the Jin and Song dynasties. Then China
entered the Yuan dynasty's era of paper currency, followed by the Ming
dynasty's era of silver. In Europe, the rise of the Italian banking houses
in the twelfth century and France's Champagne trade fairs went down in
history. By the thirteenth century, Italy had undergone a number of further financial changes; in 1252, Florence minted the first gold coin in
Western Christendom, the florin (weighing around 3.5 grams), and the
Italian city-states had already begun a number of financial innovations
by then.

Chinese and foreign historians enjoy discussing the Great Divergence between China and the West, arguing that it occurred either in the
fifteenth century or the eighteenth century. Even more important, however, is that East and West had already experienced a major financial
divergence in the thirteenth century. In the West, the financial revolution and its progression eventually triggered the Industrial Revolution,
while in the East, the failure of the Song's and Yuan's paper-currency
experiments necessitated a retreat to the stagnation and mediocrity of
the early Ming's Hongwu reign. Centuries were wasted on supplemental
lessons in the monetization of precious metals (silver), and modern
finance never had an opportunity to grow, right up until the Western
"barbarians" appeared at the gates with their gunboats and cannons.
Starting in the twentieth century, China spared no effort to catch up and
established modern banks, and China's state-owned banks took the lead
in globalization in the twenty-first century. Looking back at history in
the financial sphere, has the relationship between the state and the market been clarified? Have China's bankers been able to find a relatively
equal seat for themselves at the table?

The Ming Dynasty

The Silver Standard and Globalization

He is one of the wealthiest men in our district and a very good friend of the magistrate. It is Master Ximen. He has thousands and thousands of strings of cash and keeps a medicine shop near the Town Hall. The money in his house is piled so high that it touches the North Star, and even his spoiled rice is enough to fill many barns. His gold is yellow and his silver is white. His pearls are round and his precious stones brilliant. He has rhinoceros horns and elephants' tusks.

Lanling Xiaoxiaosheng (Ming), The Golden Lotus

Dethe is my finaunce.

Anon. (late 15th–early 16th c.), "The Lamentation of Mary Magdalene"

All the other enterprises of the Spaniards in the new world, subsequent to those of Columbus, seem to have been prompted by the same motive. It was the sacred thirst of gold . . . When those adventurers arrived upon any unknown coast, their first enquiry was always if there was any gold to be found there; and according to the information which they received concerning this particular, they determined either to quit the country or to settle in it.

Adam Smith (1723–1790), The Wealth of Nations, *Book 4,*
"Of the Motives for Establishing New Colonies"

The Establishment and Breakthrough
of the Hongwu Regime

Historians have conflicted feelings toward the Ming dynasty. Some people see it as a medieval government, while others believe that the late Ming was a bridge to the modern world. Scholars in the California School have argued that in the mid- and late Ming, the Jiangnan economy flourished to a degree that rivaled European countries at that time. They believe that Jiangnan's industrial and commercial development, flourishing trade, and meticulous division of labor suggest the emergence of the sprouts of capitalism, and that if not for the Qing invasion, China might have had the opportunity to embark on industrial revolution.[1]

This view is undoubtedly too simplistic. In fact, the Ming dynasty seemed to shuttle back and forth in time and space, from a medieval-type system under Emperor Hongwu (Zhu Yuanzhang) to modernistic commercialized economic development. The Ming dynasty stands out in thousands of years of Chinese history, and its lessons as well as its successes and failures can be considered a composite of Chinese history.

The Ming replaced the Yuan dynasty, and in its call for the restoration of Han rule, it inherited some aspects of its systemic design from the Yuan, while a considerable portion harked back to the Song dynasty framework. Historian Li Xinfeng observes: "The extreme expansiveness of the early Ming rulers originated with the Song, Jin, and Yuan traditions; the division of the central government's power among three main institutions resembled the Han system; the expropriation and division of local authority resembled the Song system; the mapping of local districts combined the Yuan and Song systems; and the stripping of power from the nobility, ministers, and the armed forces and the limitations on combining military forces were a legacy of the Tang and Song."[2]

Zhu Yuanzhang reverted to the conscription system and divided up the training, commanding, and deployment of troops, abandoning the Song dynasty's enormous outlay on a mercenary system. Correspondingly, finance and taxation reverted to a barter economy, with a forceful emphasis on agriculture and deemphasis on commerce at the expense of Jiangnan's industrial and commercial prosperity, and a ban on maritime trade. In terms of social controls, the Song government had gradually withdrawn from managing the grassroots level, allowing local governance to be largely taken on by local elites and granting a considerable degree of personal freedom. The Ming government, however, went in the opposite direction, expanding its control over society to unprecedented levels through its harsh village organization (lijia) system,[3] a "yellow registry" system of households, the hereditary allocation of duties to households under the classifications of soldier, civilian, artisan, and (salt) stove, and the imposition of corvee labor. This Hongwu system covered the early to middle periods of the Ming dynasty, and with social tranquility, the economy reverted to the placid ripples of small-scale peasant economy. In contrast to the Song dynasty's flourishing commodity economy, when 260 million strings of coins were minted, the Ming dynasty's total coinage never surpassed 6 million strings, less than 3 percent of Song levels. Archaeologists in Malaysia's Sarawak state discovered a large amount of Song dynasty stoneware and porcelain, but none from the Ming dynasty. This "Ming window" reflects the Ming's retreat from international trade, in contrast with the Song.

However, the Hongwu system did not "continue for ten thousand generations," as Zhu Yuanzhang hoped. Like all Central Plains dynasties, the Ming experienced frequent border conflicts that required permanent frontier forces, rather than the set-up Zhu Yuanzhang envisaged, with soldiers dispersed and separated from commanders except when engaged in battle. A system therefore gradually developed that combined border-area forces under a garrison commander with an immense standing army at the capital. Even more crucial, as with the garrison militia system of previous dynasties, the garrison forces over time inevitably suffered shortages and declined in combat effectiveness. The Ming's main forces collapsed during the Tumu Fortress crisis[4] in what one might call a massive implosion of military power. After the bitter defeat at the Tumu Fortress, the Ming dynasty's military system gradually reverted to the mercenary system; from establishing crack regiments to Qi Jiguang's[5] training of troops, the Ming army partially restored its combat effectiveness.

On the economic side, the early Ming's reliably self-sufficient garrison farms suffered seriously shrinking productivity, and the lijia household registration field allotment system on which the regime depended for its grassroots administration also headed toward decline. The traditional corvee system was already unequal to the burden of the state's enormous expenditure, and the system of taxation in kind had long proven inefficient and insufficient. It became increasingly common for taxation in kind to be discounted with silver, and to pay off statutory corvee service with silver.[6]

As the population increased during peacetime, Jiangnan's agricultural patterns underwent constant change, maritime bans were continuously broken, and commerce and the handicraft industry gradually developed. By the mid-Ming period, the Hongwu system was already scarred and battered, and under the subsequent assault of massive foreign silver imports, Zhang Juzheng's "Single Whip tax system," and other such political reforms and acts, it came to exist in name only. The economic conditions of the Ming's middle and latter periods were so entirely different from those of its early period that some historians refer to the transformation of the Ming's middle period as a distant echo of the Tang and Song reforms. This immense tidal transformation also brought changes in the Ming's currency system, with a shift from the hard-pressed Great Ming *baochao* to the ultimate establishment of a silver standard.

Issuing Paper Currency Couldn't Save the Ming

The Ming dynasty can be considered the final act in the history of paper currency in premodern China.

The early Ming paper currency was to a great extent modeled on that of the Yuan dynasty. The linkages in the evolution of the monetary system from the Sui and Tang to the Northern and Southern dynasties, and from the Jin and Yuan to the Southern Song, were very strong. Radical reform was not only strongly resisted by the general population, but also regarded with suspicion in the upper strata. Monetary policy alternatives within localized networks had powerful externalities, so it is understandable why later dynasties followed the example of previous dynasties.

When the Ming dynasty was first established, it had great expectations of issuing currency. The first Ming emperor, Zhu Yuanzhang, issued currency and also made it unconvertible by prohibiting the general populace from using silver, as in the Yuan dynasty: "The people were prohibited from using gold and silver in trade, which was made a crime, or from exchanging paper currency for gold and silver."[7] The face of the *baochao* (treasure certificate) was inscribed with the words "Great Ming Baochao, for use throughout the country," and the money stated clearly that a reward would be paid for information on counterfeiting. It is interesting to note that during the Yuan and Ming dynasties, the reward for information on counterfeiting was paid in silver. The *baochao* was valued at "each note worth one *guan* equivalent to 1,000 *wen* in bronze coins or one tael of silver, and four *guan* equivalent to one tael of gold." This shows that in the early Ming the exchange ratio of gold to silver was around 1:4. The stipulation that the Ming dynasty's Great Ming *baochao* could not be exchanged for bronze coins or other kinds of metal money effectively made it a forerunner of fiat currency, but the lack of adequate reserve funds to guarantee its value had predictable results. The Great Ming *baochao* was unpopular in the market from the outset; people refused to use it and bronze coins and silver continued to circulate, while the first Ming emperor stubbornly continued to ban the use of silver until the last years of his rule. It was not until the reign of Emperor Yingzong [the sixth and eighth Ming emperor] that the ban on silver began to be relaxed, but refusal to use paper currency was still punished as before: "Those who resist paper currency were fined 10,000 *guan,* and the entire family banished to the frontier."[8]

The Ming monetary system could be considered comprehensive, combining paper currency with copper cash and silver ingots (*yinding*). But in actual practice, the Ming went from "using paper currency and not coin" to "using both coin and paper currency" and then to "everything paid in silver and coin." This wasn't because the rulers were open-minded, but rather because the paper currency had been too greatly devalued, and silver and copper had regained favor among the general population. Even the imperial censor at that time, Chen Ying, stated: "For years the paper currency law has been unenforceable, the reason being that the imperial court issued too much currency and had no way to reclaim it, so that goods were valued more highly than currency."[9] The Board of Revenue also stated, "In private trading, only gold and silver is used, while paper currency stagnates," as a result of which "the price of goods has soared, and the currency law is ineffective." During the Hong-wu era (1368–1398), paper currency experienced substantial devalua-tion; officially, one string in currency was equivalent to 1,000 copper cash, but in actual use in the private sphere, a one-string bank note was exchanged for only 160 cash. By the Xianzong era (1465–1487), taxes and official and military salaries and emoluments were paid in a combi-nation of coin and paper currency, as a result of which one string in paper currency was worth less than one copper coin. By the fourth year of the Jiajing era (1525), even the government acknowledged the mas-sive devaluation of the paper currency, and the exchange ratio became one string in paper currency exchanged for three *li*[10] of silver. Paper cur-rency became impractical, and silver took over: "At this time paper cur-rency has long been unusable, and copper coins are also blocked, so it is advantageous to use silver."[11]

What effect did the devaluation of the paper currency have on the Ming dynasty? In view of the inflation that had occurred in previous dynasties, the Ming promptly pulled back on issuing paper currency. Unlike the Southern Song, Jin, and Yuan, which stopped issuing cur-rency because they fell, the Ming gradually ceased issuing paper cur-rency almost before its failure became evident. The whys and wherefores can be analyzed from the logic of public policy. The relative incentives and interests of all sides should be taken into account; all major policies, whether progressive or regressive, are inseparable from their incentive compatibility to the bureaucratic clique; put plainly, it is done if advanta-geous, and not done if disadvantageous.

In terms of official salaries, Ming dynasty officials, who ranked among the interest class, were at first paid in paper currency, but salaries shrank due to inflation. Contemporary historical records verify that official salaries were greatly discounted by inflation, because the pur-chasing power of the currency with which they were paid suffered cata-strophic decline.

According to one scholar's calculations, a grade-nine official in the early years of the Hongwu era received eight piculs of rice per month; in the middle years of the Zhengtong era this was reduced to two and a half piculs; and during the Chenghua era it was reduced to one picul seven *dou:*

At the beginning of Hongwu [1368], a regular first rank official got 120 hectoliters of rice per month. At that point, the entire amount was paid in rice. In xuande 8 [1434], a portion was drawn in Treasure Certificates, and as a consequence such a salary was only equal to 46 hectoliters of rice. During the zhentong period [1436–1450], the proportion in Treasure Certificates increased, and a regular first rank official's monthly income was only equal to 34 or 35 hectoliters of rice. By chenghua 7 [1471], it had been reduced to less than 20 hectoliters, equal to that of a seventh rank official of Tang's Kaiyuan period.[12]

As it became impossible for officials to make a living, policies naturally had to be amended. In the third year of the Zhengde era (1508), payments were made entirely in silver.

When paper currency became devalued, the Ming dynasty government had to wield its administrative power to force everyone to use it. But this administrative force could never be sustained for long, because the bureaucratic clique that represented it was the first to resist this kind of action. With the welfare of officials also affected by devaluation, continued expansion of the paper currency system naturally became difficult. Whether due to active resistance or passive execution, the administrative measures would be difficult to enforce. Ultimately, the emperor would discover that he was fighting his battle alone, and that the bans existed on paper only. A further point, as Tullock emphasizes, is that from the perspective of the economics of government, when paper currency becomes increasingly unpopular, the excessive issue of paper currency also becomes increasingly unprofitable. When the profit becomes lower than the cost, the government has no motivation to continue it.

Even so, paper currency was a straw that emperors found difficult not to clutch. Even in the last stage of the Ming, rulers still hoped that paper currency would help them forestall decline. According to the work *Remnants of Memories of the Ming in the Spring* by a statesman of the late Ming and early Qing, Sun Chengze, another major conversion to paper currency was made at the end of the sixteenth year of the

Chongzhen era (1643). Emperor Chongzhen, at wit's end to raise money for military expenses, adopted the suggestion of the scholar Jiang Chen to absorb the silver in private hands by once again issuing paper currency and offering a reduction in rent tax as an additional incentive. One of his ministers assessed the plan at the time: "However ignorant the people might be, who will pay silver for a piece of paper?"[13] Citing Zhu Yuanzhang's issuing of paper currency, Emperor Chongzhen replied: "Would the founding emperor have acted wrongly?" Like his ancestor Zhu Yuanzhang, Chongzhen had blind faith in the power of rule by law. Ignoring his counselor's advice that "when the people are living in extreme hardship, peace is best," he believed it was enough to "make the law severe." Unfortunately, no one would buy the paper currency, in spite of relentless pressure, and shops closed their doors. The farce didn't end until rebel Li Zicheng invaded the capital. Subsequently Li Zicheng and the Southern Ming loyalist rump states continued by minting coins.

Paper currency died out and silver revived according to the usual hypnotic and painfully swinging pendulum of history. The lure and danger of paper currency are that it can seemingly be issued at will but is ultimately doomed to self-combust. Generations of rulers have always forgotten this point. When the paper currency farce came to an end in China, it reclaimed an air of legitimacy hundreds of years after being widely adopted by foreign countries. In the 1930s and 1940s it triggered China's most shocking episode of runaway inflation and contributed to a major transition in Chinese history.

Unbannable Silver

Posterity has always credited the Ming dynasty with the establishment of the silver standard. But the Ming government's attitude toward silver was particularly conflicted, and silver was resisted before ultimately being accepted. The Ming initially continued the practices of the Yuan by attempting to replace bronze coin and silver with paper currency. The basic approach to the Great Ming *baochao* was that gold and silver in private hands could only be sold to the government.

Silver was banned in order to promote the paper currency and prevent competition with it, but contrarily, the decline and withdrawal of paper currency marked the victory of silver and establishment of its status. Research by economist Gordon Tullock pinpoints the mid-1390s as the critical point in the withdrawal of the Ming dynasty's paper currency. The circulation of bronze coin was temporarily prohibited in the twenty-sixth year of the Hongwu era (1393), but by 1400 the paper currency had been devalued to 3 percent of its face value, stoking the ire of even Ming officials.[14]

"All territory under heaven belongs to the emperor," but the emperor's will is not the sole determinant of historical developments, especially in the case of money. The early Ming ban on silver was never strictly enforced, especially as paper currencies are inevitably devalued when issued in excess. When Yingzong ascended the throne in 1436, he had no choice but to "apply the silver ban laxly." *History of the Ming* states: "The court and commoners all used silver, or else [copper] coin for small purchases, and only a portion of official salaries were paid in paper currency."[15] This pattern was repeated again and again, to the point where "in the thirteenth year the ban was revived, and those who resisted paper currency were fined 10,000 *guan* and their entire families were banished to the frontier." Finally, in the first year of the Longqing Emperor's reign (1567), the government proclaimed that "anyone buying or selling goods worth more than one cash can use silver and coin; for [goods valued] below one cash, coin can be used." From then on, silver officially enjoyed the status it deserved and was completely monetized as a bona fide currency. Official salaries were increasingly paid in silver, and the Ming dynasty finally crossed the threshold of the silver standard.

In history, between the flesh and bones of politics, taxation is always a principal artery of historical change, and money its network. The Ming dynasty silver ban ended mainly because silver proved itself. The empire needed taxes to sustain itself, and reforms like the "Single Whip tax system" led to more efficient land taxation. Grand Secretary Zhang Juzheng extended the Single Whip tax system throughout the country in the ninth year of the Wanli era (1581). Scholars have long noted the effect of the Single Whip tax system on silver. For instance, economist Liang Fangzhong pointed out in 1936 that this was not only a major turning point in the history of land tax, but could be considered the beginning of the modern land tax system. From then on, land tax was paid mainly in silver, breaking the 3,000-year practice of payment of land tax in kind.[16] The Qing dynasty scholar Wei Yuan holds that the use of silver as currency actually spread because of the shift in tax revenue from coin and grain to silver: "Before the Song and Ming, silver wasn't money . . . After the change from coin and grain to silver, silver spread throughout the land."[17]

Superficially, the silver standard was directly related to the Single Whip tax system, but it also had hidden links to the influx of silver. The Single Whip tax system meant the conversion of corvee labor and other miscellaneous services into payments of silver. It is worth pointing out that this policy was initially practiced in the southeastern coastal provinces, which had been infiltrated by silver. *The Cambridge History of China* notes that silver was plentiful in those places, and large-scale trade and commerce had long made the use of silver taels a preference in commercial affairs. Once this policy was extended throughout the country, the silver standard was gradually established.

Money is the economic lifeline of an empire's political power, and defeat always begins and ends with fiscal administration. Whether it's the Yongle Emperor Zhu Di moving the capital to Beijing or Zheng He setting off on the South Seas, major political enterprises required economic support, and these changes helped silver exploit a loophole in the official system. In the case of moving the capital, in the early Ming, officials of all ranks were originally paid with government-owned farmland in Jiangnan, but this was soon changed to payment in rice, and after the mid-Ming a portion was paid in coin.[18] When Yongle moved the capital, it became inconvenient to pay officials with rice, so they were paid with vouchers instead, often at discounted value. During the Xuande period (1426–1435), the Jiangnan region promoted "golden flower silver" for payment of land tax. "Golden flower silver" was originally two taels of pure silver ornamented with gold, but the name was later applied throughout China to silver paid in place of grain. By the first year of the Yingzong Zhengtong reign (1436), this method became even more widespread, and silver became the main form of tax payment. A century later, Zhang Juzheng's reforms completed the commutation of all tax payments into silver.

In the early fifteenth century, the Ming government finally abandoned the Great Ming *baochao* and acknowledged the status of silver. With silver taking on a leading role, large amounts of it flowed in from Japan and the Americas. The Ming dynasty also began mining silver during the Wanli era. Scholars emphasize that the "silver smelting fever" in this stage of the Ming dynasty was part of a world trend that was taking place concurrently in Japan and Germany.

The notebooks of Ming authors around this time recorded varying assessments of paper currency and silver: "The Song and Yuan used paper currency, and it was especially inconvenient: with the dampness of rain and nibbling of rats it turned to naught; stuffed at the bottom of a bag in one's bosom, it became worn; people enslaved themselves to daily guarding their paper currency. Silver coins were convenient in that water or fire could not destroy them, rats and insects could not invade them, and they could be passed around 10,000 times and retain their original quality."[19]

Apart from banning silver, the Ming dynasty also closed off the country and even prohibited tilling coastal land. The first Ming emperor, Zhu Yuanzhang, issued the order: "Not a single plank can enter the sea."[20] If silver could not be banned, a ban on maritime trade was just as hard to enforce. It is well known that the Ming eunuch Zheng He sailed to the West seven times in the fifteenth century. Smuggling was also widespread among the general populace, maintaining a steady undercurrent of foreign trade in the private sector. China established trade relations with Europe and the Americas in the sixteenth century, and this continued for another 100 years.

It is worth mentioning that not only Chinese are familiar with Zheng He's maritime journeys; they are also recorded at length in foreign accounts. China and Europe cast their eyes on the high seas at the same time in the fifteenth century, but with completely different motivations. At that time Chinese ships virtually led the world in maritime navigation, and Zheng He's explorations occurred nearly a century earlier than those of Europe, but most of this effort was insignificant in the course of history's enormous changes. In his book *World Order*, American statesman Henry Kissinger emphasizes that while Zheng He had the advantage of taking the lead, and China's maritime technology was more advanced than that of pluralistic and fragmented Europe, Zheng He's voyages focused on exchanging gifts with dignitaries in India and Southeast Asia and striving to enroll them in China's imperial tribute system, and all he came back with were cultural and zoological curiosities.[21]

Zheng He's failure was not one of technology or funding. Posterity has borne out that Zheng He's fleet was ten times larger than Columbus's armada in both scale and tonnage, but he was flaunting national prestige while Columbus was exploring the unknown. Added to that, after Zheng He there was no mechanism to continue sea voyages, so the ultimate results were different. Sinologist John King Fairbank emphasizes the enormous divergence between the forces driving Zheng He and Columbus, noting that Chinese fleets lacked the motivation to circumnavigate Africa to reach Europe, or even to establish trading posts: "The similar capabilities of the Chinese and Portuguese voyagers make the contrast between their motivations all the greater. The Chinese simply lacked the expansive urge which the Europeans had, and this fact made all the difference."[22]

Subsequent events showed that the first Ming emperor's bans were worth little more than the paper they were written on, whether applied to silver or to seafaring. There was in fact a logical relationship between the two: Silver's consolidated status in the Ming dynasty, and its subsequent adoption as the value standard for the Ming and Qing dynasties, are inseparable from the flow of enormous amounts of foreign silver into China, and foreign trade also encouraged this trend. Economist Quan Hansheng has carried out a great deal of research on silver in the premodern era, which has also been endorsed by international colleagues. He places silver in Chinese history for points of comparison: The late Tang to the middle period of the Northern Song marked the apex in the use of copper coins; in the mid-Ming, silver gradually won favor, as is especially evident in the growing proportion of silver coin in government revenue. His conclusion is that the proportion of copper coin in government revenue gradually decreased from the Song to the Ming, while the amount of silver continually increased, verifying the trend of "using silver and scrapping copper coins" (see Table 3-1).

China lacked silver and produced little of it, so where did silver currency come from in the Ming dynasty? The general consensus is that

Table 3-1. Song and Ming Government Revenues in Silver and
Copper Coin

Era	Copper coins	Silver coins	Source
Tianxi fifth year	26,530,000 (+)	883,900 (+)	*Extended Continuation of Comprehensive Mirror in Aid of Governance*, Vol. 97, "Tianxi Fifth Year"
Yuanyou first year	48,480,000	57,000	Su Che, *Luancheng Latter Collection*, Vol. 15, "Yuan Weizhan Accounting Records of Revenue and Expenditure"
Wanli eighth year	21,765.4	2,845,483.4	Sun Chengze, *Record of Spring Dreams in the Capital*, Vol. 35
Yueli ninth year	21,765.4	3,704,281.6	*History of the Social-Economic System in the Ming Dynasty*, Vol. 36, pp. 15–16

Source: Quan Hansheng, 1967, "Fluctuations in the Purchasing Power of Silver in the Song and Ming Dynasties and the Reasons for It"

the decisive factor was the influx of silver into China from the sixteenth century onward. In the words of Wei Yuan, "In former times, most of China's silver came from foreign countries. Foreign countries also used silver currency first in China. Before the Song and Ming, silver was not currency."[23]

China's natural silver reserves were concentrated in Yunnan. The Song dynasty work *Exploitation of the Works of Nature* records: "Any silver that can be spoken of in China . . . comes from eight provinces. None add up to half of that from Yunnan." Some Japanese scholars believe that after the Ming dynasty's Tianshun period (1457–1464), most silver was Yunnan silver, while from the Long-Wan periods onward

(Longqing 1567–1572, Wanli 1573–1619), most silver came from overseas, mainly Luzon in the Philippines.[24]

Apart from the Ming dynasty's production of silver, several previous dynasties, especially the Song, produced far more silver than the
Ming. Scholar Song Lingling estimates that during the Southern Song
period, more than 3 million taels of gold and silver entered the government coffers every year. Scholars synthesizing various estimates believe
that in the late Song, the amount of silver totaled 100 million to 150 million taels. However, this silver didn't all remain in China. The Yuan dynasty used paper currency and strictly prohibited the use of silver, while
various kingdoms in the western regions traditionally used silver and
valued it much more highly than China did; consequently, during the
Yuan dynasty, Chinese silver flowed into the western kingdoms through
the Silk Road. The Japanese scholar Otagi Matsuo estimates that as much
as 90 million taels of silver flowed out of China in the Yuan dynasty. If
that is the case, only around 30 million taels of silver carried over from
the end of the Song into the Ming dynasty.

Even so, that is still more than the amount produced during the
Ming dynasty, which is estimated at 15 to 25 million taels. Added together, the amount of local silver during the Ming dynasty totaled
around 50 million taels.

In comparison, the great tide of silver that entered China from Japan, Latin America, and Europe during the Ming dynasty played a much
more important role.

Trade has always fueled globalization. First it was the Portuguese,
who after great effort finally obtained permission to trade in Macau,
which became an important gateway to the world for China's Ming and
Qing dynasties just as the pace of globalization was accelerating. One of
the things that "greased the wheels" was naturally silver, especially the
silver flowing into China. Certain scholars have even summarized this
trade model as another form of "payment": "That these payments were
ideologically called 'tribute' did not change their essential function,
which indeed did express the commercial 'tribute' in silver that others,
including of course the Europeans, were obliged to pay to the Chinese in
order to trade with them."[25] The degree to which China relied on silver
nevertheless greatly exceeded the West's dependence on Chinese silk

and tea, especially as silver became the economic lifeblood of a steadily monetizing China. The failure of both the Europeans and the Chinese to pay close enough attention to this major historical truth resulted in China's series of tragedies from the late Ming onward, as will be related in greater detail later.

Even more important was trade with the Philippines, and here we must also mention the Spaniards. Of course, this did not begin with their contribution to trade. After the "discoverers of the Orient," the Portuguese, made contact with China, Macau became an international trading base for centuries. Then the "discoverers of the world," the Spanish, also came to Asia, and reportedly introduced the smallpox vaccine to China in the early nineteenth century. Chinese merchants, most of them Fujianese from Xiamen (Amoy), Quanzhou, and Fuzhou, became increasingly influential in the flourishing trade with the Philippines. Records indicate that the Spanish were uneasy about this but had to rely on the Chinese for trade. Tens of thousands of Chinese merchants were massacred in 1603 and 1639, but even when subjected to population limits, poll taxes, and expulsion from the country, the number of Chinese merchants continued to grow.

After the Spanish occupied Latin America, they gained enormous silver resources. From the sixteenth century onward, New World silver began flowing around the globe through various conduits. The Philippines became the main transit point through which silver flowed into China, not only silver from colonial Latin America, but also silver from Europe detouring through Southeast Asia.

Quan Hansheng estimates that 75 million pesos or around 60 million taels of silver flowed into China from the Philippines during the Ming dynasty. Another calculation is that some 400 million pesos' worth of Latin American silver was imported to Manila between 1571 and 1821, mainly for the purchase of Chinese raw silk and silk fabric, which were then shipped back to be sold in Latin America. Probably one-fourth of this silver also passed to China.[26] Furthermore, Chinese scholar Qian Jiang calculates that from 1570 to 1760, China's actual trade with Luzon reached 300 million pesos, to the point that even the Spaniards grumbled in 1639 that the "king of China could build a palace with the silver bars from Peru which have been carried to his country . . . without . . . having

been registered and without the king [of Spain] having been paid his duties."[27] Many scholars believe that at least 200 million pesos in silver
flowed into China through the Philippines, the equivalent of 7,200 tons.
Apart from the Philippines, much of the silver first went to Europe and
then flowed from there into Asia. Ward Barrett believes that from 1493 to
1600, the worldwide production of silver totaled 23,000 metric tons, of
which the Americas produced 74 percent. Seventy percent of the New
World silver was imported into Europe, and 40 percent of that silver then
flowed into Asia.[28] Scholar Wan Ming estimates that some 12,620 tons of
American silver flowed into China from 1570 to 1644.[29] Andre Gunder
Frank's estimate is rather exaggerated. He believes that 98,000 tons of
silver were shipped from America to Europe from 1500 to 1800, and that
of that, 39,000 tons were remitted onward to Asia, with 59,000 tons remaining in Europe.[30]

Generally speaking, the consensus is that apart from Japanese
silver, one-third to one-half of American silver flowed into China. Research indicates that around 200 million taels of silver flowed into
China, greatly facilitating the silverization of China's economy.

In other words, although China invented the *jiaozi* early on, its
subsequent excessive issue of paper currency and retreat to commodity
currency, and its resort to the use of copper cash and bartering with rice
and other such tangible goods, ultimately led to metal currency winning
the market's endorsement. The first 500 years of this millennium was a
process of trial and error with paper currency and its ultimate collapse,
while the second 500 years brought the affirmation and victory of silver.
Silver took on a leading role in the Chinese economy, and China did
not abandon the silver standard until the 1930s. The circulation of silver
had such far-reaching and profound effects in China and throughout
the world that even a writer who gladly resists "West-centered thought"
has used the flow of silver into China to affirm China's past status, and
has declared that "the wheels of this global market were oiled by the
worldwide flow of silver."[31]

But that is to be recounted later. Silver arrived uninvited, and in the
twilight years of empire it hastened the emergence of a completely new
end-time landscape.

The Monetization of Silver and China's Ximen Qings

The use of silver was not only the result of flourishing overseas trade, but was essential to the shift from a barter economy to a money economy, and was rooted in the economic development of Ming dynasty society. This also caused the Ming dynasty economy to take on a very different appearance from the past.

Silver not only stimulated the Chinese economy, but also hastened the birth of many social transformations. The inflow of silver was of major significance to the late Ming; it was just at that time that China was rapidly becoming more worldly and materialistic because of commerce: "... By facilitating rapid monetary growth, enhancing the efficiency of exchange, and enabling Chinese officials to carry out long overdue tax reforms, Japanese and Spanish-American silver played a crucial role in the vigorous economic expansion for which the late Ming period in China is justly famous. That expansion affected many regions of the country, but it was particularly noticeable in the south and southeast, where the urban population increased dramatically, agriculture became more commercialized, and trade and industry flourished."[32]

The Golden Lotus was written just at the time when the late Ming economy was undergoing silverization, and in a sense, it is silver that helped China's Ximen Qings achieve their aims. Careful reading and comparison show us that this is a completely different economic world from that depicted in other novels. Scholars observe that The Golden Lotus has more than 300 named characters representing nearly every kind of person and business, and even those who are not engaged in commerce have a certain commercial quality. "Apart from prostitutes and the members of Ximen Qing's family, the main characters in the novel are mostly made up of two types: merchants and officials. Some officials are directly or indirectly engaged in commercial activities—for example, Zhou Shoubei putting up the capital to run Xie's restaurant in Linqing; others, although not engaged in business, regard officialdom as a tool for making money and seeking personal gain. It can be said that almost all of the officials in The Golden Lotus give off a strong whiff of commerce."[33]

Officialdom is the natural outlet for merchants; Ximen Qing is undoubtedly a key character and an excellent metaphor for late Ming society. Pushing aside moral judgment, this man struggled his way up from a family in decline to make a fortune from his herbal medicine shop, and can be credited with an entrepreneurial spirit. He's a classic "economic man," his home life and his power network revolving around silver.

What is the silver-tainted life of Ximen's family in Qinghe County actually like? Apart from the sex that everyone loves talking about, food also makes a deep impression; someone calculated that *The Golden Lotus* mentions more than 200 kinds of food, 24 types of liquor, 19 types of tea, and at least 247 eating scenes, large and small, compared with only 105 explicit sex scenes.[34] Look at how the visiting Count is received: "First were put out four dishes of fruits and nuts, then four dishes of delicacies: rosy Taizhou duck eggs, curvaceous cucumber with Liaodong prawns, fragrant deep fried ribs and a plump steamed cured chicken. The second course was likewise four dishes: roast duck, jellied wings and trotters, fried pork and sautéed kidneys. After that came an imported blue and white platter filled with red, fragrant, willow-steamed shad, absolutely delicious and melting in the mouth; even the bones were tasty."

The reception given to hangers-on is also described colorfully. If the extravagances of county-seat nouveaux riches are so ubiquitous, the atmosphere in the imperial court can only be imagined. This shows the changes to the quality of life triggered by the monetized economy resulting from the influx of silver. In terms of increasing conspicuous consumption, the early Ming dynasty and late Qing come close to eighteenth-century Europe. In Europe, however, it also brought about major social transformation. In David Hume's words: "Since the discovery of the mines in AMERICA, industry has increased in all the nations of EUROPE, except in the possessors of those mines; and this may justly be ascribed, amongst other reasons, to the encrease in gold and silver . . . It is easy to trace the money in its progress through the whole commonwealth; where we shall find, that it must first quicken the diligence of every individual, before it encrease the price of labour."[35]

Unlike the analysis of the rise of capitalism by Hume, Max Weber, and others, the great socialist theorist Werner Sombart gave a more sensual explanation for the rise of capitalism in eighteenth-century Europe:

"Luxury, then, itself a legitimate child of illicit love—as we have seen—gave birth to capitalism."[36] Whatever is popular always circulates from top to bottom, and the spread of luxury and capitalism is no different. Starting with the royal courts, especially the French royal courts, it spread to different classes, and festival celebrations and parading around in costume became increasingly common: "All the follies of fashion, luxury, splendor, and extravagance are first tried out by the mistresses before they are finally accepted, somewhat toned down, by the reputable matrons."[37]

In fact, the view that conspicuous consumption benefits the economy can be verified today; the American economist Thorstein Veblen stated a similar viewpoint in *The Theory of the Leisure Class*. But it is rare to take Sombart's view, which defined the dissipated and licentious fashionable circles as a trend of the times and even a force for progress, and placed them in the position of "the first driving force." He believed that it was consumption beyond necessity that spurred the emergence of capitalism, and that the great cities of the early stage of capitalism were basically consumerist cities:

> The rich soon become insensible to new pleasures. The furnishings of their houses have the character of changeable stage settings; to dress up becomes a real task; their meals are pageants. In my opinion luxury is to them as much an affliction as poverty is to the poor. Oh, it has indeed been worth while to sacrifice everything for luxury! The great scourge of the rich in Paris is their frenzy of spending; they always spend more than they intended to. Luxury has taken on such dreadfully expensive forms that there is no longer any private fortune which is not undermined by it. Never has there been a more profligate age than ours! People squander their income, devour their substance; and everyone seeks to outshine his neighbor by a display of shocking extravagance.[38]

In Sombart's theoretical world, physical and sensual liberation are among the motivating forces of luxurious consumption. His book is full of descriptions such as "it became 'the thing' to keep an elegant mistress instead of, or besides, a lawful spouse,"[39] and "It became good form for a young man to seduce a married woman; he must do it lest he be laughed at by his friends."[40] Finally he asserts, "I know of no event of greater importance for the formation of medieval and modern society than the transformation of the relations between the sexes which occurred during the middle ages and through the eighteenth century."[41]

In retrospect, this parallels the world depicted in *The Golden Lotus*; the two seem to have the same starting point, but *The Golden Lotus* was written 200 years before Sombart's writings. The late Ming was in fact an era that emphasized enjoyment and commerce, so why did its apparently identical luxury not give rise to a modern banking system and other financial innovations, and then proceed to give birth to capitalism?

Needham's Puzzle in the Ming Dynasty

China's silver-tainted late Ming developed a highly commercialized economy, and silver constantly flowed into it from all over the world, so why didn't it produce capitalism? This is one of the great questions of history that has enticed subsequent generations and vast amounts of research.

One of the prominent people who raised this question was the sociologist Max Weber, who asked: Why did the Industrial Revolution not first occur in China, which nurtured the sprouts of capitalism? This is the legendary Weber question. Subsequently, the British scientist Joseph Needham, while researching China's scientific discoveries, also came up with the famous Needham's Puzzle: China's discoveries put it far ahead other civilizations in ancient times, so why didn't the Industrial Revolution occur in China?

From Weber's question to Needham's Puzzle, what are possible answers? The Chicago School believes in simple answers for complex questions, but the historical reality has often been that simple questions have complex answers. Needham's interest in China may have originated from curiosity that overflowed from his area of specialty, but he left China with a riddle that has lasted for decades. Countless explanations have been hurled into this enormous theoretical black hole, but silver is a common thread in the weave of history.

The influx of silver triggered a series of economic changes: With the establishment of the silver standard, banks emerged in Europe, and small local banks, or *qianzhuang,* emerged in China—almost all the vernacular novels of the Ming dynasty mention these small banks. The banks of Venice originated with the money-changing profession, and the earliest bank resembling a central bank emerged in Venice during the thirteenth year of the Wanli era (1585); the Banco della Piazza di Rialto was established in Venice in the fifteenth year of the Wanli era (1587), and the illustrious Bank of Amsterdam was established in the thirty-seventh year of the Wanli era (1609).

Silver gradually became part of the mainstream in the Ming dynasty, rewriting society on the currency and commercial levels and infiltrating the daily lives of ordinary people in a way that drew the various classes into a more materialistic and marketized existence.

The prevalence of silver brought innovation to the financial industry. As is well known, the money-changing industry has a long history in China, and during the Tang dynasty gold and silver shops emerged, mainly for trading but with exchange as a supplementary business, in essentially the same way that European bankers originated among goldsmiths. Early money shops are usually regarded as the progenitors of small local banks. Money shops are believed to have made their first literary appearance in *The Golden Lotus,* for example in a quote by the character Feng Jinbao: "'After I came out of prison,' she said, 'my mother died. The shock had been too much for her. Then I was sold to Madam Zheng the Fifth. But lately, few people have come to see me, and I have had to go to the street to pick up business. Yesterday Master Chen told me that you had a money-changing shop here. I was anxious to see you, and at last my wish has been fulfilled.' "42

China's local private banks seem to have emerged simultaneously with banks in the rest of the world, but their starting point was different, and this determined their different fate. Fernand Braudel has written elaborately about the banks of Genoa during almost the same era in Europe, and he believes their role was not much different from that of today's Bank for International Settlement in Basel: "For three-quarters of a century (1557–1627), 'the Genoese experience' enabled the merchant-bankers of Genoa, through their handling of capital and credit, to call the tune of European payments and transactions. This is worth studying in itself, for it must surely have been the most extraordinary example of convergence and concentration the European world-economy had yet witnessed, as it re-oriented itself around an almost invisible focus."[43] The Medici clan were already powerful players during that same period, and dominated thirteenth-century Florence even more; the clan produced three popes, two French queens, and many noblemen. While Europe's top bankers had monarchs and popes as their biggest clients, the richest man in Qinghe County, Ximen Qing, found it difficult to forge a connection with the comptroller of Imperial Tutor Cai, and entered the palace in the eastern capital only after exhaustive effort and many setbacks; multiple rounds of servile pleading were required for him to be granted an audience.

This shows that the influx of silver apparently only flowed into the historical black hole of China's traditional system, and only partial change was possible without a systemic leap. To a certain extent, Ximen Qing qualified as an entrepreneur of the silver era, but he could not escape the historical inertia of Qinghe County because China lacked the soil to cultivate a modern entrepreneur. In other words, without the necessary systemic environment, in particular a rule-of-law environment supported by a spirit of contract, capitalism is out of the question. Definitions of capitalism may differ, but most research supports the role of capital in expanding markets and molding the system, and one of the most important links happens to be the support of the state government. It has been observed that environment, ambition, and even a sense of responsibility have lured many monarchs of past regimes into capitalistic activities. Economic historians believe there are two kinds of entrepreneurs: those who wield political power and those who wield their personal organizational and mobilization abilities. The latter type have gradually blended with the first type in the new era, and through the first type, or through the government, they have been able to pass laws beneficial to their personal business activities.

Comparatively speaking, China's system didn't encourage entrepreneurs or entrepreneurial activity. Human beings have engaged in commerce throughout the ages, and China is no exception. *Gu Liang's Commentary on the Spring and Autumn Annals* states: "In remote antiquity there were four types of people: scholars, merchants, farmers, and workers." This shows that merchants already existed back then and were ranked before farmers and workers, but soon afterward the order was changed to scholars, farmers, workers, and merchants. Scholar Yu Ying-shih believes that scholars, merchants, farmers, and workers are professional classifications: "Scholars and merchants were undoubtedly the most active classes at the time," and the subsequent sequence of scholar, farmer, worker, and merchant was changed because of "emphasizing farmers over merchants." This shows that from ancient times, China's industry and commerce were relatively developed, and the status of merchants in fact could not have been very low (prohibiting merchants from "wearing silk clothing or riding in carts" was for appearances' sake), but some aspects of Chinese historical tradition are inconsistent with or even counter to commercial logic. Qian Mu once said: "China's historical tradition is often able to warily grasp a low-standard economic viewpoint that puts human life first and the economy second. Therefore, when discussing economic issues, there is often a special focus on the words 'thrift and decorum.' " For this reason, the Chinese government's ideal standard for the economy is "equality," and its ultimate criterion is "peace under heaven," while Western history has mainly pursued "inequality."

In the final analysis, entrepreneurs are a crucial social group, and they emerge through "inequality." Chinese and Western entrepreneurs have encountered different systemic environments; one constrains industry and commerce, and the other devotes itself to protecting property rights. Premodern China, although not lacking individual wealth or even the possibility of extreme wealth, could not easily engender collectively promoted systemic change. Because of that, both Weber's so-called Protestant work ethic, which stresses diligence and abstinence, and Sombart's so-called capitalist spirit, combining entrepreneurial spirit with civic spirit, may have been sparked sporadically in China but were never able to amount to anything or escape the cycle of the "merchant in an official's cap." They could only produce entrepreneurs who relied on the system for easy gain, rather than entrepreneurs who pushed for systemic reform.

Beginning with the Renaissance, Western history's direction began to shift, and the role of intangible systemic innovation began to expand.

Peng Xinwei believes that Asian banks developed from money-changing to deposit and remittance services, which led them to gradually increase in scale, since the financial industry is established on credit, and the accumulation of credit drives forward-directed money-creating capabilities. This path is not a smooth one; Venice's money-changing shops also had their bad debts; Charles I seized control of the London Mint during the thirteenth year of the Chongzhen reign (1640), and even John Law's games with paper money in France were really just a passive form of plunder. Even after suffering setbacks, however, the West's modern banking system finally took shape. By way of contrast, China developed from money-changing to lending services, but savings deposit services did not develop, and neither the public nor the private sector had the habit of external money storage. Indeed, the Ming dynasty's famously corrupt official Yan Shifan simply hoarded silver in a cellar, while rulers always engaged in active rather than passive pillage.

China was actually a step ahead when it came to remittances, which were commonplace from the Northern Song onward, but later generations appraised the trade as "unnoticeable," while the money-exchange shops and local private banks can be considered the major backdrop of the late Ming, as will be related in detail later. The Ming dynasty's remittance service was operated by the government; the general populace referred to it as bank checks, or what in the Song dynasty was called the *qianyin*. This kind of traditional remittance method couldn't keep pace with the evolution of commerce and was typically subject to collusion between officials and merchants. Europe, however, developed the practice into even more credit services, and eventually used it for international trade. Ultimately, in the seventeenth century it developed into checking accounts, savings reserves, cashier's checks, and other financial innovations, triggering major transformation in commercial society.

China's local private banks enjoyed a head start, but ultimately they fell behind and even disappeared in the dust of history. What factors contributed to the widely diverging fates of the private banking industry in China and the West? Taken a step further, silver drove the rise of new merchants like Ximen Qing, but their rise was in the form of joining the old class or becoming officials. The contribution that this kind of entrepreneur made to society and to the economy's market expansion seemed to have been more a matter of dividing up the cake than of enlarging it.

Regarding the special characteristics of the Chinese economy, Qian Mu gave an explanation not lacking in humanitarian sentiment:

> China's industry and commerce always developed toward prosperity and not decline. It is only when socioeconomic material conditions were adequate to satisfy the populace that Chinese people became wary and stopped going further or changing directions to take human and material resources to a higher plane of human existence . . . Therefore, although the upward development of the economy was materialistic in both cases, the West tended toward a scientific mechanistic aspect while China leaned toward the skill-molding aspect . . . This shows that China's traditional economic viewpoint has a humanitarian and ethical standard and emphasizes human life over the economy. The economy is meant to assist human life and not dominate human life. Therefore economic development was limited.

Qian Mu believes that restraints on the development of industry and commerce were conscious and voluntary. Opinions differ on this explanation, but both Qian Mu's personal opinion and the moralized thinking it references reveal China's economic policy mindset. In this way of thinking, the economy always settled for a low-standard balance, while merchants usually had no real status, ability, or power to participate in the government's systemic chess games. As a result, property rights and capitalism could not develop. If the state obstructed capital and entrepreneurs, even people as shrewd as Ximen Qing could only make a splash within Qinghe County.

Delving deeper, even back in ancient times China had both government and private lending, which in premodern times distinguished between "buying/selling on credit" and "borrowing/lending." The Tang dynasty had remittance services in the form of the so-called flying (*fei*) money, and the subsequent proliferation of silver shops and local private banks demonstrated the popularity of silver and the flourishing of commerce. But this was not necessarily a sprout or harbinger of Chinese capitalism, and there is sometimes a degree of wishful thinking regarding commercialization in the Ming dynasty. Some scholars counter that commercialization is not the same as capitalism; modern Western capitalism is different from early commercial systems that existed in China, India, Babylon, Egypt, and the Mediterranean region. The former is especially reliant on accuracy in the natural sciences, while China lacked anything like laboratories, even in the late Qing dynasty. This argument corresponds to the management level, resembling Ray Huang's "numerical management" train of thought.[44]

This is just one aspect of the causes; in fact, apart from cultural, ethnic, and other explanations, the economic system is still worth considering. The different attitudes toward trade and maritime pursuits in Asia and the West put their respective economies on different trajectories, and the protection of property rights remains key. This protection relies on rule of law. As Douglass North says: "An institutional arrangement will be innovated if the expected net gains exceed the expected costs. Only when this condition is met would we expect to find attempts being made to alter the existing structure of institutions and property rights within a society."[45]

Comparatively speaking, in Europe the influx of New World gold and silver is regarded as a harbinger of the rise of the Western world. These precious metals helped create a new elite; in fact, it is said that the cost of seeking precious metals was about the same as the value of the precious metals, which made this more a redistribution of wealth than a process of creating wealth. But in this process, wealth took on new meaning, and a new class was born in Europe. Werner Sombart noted that in the Middle Ages, anyone with power and influence was assumed to be very wealthy; now anyone who was wealthy was assumed to have power. Before, power brought wealth; now, wealth brought power.[46] The new elites differed from the former elites in that their wealth had nothing to do with birth or power, therefore hastening the emergence of a larger middle class. The middle class found opportunities in overseas trade and other new economic activities, and consequently created a new category of entrepreneur, the cumulative power of which ultimately became a major driving force for historical change, including the nurturing of capitalism.

As the world changed, the meager efforts of China's merchants, although aided by silver's splendor, were as sluggish as ever. Constrained by the boundaries of Qinghe County, there was no way for the various Ximen Qings to escape history's bell jar. Without rule of law and credit, there was no space or historical environment for entrepreneurs to grow, much less for modern capitalism to emerge.

The Influx of Silver and the Fall of the Ming Dynasty

The use of silver spread during the Ming dynasty, first of all because the economy required monetization and relied on the influx of foreign silver for external supplies. This brought the fateful encounter between China's overseas trade and the great geographical discoveries. Silver's flourishing during the Ming empire unintentionally also contained the seeds of its destruction.

Tracing the fall of the Ming dynasty in 1644 requires going back even further. The Ming dynasty was a node in China's new and old world. The Ming dynasty continued the evolutionary logic of its preceding dynasties, which also foreshadowed the transition from the Ming to the Qing. On a coordinate axis of time, the Ming Empire corresponds with Europe's groundbreaking transformation. Out of comparative inertia, historians like to analyze the gains and losses of the millennium starting with the Ming, and even years of no significance are annotated and endowed with profound and far-reaching implications: for example, Ray Huang's 1578 and Sinologist Valerie Hansen's 1600.[47]

For China, 1600 was a watershed. Hansen, who has been captivated by China all her life, has a different perspective from customary Chinese thinking. She points out that before 1600, China was an "open empire."[48] She abandons the customary dynastic divisions to define three eras for China before 1600: The first stage is from the Shang and Zhou to the Qin dynasty, from 1200 B.C.E. to 200 C.E., the period of building China. The second stage begins with the unification of China by the Qin dynasty in the third century C.E., when indigenous Daoism began to rise in an organized fashion, many Buddhists also arrived in

China, and China began to look to the West and India for more than 1,200 years. The final stage is the shift toward the north from the tenth century to the seventeenth century, the large amount of time during which China was under the rule of northern nomadic tribes, who at the same time became gradually Sinicized. The Mongols remain the Ming dynasty's greatest worry until the Manchus of the northeast finally rise to prominence.

What actually happened around the year 1600? With the influx of enormous amounts of silver, the status of silver continued to rise in China during the mid-Ming dynasty, consolidating the status of the silver standard in every respect. Many scholars emphasize the role of Zhang Juzheng's "Single Whip" tax system. Implementation of the Single Whip tax system thoroughly nullified the Hongwu system and formed a link between Yang Yan's tax law reforms in the mid-Tang and the "merger of the poll tax with the acre tax" (tanding rumu) of the Yongzheng period in the early Qing (1723–1735). This put an end to the use of payment in kind in China's state revenue system and transitioned into the payment of tax in money. Scholars generally agree that it further expanded the silverization of the Ming dynasty economy. Scholar Peng Xinwei calculates that in 200-plus years, the exchange ratio of gold to silver went from 1:4 and 1:5 at the beginning of the Ming to 1:10 and even 1:13 in the late Ming.[49] The flow of precious metals looks like merely economic behavior, but its effects and side-effects were endless and even influenced the fall of an empire.

After silver was discovered in Peru, most European silver mines were abandoned. Adam Smith subsequently asserted that American silver mines affected not only the price of European silver, but also the price of silver from Chinese mines. He personally witnessed the effect of precious metals on Europe in the seventeenth century, and noticed the mutual influence of trade between the New and Old Worlds:

> It is more advantageous too to carry silver thither [to India] than gold; because in China, and the greater part of the other markets of India, the proportion between fine silver and fine gold is but as ten, or at most as twelve, to one; whereas in Europe it is as fourteen or fifteen to one. In China, and the

greater part of the other markets of India, ten, or at most twelve, ounces of silver will purchase an ounce of gold: in Europe it requires from fourteen to fifteen ounces. In the cargoes, therefore, of the greater part of European ships which sail to India, silver has generally been one of the most valuable articles. It is the most valuable article in the Acapulco ships which sail to Manilla [*sic*]. The silver of the new continent seems in this manner to be one of the principal commodities by which the commerce between the two extremities of the old one is carried on, and it is by means of it, in a great measure, that those distant parts of the world are connected with one another.[50]

During the late Ming, the exchange relations between the monetary systems of China and the rest of the world were similar to the trade deficits and hot money of the early twenty-first century. At the earliest point, from the Roman era, China was considered to come under European currency. Because the international payment structure was advantageous to China, silver streamed into China from all corners of the world. This was even more the case under the push of American silver in the seventeenth century: "As much as twenty percent of all silver mined in Spanish America came directly across the Pacific via galleon to Manila and thence to China to pay for silks and porcelains. Other American bullion found its way indirectly through the Central Asian trade to Bokhara. As much as half of the precious metals mined in the New World may in this way have ended up in China."[51]

It was once believed that the vitality of the great Roman Empire was sapped by the massive outflow of precious metals, and the situation was similar for silver in the Ming empire. American scholar Frederic Wakeman believes that the fall of the Ming dynasty and the rise of the Qing in 1644 was the most dramatic dynastic shift in Chinese history, and that silver played a key role in it.[52]

Historical fact must be based on comparison, and Europe was concurrently experiencing its famous "crisis of the seventeenth century"— historian Eric Hobsbawm invented this name, mainly to express a series of crises that included economic recession, population decline, and social unrest.[53] Taken a step further, this was in fact a global crisis, and one school of historians believes that the different ways that the crisis was dealt with almost simultaneously in Asia and the West led to a great divide in history.

It is believed that under the "crisis of the seventeenth century," Asia continued with its model of dynastic change, while in the West the crisis spurred the stride into modernized society: "In every general conjuncture, different countries react differently, whence the inequalities of development which, in the end, make history."[54] Consequently, the strategic decisions of a moment become permanent history, and what looks like a trivial divergence brings about completely different outcomes.

In comparison, China's traditional narrative of dynastic change often covers up historical truth. It is worth pointing out that over the course of thousands of years, prosperity and diversity have usually been associated with division rather than with great unity. China's period of great unity under the Qin dynasty was actually very brief: "If calculated from when the First Qin Emperor Qin Shihuang completing the expansion of his territory, unity was preserved for only six years."[55] But these six years planted the seeds for what was to follow.

As the shrewd statesman Henry Kissinger once said, "European-style ideas of interstate politics and diplomacy were not unknown in the Chinese experience; rather, they existed as a kind of countertradition taking place within China in times of disunity. But as if by some unwritten law, these periods of division ended with the reunification of All Under Heaven, and the reassertion of Chinese centrality by a new dynasty."[56]

Through silver China's upheavals became secretly bound to world trends. Frederic Wakeman sees a resonance between China's crisis and that of the rest of the world in the seventeenth century:

> We can speak of the major conjunctural domination of China in Manila to the degree that there is a conformity between the secular and intercyclical fluctuation of the Chinese trade and the global trade; to a degree even more where the amplitude of the secular and intercyclical fluctuation of move-

ments with China is much greater than the amplitude of the indices of total activity. We can therefore conclude that in spite of appearances, it is the ups and downs of trade with the Chinese continent which commands the ups and downs of the galleon trade itself.[57]

As Laozu said, "Happiness is found alongside misery, and misery lurks beneath happiness." Historians differ over whether silver's increasing prominence bound its fate more closely to that of the Ming empire. Some emphasize that China's economy would have developed even without silver, and that the flood of overseas silver symbolized China's loss of monetary sovereignty, and even the beginning of centuries of transference of monetary sovereignty overseas.[58]

Even today, some believe that transfer of monetary sovereignty overseas led to the fall of the Ming dynasty and the decline of the Qing. I actually believe that monetary sovereignty is not that significant in the age of precious metals, and that precious metals are a natural leap for classical economic activity. Even in modern times, monetary sovereignty is not a power that can be fought for. The Ming dynasty had no choice but to go from banning silver to using silver; monetary sovereignty could not be obtained by fighting for it. It is also a fact that China produced too little silver, and that deflation was far from the only effect of receding inflows of silver. Possession of precious metals was the great desire of virtually all ancient empires, and foreign silver and the Great Ming Empire helped each other achieve their respective aims. In the words of historian Fernand Braudel, "Asia had retaliated from the days of the Roman Empire by consenting to exchange her goods only for precious metals—gold (which was preferred on the Coromandel coast) but above all silver. China and India in particular became . . . bottomless pits for the precious metals in circulation: they were sucked in, never to re-emerge."[59] China's thirst for silver and ability to draw a continuous inflow of silver initially looked advantageous, but in fact also constituted its weakness. The continuous influx of silver helped China establish a silver standard and led to the monetization of commodities to an unprecedented degree, but once that inflow dried up, it dealt a fatal blow to the Ming economy.

In the first half of the seventeenth century, several major famines broke out in China. Past explanations always attributed them to natural causes, but in fact, as historian William Atwell observes, they were the tragic outcomes of larger economic and social problems that had been festering for some time, many of which seem to have been directly related to the large amounts of bullion that had flowed into circulation in East Asia after the middle of the sixteenth century. "That bullion facilitated high levels of public expenditure, rapid urban growth, and intense economic competition, all of which proved to be socially and politically disruptive."[60] Atwell believes that China's difficulties stemmed in part from its almost total reliance on bullion imports to increase its money supply. When the amount of silver flowing into China from Spanish America dropped sharply, the Ming government was soon confronted with an economic nightmare. "The Ming dynasty fell, in part, because it simply did not have the funds to continue its operations."[61]

In retrospect, a series of nearly coincidental and mutually intertwined incidents drove the nail into the coffin of the Ming Empire. From 1634 to 1636, the Spanish decided to limit the amount of Latin American silver flowing into the Philippines; in winter 1636, the strained relations between Chinese and Spanish in Manila finally broke out in violent conflict, and more than 20,000 Chinese were killed. After that, the amount of silver flowing into China through the Philippines greatly decreased. In summer of that year, the Japanese Tokugawa shogunate decided to ban merchants from Macau from trading in Nagasaki, and the route that had brought a large amount of Japanese silver to China was also shut down. Affected by this series of factors, China's silver imports plunged. The sharp reduction in the inflow of silver was accompanied by a collapse in the silver exchange rate. These historical threads silently tightened the economic rope around the neck of the Great Ming Empire.

Reduced silver supplies led to all kinds of hoarding and "manmade illnesses." Because many taxes and levies had to be paid in silver, the tax burden became unbearable, and many people went bankrupt as a result. The phenomenon of ghost towns emerged in rich and populous regions, and the income extorted by the imperial court's fiscal administration radically declined. As silver supplies dried up, the exchange ratio between silver and copper coins rose sharply, and the ability of poor people to buy the necessities of life with copper cash greatly decreased. Added to that, a Little Ice Age occurred at that time, bringing constant natural disasters; food production dropped and food prices exploded. After a famine in Henan in 1640, rice sold for 3,000 copper cash per *dou* [ten liters], and wheat for 2,700 cash per *dou*, and many people starved from north to south. Starvation and epidemic illnesses caused the population to plummet by tens of millions and made violent popular revolution virtually unavoidable.

Silver was the fuse, and the economic, natural, and population crises that accompanied the silver crisis combined to change the course of the Ming dynasty's history. Behind the famine and eyewitness accounts of "streets filled with refugees" and cannibalism was popular revolt, and all kinds of rebellions arose. The army of Li Zicheng, who destroyed the Ming dynasty, appeared in the northwest, and later generations of historians believe this was more than coincidence, because it was a territory far removed from that silver-stained and famine-ravaged land.

The havoc wreaked by inflation led to complete social collapse, not only causing famine, death, and suffering and triggering rebellions all over the country, but also causing bureaucrats' salaries to shrink, which in turn caused the Ming regime's legitimacy to be shaken by corruption. Food prices steadily increased, while official salaries calculated in silver remained relatively stable, which meant that official incomes were eroded by inflation. "By 1629, the annual subsidies to civil officers and imperial clansmen (of which there were approximately 40,000 in the capital alone) in Beijing amounted only to 150,000 taels or less than one percent of the national budget."[62]

Plummeting official income was obviously undesirable, because this inevitably meant even more rampant fleecing of the population. The existence of Hai Rui as the image of an honest and upright official seems a confirmation of the Ming dynasty's decadence. For imperial officials such as Hai Rui, relying on official salaries meant a spartan existence as long as they lived, and buying his mother a kilo of meat for her birthday was a major event. Although he ultimately rose to the position of imperial censor and was posthumously awarded the title of Grand Guardian of the Crown Prince and the name Zhong Jie, meaning "faithful and pure," Hai Rui died without issue and left behind only twenty taels of silver, requiring others to donate funds for his funeral. *History of the Ming* records: "People in white mourning garments lined the river banks for miles ... Throughout the land he was known as Mr. Gang Feng."[63] But how many people were willing to live like Hai Rui and die under such straitened circumstances? Hai Rui lived through the reigns of the Zhengde, Jiajing, Longqing, and Wanli emperors and became famous throughout China, but his official career had its ups and downs, and he was never entrusted with important political positions.

As might well be imagined, upright officials like Hai Rui not only were a minority, but were out of step with the times. Striving for unofficial sources of income became an unspoken rule in the political world, and even the Ming dynasty's emperors did all they could to enrich the palace coffers, treating the entire country like their private property. Military expenses became tight, but "it was not possible to request funds to be issued from the privy purse." Ironically, when Li Zicheng finally occupied Beijing, all that remained in the palace and public treasuries were 170,000 taels of gold and 130,000 taels of silver. When corruption becomes a systemic phenomenon and the upper classes brutally squeeze the lower classes, social unraveling becomes inevitable and the death of the regime is not far off. Some scholars therefore "attributed the economic difficulties of the late Ming to a systemic breakdown affecting the entire social order."[64]

Indeed, silver had a profound and far-reaching effect on the monetization of China's economy and on systemic reform. From the establishment of the silver standard to the collapse of the Ming dynasty, persistent trade deficits also created follow-up problems such as the Opium Wars—in a certain sense, it would be no exaggeration to call the Opium Wars the Silver Wars instead. The monetization of silver and the late Ming's commercialization mutually stimulated each other, causing China to partially merge into the world economy and also to know the meaning of depression after prosperity. That is why thinkers such as Gu Yanwu and Huang Zongxi typically had negative appraisals of silver. Huang Zongxi believed that abolishing the use of silver would have seven major benefits: 1) grain and cloth would be available to ordinary people, with enough for all; 2) constantly minting cash to meet all needs would mean no shortage of the medium of exchange; 3) without the hoarding of silver and gold there would be no rich or poor families; 4) carrying heavy metal currency made it inconvenient for people to leave their hometowns; 5) government officials could not so easily hide their ill-gotten wealth; 6) thieves and burglars would be easily traced by their heavy loads; 7) the interchange of cash and paper currency would be facilitated.[65] Scholar Wang Fuzhi, like many other enlightened scholars, concluded that silver increased the gap between rich and poor, and that the more silver, the greater the gap: "The more of this substance there is, the poorer the realm is."[66]

Writing something down makes it eternal; text is after all the foundation of history. In contrast with the indignant denunciations of silver by great minds, the silver-tainted Ximen Qings have no voice; they are China's persistently silent commercial class. In his book *Macrohistory Will Not Shrink*, Ray Huang compares China's Ming and Qing social structures to a submarine sandwich: Civil officials and intellectuals formed the long piece of bread on the top, the undifferentiated peasantry formed the long bottom piece, and the middle structure was always fragile and inconsequential: "The existence of the merchant class had no intrinsic value," so their legal and social status can easily be imagined.

By contrast, the enlightened personages of China's Ming dynasty sniffed out money as a factor in epochal transition, while the hardships of the people also spurred them to raise trenchant criticisms. This discussion greatly influenced the judgment of subsequent generations, albeit in more modern and scholarly form. But most of these judgments, whether in premodern times or today, neglect economic logic. Silver was not the active choice of the Great Ming Empire, but rather the passive result of the chess game between imperial authority and the market. This is not to say that the decreased inflow of silver was irrelevant to the rise and fall of the Ming dynasty—silver can be credited with the Ming dynasty's prosperity, as well as with bringing about its extinction. The even larger backdrop, however, is China's inability to escape the restraints of a broken government system; it was major systemic failure.

No single cause can explain history or drive it forward; Chinese bias in favor of Big History typically disregards real-life complexity. The search for historical truth means approaching probable truth rather than seeking out a single driving force. Silver forms the veins and arteries of history, but is not the cause or objective of history. The influx of silver originally coexisted with international trade, economic marketization, and monetization, and its acceptance was not a matter of the government's hope or promotion alone. As before, the popularity of silver was decided by the flourishing of the Ming dynasty's commodity economy. Regardless of the currency, its ultimate endorsement by the market still originated with the choice of the general public. China's *jiaozi,* European currencies, and even the Ming dynasty's final paper currency farce all prove that monarchs can choose a certain currency and even put their own image on it, but they cannot force people to use it. Just as the influx of silver coincided with the late Ming's commercial and economic prosperity, its constricted flow became one of many ropes around the neck of the Ming dynasty.

Chinese Money and Toyotomi Hideyoshi

The world revolves around money, and the new money of each era will create new tycoons and even new eras.

The most influential such development in modern history was the inflow of New World silver resulting from the great geographical discoveries. The flow of this silver into Europe spurred a revolution in commodity prices in Spain, but also led to a series of inflationary developments in Europe: In the sixteenth century, the price of goods in Andalusia increased 500 percent, and the situation was similar in Great Britain and France; wages were unable keep up with the rising price of goods. At that time inflation was not an entirely bad thing; in the words of one economist, "The high prices and low wages meant high profits."[67] This encouraged foreign trade, and the overflow of wealth created ambitious and zealous merchants. The assault of inflation on the low-income stratum and the drop in labor costs also spurred new arrangements at the systemic level. This reallocation of social wealth created chain reactions credited with "adding fuel to the flames" in the emergence of capitalism in Europe.[68]

In Asia, silver likewise had profound influence on China, but also on Japan.

Prehistoric Japan was a hunter-gatherer society. When rice paddy cultivation was introduced to Japan around the third century B.C.E., its community ecology gradually evolved and social order also emerged in the form of multiple small states. The emperor politically unified the country in the seventh century, and Buddhism also began to flourish. This was the stage in Japan's history when the emperor achieved actual power. This unification did not last long, however, and China's Ming dynasty coincided with a warring states (Sengoku) period in Japan.

At that time, Japan was one of China's sources of silver. Japan had such abundant silver mines that one of its islands was known as Ginsima, or Silver Island. According to one record, "Japan merchants use only silver for barter, unlike the cargo trade of Western barbarians."[69] This inflow, while not comparable to other channels, added up to a considerable amount. Some Japanese scholars point out that after the Tokugawa shogunate established its rule, it exported nearly 2 million kilos of silver to China, or around 30 million taels.

Corresponding to the flow of silver into China was the flow of Chinese copper coins into Japan before the Ming dynasty. For example, when shogun Ashikaga Takauji decided to raise funds to build the Tenryū temple, Japan dispatched the "Tenryū-ji bune" trading vessels to resume trade with the Yuan dynasty. Whether profitable or not, each ship returning to port had to pay 5,000 *guan* toward the construction of the Tenryū temple.

Just as American silver triggered dramatic changes in Europe, money had the effect of not only changing the price of goods, but through those price changes also creating a redistribution of wealth that affected the social structure. Before the Toyotomi era, Japan basically used Chinese currency, typically obtained through tribute payments, trade, and plundering, and the influx of large amounts of Chinese currency had an enormous effect on Japan.

Historian William S. Atwell quotes the observations of a Western priest in Japan at the time: "The laws, administration, customs, culture, trade, wealth, and magnificence were restored throughout the kingdom, and populous cities and other buildings were raised everywhere as a result of trade and peace. Many people became rich, although the ordinary folk and peasants were impoverished by the taxes they were obliged to pay. The lords of the land became very wealthy, storing up much gold and silver. Throughout the kingdom there was a great abundance of money, new mines were opened and the kingdom was well supplied with everything."[70] He believed that Japanese silver flowed into mainland China through Macau, Taiwan, and other territories, and that this in turn stimulated the expansion of Japan's domestic market. A key factor in Japan's economic development in the late sixteenth and early seventeenth centuries was the rapid development of a monetized economy, which gave powerful impetus to the political unification movement initiated by the samurais Oda Nobunaga, Toyotomi Hideyoshi, and Tokugawa Ieyasu. At the same time, the substantial investment by feudal lords in foreign trade resulted in a sharp increase in the export of Japanese silver in the late sixteenth and early seventeenth centuries.

The economy is typically the first driving force for social cohesion and cultural mindset, and there were already portents that times were changing. Zhu Yuanzhang and Toyotomi Hideyoshi were among the few people from time immemorial who rose from humble beginnings to become powerful overlords. Toyotomi Hideyoshi, one of the three great warriors of Japan's warring states period, can be considered a "local tycoon" who emerged because of favorable conditions in Japan at that time. Born in 1536, he succeeded Oda Nobunaga and was succeeded by Tokugawa Ieyasu. This fierce and ambitious leader of Japan's warring states period, born in humble circumstances to a low-level samurai (some say a peasant), eventually followed Oda Nobunaga and then took over as Daijō-daijin;[71] Toyotomi was the surname of the imperial family. This warrior from a common family not only united Japan, but also attempted to encroach on East Asia, from Korea to China. The Osaka Castle that Toyotomi built was destroyed, and the existing Osaka Castle was built after Tokugawa Ieyasu defeated Toyotomi Hideyoshi's son Toyotomi Hideyori. Toyotomi Hideyoshi's achievements are evident everywhere, and Tokugawa Ieyasu virtually existed in his shadow; after gaining the kingdom he became lost to history.

The rise of Toyotomi Hideyoshi is inseparable from economic power, and the massive inflow of copper coins from China was crucial to that. The influx of Chinese coins corresponded to the flourishing of Japan's external trade and resulted in commercial capitalists gaining ground. The iron-fisted rule of the shogunates began to disintegrate, and Japan's warring states period emerged from that. At the same time, the social structure began to change and the status of commoners rose; some scholars have even stated that Toyotomi Hideyoshi was "groomed" by Chinese money.[72] It is interesting to note that Japan began minting money in the Toyotomi era, and during the late Qing, Japan preceded China in producing milled (machine-struck) coinage.[73] There were even Japanese silver dollars that flowed into China, colloquially known as "Great Japan" after the words that were engraved on the face of the coins.

The outbreak of Japan's Ōnin War launched the warring states period within Japan and triggered the Ningbo Incident,[74] resulting in the Ming dynasty repeatedly rejecting Japan's tributary trade, even if the trade ban existed in name only. This resulted in an upsurge in Ming dynasty smuggling and Japanese piracy (*wokou*) as well as the Portuguese grabbing a share of China's foreign trade, and Japan began repudiating Chinese suzerainty, especially beginning with the "three heroes of the warring states."[75]

Toyotomi Hideyoshi not only completed the reunification of Japan after the dissolution of the Ashikaga shogunate, but ambitiously launched two wars with Korea (known in Japan as the Bunroku and Keichō wars) in the twentieth and twenty-fifth years of the Ming's Wanli reign (1592 and 1597), in hopes of using these wars as a springboard to encroachment on China.

The effect on China of Japan's wars in Korea is routinely overlooked; in fact it may have been the first dirty stuffing to soil the Ming dynasty's rich brocades. Scholars have typically held that the foundations of the Ming economy already showed signs of weakening after the Hongzhi and Zhengde periods, and began to shake during the Wanli years; Ray Huang's *1587: A Year of No Significance* endeavors to depict this moment as the watershed dividing East and West. Symbolically, what draws the most notice are the three wars during the Wanli period, among which the wars in Korea stand out as the only battles fought on foreign soil. The records show that Toyotomi Hideyoshi mobilized around 300,000 troops, and the Ming dynasty mustered an expeditionary force of 100,000 troops to recapture Korea, reportedly including fighters from Siam (now Thailand) and the Ryukyu Archipelago. Historians still find

Toyotomi Hideyoshi's actual intentions toward China inexplicable, especially his repeated negotiations with the Ming dynasty special envoys;
each side also has different assessments of who won and who lost, but
in any case the seven-year war collapsed after the death of Toyotomi
Hideyoshi.

Toyotomi Hideyoshi reportedly at one point demanded the parti-
tioning of Korea, taking a Korean prince hostage and marrying a Ming
princess, but obviously he never achieved these aims.[76] Japan's intentions
during the Ming dynasty seem fortuitous, but in fact they originated
in the conflict between Japan's development and China's order; that is,
Japan was not content with its marginal status, while the concept of the
Middle Kingdom was a symbol of legitimacy for China and could not be
abandoned; the concept remained the same under Qing rule 100 years
later, even with the hope of continuing the tributary model in foreign
trade.

This war was like a preview of subsequent historical events. As a
tributary in the eyes of the Celestial Empire, Japan's rise undoubtedly
challenged the imperial order envisioned by the Ming dynasty, hinting at
a series of clashes between the Celestial Empire and the outside world
and suggesting a vague connection with the subsequent Sino-Japanese
War of 1894–1895. *The Cambridge History of China* assesses the war in
Korea as "utterly futile" and a "folly,"[77] in which inept handling by both
sides caused a stalemate situation; if not for the death of Toyotomi Hideyoshi, it's hard to know how it would have ended.

Although ultimately the Ming dynasty concluded the war in Korea
through military means, it suffered heavy economic casualties; it might
be said that Japan's offensive was a symbol or harbinger of the collapse of
the Great Ming's flourishing age. Soon afterward, the Ming court fell
into difficulties and its currency system began to deteriorate. The purchasing power of China's copper coins was very strong before the Wanli
period, but began to slide from then on. The fall of the Ming actually
began during the Wanli reign, and the effect of Japan and the war in Korea cannot be discounted. Looking back at Japan, when Tokugawa Ieyasu
took over from Toyotomi Hideyoshi and established the Edo shogunate
in 1603, Japan was unified again and embarked on its flourishing Edo
era. In terms of currency, Japan went from relying on the Ming dynasty's

"cross-over money" to gradually developing its own monetary system. Tokugawa Ieyasu not only launched the Edo era, but also developed an independent currency system combining the use of gold, silver, and copper coins.

The last years of the Ming dynasty coincided with the beginning of Japan's Edo period. As Japan's last feudal period, lasting 265 years from 1603 to 1867, the Edo is typically regarded as critical to shaping Japan's collective consciousness and national identity. For example, Japan always brags about being a nation of rice paddies, but in fact the widespread use of rice paddies and even the Japanese style of eating mainly took shape during the Edo period.

The seventeenth century was an era of globalization, and there was synchronicity in the crises experienced in various countries. Natural disasters and famines occurred not only in Europe, but also in China and Japan. The fall of China's Ming dynasty has been recounted many times, but why did Japan's response bring in an era of self-sufficiency and peace? Historian William Atwell believes that part of the reason is the trade and monetary policies carried out by the shogunates, for example, reducing the export of silver in response to local demand, and that another part was the greatly increased production of copper. This allowed Japan to recover more quickly than China from the "crisis of the seventeenth century."[78]

The fates of the two countries diverged even more in the eighteenth century, and they grew further apart on the silver issue. Atwell points out that as the productivity of Japan's silver mines was unable to keep pace with economic demand, the shogunal government was forced to impose new restrictions on the export of silver, and the drop in precious metal output spurred Japan toward more than a century of vigorous international economic activity. From then on Japan settled into a self-sufficiency that colored its history for the next 150 years. As for China, its continued reliance on foreign silver involved it even more deeply in the "emerging world economy."[79]

The "crisis of the seventeenth century" has become a catchphrase, and overseas scholarship has attributed the fall of the Ming dynasty to it, along with the disastrous effects of the Little Ice Age. The Ming dynasty and the Tokugawa shogunate in fact faced similar challenges, with

Japan's first large-scale famine occurring during the Kan'ei era (1624–1643). Some scholars attributed the extremely disparate political fates of the two regimes to the different responses of their economic, political, and monetary systems.

Comparison is just a form of imagination; history cannot be replicated, but it can be replayed to some extent. Relatively independent silver and copper production was of great benefit to Japan in dealing with the seventeenth-century crisis, but the real difference between China and Japan was probably not reflected until the nineteenth century.

The Late Qing

Collapsing in Chaos

Official careers crumbled;

The gold and silver of the wealthy vanished;

The kind-hearted escaped with their lives;

The ruthless received their just deserts . . .

Cao Xueqin, "The Birds into the Woods Have Flown,"

The Dream of the Red Chamber *(Qing)*

He who can forge this gold into a ring will rule the world,

but only if he foreswears love.

Richard Wagner (1813–1883), The Ring of the Nibelung

If Chinese banks are not established as a matter of urgency, it will be impossible

to use the vital energy of Chinese merchants to constrain foreign merchants.

Sheng Xuanhuai, "the Father of Chinese Industry" (1844–1916)

The Currency Chaos of the Qing Dynasty

As mentioned earlier, the most direct reason for the fall of the Ming dynasty was military defeat. Just when the Ming Empire was in greatest need of armed strength, its military apparatus became least effective. If it could have fully employed its limited armed force to pacify the peasant uprisings in the northwest, or to defend against the Qing's armored cavalry in the northeast, it might have attained a measure of success, but it lacked the capacity to wage war on both fronts simultaneously. When the Ming forces saw a glimmering hope of stamping out the peasant uprising in 1638, the Manchu Huang Taiji staged a massive invasion that forced the Ming army to reinforce the northeast, nullifying their previous battle gains; the peasant rebel leaders Li Zicheng and Zhang Xianzhong swept across half of China.

On further examination, this was in fact the same old problem faced by traditional Central Plains Han empires, that is, how to deal with military threats from the steppes. The conquering Qing dynasty employed a much more effective method than the Ming Empire to deal with this problem: it constructed a northern and southern bicameral monarchal system consisting of a khanate ruling the Jurchen and Mongolian tribes north of the Great Wall, and an imperial bureaucratic system ruling its subjects south of the Great Wall. Tax revenues in the south were enough to help the Qing Emperor thwart the nobility's attempts at division of power, and the cavalry on the steppes provided the empire with its greatest military power in the "cold weapon" pre-firearm era. Consequently, once the bloodbaths were ultimately followed by peace, China's economy quickly revived in the early Qing, shielded and sustained by policies such as "no new taxes" and "giving the populace a rest."

The story of silver continued to play out in China from then on. Silver flowed from the West to the East, enrichening the Great Qing Empire but also bringing greater uncertainty to China's future. The Qing carried over the main systems of the Ming, and silver continued to be widely used under a policy of "using silver for large sums and copper coins for small sums." Currency from previous dynasties could also be used, and silver and copper coins were mixed together, as in the case of soldiers' pay and provisioning made up of "eight parts silver and two parts coin."

The common use of silver and copper coins together as early as the Wanli era of the Ming dynasty is exhaustively described in the contemporary *Fivefold Miscellany* of Xie Zhaozhi:

Using copper coins is convenient for poor people. Wherever
people gather, there is gambling. In the capital there is a
daily minting of 100,000 cash, which does not go north beyond Lulong or south beyond Dezhou, some 2,000 *li*. If
the number of coins is not increased, what then? Shandong
uses a mixture of silver and coin. All of the coins have Song
reign marks. Two are equivalent to one new coin, but the
new coins are discarded and not used. Yet, Song coins are not
being minted, and most are dug from the ground, so how
many can be obtained that way? The south does not mint
many coins, and its coins are thinner than those of the capital; there also may be illegal minting among the populace.
Fujian and Guangdong never use coin, but rather silver certificates. Treacherous forgeries in the market are especially
loathsome.

Although silver taels were established as legal tender in the Qing
dynasty, silver had not yet evolved into coin form in China. Qian Jiaju
believes that on the official level, silver taels qualified as a monetary
standard,[1] for three reasons: Taxes equal to or greater than one tael of
silver had to be collected in silver, while those under one tael could be
paid according to the convenience of the taxpayer; the legal exchange
ratio was 1,000 copper cash to one tael of silver; full fine silver (*wenyin*)
was stipulated at a standard percentage content, and the government's
accountants made their calculations in silver taels. Ostensibly silver was
not unlimited legal tender, but large transactions could not be carried
out in copper cash.

Even so, defining the Qing dynasty's monetary system as a silver
standard easily overlooks its complicated and chaotic aspects. There has
been much discussion and varying definitions of the Qing monetary system, but in terms of practical function, the status of silver was enhanced,
while copper coin continued to enjoy the advantage in designated spheres.
Scholarly research has ascertained that government expenditure was almost completely in silver, and the Qing dynasty also encouraged the use
of silver in the private sector. An edict issued in the tenth year of the
Qianlong era stated: "Hereafter wherever the government issues silver

taels, it will disburse payments in silver taels, except for the Ministry of Works continuing to issue copper cash. Silver should also be in predominant usage in everyday transactions among the people."[2] The Qing avoided the paper currency–issuing malady of previous dynasties, and therefore did not suffer from massive inflation, but its currency system was maddeningly chaotic.

Setting aside the multitude of copper coins, silver currency alone was a headache. As noted earlier, many world currencies are named after units of weight, for example the British pound, but these weight units ultimately had no direct connection to the currency. In China, however, silver taels continued to serve as a monetary unit for a very long time, evolving very little from their primitive state. Ironically, when China had to pay reparations to foreign entities at the time of the Opium Wars, it was obliged to pay 6 million Mexican silver dollars because its own silver tael system was too confusing.

The American Hosea Ballou Morse (1855–1934) served as an official in the late Qing Imperial Maritime Custom Service for many years starting in 1874, and was considered a protégé of Sir Robert Hart. A great deal of subsequent research is based on the first-hand information he provided. Morse once complained:

> Another element of perplexity, sufficient to prevent the ordinary mind from penetrating the mysteries of taxation in China, is found in the question of exchange. China has no coinage except the copper "cash," of which to-day it takes about 10,000 to equal a pound sterling and 2,000 an American dollar. Her silver currency has no one uniform standard, and the hundreds of standards known in the empire, or the dozen known in one place, vary within a range of over 10 per cent. Even the Imperial Treasury tael is an actuality only at the Imperial Treasury itself, and elsewhere in China is merely a money of account.[3]

This confusion continued for hundreds of years, and accounting was bewildering even in modern times. China is regarded as having employed a silver standard from the late Qing to the Republican era, but it would be more accurate to say that China had no currency standard whatsoever; as the Beiyang government admitted in 1914, "China's greatest ill today is its lack of a currency standard."[4] During this time, China used not only a mixture of silver taels and various kinds of silver dollars, but also copper cash and foreign currency, as well as paper currency issued by foreign banks and "private notes" from small private banks. Silver taels included both virtual silver (*xuyin*) and physical silver (*shiyin*), and physical silver included *baoyin* (silver ingots, *yuanbao*), *zhongding* (medium-sized ingots), *luozi* (ovule ingots), *xiaoluo*, fragmentary silver, and so on. Silver ingots were also subdivided according to their silver content in various regions, such as Shanghai's "2-7 *baoyin*" and Tianjin's "white silver." There were reportedly more than 100 types of scales for weighing physical silver during the Beiyang era. Virtual silver also existed in every form and description, including treasury silver, customs silver, and tribute silver.

Calculating exchange rates among the virtual silver for every locality and industry became the main occupation of the financial sector. A "silver song" popular among the money-exchange shops of Shanxi at that time combined the various silver units into a jingle, from the *huabao* of Tianjin to the *gubao* of Wuhan, the *xiangyin* of Changsha and the *biaoding* of Yunnan.[5]

The chaotic situation of Chinese currency was due first and foremost to the separate regimes of the central government and the localities, which led to money being minted and circulated within localities. It was also due to the flourishing of all kinds of private minting.

Finance scholar Shi Junzhi observes:

The Western Han dynasty further perfected the monetary system legislated by the Qin dynasty, in the form of three key principles: 1) the imperial government held the monopoly on minting copper coins, and civilians were strictly forbidden to do so; 2) the law protected the circulation of money minted by the imperial government, and all levels of government and the general populace had no choice but to accept all of the copper coins minted by the imperial government, regardless of quality; 3) the circulation of copper coins smelted or altered by

members of the public was strictly prohibited. These three
principles had a crucial effect on the circulation of currency at
that time.[6]

In actuality, however, it was not easy to effectively ban the circulation of
privately minted coins, and the Song dynasty completely abandoned this
policy. The private minting of coins flourished from a very early stage
and continued throughout successive dynasties. Some libertarians consider the private minting of coins to be a traditional civil liberty, while
statists castigate it as demonstrating a lack of consciousness of monetary
sovereignty. Wan Zhiying points out that in the fifteenth century, silver
ingots and privately minted copper coins largely replaced the official
currency minted by the imperial court, and that the Ming dynasty even
abandoned minting coins for a time.

The prevalence of private minting was in fact a classic paradox of
Chinese rule by law: the harsher the ban, the more indicative it was of
the government's loss of control. Private minting had been prohibited
throughout history but had rarely been curtailed because of that, as in-
dicated by eyewitness accounts and related records: "Privately minted
coins went under names such as sand shells, wind skins, fish eyes, old
sandboards, hair coins, dust boards, goose eyes and floaters. All were
thin and small and minted from mixtures of clay, sand, copper, lead and
tin. People sandwiched these small coins between copper cash, and the
market value and the names of coins differed according to the amount
of privately-minted coins mixed in."[7]

Private minting was not only immune to repeated bans, but even
came out into the open and attracted both official and private-sector
participation. Public officials are believed to have always engaged in private minting. Economist Ma Yinchu mentioned one minor case: "The
Copper Coins Department minted copper coins daily at a set time and
in amounts that were not too excessive." But Copper Coins Department
functionaries involved in the minting process could extend the minting
time by one or two hours, and the profit from the extra minted coins
became their private possession, openly and legally referred to as "department personal property." Furthermore, foreign powers were not
constrained in China, and foreign banks that satisfied stipulations on

reserves were allowed to issue currency that enjoyed the same level of credit as China's domestic currency.

The low threshold for privately minted coins shows that the technical threshold for premodern coins was not high. At that time not only foreign currencies but also the currencies of previous dynasties were used, and official currency and privately minted currency circulated together. From another perspective, cost factors may help explain the situation. In the pre-industrial era, if it was technically impossible to eradicate the forgery of official currency, it was likewise hard to eradicate privately minted currency. In fact, the success of Britain's gold coins lay in technological innovation following the invention of the steam engine. But minting standards remained low in China at that time, and the cost of minting was very high; during the Qianlong era, minting costs composed upward of 15 percent of the value of the metal. This often made officially minted currency only barely profitable, and minting actually ceased at certain times in history for that reason, while private minting continued to flourish.

Chaotic currency values could be considered a boon to money-changers. Apart from its benefits to China's money-changing profession, the system also created considerable space for officials to manipulate circumstances to their own advantage, and along with the involvement of various interests, this is one of the main reasons why subsequent monetary reforms made no real progress. Morse described the trouble involved in silver tael conversion during that time:

In a typical case, Treasury taels were converted into cash at the rate of 2600 per tael and converted back at 1105, whereby a tax of Tls. 70.66 was converted into a payment of Tls. 166.29. But let us take an ordinary everyday incident of revenue collected in Kiangsu and remitted as a grant in aid of Kansu. The tax-note will be in Treasury taels; it will be paid in local taels; the proceeds converted into Tsaoping taels for remittance to Shanghai, where it is converted into Shanghai taels; again converted in Tsaoping taels for remittance to Kansu (assuming it is remitted by draft), where it is received in local taels; these are converted into Treasury taels for

accounting with Kiangsu, and back again into local taels for
deposit in a bank, and again into Treasury taels for accounting with the Imperial Treasury, and again into local taels or
copper cash for disbursement.[8]

Not only were silver and copper coins used together, but local factors
were also very strong; apart from the various local currencies, even the
exchange value of the government-issued copper coins differed at the
local level. George Ernest Morrison, a reporter for *The Times* of London
who traveled in China early as a student, recorded the exchange value of
copper coins in different places at the same time: In the eastern provinces, one string of cash consisted of 100 copper coins, and ten strings
was equivalent to one Mexican silver dollar. But at that time China had
eighteen provinces, and the number of coins in a string of cash differed
among them. For instance, in Taiyuan it was eighty-three, and in Zhili
(Hebei) Province it was thirty-three. Japanese intelligence reports provided even more detailed observations. In the 1880s, the value of copper
coins in various places was as follows: in Beijing (*daqian*, equivalent
to ten copper coins), five equaled 100 cash and fifty equaled one string,
one American dollar was nine strings and 500 cash; in Tianjin (*xiaoqian*
or "capital coins"), fifty equaled 100 cash, 500 equaled one string, one
American dollar equaled two strings and 400 cash; in Tongzhou (*xiaoqian* or "capital coins"), fifty equaled 100 cash, 500 equaled one string, one
tael equaled three strings 400 cash; in Shanghai (*xiaoqian*, or "old money"), 100 equaled 100 cash, 1,000 equaled one string, one American dollar equaled one string and 250 cash; in Yantai (*xiaoqian* or "old money"),
100 equaled 100 cash, 1,000 equaled one string, one tael equaled one
string and 730 cash; in Mongolia (*xiaoqian* or "old money"), 100 equaled
100 cash, 1,000 equaled one string; at the Shanhai Pass (*xiaoqian* or "east
money"), sixteen equaled 100 cash, 160 equaled one string; in Chengjing
(today's Shenyang), thirty-three equaled 200 cash, 160 equaled one
string, one tael equaled nine strings and 600 cash.[9]

This sounds completely fantastical, but it is a true story. A process
loaded down with so many trivial details also provided many opportunities for embezzlement; the bureaucratic structure will always seek to
maximize personal material benefit. Foreign observers in the late Qing

witnessed the phantasmagoric money exchange while emphasizing that their descriptions were "no burlesque, but an actual account of what happens":

> We have a series of nine exchange transactions, each of which will yield a profit of at least a half of 1 per cent. on the turn-over, apart from the rate of exchange on actual transfer from place to place, and altogether outside any question of "squeez-ing" the taxpayer. Moreover, as we are dealing with the past more than the present, it is right to record that regularly in the past and frequently in the present the remittance is made by actually sending the silver from Kiangsu to Kansu, not reduc-ing the exchange operations above noted by a single step.[10]

Clearly, Qing dynasty corruption was virtually systemic corruption, and the ability of this currency chaos to persist for years was a by-product of this corruption, as the exchange procedure left a great deal to official discretion. History tells us that any system, good or bad, has a tradition, and the confusing monetary system was no different.

When tax paid in kind changed into tax paid in silver taels from the mid-Ming onward, it became necessary to recast fragmentary silver and then the subsequent Qing dynasty silver dollars into silver ingots (*yinding*) of greater weight. The wastage from the process of smelting fragmentary silver always became part of the additional taxes that offi-cials demanded, but this portion never reached the government coffers, remaining with the local government. "Mint wastage" or "redundancy" was sometimes half the scheduled tax; it was typically allotted among various levels and increased rather than decreased. For example, in *The Golden Lotus*, probably set somewhere in the north, Ximen Qing and Uncle Wu talk about self-supporting garrisons and taxes collected in units of silver: "In Jinzhou, not counting barren land and marshes, we have twenty-seven thousand acres, and each acre must make a contribu-tion of one tael and eight *qian*, so all together we have more than five hundred taels. At the end of the year we send the contribution to Dong-pingfu. There, arrangements are made for buying grain and hay for the horses."[11] That is to say, the total is 500 taels of silver in tax, of which so-called redundancy profit accounts for 20 percent ("I think I ought to make more than a hundred taels every year"). In the Qing dynasty's Yongzheng period, mint wastage was abolished and converted into official living allowances, which could be ten or 100 times an official's salary. That didn't help matters, however, because the lack of a unified currency measure gave officials opportunities to make money change hands.

The price of systemic failure is obvious. It greatly increased transaction costs for no reason, and for the local private banks it "add[ed] enormously to the cost by the expenses of transport and escort for a journey which must be counted by months and not by days."[12] The emperor had no means of changing the situation once and for all, and as the bureaucratic clique became increasingly strong, eradicating corruption would require killing the state. As a result, later attempts to unify the currency system faced many obstacles.

"Huang Zongxi's Law" Encounters the "Malthusian Trap"

Finance and taxation have a symbiotic relationship; people regard taxation as the source of circulation and reallocation of wealth throughout the country. China's currency chaos requires mention of China's taxes and levies. Most of the time, fiscal reform was genuine history. The Han dynasty dictionary *Shuowen Jiezi* states: "Tax, that is, rent," linking tax to the economic concept of rent, that is, seeking to gain wealth without benefit to society. So-called taxes are essentially protection money collected by rulers.

The Ming and Qing dynasties epitomized the backwardness of the finance and taxation system. But corresponding to that, China did not have high taxation rates in the past, especially in the Ming and Qing dynasties; the stereotype of "heavy taxation and impoverished citizens" and its causal logic are in fact a misapprehension. Taking the Ming dynasty as an example, Ray Huang points out that the entire country's highest land tax rate was in the southern jurisdictions under the Suzhou government, which was around 20 percent of rural income and averaged less than 10 percent. Comparatively speaking, the Japanese daimyō (feudal lords) took 50 percent of income. Late seventeenth-century

China had a population thirty times larger than that of England, but the total tax revenue of the two countries was virtually the same.[13]

As for the Qing tax system, after the Qing dynasty crossed the Shanhai Pass and established rules (stipulating set quotas), the tax burden actually decreased with the rise in population and changing commodity prices. Even in the late Qing, when taxation was highest, it was still relatively light by modern standards. Survey calculations by the American agricultural economist John L. Buck found that direct tax made up 5 percent of China's agricultural income in the early twentieth century, while economist Yeh-Chien Wang calculated 2 to 4 percent; even high-tax regions such as Suzhou and Shanghai didn't exceed 8 to 10 percent.[14]

Yeh-Chien Wang calculates that in the last stage of the late Qing, the land tax burden was even lower than in previous dynasties. At the peak of the Kangxi-Qianlong flourishing age, in the eighteenth year of the Qianlong period (1753), tax revenues totaled around 73.79 million taels, of which land tax was 54.21 million taels, or 73.5 percent of the total. In the thirty-fourth year of the Guangxu period (1908), total tax revenues were 290.2 million taels, of which land tax was 102.4 million taels, or 35.1 percent of the total. By way of comparison, the cultivated area increased by 50 percent during that same 155-year period, and the land output increased by 20 percent, while commodity prices tripled. Total tax revenues nearly quadrupled, while land tax only doubled, a relative one-third decrease in the tax burden.

Some Chinese leftist scholars have affirmed the stability of China's dynasties, claiming it was based on implementing passive fiscal policies and stable monetary policies. They regard so-called passive fiscal policy as "taking little and giving little" to citizens and industry, or even "neither giving nor taking." Under this policy, the main financial expenditure is applied to the bureaucracy while taking a categorically passive attitude toward developing the people's livelihood and industry, under a principle of "absolutely no meddling." This explanation is undoubtedly imagination after the fact and overinterpretation. These seemingly passive fiscal policies qualify as predetermined choices and in fact were a matter of no choice at all. First of all, the low Ming and Qing tax rates were a consequence rather than an objective; their backdrop was rampant corruption and an inefficient revenue system. The Qing dynasty quota tax was ostensibly a baseline to stabilize popular sentiment, but in fact it was the final criterion in the chess game between the two sides: The government stipulated the minimum payment quota, while the people saw that quota as the maximum payment and strove to minimize it. In other words, the rulers put great effort into plunder, but their abilities were limited, and the beneficiaries were not the peasants. Historians have also said that it was the system rather than high taxes that "impoverished the populace." Low tax rates brought no benefit to ordinary peasants, but encouraged large and small landowners to increase exploitation and officials to collect all kinds of additional fees.[15]

Second, tax revenue quotas were ostensibly a good thing, but lacked systemic support consistent with the rules of economics, so even with the best of motivations they were certain to go wrong. In the Qing dynasty, additional taxes that materialized when the rules were established became "systemized" and inevitably accumulated. As the population expanded in the middle and late stages of the Qing dynasty, the number of people relying on the government for their livelihood increased, accompanied by an increase in all kinds of surtaxes.

Additional levies can be considered a major characteristic of the Ming and Qing dynasties. People typically quote the reflections of the Ming Confucian Huang Zongxi regarding the failings of old-era tax reforms. Huang Zongxi was born during the Ming–Qing transition, and in an era of major reform he leaped from the set patterns of traditional Confucianism and began reconsidering the traditional system, proposing some ideas that were considered extraordinary at the time. He did not fail to deeply ponder the traditional tax system, especially the "evil of taxes that pile up without ever being repealed," from the Tang dynasty's dual tax law to the tax consolidation reforms around the time of the Ming dynasty's Single Whip tax system.[16] Subsequent generations, from Liang Fangzhong and others in the Republican era to the scholar Qin Hui more recently, have summarized his viewpoint as "Huang Zongxi's Law," that is, "To remove the evils of random charges and exactions and reduce the leaching of tax revenue embezzled by officials at various levels, merging nontax exactions with tax and simplifying tax itself became the mainstream concept of tax reform."[17] Reforms of this kind included the unified taxation method, the fusion of the poll tax with the field tax, the Single Whip tax system, and so on. Subsequent generations have argued over the Single Whip tax system, with Qian Mu's assessment relatively neutral. A system combining taxes and corvee is usually considered a simple method, but there were also many opposing voices, and as in the disputes over the Song dynasty tax exemptions, the southerners were in favor and the northerners opposed.

Was this method effective? In the short term yes, but not in the long run. It is only rational that when the higher-ups have a policy, those lower down have a counterpolicy; without systemic oversight and management, every reform becomes an opportunity for officials in each session to apply it to their advantage. Top-down supervision has been played as a cat-and-mouse game for millennia without any real progress. When corruption becomes too serious, a few officials are always punished to allay public wrath. Japanese scholar Iwai Shigeki points out that there were limits to the Single Whip tax system; it made history by combining corvee, fees, and additional tax burdens into the financial administration, but it also reduced the fiscal elasticity of local governments. As a result, when localities increased their expenditure (for example, for sudden incidents such as military action), they would naturally expand the various corvee items outside of the Single Whip tax system. For this reason, Iwai Shigeki describes the Ming and Qing fiscal systems as "original-amount fiscalism." The decline of empire can be attributed to the pendulum constantly swinging between financial crisis and reform crisis.[18]

In short, these tax reform methods were still unable to escape what Huang Zongxi described as a model of "light overt tax, heavy hidden tax, and an extortionate bottomless pit of miscellaneous exactions." It was essentially the criticism that Huang leveled against the Single Whip tax system as a vicious circle of order and disorder that the autocratic government could not escape. Scholar Qin Hui summed it up this way: "Every case in the history of tax reform by merger heralded the appearance of a wave of sundry taxes."[19]

The reason why the Ming and Qing fiscal systems are summed up as "original-amount fiscalism" is that although the Ming and Qing financial administrations had some differences (for example, the Ming dynasty implemented physical commodity finance, while the Qing implemented money finance), their fiscal structures had common features, specifically a rigidly stipulated portion complemented by a highly flexible additional portion.[20] Furthermore, for lengthy historical periods, original-amount fiscalism resulted in insufficient funding for local government, so the number of additional tax items gradually expanded, and the increasing tax burden was not borne equally by the various social classes.

The proliferation of sundry additional taxes also corresponded to the Qing dynasty's population situation, as well as the empire's prosperity and stagnation. Under prolonged peace, the Great Qing Empire confronted the "Malthusian trap" as the population exploded from the eighteenth to the nineteenth century. Scholars estimate that China's population more than doubled, from 150 million to more than 300 million, from the end of the seventeenth century to the White Lotus Society rebellion at the end of the eighteenth century, increasing by 56 percent from the years 1779 to 1850 alone. In the eighth year of the Shunzhi period (1651) the population was 165.1 million, in the fiftieth year of the Kangxi period (1711) it was 171.1 million, in the fourth year of the Yongzheng period (1726) it was 172.6 million, in the fifty-ninth year of the Qianlong period (1796) it was 313.28 million, in the second year of the Daoguang period (1822) it was 372.45 million, and twelve years later it was 401 million.[21]

With such a large population, per capita productivity could not increase without an economic or technological leap, but could only struggle to preserve the status quo, mainly through the propagation of high-yield crops such as early-maturing rice and corn. This technical progress and the increase in cultivated land were offset by population growth, and per capita income barely increased or simply stagnated. This was the basic trend in the Ming and Qing. According to research by Harvard University professor Dwight H. Perkins, China's grain yields and population both increased tenfold from 1368 to 1968, but its cultivated land area only increased fivefold. Agricultural development managed to keep up with population growth, but the amount of grain per capita did not change, manifesting as a constant actual income.[22] In spite of war and chaos, China's agriculture still showed powerful stability and a consistent low-level equilibrium. The population continued to increase after experiencing war and famine, but income from surplus labor actually trended lower rather than increasing.

One of the classic effects of population surplus was that increasing numbers of educated people were no longer able to satisfy their dreams of distinguishing themselves through the imperial civil examination system. As a result, the administrative structure constantly expanded and its functionaries became redundant. The bureaucratic social class expanded, and many people who were unable to join this class began pursuing similar occupations, with the proliferation of various hangers-on, aides, and clerks forming the landscape of the late Qing. At the local level a class of contracted tax collectors and beadles along with the immense rentier class doomed the empire's enormous apparatus to inefficiency and even stasis.

Inefficient tax collection and the levying of all kinds of additional fees exposed the abuses of the imperial governance system, typically manifested in budget chaos. The budget is a state's means of livelihood, and even today the Budget Law is known as the Economic Constitution, with the objective of managing unconstrained power. Western and Chinese budgeting systems were clearly divided from the outset in terms of managing income and expenditure. In the West, detailed figures were provided for budgeted income and expenditure, but in China there were serious imbalances and a random quality to income and expenditure.

Again it was Morse, with the curiosity of an outsider, who described budgeting differences between the East and the West. In the West, budgets were divided among different administrative areas—national, state, and municipal in America; national, county, and municipal in Great Britain; and imperial, royal, and municipal in Germany. "Furthermore, the underlying principle, more or less lived up to, in the West is that every penny taken directly from the taxpayer is covered into the official treasury, and from the same source is provided every penny of the cost of administration."[23]

Comparatively speaking, since there was no correspondence between rights and taxes, or between taxes and the budget, the citizenry had no desire to pay even more taxes to sustain the administrative apparatus, and China's budgeting system became a morass. Existing systemic inertia and the growing bureaucratic clique were mutually reliant, and economic inefficiency and the systemic failure of the imperial bureaucracy formed a vicious circle that resulted in the ubiquity of phenomena such as over-staffing and organizational bloat. In Morse's words, "The administration of justice in China creates no charge upon the official revenues, but maintains itself from fees and exactions," and "the Chinese official is nowadays less an administrator than a tax-collector."[24]

The budget is the foundation of the taxation system; taxes form the foundation for building the country, and the use and management of taxes reflect a country's level of civilization and standard of governance. Modern states are typically born through reform to the finance and taxation system. Comparing the experiences in China and the West, it could even be said that the backward imperial system bred a backward financial and taxation system that could only prop up the empire's backward administrative system.

A finance and taxation system such as China's is one of the causes of economic inefficiency, as well as the result of being trapped in the bell jar of history. The economy's inability to escape the traditional agricultural model prevented population increase from becoming a population dividend, as happened in the industrial age; instead, bogged down in the Malthusian trap of the pre-industrial era, it became the empire's unbearable burden.

Among the European countries, France's financial and taxation system in the seventeenth and eighteenth centuries was the most similar to China's, with its tradition of "rural tax collectors feathering their own nests." The contracted tax collection system carried the remnants of feudalism, and tax farmers in France were at one point attacked as one of the "monsters to be demolished" because they "pillage with impunity, and with their vexations have destroyed nearly all the commerce and the manufacture of the Kingdom."[25] The fury of the French Revolution ultimately buried this system and France's ancien régime.

In comparison, England had higher taxes than France at that time, and much higher taxes than China's Ming and Qing dynasties. Although France's tax rate was much lower than England's, that didn't prevent the outbreak of the French Revolution, because of the great inefficiency, corruption, and arbitrariness of the system. The advantage of England's "square of power" was first of all its efficient taxation system, especially compared with France's contracted tax collection apparatus. This system also imposed effective constraints on power, with the British king transferring part of his authority to Parliament, and Parliament guaranteeing that the king would not arbitrarily abuse his power. Adding in a powerful national debt system in collaboration with the relatively independent Bank of England, Great Britain solved the problems of tax collecting and economic fluctuation. These achievements provided the country with stable and generous financial support, so England could rely on its modern financial prowess to make its rise during the Age of Sail, even while missing out on New World gold and silver.

The silver-dependent Great Qing Empire was already facing latent crisis before the outflow of silver and the incursion of gunboats. This slow but lethal crisis laid the foundation of corruption during the empire's flourishing age. Suffering the pincer attack of "Huang Zongxi's Law" and "the Malthusian trap," the overheated flourishing age of the Qianlong era was only a flash in the pan. Under a series of factors, China's silverization increased unabated, and the foreign warships arrived at a low ebb in China's cycle of order and disorder. One historian observed, "Unfortunately, by the nineteenth century, our society, political system and economy were all unbearably corrupt . . . By the Jiaqing era, China had reached a cyclical nadir. The invasion by Western forces came just when our resistance was weakest. By the Daoguang era, our legal system existed in name only, officials were corrupt, the people lived in abject suffering and morality had lost part of its cohesive power."[26] When China finally collided with the West, the disparity of strength was self-evident, not to mention the role of silver as the catalyst for conflict.

The Tribute Mentality and the Celestial Empire Mentality

Most silver came from abroad, so how did China acquire silver under its closed-door system? It all began with the Great Qing Empire's entrenched tribute system and the East Asian trade bloc. People associate the closed-door policy with the Qing dynasty, but that door had already begun to close during the Ming dynasty. The first Ming emperor's ban on maritime trade was not comprehensively enforced, but its influence remained deep, and the diplomatic tribute system cohered at that time.

Historians often cite the *Collected Statutes of the Ming Dynasty* regarding "foreign states and barbarian border tribes paying tribute to the imperial court": "Southwestern barbarians: Korea, Japan, Ryukyu, Annan (Vietnam), Zhenla (Cambodia), Siam (Thailand), Champa (Vietnam), Java, Sumatra (Indonesia), Suoli [an island nation in the South China Sea], Sulu (the Philippines), Kerala (India), Malacca (Malaysia), Bengal (Bangladesh), Ceylon (Sri Lanka), Luzon (Philippines), Mogadishu (Somalia), etc.; Northern barbarians: Tatar, Eleuth (Mongolia), etc.; Northeastern barbarians: the Jurchens of Haixi and Jianzhou, etc.; Western barbarians: Hami, Uyghurs, Samarkand (Central Asia), Mecca (Arabia), Medina (Arabia), Ü-Tsang (Tibet), etc."[27] The Qing dynasty added Laos, Burma, Portugal, the Netherlands, and other countries.

The sequence and changes in these names typically represented the remoteness or intimacy of China's relationship with them. In fact, the concept of Cathay and peripheral people existed during the Western Zhou and Spring and Autumn periods. The *Book of Rites* records:

> The people of those five regions—the Middle Kingdom and the Rong, Yi, and other surrounding tribes—had their own unalterable natures. The tribes on the east were called Yi. They wore their hair unbound and tattooed their bodies. Some ate their food uncooked. Those on the south were called Man. They tattooed their foreheads, and their feet turned in toward each other. Some also ate their food uncooked. Those on the west were called Rong. They wore their hair unbound and were clothed in skins. Some did not eat grain. Those on the north were called Di. They wore the skins of animals and birds and dwelt in caves. Some also did not eat grain.[28]

As conceptions of the Yi, Man, Rong, and Di have evolved in subsequent generations, modern appraisals of the tribute system have tended to be negative. For example, historian Fan Shuzhi found the tribute system incompatible with the "globalized" trade that was coming to the fore at that time.[29] The famous Sinologist John King Fairbank once stated that the tribute system "functioned as both a mechanism for managing trade and diplomatic relations and a ritual affirming the universality of the Confucian order. The very success of the system, its complete integration with the institutions and world of Imperial China, pointed at once to both its stability and its vulnerability."[30]

Indeed, the tributary system was not only part of the economy, but also part of imperial rule and the order of the Celestial Empire. The Qing government carried on the Ming system and also inherited its mantle in the tributary system; in fact, several Manchu branches had joined the Ming tributary system.

Yet, globalization's waves were beating against the gates of the tribute system; it was only that Asia, and especially China, seemed unmoved by it. As Fairbank points out, China's maturity differed strikingly from the blank slate of the New World:

> The sixteenth-century Portuguese and the seventeenth-century Dutch and British adventurers and merchants who opened the China trade discovered unknown regions, just as their contemporaries were opening up the New World. The all important difference was that East Asia, far from being a virgin continent, was already the center of an enormous and ramified commercial life of its own. The early Western ventures were but small increments in channels of commerce already centuries old.[31]

In a broad historical perspective, horizontal comparisons often reveal the essence. Sinologist Fairbank once compared China with New England. In 1637, Great Britain opened trade with Guangzhou, and in 1620 the *Mayflower* reached Plymouth, Massachusetts, but the development of the two places over the subsequent centuries cannot even be mentioned in the same breath: "British trade with China was not able to expand outside Canton until the nineteenth century, when New England had long since become part of a new nation ready itself to aid in expanding the Canton trade."[32] This frustrated the ambition of Western merchants, but what result could come of an encounter between tributary logic and trade logic? Western countries such as England clearly hoped to gain much more than tributary states.

That is how the "historical diplomatic mission" by British envoy George Macartney came about in 1793 on the occasion of the eightieth birthday of the Qianlong Emperor. Jiang Tingfu says that at that time, Europe regarded the Qianlong Emperor as an enlightened ruler, and the British believed that the difficulties they experienced in opening up trade with China were due to local officials. Diplomatic envoy Macartney put a lot of thought into preparations for the mission: "The special envoy sailed first class in a naval vessel with armed escorts. The gifts presented to Emperor Qianlong were Britain's very best products. The intention was for China to know that Great Britain was a powerful and civilized country. The British government instructed Macartney to do his utmost to accommodate Chinese etiquette and custom, but to indicate that China and Britain were equal."[33]

Although delighted with this ceremonious approach, the Qianlong Emperor naturally treated Macartney as just another representative of a tribal nation, and a dispute developed over the rite of kowtowing. Previously Dutch, Portuguese, Russian, and other Western diplomatic envoys had conceded in varying degrees to Chinese rites, but the British did not regard them as international protocol.

Thus there ensued interminable rounds of persuasion and refusal. Macartney initially refused but then conditionally agreed: "When China sent an envoy to London in the future, that envoy would also have to bow to the British King; or the Chinese could have an official reciprocate by bowing in front of the portrait of the British King that [Macartney] had brought. His objective was to show that China and Britain were equal. China did not accept this condition, so [Macartney] again refused to kowtow."[34]

Macartney's demands to open trade drew this now famous reply from Emperor Qianlong:

> Our Celestial Empire possesses all things in prolific abundance and lacks no product within its borders. There was therefore no need to import the manufactures of outside barbarians in exchange for our own produce. But as the tea,

silk, and porcelain which the Celestial Empire produces are absolute necessities to European nations and to yourselves, we have permitted, as a signal mark of favour, that foreign hongs should be established at Canton, so that your wants might be suppled and your country thus participate in our beneficence.[35]

This vivid historical episode has typically been interpreted as demonstrating the arrogance and closed-off nature of the Celestial Empire, but in an economic or even political sense, the Qianlong Emperor's reply was not unreasonable. More in-depth research has led scholars to regard the tribute system in new ways. According to research by Japanese scholar Takeshi Hamashita, Asia had long had its own trade bloc, and the tribute system was its foundation. China's handling of the system did not lack shrewdness, and was quite flexible in encompassing various countries, religions, societies, and ethnicities: "As tributary relations were not based exclusively on relations of control, but also had an important basis in trade, they were multidimensional, embodying multiple elements and multidirectional demands."[36]

It was because of this that China possessed an internal market as well as an external tributary trade bloc. For China, goods from outside were not necessities, and trade was not essential to national construction. One characteristic of the tribute system was that it was founded on commercial trade: "The tribute system in fact paralleled and was intertwined with commercial trade relations."[37]

The fact is that purely in economic terms, China seemed to get along very well without the rest of the world, and in political terms, China could achieve its aims through selective commercial relations; the tribute system seemed to kill two birds with one stone. Takeshi Hamashita summarizes the essential nature of the tribute system in the political structure as follows: Regional rulers presented themselves to the emperor (Son of Heaven) in Beijing and were conferred with titles, confirming the mission of the tribute, that is, submission. The nature of this relationship was that between a suzerain state and a vassal state, and tributary countries, regions, and tribes had to regularly pay tribute and express fealty to China. In exchange, the tribute entity not only gained the ruler's acknowledgment, but also obtained gifts in exchange along with opportunities to trade in luxury items.

Correspondingly, the tribute system included three aspects: bilateral formal tribute exchange—tribute gifts from diplomatic missions and the gifts the emperor gave in return; trade specially authorized by the Beijing Bureau of Interpreters—the government limited the number of merchants allowed to accompany diplomatic tribute missions; frontier trade—merchants accompanying diplomatic tribute missions would engage in trade with Chinese merchants at designated customs points and ports.[38]

Therefore, simplistically regarding the Qing dynasty's interactions with the West as ignorant or blindly arrogant may lack a measure of understanding. The tribute system can be seen as a footnote in the Celestial Empire's attitude, and also as a conciliatory policy when foreign military power was inadequate. Historian Fernand Braudel noted that China's control over vast neighboring territories formed a self-contained world economy: "China . . . from earliest times took over and harnessed to her own destiny such neighbouring areas as Korea, Japan, the East Indies, Vietnam, Yunan, Tibet and Mongolia—a garland of dependent countries."[39]

At the same time, tribute-paying countries began looking at China from a slightly different angle. As the tribute system continued, the Celestial Empire suzerain state changed; the garb of the Central Plains changed into that of the northern barbarians, and the Koreans who continued to wear the garb of the Great Ming felt a sense of superiority. The change in the title of the travel journals of Korean envoys from *Being Presented at Court* to *Swallow Journeys* expressed their farewell to former times. In the ninth year of the Jiaqing era (1804), Korean envoy Seo Jang-bo wrote, "The entire country is filled with odors and filth; its destiny looks unpropitious. The imperial jade seal is unclaimed; the Jurchens dared to snatch it."[40] This subtle view of China under Qing rule can in fact be seen as a source of Japan's subsequent propaganda pitching the Sino-Japanese War of 1894–1895 as a war of civilizations.

It is worth noting that silver was also a focal point in the tribute system. Silver was not only widely used domestically, but was also a medium of international trade, and the inflow of silver gradually formed the so-called Asian silver circulation sphere that had a profound effect on China, and even Asia more generally. It accelerated the silverization of China and swept China into the global monetary system, triggering a series of profound changes. The status of silver had already been enhanced by the inflow of New World silver after the sixteenth century, and by the mid-nineteenth century, with the exploitation of gold and silver mines helping Western Europe gradually transition to the gold standard, Asia's silver circulation sphere became one of the currency systems channeled into the international gold and silver exchange system.[41]

China's central position in the Ming-Qing tribute system was related to China's economic status as well as political factors. Through its relations with the tribute trade network and the world, China had a subtle status in the world economy—some economists even believe it had a central status.[42] The reason lay in China's uniqueness: China held the monopoly on porcelain, silk, tea, and other products while at the same time serving as the ultimate "sink" of the world's silver.[43]

China's importance was in fact due to the division of labor in the global economy, which China was swept into, more through passivity than anything else. That is why the long-term trade surplus that China maintained until the nineteenth century kept silver flowing into China in a steady stream, and also why, when the flow of the world's silver changed direction, China's tribute system became hard to hold together.

From Tribute to Treaties

China's tribute system originally functioned according to its own logic, but when this logic encountered the logic of globalization or the West, it experienced something like a planetary collision. The Ming and Qing tribute system shows that the West did not march straight into the ranks of "barbaric nations and tribes." This was because China had not yet formed a Western logical sequence, and also had difficulty (and lacked interest in) differentiating between Westerners and "barbarian nations and tribes."

The aforementioned tribute system occasionally mentions various Western countries, requiring the Netherlands to pay tribute by way of the Bogue [*Humen*] in Guangdong every eight years. The diplomatic envoys of Portugal, Italy, and England also came by way of the Bogue at unfixed intervals, with strict limits on the number of personnel and ships: "Each embassy may have three ships, with not exceeding one hundred men in each; only twenty-two may proceed to Peking, the rest remaining at Canton."[44]

In the eleventh year of the Ming dynasty's Zhengde era (under Emperor Wuzong), the Portuguese explorer Rafael Perestrello took a native ship from Malacca to China in what is believed to be one of the earliest contacts between China and the West.[45] The Portuguese may have had the most successful dealings with China; they settled in Macau and turned it into a trading base for various countries. More than 4,000 foreign nationals (apart from clergy and military) lived there in the nineteenth century.[46]

Apart from the Portuguese, the Spanish and Dutch also had contact with China. The Spanish entered the historical annals due to the massacre of Chinese merchants in Malacca. The Dutch hoped to trade with China in spite of the humiliating tribute model, and a diplomatic mission that went to Beijing in 1655 took a humble approach:

> These envoys conformed in every way to the requirements of
> the Chinese. They carried rich presents, and allowed them to
> be called, and called them, tribute; and they received the gra-
> cious offering of gifts in return; they prostrated themselves
> before the emperor; they performed the three kneelings and
> the nine prostrations (the kowtow) before his sacred name,
> his letters, and his throne; and they comported themselves as
> representatives of an Asiatic princeling bearing tribute and
> homage to their Asiatic suzerain. They hoped by this conduct
> in China to secure the trading privileges which they had ac-
> quired by the same means in Japan, but all they gained was
> permission to send an "embassy" once in eight years, and that
> four trading ships might accompany each such embassy.[47]

The Dutch seemed to have trouble competing with the Portuguese in China, and they looked particularly backward after being expelled from Taiwan. After George Macartney returned to England empty-handed,

Holland once again sent diplomatic envoys, Isaac Titsingh and A. E. van Braam, to Beijing in 1795: "They resolved to avoid the errors which had caused the failure of the British embassy under Lord Macartney; he had refused to perform the kowtow; they were ready even to improve on the methods of the preceding Dutch embassies, and to make whatever recognition of suzerainty the Chinese might demand."[48]

For this reason, the Dutch were "brought to the capital like malefactors, treated when there like beggars, and then sent back to Canton like mountebanks to perform the three-times-three prostration at all times and before everything their conductors saw fit."[49] Even so, their mission failed to produce results. The diplomatic efforts of the British and Dutch, regardless of their attitude, led the West to believe that the diplomatic route was blocked. The Dutch were adaptable "coachmen of the sea," but their methods and the resulting benefits did not impress the British, and trade relations inevitably became strained.

In the face of constant trade requests from foreign countries, the Celestial Empire had established a foreign trading cantonment in Guangzhou (then called Canton), with thirteen "hongs." Initially trade could be carried out in several cities, but later it was limited to Canton alone. The imperial court didn't initially attach much importance to customs revenue, and the government set customs tax very low. This led to extreme levels of corruption among Canton's customs officials, their enormous discretionary power resulting in constant demands for bribes. Western merchants detested the waste of time and money that this practice entailed:

> The customs tax set by the imperial court was originally very light, averaging no more than 4 percent. The Qing government did not place much importance on this customs revenue, but the venality of government officials made it extremely onerous, amounting to about 20% of the value of the goods. Chinese law stipulated that taxation should be a matter of public record, but officials kept it top secret in order to facilitate their own evil purposes. Foreigners paying tax had to go through a haggling-type negotiation that sorely taxed their patience.[50]

County officials were not as they are now; trade relations were not carried out through transparent management or explicit regulations. One version is that Chinese customs duty was indeterminate and often required paying ten times the normal customs duty. According to contemporary accounts, an arriving ship would first dock in Macau and obtain various permits, after which it anchored for about three months: "While there, [a ship] continued to give a steady stream of profit to the interpreter and comprador, to the bumboatmen and other small fry, and to the minor officials from daily and monthly fees, and gratuities to facilitate her working and expedite her departure."[51]

One reason Macartney went to China was in hopes of dealing with the corruption at Canton customs and perhaps even bringing it to the attention of the emperor. The rules between China and Britain were different and could not be compared with missions from Holland and Portugal: "This can only be explained by the dignified bearing, as of a royal envoy, assumed by Lord Macartney himself, and his avoidance of any appearance of being a mere commercial emissary."[52] Macartney's assessment of the Qianlong Emperor himself was quite favorable: "dignified, but affable," a "very fine old gentlemen," and his journal included many rather good recollections of China. Ultimately, however, his journal had such an enormous effect on the Western world that China's image began to crumble, and the West's attitude toward China began its descent from idealistic praise to practical disdain.

Although Macartney was treated well enough, his commercial demands were not met. One of Macartney's objectives was trade, especially addressing the various obstructions to normal trade posed by Canton customs as well as expanding the treaty ports, but ultimately the authorities in Canton scored a major victory. Macartney's appeal would be considered normal in modern society. If everything is business, then anything is up for negotiation; it is merely a matter of conditions, especially in diplomacy between great nations. The Celestial Empire, however, had no interest in "business" that seemed beneficial to both sides.

What was the reason? Apart from China being economically self-sufficient, there were also political reasons—that is, that the Celestial Kingdom's order was in conflict with the world alignment. As Jiang

Tingfu puts it, the Celestial Kingdom did not recognize the equality of other nations:

> When Westerners came to China, we always treated them like people from the Ryukyu Islands or Korea. If they didn't come, we wouldn't force them. If they came, they had to acknowledge China as a suzerain state and themselves as a vassal state. This matter of decorum and ceremony became a major obstacle to diplomatic relations, as "the Celestial Empire" was absolutely unwilling to stretch the rules. China at that time did not feel the necessity for contact with foreign countries, and after all, if the foreign barbarians were so lacking in decency and propriety, what benefit was there in contact with them? They came greedy for profit, and the Celestial Empire bestowed its favor on them by allowing them to do business, merely to humor them and keep them in line. If they didn't know their place, the Celestial Kingdom would "exterminate the barbarians." At that time, China didn't know there was such a thing as diplomacy, but only knew about "exterminating or cultivating the barbarians." The government was divided only between those who advocated extermination and others who favored cultivation.[53]

In general it can be seen that although there was profit to be made in trading with China, what provoked foreign merchants most about the Chinese side's "hidden but irritating extractions" was the lack of a free market, without which "they were helpless under conditions in which they could be robbed wholesale,"[54] a feeling very different from in their home country. Holland, Portugal, and other countries had always tolerated China's rules as "humiliation in exchange for trade," but the British tried to bring about substantive change.

At this moment, with England's steadily increasing power and the end of war in Europe, England needed clarity in its Far East markets in order to improve its domestic commerce. The British already enjoyed a leadership status among the foreigners in Canton, and the China overseas trade stake belonged to the East India Company:

By then the Industrial Revolution had begun in England, and
the handicraft industry of former times was slowly turning
into machine manufacturing. The overseas market became
more crucial by the day to England's national economy, and
England felt that China's trade restrictions were most detrimental to England's commercial development. During that
time, England emerged victorious over France in India, and
the Indian subcontinent fell into Britain's grip. From then on,
developing business in East Asia was even easier, because the
British had India as a base area.[55]

Under these circumstances, England hoped to once again engage in negotiations with the Qing government. Envoy William Pitt Amherst set
off on his diplomatic mission to China in 1816. As before, the reason was
the obstacles local authorities were creating to trade; his object was to
obtain "a removal of the grievances which had been experienced, and an
exemption from them and others of the like nature for the time to come,
with the establishment of the Company's trade upon a secure, solid,
equitable footing, free from the capricious, arbitrary aggressions of the
local authorities, and under the protection of the Emperor, and the sanc-
tion of regulations to be appointed by himself."[56]

By then the Jiaqing Emperor had taken the throne, and although
Lord Amherst's boats bore the flag of "tribute bearer," the ceremonial
kowtow remained an issue, and ultimately Lord Amherst went home
empty-handed. This diplomatic mission was such a failure that Amherst
was not even treated as well as Macartney had been, and both sides, especially England, were left with very different impressions.

In this situation, very few options were available to England and
the Qing government. Missionary Samuel Wells Williams, who as the
first American missionary to go to China was among the first batch of
China watchers, felt that England had only three possible avenues at that
time: "a resort to force to compel the Chinese to regulate the trade on
reasonable terms, absolute submission to such rules as they might pre-
scribe, or abandonment of the trade."[57] And even Chinese such as Jiang
Tingfu have been forced to concede that these two failures left England
with no further recourse to peaceful negotiations.

How to deal with this series of mediations remained a problem that tangled emotion with conviction, resulting in the series of disasters that followed. Morse believed that both sides were in the wrong:

> The actual events which gave rise to the proceedings of which complaints were made, were such as to put England technically in the wrong, when judged by the standards of the twentieth century; while, as was also usual, the Chinese conduct of their case was such as could not be endured by any nation which was not, in fact, vassal to the empire, or would not, like the Dutch, assume a vassal's attitude in the hope of obtaining trading privileges.[58]

In other words, the trading logic represented by England, as world overlord, and the Celestial Kingdom's self-regarding tribute logic hinted at the conflict to come decades before the first Opium War was launched. "China had a special relationship with the West. Before the Opium Wars, we were unwilling to treat foreign countries as equals; after the wars, they were unwilling to treat us as equals."[59]

Conflict with the West led to the tribute system gradually transitioning into a treaty system. Comparing the tribute system with treaties between China and foreign countries, John King Fairbank believes that the tribute system reflected "Sinocentrism," and he even ties the tribute system to the inequality of the West's treaties: "To understand the onesidedness and inequality of the unequal treaties which the Western powers imposed upon the Chinese empire, one must look at the ancient tribute system which China first imposed upon Western visitors. This old Chinese system was just as unequal as the treaty system that supplanted it."[60] While not unreasonable, this naturally leaves a sour taste in the mouth for Chinese, especially as the unequal treaties constituted a major impetus for campaigns to save the nation from extinction, and even though the treaties eventually also brought improvements to China's management, legal, and other systems.

Humanity comes before nationhood; from a neutral standpoint, is it just to exchange one form of inequality for another? In any case, history has no hypotheticals. As the treaty system replaced the tribute system and was carried out under armed force, the treaties not only changed China's relationship with the rest of the world, but also Chinese society's own workings, and was the beginning of a forced modernization.

Trade Deficits, Hot Money, and the World Out of Balance

Globalization is in fact an impulse that history cannot restrain; sometimes it is a torrent and other times an undercurrent, but behind trade and war there is always the sound of silver flowing.

Even during the Ming and Qing eras, which were closed off according to traditional narratives, China still had close ties with global trade. The Asian trade bloc, while self-sufficient, was linked to the rest of the world through many channels. Historically, China obtained silver through Manila, Macau, Japan, and other channels, and the West used these same channels to join the Asian trade network, in which Asia, and especially China, discharged tea and raw silk while silver flowed ceaselessly into China. Takeshi Hamashita believes that this resulted in New World silver opportunistically pouring into China; using today's expression, it was a kind of "hot money."

Hot money brought the flourishing and growth of many trades and industries and gave rise to many wealthy merchants; even salt merchants and hongs closely allied with government officials benefited substantially—for example, the leader of the Thirteen Factories (Hongs), Wu Bingjian, known in the West as Howqua. The assets of the hongs reportedly reached 26 million silver dollars in 1834. At that time many people envied China's silver inflow; the Russians described the situation of China and India in this way: "These nations carry on much trade with the Portuguese, the French and the English, [who] buy from them all their manufactured goods and some raw materials. But neither the Indians nor the Chinese buy the slightest amount of European goods, except for watches, ironware, and a few arms."[61]

Back in the eighteenth century, Adam Smith already noticed the different exchange rates for silver in Canton and London, hinting that trade would result in changing silver prices:

At the same time and place the real and the nominal price of
all commodities are exactly in proportion to one another . . .
Half an ounce of silver at Canton in China may command a
greater quantity both of labour and of the necessaries and
conveniences of life than an ounce at London. A commodity,
therefore, which sells for half an ounce of silver at Canton
may there be really dearer, of more real importance to the
man who possesses it there, than a commodity which sells
for an ounce at London is to the man who possesses it at
London. If a London merchant, however, can buy at Canton
for half an ounce of silver, a commodity which he can after-
wards sell at London for an ounce, he gains a hundred per
cent by the bargain, just as much as if an ounce of silver was
at London exactly of the same value as at Canton. It is of no
importance to him that half an ounce of silver at Canton
would have given him the command of more labour and of a
greater quantity of the necessaries and conveniences of life
than an ounce can do at London. An ounce at London will
always give him the command of double the quantity of all
these which half an ounce could have done there, and this is
precisely what he wants.[62]

As in the Ming dynasty, the inflow of silver in the Qing dynasty was a
double-edged sword, bringing the empire prosperity, but also planting
the seeds of instability. The further silverization of the Chinese economy
meant that the lifeblood of the currency was not in the government or
even the populace, but was passively linked to the world. The subsequent
outflow or reduction in silver would affect the empire's lifeline, as the
prosperity of the Qianlong era was founded on "subsidiary" rather than
"basic" wealth, and was therefore unstable.[63] The reduced inflow of silver
also meant an upsurge in commodity prices, of which rice prices were
the most representative. In the thirteenth year of the Qianlong period
(1748), Hunan provincial governor Yang Xifu wrote, "I was born and
raised in the countryside, with generations of diligent cultivation. In the
Kangxi years the rice gathered to the threshing ground cost two or three
strands for one [picul]; in the Yongzheng years, however, it cost four or

five strands, and now it requires five to six strands."[64] This implies that the price of grain doubled from the Kangxi to the Qianlong period.

Changes in the empire's commodity prices were felt even by foreign guests. British envoy Macartney's vice-consul, Sir George Leonard Staunton, asserted that the prices of some necessities in China were about the same as in England: "The influx of silver from Europe into China within a century [he was writing in 1793] has occasioned a great increase in the price of all articles of consumption, and has altered the proportion between the fixed salaries of the several officers of government and the usual expenses by their respective stations. The ancient missionaries mention in their accounts the extreme cheapness of living at that time in China, but many of the necessaries of life are not now lower than in England."[65]

Silver was important, but having silver didn't mean having everything. The Great Qing Empire only saw the inflow of silver and not the wind of globalized trade looming ahead. Relying on a domestic market spanning the length and breadth of the land and on a scale nearly equal to the European market, China's Ming and Qing economies were self-sufficient, and the controversial tribute system was not without its uses. In economic terms, the tribute system was essentially a trade monopoly, and many of the Ming dynasty's "Japanese pirates" were actually smugglers and traffickers. The empire's trade considerations were more political than economic, and the tribute system was seen as a means of supplementing its inadequate foreign military capabilities. This concept still exists in international trade today: As one East Asian statesman has said, international trade has never been merely trade, but rather a choice between "who is your friend and who is your ally."[66]

Trade has never been only about rule and politics, but also about exchange and freedom. In epochal terms, China missed out on the eighteenth and nineteenth centuries, ostensibly gaining silver but in fact suffering enormous loss. What it lost was not only trade in goods, but even more the information exchange and systemic shock accompanying trade. Ultimately it could only passively join the latter half of globalization's mighty stir.

The great British Empire rose almost simultaneously with the fall of the Great Qing Empire. If the British navy established the military basis for England's global trade, then China's story took another direction. Soon after suffering military defeat, China saw its trade superiority begin to crumble. Large quantities of opium began flowing into China, while its tea, silk, and other commodities began losing their monopoly status in the international market. Takeshi Hamashita points out that Japanese and Indian tea began appearing on the international market from the 1850s onward. By the early twentieth century, Japan had largely taken over China's monopoly on green tea in the U.S. market, and Indian black tea had already replaced Chinese tea in England in the nineteenth century. Tea was no longer a specialized project limited by geographical circumstances.[67]

After observing the historical processes of tea leaves and silver trade in Asia and the West, Takeshi Hamashita concludes that the Opium Wars were located on a continuum between the two, and originated with the intention to legalize the opium trade and expand the purchasing market for tea.

1840: Opium War or Silver War?

The shift from tribute to treaty did not happen overnight; history's dramatic changes always need the impetus of a trigger. In China this factor looked as if it was opium, in the West it looked as if it might be trade, and what linked them was silver. Subsequently opium was subjected to considerable moral censure and was even seen as a conspiracy against the "weak man of Asia," but what lay behind it was the pursuit of profit.

As a topic, the Opium Wars have mystified people. Opium has a long record in the history of humanity, the term itself tracing back to Greece. Opium was introduced to China very early, with many records of it in the Ming dynasty, and some scholars believe that opium and poppies were introduced to China no later than the Tang dynasty.[68] Opium originally emerged as a medicinal product; according to one telling, opium was more readily available in 1870 than cigarettes were in 1970. Opium was also a source of inspiration for literary people, with the British essayist Thomas De Quincey's *Confessions of an English Opium-Eater* a notable example. Excessive use of opium, however, caused addiction to increase dramatically, especially after the smoking method emerged in

Fujian and Taiwan. By the nineteenth century, opium had become a symbol of evil in the West, and China became trapped between image and reality as a languid Oriental empire.

History's amazing twists and turns always include chance details. The popularity and even the harm of opium in the Qing dynasty were closely related to changes in the manner of consumption. The British drank it dissolved it in water (consuming ten to twenty tons per year), a method that produced a mildly narcotic effect but nothing to worry about. The more addictive smoking method prevalent among the Chinese reportedly originated in Java and spread to mainland China through Taiwan (or Fujian). "The difference was not unlike that between chewing coca leaves and lighting up a crack pipe. British drug dealers contrived to overlook this difference but the Daoguang Emperor did not, and in 1839 declared war on drugs."[69]

The First Opium War, or Sino-British War, was not only a crucial turning point in Chinese history, but also a source of powerful national sentiment among many Chinese. Yet, history is not decided by a single incident, and our knowledge of the Opium War may be inadequate; different standpoints often lead to different inferences, especially in the case of emotionally charged historical incidents.

The lure and effects of opium are similarly confusing, both in China and in the rest of the world. Is opium a medicine or a hard drug? Did opium addiction originate in Asia or the West? Is opium consumption a moral problem or an economic problem? Was this war an opium war or a silver war? . . . Solving one problem often leads to another problem. Opium was the catalyst for war, and even more a dual metaphor for moral anxiety and national peril in China's modern history: Foreign opium took away China's silver and left China with the image of the "sick man of Asia"; opium addiction even became a vice exported by China. Opium went on to become a status symbol; many military regimes from the late Qing to the Republican era had a critical relationship with opium. Under the name of opium, China became a morally flawed victim of persecution.

On this point, Li Hongzhang did not lack discernment. In an 1881 letter to the British Society for the Suppression of the Opium Trade he wrote that the Chinese viewed this problem from a moral standpoint, while the British saw it as a fiscal matter.[70] This viewpoint might not have been his own; an aide to the official Zeng Guofan held: "The English barbarians originally had no thievish intentions in their trading, and the imperial court therefore acted with great magnanimity."[71]

The Opium War started with trade; China and England were linked by tea and opium, and the channel between them was silver. Everyone finds precious metals irresistible; not only the Chinese but also the British resented the outflow of silver. Well before the Chinese began grumbling about "leaking silver," Western Europe was criticizing its own outflow of silver, and this created favorable conditions for the smuggling of opium.

By the Victorian era, British people of every social class were addicted to tea. How great was the profit on tea? The 1785 tax reduction law had reduced the tax on tea leaves to 12.5 percent from the previous hefty 119 percent, which had led to pervasive smuggling. The reduction in customs tariffs stimulated the export of Chinese tea, which composed 80 to 90 percent of the East India Company's China trade; by the 1790s, the company's tea trade had reached 23 million pounds sterling.

In spite of mouthwatering tea profits, the East India Company was thwarted in its plans to sell woolens to China. This meant that the East India Company's exports to China were only one-third of its imports, and this enormous difference was the reason that silver flowed steadily into China: "The company was having trouble raising enough [silver] to keep the trade going. So there was much joy when the traders realized that whatever the Chinese government might want, the Chinese people wanted something else: opium."[72]

That is why the Opium War was in fact a silver war, and the Opium War has even been referred to as a trade war, which shows the significance of the economic factor. Initially trading was profitable for China; the world needed China's silk, tea, and other goods, while the Chinese had no intention of buying foreign goods. The tea trade increased exponentially, from five crates in 1648 to 400,000 pounds in 1720 and then 23 million pounds in 1800. England was the main purchaser of Chinese tea; reportedly one-seventh of China's tea leaves entered England, and customs duty on tea imports made up one-tenth of England's tax revenue.

Behind the trade was the transmission of currency, and silver began pouring into China as trade developed. Silver flowed into China at a rate of 3 million taels per year in the 1760s, and increased to 16 million taels per year in the 1780s. Trade wars have existed from antiquity; now they tend to be carried out in intense battles of words, but naked violence was more likely in the past. England launched a counterattack, and opium began flowing into China. As opium from Bengal began entering China in an organized fashion, China and England's trade evolved into triangular trade between China, India, and England. Other British and Indian merchants also began engaging in trade in Asia with the permission of the British East India Company; as "country merchants" they played an even more important role in the opium trade and even in the China trade, foreshadowing subsequent disputes. In spite of China's bans on the import of opium, more than 4,500 crates of opium were imported to China in 1800, reaching 40,000 crates in 1838. Scholars have ascertained that a crate of opium measuring one meter long, half a meter wide, and half a meter tall contained forty opium balls of various sizes, enough to supply 100 addicts for one year. Under the ban, opium continued to spread and the trade balance began to shift. In the 1820s, 2 million taels of silver flowed out of China every year, but by the 1830s, this number rose to 9 million taels.[73]

China issued its first imperial edict banning opium back in the seventh year of the Yongzheng era (1729). The "Regulation on Selling Opium and Opening Smoking Dens" stated: "Anyone engaged in selling opium in violation of the ban will be pilloried in public for one month and banished to the frontier for military servitude; anyone who opens an opium smoking den and lures the sons of good families like those who delude people with cult teachings will be imprisoned, lashed with 100 strokes of the cane and sent 3,000 *li* away. Boatmen, constables, neighbors and so on will receive 100 strokes of the cane and will be imprisoned for two years. Conscripted soldiers etc. who use the pretext for extortion will be punished according to the amount of the bribe. Civil and military officials who neglect their duty to supervise customs control will be handed over to their departments for stern punishment."[74] The early opium ban was not very strictly enforced, however; it was more common to regard opium as a local issue or practice in

Guangdong, Fujian, and such places, and opium even continued to be taxed at customs for a period of time after the ban was issued. During the Jiaqing era (1796–1820), repeated bans were proclaimed on the import of opium, but when the governor general of Guangdong and Guangxi memorialized the emperor to reaffirm the ban, Jiaqing showed greater concern for the foreign trade in clocks and watches, glass, and other such items that led to "China's silver being considerably squandered," and demanded careful attention to prevent "domestic silver taels to be connivingly acquired by the barbarians."[75] The Daoguang era brought a change for the better, and the opium ban became a grand slogan and campaign. Jiang Tingfu attributes the resolve of the Daoguang Emperor's opium ban to the rapid increase in imports at that time: "In the first year of the Daoguang era (1821), only 5,000 crates were imported, but in the fifteenth year (1835) it had increased to 30,000 crates, at a value of around 18 million *yuan*."

The inflow of opium and outflow of silver sparked discussion of impending crises, but the prevailing stand at that time was to "increase customs duty while encouraging planting and using domestic products to resist foreign goods." In retrospect, this could be considered a normal trade countermeasure, but leaders typically want to resolve issues as quickly as possible, and the Daoguang Emperor's demand for a quick solution now looks something like a historical tragedy.

Officials conceded in private that banning opium would be a challenge, but they gave the outward impression of advocating strict bans in order to curry favor with the Daoguang Emperor. This is not the only time this phenomenon has emerged in Chinese history, just as the hawkish faction always enjoys contemporary public support and posthumous historical favor. This is why the Daoguang Emperor was extremely pleased when opium ban advocate Lin Zexu appeared on the scene, and he appointed Lin, who had never handled "barbarian services," as his imperial commissioner.

Changes were also under way in England. In the eleventh year of the Daoguang era (1831), the fourth prince regent, Aisingioro Yizhu, the future Xianfeng emperor, was born at the Summer Palace in Beijing. That same year, the British East India Company's monopoly was abolished and the British appointed a new *taipan* (this term, originating in

Cantonese, referred to a manager of business affairs). Previously Chinese customs officials negotiated with the *taipan* to manage British merchants, but after the East India Company's monopoly was abolished, "country merchants" gained even more independence and say-so in Sino-British trade, and the role of the *taipan* also changed; he was no longer merely a merchant in the normal sense but an official with government authority:

> The chief superintendent was instructed that every effort was to be made to conform to all Chinese regulations and to consider all Chinese prejudices, and at the same time was forbidden to call in the aid of the armed forces of the crown; and yet he was required to adopt a course which would convert him from a mere superintendent of trade—a taipan, as the Chinese would consider it—into a royal envoy, and would break every Chinese regulation and offend every Chinese prejudice.[76]

The Qing government did not perceive the change in circumstances; for China, the chief superintendent of business affairs was only another *taipan* or "barbarian headman." This led to conflict as unyielding head negotiators from both sides mounted the stage: on one side Lin Zexu, and on the other Charles Elliot. Canton announced a ban on opium at the beginning of 1839, and Imperial Commissioner Lin Zexu arrived on March 10. The next day he ordered the foreigners to hand over their opium and banned them from leaving Canton. On March 27, chief superintendent of business affairs Charles Elliot ordered the British merchants to hand over their opium and leave Guangzhou, and an embargo was placed on British trade with Canton.[77]

Disregarding the two sides' tit-for-tat pretexts, an American historian subsequently described this historical interlude as a bizarre war. When Elliot told the British opium dealers to hand over 1,700 tons of opium to Lin Zexu and guaranteed that the British government would compensate their losses, it seemed that the story would have a happy ending: "Lin got his opium; Elliot saved face and kept the tea trade moving; and the merchants got top price (plus interest and shipping) for their drugs. Everyone won."[78] The story didn't end there, however; the winners didn't include British prime minister Lord Melbourne, who was expected to compensate the drug dealers for their losses—a total of 2 million pounds sterling. Under lobbying and pressure, the prime minister had "no choice" but to pay out the compensation, but he then sent an expeditionary force to recover the costs from China.

Many people may be familiar with what followed, but few may be clear on the details. Based on Morse's chronicle of events, what exactly happened?

1839   July 7th. Lin Wei-hi killed in affray at Hongkong.
        Aug. 25th. British expelled from Macao.
        Aug. 31st. Commissioner Lin calls on villagers to arm.
        Sept. 12th. Spanish brig *Bilbaino* burned at Macao.
        Nov. 3rd. Naval action at Chuenpi [Chuanbi]. War opens.
        Nov. 26th. British trade prohibited forever.
                . . .
1841   Jan. 7th. Batteries of Chuenpi and Taikoktow [Dajiaotou]
            captured. Armistice.
        Jan. 20th. Convention signed by Captain Elliot and Kishen
            [Qishan]. Hongkong ceded.
        Jan. 30th. Convention denounced by Chinese government.
        Feb. 23rd. Hostilities renewed.
        Feb. 25th. Proclamation issued offering rewards for English
            heads.
        Feb. 26th. Bogue batteries captured.
        March 20th. Suspension of hostilities. Trade reopened.
        April 30th. Convention of Jan. 20 denounced by British
            government.
        May 21st. Renewal of hostilities at Canton.
        May 27th. Convention signed. Canton ransomed.
        June 7th. Hongkong declared a free port.
        June 14th. First sale of land at Hongkong.
        Aug. 10th. Sir H. Pottinger, sole plenipotentiary, arrives.
        Aug. 26th. Amoy [Xiamen] taken and occupied.
        Oct 1st. Tinghai [Dinghai] taken and occupied.
        Oct. 10th–13th. Chinhai [Zhenhai] and Ningpo [Ningbo]
            taken and occupied.

1842   Feb. 16th. Hongkong declared a free port. Also Tinghai.
        Feb. 27th. British government offices transferred to
            Hongkong.
        May 18th. Capu [Zhapu] taken; severe loss to Manchu
            garrison.
        June 16th. Wusung [Wusong] batteries taken.
        June 19th. Shanghai occupied.
        July 21st. Chinkiang [Zhenjiang] taken; Manchu garrison
            exterminated.
        Aug. 9th. Plenipotentiaries arrive at Nanking [Nanjing].
        Aug. 29th. Treaty of Nanking signed.
1843   June 26th. Ratifications of treaty exchanged. Cession of
            Hongkong proclaimed.
        July 22nd. General Regulations of Trade published.
        Oct. 8th. Supplementary treaty of the Bogue signed.
        Nov. 17th. Shanghai opened to foreign trade.[79]

Those who opposed the opium trade most stridently, Lin Zexu and
the Daoguang Emperor, became history's losers and ended their days in
dejection. Although endorsed by their compatriots while alive and after
their deaths, both undeniably had intellectual limitations, and the best
of intentions doesn't put them at the front ranks of history. England saw
itself as preserving both opium profits and unobstructed trade, and both
were related to silver. Jiang Tingfu believes that in terms of world trends,
war was unavoidable, and that it had its reasons, whether as what we
refer to as the Opium War or what the British called a trade war: "On
the opium problem, the Chinese side strove to completely ban it, while
the English hoped to maintain the status quo: their defense against our
attack. Regarding the trade issue, the British strove to gain even more
opportunities and freedom, while our side insisted on maintaining the
status quo: our defense against their attack."

In retrospect, one cannot help but sigh over Macartney's early
peaceful diplomatic efforts. The Qing dynasty's refusal to negotiate may
have been what began to make war unavoidable. Jiang Tingfu's view may
be even closer to reality: "The British objectives in China were entirely
trade-related; people engaged in business, whether Chinese or foreign,

past or present, all hope for a stable situation. The British government's actions are what we call 'muddling along.' " The Opium War looks inevitable today, but at that time it had its chance aspects, and in fact was related to the damage to British trade and demands for compensation for the destroyed opium. It was a clash between two cultures as well as a collision of two viewpoints, and perhaps it can only be completely understood by dissection from both sides.

Reality, especially war, can dispel romantic illusions. In the process of Europe's modernization, there were utopian fantasies toward China; for example, the French author Voltaire once praised China as the world's first civilized country. With increasing exchanges, however, this enthusiasm gradually dissipated, and China acquired a basically negative image. Adam Smith noticed China's social stagnation and the privations of its ordinary people compared with the Marco Polo era:

> Instead of waiting indolently in their workhouses, for the calls of their customers, as in Europe, they are continually running about the streets with the tools of their respective trades, offering their service, and as it were begging employment. The poverty of the lower ranks of people in China far surpasses that of the most beggarly nations in Europe. In the neighbourhood of Canton many hundred, it is commonly said, many thousand families have no habitation on the land, but live constantly in little fishing boats upon the rivers and canals. The subsistence which they find there is so scanty that they are eager to fish up the nastiest garbage thrown overboard from any European ship.[80]

Compared with the imaginings of literary philosophers, British envoy Macartney's report was subsequently considered more insightful. He felt that China was basically unprepared to wage war with the great powers of Europe because it was filled with poverty, its scholars had little interest in material progress, and its soldiers were still using bows and arrows. Macartney's negative assessment of China had a profound effect on Western society. Quotes of his such as, "We keep aloof from them as much as possible," and that the Qing dynasty was "an old crazy first rate man-of-war," which its leaders doomed to be "dashed to pieces on the shore,"[81] proved prophetic in history's transmigration.

The Opium War is a wound in the national psyche of the Chinese, but the British subsequently played it down; the understanding of both sides was full of ignorance and misreading. It was only after the Great Qing Emperor expended countless lives and silver in two years of war-fare that he thought to ask his top officials where England even was.[82] Even today, we still know too little about the Opium War. Like all wars, the Opium War is full of narratives from different angles as well as dis-tortions and amnesia, but what cannot be ignored is that the war dragged China kicking and screaming into an alien and rapidly changing era of globalization.

Reprise: What Caused the Empire's Money Famine?

Modern history has been a nightmare for the Chinese. The Opium War became the first wound in the heart of Chinese, and nationalist sentiment was the after-effect. One of the invisible threads that influ-enced this drama was silver. "Costly silver and worthless cash" could be considered a key phrase of late Qing society, with many related histori-cal records from the Daoguang era.

Looking back, premodern people's excessive focus on precious metals remains an issue worth exploring. Although not without psycho-logical motivations outside of economics, from the classical economic perspective, the flow of precious metals could in fact easily create pain-ful deflation. Even today, trade wars often unfold around exchange rates; in the era of hard currency, the flow of precious metals triggered even more discussion. The famous petition submitted by Minister Herald Huang Jueci to the emperor in the eighteenth year of the Daoguang era (1838) can be considered a classic example. He emphasized that "China's silver taels are being secretly wasted on the filth of foreigners," and "the price of silver has continued to increase in recent years; one tael of silver costs 1,600 copper cash. The silver is not spent in-country, but is leaking out to foreign countries. Since opium has flowed into China, my far-sighted Emperor Renzong has known its inevitable harm and has issued bans, but ministers and officials at that time did not expect it to have such extremely bad influence!"

Contemporary histories contain numerous accounts of the high cost and outflow of silver. *Veritable Records of the Qing,* for instance, records how the situation varied greatly north and south of the Huai River. In the south, river transport costs had increased ten times, making people reluctant to travel long distances. The cost of annual repairs to irrigation works in various places was also affected, with not enough money available to remedy the situation.[83] Standing back may allow us to view the complete picture. What is historical truth? Perhaps it can only be approached through step-by-step "disenchantment." This war pitted empires of the East and West not only over opium, but even more over silver.

In the early years of the Qing dynasty, the exchange ratio between silver and copper cash of 1,000 cash per tael remained very stable until the Jiaqing era (1760). Occasionally there was a local phenomenon of "silver devalued and copper cash more valuable," and people seeing an opportunity for profit privately minted copper coins. With the outflow of silver, the problem became one of "costly silver and worthless cash." The shortage of silver was evident in the exchange ratio between silver and copper cash. The Qing government stipulated that one tael of silver was equal to 1,000 cash, but this exchange ratio increased steadily before the Opium Wars to 1,560 cash. After the Treaty of Nanking, the Qing government paid compensation of nearly 28 million dollars as redress for the destruction of opium as well as war reparations and paying the debts of merchants:

> The Emperor of China agrees to pay the sum of Six Millions of Dollars as the value of the opium which was delivered up at Canton in the month of March, 1839, as a Ransom for the lives of Her Britannic Majesty's Superintendent, and Subjects, who had been imprisoned and threatened with death by the Chinese High Officers . . .
>
> The Government of China, having compelled the British Merchants trading at Canton to deal exclusively with certain

Chinese Merchants, called Hong Merchants (or Cohong), who had been licensed by the Chinese Government for that purpose, the Emperor of China agrees to abolish that practice in future at all Ports where British Merchants may reside, and to permit them to carry on their mercantile transactions with whatever persons they please; and His Imperial Majesty further agrees to pay to the British Government the sum of Three Millions of Dollars, on account of Debts due to British Subjects by some of the said Hong Merchants or Cohong, who have become insolvent, and who owe very large sums of money to Subjects of Her Britannic Majesty . . .

The Government of Her Britannic Majesty having been obliged to send out an Expedition to demand and obtain redress for the violent and unjust Proceedings of the Chinese High Authorities towards Her Britannic Majesty's Officer and Subjects, the Emperor of China agrees to pay the sum of Twelve Millions of Dollars, on account of the Expenses incurred; and Her Britannic Majesty's Plenipotentiary voluntarily agrees, on behalf of Her Majesty, to deduct from the said amount of Twelve Millions of Dollars, any sums which may have been received by Her Majesty's Combined Forces, as ransom for Cities and Towns in China, subsequent to the 1st day of August, 1841.[84]

This compensation was a major blow to the empire's finances at that time. The feudal imperial court's tax-levying capacity had always been weak, and there was little surplus of revenue over expenditure. In 1843, for example, revenue was 42.26 million taels and expenditure was 41.9 million taels, for a surplus of 350,000 taels. In the above compensation funds, the Canton cohongs and other private parties put up 15.1 million taels, more than half, with the rest coming out of the government treasury (at that time, one Mexican dollar was equal to 0.73 taels of silver).[85]

Already suffering from a money famine, the Qing dynasty was hit by an even more devastating retrenchment crisis. The exchange ratio between silver and copper cash rose again, and ultimately an exchange rate of 2,000 cash per tael of silver became prevalent: "Today's silver price is

2,000 per tael, an increase double the usual value in copper cash, and sometimes up to three times."[86] "The price of silver has never been higher than today. In the capital each tael of fine silver [*wenyin*] is changed for 2,000 copper cash; in the outer provinces each tael is changed for 2,200 or 2,300 cash or more."[87] "In the south the standard is 2,000 per tael of silver; in the north I hear it is even more."[88] This trend intensified in the years that followed. Scholar Peng Zeyi calculated from contemporary data that the exchange rates between silver and copper cash were as follows: 1847: 2,167.44 cash; 1848: 2,299.34 cash; 1849: 2,354.98 cash; 1850, 2,230.32 cash.[89]

The fluctuating exchange rate between silver and copper cash caused tax revenues to shrink, and the farmers who mainly dealt in the production of commodities suffered in the exchange. People's inability to sustain their livelihood was fatal to a regime beset by crisis. According to Lin Zexu's account, the average family spent an average of 100 cash worth of silver per day, so the rising cost of silver created hardship for ordinary people.

In the final analysis, what caused the empire's silver famine? The mainstream explanation in China has always been the outflow of silver, especially as triggered by the Opium War. According to Peng Zeyi's research, in the years 1843 to 1846 alone, China experienced a trade deficit of 39 million to 47 million silver dollars.[90] Comparatively speaking, from the eighteenth century to the first thirty years of the nineteenth century, Morse calculated that the amount of silver flowing into Canton totaled 90 million to 100 million pounds sterling, or an average of 3.08 million silver dollars per year.[91]

There is another explanation. Around the time of the Opium War, a drop in the production of American silver had an even greater effect on the Great Qing Empire.[92] Lin Man-houng believes that the sudden reduction in New World silver almost toppled the Qing dynasty, and that the subsequent inflow of silver helped the "resurgence" of the Qing dynasty, but also caused it to become even more dependent on foreign silver, and weaker than its silver-producing Asian neighbors.

China's silver production capacity was long insufficient, so foreign silver was of utmost importance. Scholar Wei Yuan (1794–1856) once spoke of China's dependence on foreign silver:

> Silver from mines is three or four parts out of ten. That com-
> ing by foreign boats is six to seven parts of ten. China's silver
> mines have already extracted three to four parts of ten. Left
> to be extracted are six to seven parts of ten. The vital energy
> of heaven and earth disappears with each breath and each
> morning and evening tide. Silver has come by foreign boat
> for thousands of years. Now the foreign boats are taking it
> away. China's secret treasure has been in its mountains and
> rivers for thousands of years, and they must be opened today.
> China fights for use of the West's silver money. It is more
> costly than domestic silver.[93]

Initially, Japan was the main source of silver used in China, but from the
late eighteenth century onward, New World silver became the mainstream. That meant that this enormous but fragile empire imperceptibly
laid bare its "crucial seven inches" in the chaos of globalization. Lin
Man-houng goes a step further to claim that there were two reasons for
the reduction in China's silver. First was a worldwide reduction in silver
production. The turning point occurred in 1775, when Japan began retaining silver for its own use and China became entirely dependent on
New World silver. Affected by the Napoleonic Wars and the American
War of Independence, Latin American silver exports dropped by half in
the first thirty years of the nineteenth century and didn't return to the
1800 level until 1850. Second, the worldwide silver shortage led to an
adjustment in Chinese exports. In the first part of the nineteenth century, the worldwide demand for Chinese silk and tea declined, with the
tea trade only maintaining its past levels, while British opium imports to
China increased, resulting in the outflow of silver for forty years. China's
economy suffered because of that. If not for these two factors, China
would not have experienced a silver shortage.

   If we know that the outflow of silver was not only because of opium, can we go a step further to explore whether the outflow of silver
actually led to the fall of the Qing dynasty according to the same logic as
for the Great Ming Empire?

   As soon as the silverized late Qing economy encountered a tightening of the silver supply, it unavoidably became unstable. With taxes

and levies unified and paid in silver, the silver famine put the general public, especially the lower strata, under enormous pressure. It goes without saying that tax pressures led to hardships in everyday life, and this in turn led to the state treasury suffering losses under the official silver and copper cash exchange ratio. The ultimate result was "the state not adding taxes, but the people paying more taxes in reality." "Every *qian* of treasury-standard *wenyin* [fine silver] equals 200 copper cash. Each bag [of salt] costs more than 530 cash and up to 560 cash or more. At a partially reduced price, each bag [of salt] costs at least two *qian* and nine *fen* of silver. Although salt on the Chu coast has not yet reached this cost, the people still suffer from high prices . . . Year after year the fields suffer crop failures while silver becomes more costly. Full tax cannot be collected. There are declines in silver and cash, and there may not be enough to sustain the army."[94]

The many social changes in the late Qing were undeniably related to the changing exchange ratio between silver and copper cash. The Opium Wars and the chaos of the Taiping Heavenly Kingdom were to a great extent silver crises. One scholar believes the outflow of silver caused China to lose more than half of its wealth. Even by conservative modern estimates, the outflow of silver from 1808 to 1856 reached 16.4 percent of the total silver supply in China.[95] If not for this outflow of silver, it is possible that China would not have been forced onto the road of modernization. Whether because of opium imports or declines in the output of silver, in the early nineteenth century the empire entered a situation of "costly silver and worthless copper cash," which led not only to a monetary crisis, but also to a political crisis. Many historians believe that China was in fact tripped up by the silver rope that bound it to Mexico.[96]

Whatever the reason, it deserves further thought by later generations. The Opium War changed not only China's fate but also Japan's, and the comparison with Japan is especially lamentable. Three hundred years before 1840, China was not really so closed off; there was still space for people like Matteo Ricci and Xu Guangqi,[97] while the Japanese shogunate was still ordering people to "trample on the image of Christ." Even Chinese merchant vessels could not escape. In an effort to investigate Christians and stamp out missionaries, any mention of Christ was forbidden, and even church books were banned. Against this backdrop, is it possible that China's and Japan's different reactions to challenges may have been rooted in the spaces in China's vast mass, which also made it difficult to turn at full speed in the face of attack? Or was it that when the conflict over silver and opium began, China's silver and trade links forced it into full-scale conflict with the world, while Japan's relative silver self-sufficiency allowed it to escape the disaster of 1840? Did this lucky fluke also subsequently put Japan on its long, one-way passage to militarism?

History has no hypotheticals, but in the records of former days we can still find clues of what might have been. The period from the Opium Wars until the Sino-Japanese War of 1894–1895 marked the beginning of the Chinese people's narrative of suffering. The resulting nation-saving itinerary overwhelmed the enlightenment itinerary and buried history's foreshadowing, and the need to attack so-called backwardness became the classic conclusion. When investigating the causes of history, however, so many riddles remain to be solved. The Opium Wars broke out over the inflow of opium and ended with compensation paid in silver. Silver brought China face-to-face with the world; silver had its place as a cause and an effect, but it is not the entire history.

At this point we are obliged to mention the "two cannon theory" describing the demarcation of the "modern" and "contemporary" periods of history: "Mao Zedong tirelessly promoted the 'theory of two cannons,' initially highlighting the cannon of the Opium War between the Qing and Britain which drove China from its long period of feudal stagnation into a semi-colonial feudal society, only awakening after the cannon fire of the October Revolution in Russia after which 'the east was red and the sun rose' in China."[98] According to this theory, the first cannon thrust China from "medieval" to "modern" times and forcibly channeled it into the Western capitalist world system, while the second cannon led China from the "modern" into the "contemporary," following Soviet Russia into the socialist new world built by Lenin and Stalin. Historian Zhu Weizheng avers that he has gone from believing to doubting the "two cannon theory" and no longer endorses its demarcation of the beginning of China's contemporary history. Unfortunately, this customary narrative is still ubiquitous in China.

The Daoguang era seemed to make an abrupt descent from prosperity to decline under the British onslaught, and its subsequent brief "resurgence" did not save it from the Sino-Japanese War of 1894–1895. Is history really so dramatic?

Looking back at the late Qing situation, at that time China was not backward by economic measures. Economist Angus Maddison's figures show that in the year that the Daoguang Emperor ascended the throne (1820), China's GDP still made up nearly one-third of world GDP and it was the world's top economy, while the twelve countries of Western Europe (the United Kingdom, France, Germany, Italy, Austria, Belgium, the Netherlands, Switzerland, Sweden, Norway, Denmark, and Finland) made up only 20.9 percent. England's share was only 5.2 percent and Japan's only 3.0 percent.[99] In military terms, whether in the Opium Wars or the Sino-Japanese War, the outside world believed that China possessed an enormous armed force. Scholars have described this in detail, and I won't belabor it further here.

The problem was that China was on a downward trend and Western Europe was on the upswing. By 1860, China's share of world GDP had dropped to 17.2 percent and Japan's was only 2.3 percent, while the share held by the twelve Western European countries had risen to 30.7 percent, including 9.1 percent for England. Western Europe was in the midst of its Industrial Revolution, while China continued its low-level equilibrium. The biggest difference was in per capita income. China's population in the eighteenth and nineteenth centuries continued to grow at a same pace as its GDP, and per capita income ceased to advance, while Western Europe's per capita income greatly increased. In the words of economist Douglass North:

> In speaking of economic growth, we refer to a *per capita* long-run rise in income. True economic growth thus implies that the total income of society must increase more rapidly than population. A stationary state, on the other hand, produces no sustained rise in *per capita* income even though average income may rise and fall during cycles of quite long duration. A stationary state will result when there is no inducement for individuals in the society to undertake those

activities that lead to economic growth. Granted that individuals in the society may choose to ignore such positive incentives, and that in all societies some are content with their present situation; yet casual empiricism suggests that most people prefer more goods to fewer goods and act accordingly. Economic growth requires only that some part of the populace be acquisitive.[100]

In recent years the California School has sparked a great deal of discussion with its research on the Great Divergence, but we need to face the reality that China's systemic inertia created China and also dragged down China; China's defeat in modern times was the inevitable result of its backwardness. That is why China's backwardness did not begin with the Opium War; it was a habitual condition that can be traced back to even before the Ming.

Indeed, traces of this failure are evident after the Song. According to economist Liu Haiying's description in *China's Enormous Debt*, the Song dynasty created the supreme achievement of premodern China and its economic life achieved enormous progress: "In terms of per-capita income, from US$385 in the early years of the Song it rose to $464 at the end of the Northern Song, and then continued to rise to $585 in the last part of the Southern Song. Its economic scale far exceeded Europe's and placed it first in the world. China did not achieve this income level again until the 1980s."[101]

Systems are the crucial link in both the backwardness of the Ming and Qing and the glories of the Song. The further centralization of the Ming dynasty monarchy smothered many possibilities; the Hongwu period hobbled economic vitality for 200 years, at exactly the time that the West advanced by leaps and bounds and left the Chinese Empire far behind. Essentially, the crisis of empire stemmed from systemic crisis, and silver was merely the catalyst. With a chaotic currency system and facing threats from outside, China's officials had no control over the inflow and outflow of silver. This exposed the Great Qing Empire's fragility in terms of its inability to control domestic monetary policies and its lack of a central bank or other such organs to regulate the system. Specifically, the monetary system depends on the social system, and comparing the Song dynasty's prosperity with the *jiaozi* and the Ming's and Qing's impoverishment with silver, China's trajectory intersected with the world's and then passed it by. The backslide from trailblazer to laggard had its own momentum, which subsequently led to the late Qing's currency reform crisis and ultimately the inflation of the Republican era.

If not for the abundant supply of silver in the mid- and late eighteenth century, China may not have taken the road to a silver standard while the rest of the world, including neighboring Japan, was already on the road to a gold standard. Adopting the gold standard and linking more effectively with the world seemed an essential method for the Europeanization of civilization, and China simply brushed past it.

Foreign Silver Dollars in China

So-called foreign silver dollars, or *waiyang*, were referred to by a number of names in China, including "barbarian silver," "barbarian cookies," and "barbarian buddhas," indicating the welcome they received.

The spread of foreign silver dollars in China actually began in the Ming dynasty, mainly through Macau and the Philippines. Qian Mu writes that the Ming dynasty began using silver dollars, and by the end of the Qing the majority in circulation were Mexican silver dollars and Great Qing silver dollars, at a standard weight of 0.72 treasury ounces. Numismatist Qian Jiaju divided the Qing dynasty's use of silver into three stages: The first was the 100 or so years from the beginning of the Qing until the Qianlong period, when silver ingots (*yinding*) were in widespread use; the second was the eighty to ninety years from the Jiaqing period onward, when foreign silver dollars became currency in China; the final stage was the Xuantong period at the end of the Qing, which minted its own silver dollars (*yuan*) to be used simultaneously with silver taels. The use of two forms of silver currency continued until the government scrapped the tael and converted to the dollar in 1933.

China's foreign trade initially consisted of foreigners buying porcelain, silk, tea, and other Chinese products. The Chinese seldom bought any foreign goods, and the main trade was carried out through payment in silver by foreign merchants, typically in foreign silver dollars. Flourishing trade brought a steady increase in foreign silver dollars. By the

Qianlong period, China's high interest rates began attracting even more foreign currency. The annual interest in Guangdong at that time was reported at 1.8 to 2 percent; this was compound interest and naturally caused the influx of quite a lot of silver. For example, when Heshen's home was searched in 1799,[102] he was found to be in possession of 58,000 foreign silver dollars.

Foreign silver dollars were initially used for their stable silver content, but later they circulated by number.[103] An investigation by the Board of Revenue (*Hubu*) in 1910 found 110 million foreign silver dollars circulating in China, among which one-third were "eagle dollars." The eagle dollar, minted in Mexico in 1823 with a high silver content, took over from the Spanish doubloons that had first been used. *Life in the Age of the Silver Dollar*[104] says, "Mexican silver dollars that flowed into China were machine-minted, and their content was more accurate. Foreigners buying goods in China all used this silver dollar."

The eagle dollar circulated in the countryside as well as in the cities. American traveler William Edgar Geil (1865–1925) recorded an experience he had in Yichang. In order to make an American flag, he bought three feet of red cloth, three feet of white cloth, one piece of blue cloth, and a role of cotton thread, spending 532 *wen* in copper cash for the cloth and 100 *wen* for the thread. "I handed the shopkeeper a Mexican dollar worth eight hundred and twenty cash in 'Deserving Prosperity' [Yichang] and, just for fun, took up one of his already strung one thousand cash and pulled off two hundred. He smiled and nodded assent. So I appeared to have bought the stuff for six hundred and twenty cash. But money is China is very crazy."[105]

The proliferation of foreign silver dollars was therefore economically motivated more than anything else; in a chaotic currency system, it served as a more standard silver currency, with no political connotations. Foreign silver dollars were not regarded as legal tender, and local banks or money-exchange shops would put various stamps on them, distorting their faces beyond recognition. American missionary Chester Holcombe recorded:

Some years ago a distinguished American lady, while visiting Canton, desired to draw five hundred Mexican dollars upon her letter of credit, with which to make some purchases. Her banker advised her not to take the actual coin, but to give each merchant with whom she dealt an order upon him for the amount of her purchase. He would then deduct the sum total of her expenditures from her letter of credit. As she declined to follow this course, preferring to pay her own bills, the banker brought her the required sum in a canvas bag, and spread the money out that she might by count assure herself of its correctness. It resembled nothing so much as battered bits and scraps of old tin. There was not one piece in the lot which could be counted as a dollar, or whose value could be determined except by weight.[106]

Peng Xinwei believes that the spread of foreign silver dollars reflected the divergent development of monetary culture: One according to the Greek system, which reached an ebb during the Middle Ages and then went on the upswing after the Renaissance; and the other through the Chinese system. Chinese five-grainer coins were advanced in their own way, with similar dimensions to the later popular twenty-cent and silver coins, and close in size to the mark and shilling. Peng believes that monetary culture regressed after the Song, with easily portable silver pieces degenerating into the impractical *yuanbao* silver ingots being one example; the form of the *yuanbao* was really not practical compared with the Han dynasty's more reasonable silver cake form.[107] *Records of the Three Kingdoms: Annals of Wei* contains the expression "one thousand cakes of silver for one thousand bolts of silk," and during the Northern and Southern dynasties (420–589), silver was minted into a rectangular shape called a *ding*. "At that time gold and silver were also minted into a cake shape as well as into a *ding* shape."[108]

Chinese coins were minted by casting in a clay mold. This primitive handicraft method, which limited the amount of coins that could be produced and significantly increased the cost of production, is believed to have continued for more than 2,000 years without advancement. During a visit to the Shanghai Museum's currency hall, I found that the outward appearance of Chinese coins actually changed very little over the generations. Conversely, Europe, with its origins in Greek monetary

culture, changed with the needs of the market from the Renaissance onward. Machine minting began in the eighteenth century, but did not
spread to China until considerably later.

For this reason, the popularity of foreign silver dollars can be considered to have created a "great revolution" in China's monetary culture,
spurring the production of domestically minted silver dollars such as
the "dragon dollar" and the "Yuan [Shikai]-head." Even so, foreign silver
dollars continued to circulate until the Republican era. Numismatists
have ascertained that China's early self-minted silver dollars had about
the same silver content as foreign silver dollars, around 27 grams and a
purity of around 90 percent.[109] The popularity of the silver dollar was
ultimately due to its content and elegance. Chen Cunren records that the
eagle dollar circulated widely during the Qing dynasty, and for a time
was even assigned an equivalent value to the dragon dollar and *yuan*-
head dollar: "Every silver dollar is minted using 0.73 ounce of silver, or
0.72 *Kuping* [Treasury standard] ounce. The most standard silver dollar
is minted in Mexico with an eagle on its face, so it is called the 'eagle
dollar.' "[110] Chen Cunren analyzed the old adage "Do not expose one's
whiteness," or "Do not reveal one's wealth," as referring to the "white gold"
of the *yuanbao* or silver, and later to silver dollars.

According to Chen Cunren's record, early silver dollars were called
silver cakes in Shanghai, and he had seen one with his own eyes. These
silver cakes, minted in the sixth year of the Xianfeng era (1856), were for
the most part privately minted by wealthy families in the "sand boat"
(*shachuan*) business. They could be considered locally produced silver
dollars and appeared earlier than officially authorized silver dollars such
as the dragon dollar. It was stipulated that each cake contain 0.5 ounces
of silver, and they were struck by hand. The objective was to avoid squab-
bling over the weight of bits of silver when wages were paid every month.
The most popular of these silver cakes was produced by the wealthy
Shanghai merchant Wang Yongsheng. Some monetary historians say it
was made with a silver mold. Eventually, prolific imitation and debased
silver content brought an end to private minting.[111] It is mostly these
imitations that subsequent generations have seen, and Chen Cunren
may not have seen the genuine article.

The short-lived silver cake indicates the basic reason for the success of the foreign silver dollars. Currency is a medium of exchange in a market with fair competition, and ultimately the success of the foreign silver dollar was the result of the aforementioned Qing dynasty currency chaos. In conditions of chaotic and inferior currency production, foreign silver dollars became popular for their elegance and their standardized quality, and they existed in dozens of types. It is worth mentioning that even when silver cakes were minted in 1856, Spanish silver dollars still circulated widely in Shanghai's local markets; that was the Spanish real or "local foreign silver dollar" (*benyang*).

The popularity of foreign silver dollars, apart from creating convenience, also spurred China's further silverization, which triggered considerable controversy. The government at one point intended to prohibit the circulation of foreign silver dollars; in the ninth year of the Daoguang era (1892), an imperial edict stated:

> For years, the silver coins of the foreign barbarians, going by the names large topnot, small topnot, tanglehead, bat, double column and horse-sword,[112] have been used in-country not for buying goods, but only for buying silver; they are spent in secret, each exchanged for domestic fine silver [*wenyin*] at a discount of two to three parts. Foreign money has gradually come into vogue from Fujian, Guangdong, Jiangxi, Zhejiang, and Jiangsu to all provinces south of the Yellow River. Foreign silver dollars are used to pay taxes and in trade between merchants. Foreign vessels, in the name of trading goods, have spread foreign silver dollars to all provincial ports, purchasing *wenyin* with the result that the amount of domestic silver taels depletes by the day and the amount of foreign silver dollars increases by the day. This may be the reason why silver has become more expensive in recent years.

Yet the convenience of foreign silver dollars made them consistently popular, and the Great Qing Empire's government itself became dependent on foreign silver dollars for tax revenue and in paying foreign reparations.

Ironically, the foreign silver dollars that accumulated in private hands over hundreds of years continued to exist right up until the silver standard ended. Quite a few of these foreign silver dollars ended up in the government's coffers during the *jinyuanquan* turmoil. One foreign journalist recorded the government's policy during the *jinyuanquan* era: "It compelled the people, under threat of arrest and by forcible house search, to surrender their gold, silver, Mexican dollars and all foreign currency to the central bank."[113]

Using Silver and Losing Monetary Sovereignty?

Both the early silver and the later foreign silver dollars arrived because China could not produce enough silver to keep up with demand: "China's currency problem was that it had copper but no gold and silver; only when the Qing dynasty used the silver dollar as a monetary standard did this cease to be a problem."[114]

The enduring popularity of Ming dynasty silver and foreign silver dollars can be considered the wonder of China's monetary history. There have always been people who see this as a shift of monetary sovereignty overseas, and even believe it was related to the depressing national destiny of the Ming and Qing. The nineteenth-century observations of missionary and Sinologist Samuel Wells Williams are often cited when questioning China's lack of monetary sovereignty: "The absence of a national coinage in the precious metals among so commercial a people as the Chinese, is so singular an exception to the general usage, even of Asiatic nations, that one is led to inquire into the reasons for it."[115]

What is monetary sovereignty? An Internet dictionary defines it as "a country's ultimate and exclusive authority over its legal tender, without interference from foreign countries." This concept sounds plausible enough and is still often used today when discussing the *renminbi* issue, but is it appropriate to apply to the Ming and Qing dynasties? Does talking of monetary sovereignty without a sovereign currency show condescension to our forebears? Some people cite the late Qing minister Zhang Zhidong's[116] comment as a footnote on monetary sovereignty: "Currency is the country's great government; a country has its national authority, that is, a country has a national currency and never allows other country's money."

In fact, Zhang Zhidong had reasons for boycotting foreign currency; his attitude toward foreign currency and subsequently toward reform of the monetary system should be ascribed to pragmatism rather than nationalism. Observing the profitability of silver dollars, he was an early advocate of creating China's silver *yuan:* In 1889, the Qing government approved a test minting of silver currency by the Guangdong Silver Dollar Office. This is how China's earliest machine-processed silver dollar came into being: the Guangdong "dragon dollar" minted at the suggestion of Zhang Zhidong.[117]

Foreign silver dollars spurred the emergence of China's machine-minted silver dollars; the two were not mutually exclusive and provided people with more choices in an era of upheaval. I have repeatedly emphasized that currency is a competitive game, and even back then there were people who also thought that way. In 1890 the Ningbo provincial governor sponsored a literary competition at the arts and crafts institute. The topic of the essay was: "Foreign money circulates in all of the southeastern provinces, and Chinese feel this harms trade. Should our country mint its own gold and silver currency? Would self-minted currency be able to circulate unimpeded? Would this be better for our country, or would the drawbacks be greater than the benefits?" The provincial governor personally read the papers and awarded top prize to a Mr. Yang, who had been a successful candidate in the provincial imperial examination in Guangdong. This prize-winning essay argued as follows: "The inflow of foreign money is in fact difficult to obstruct. It is likewise difficult to prohibit its use by ordinary people. While exhausting our country's money and commodities, foreign money is popular among the people, and nothing can be done about it. I believe the only way to stem the flow of silver out of our country is to mint our own silver currency."[118] This seemed to represent the consensus at the time. Alicia Little disapproved, however: "So far each Viceroy seems to be setting up his own mint, irrespective of others. The idea of a Central Government, managing the customs, posts, coinage, or even the army and navy, is altogether alien to the Chinese mind."[119]

The problem was that even though foreign silver dollars spurred China to produce its own silver dollar, the Chinese *yuan* was never able to drive out foreign money, and its quality never matched that of the foreign silver dollars. Steven Ng-sheong Cheung, although not a numismatist, sees this as common sense: "In the past, China's currency mainly used silver as its standard, so it was a standard system. How could they make a profit? There was little profit in minting and issuing silver currency: Its currency value was only the market value of the silver itself plus the minting cost. The value would not rise above this price, because countless silver currencies were coming in from outside, and the market accepted them."[120]

Regarding the criticism that silver caused China to lose its monetary sovereignty, one contemporary train of thought traces the blame back to the Ming dynasty and holds that the Ming should not have used silver. One scholar criticizes mercantilism: "The value that the Ming dynasty attached to merchants, especially the export merchants of the southeastern coastal region, encouraged the development of commerce and foreign trade, but the price paid for that was the country's loss of monetary sovereignty and hence also its capacity for social integration."[121] This criticism of foreign silver dollars and of silver generally has reached the point of blaming it for national rise and decline.

Some scholars in Taiwan believe that China lacked a concept of monetary sovereignty; although for a time it issued paper currency and bronze and copper coins that other countries found desirable, in the Ming dynasty it used silver but didn't create a silver dollar stamped with a national symbol or portrait of a head of state, and ultimately the currency supply fell entirely under external control: "From a modern perspective, it was like some countries with unstable policies and intense commodity price inflation abandoning their own currency and adopting the U.S. dollar or the Euro. The problem is that China was a major country, and adopting such a policy was tantamount to unpinning an unstable country or region and creating one's own upheaval."[122]

Evaluating monetary sovereignty and monetary policy dependency often views the past from today's perspective. Monetary sovereignty, monetary policy dependency, and so on are part of a monetary system and reflect a country's society and economy. Understanding this "chaos" in fact means also understanding the complexity of China at that time. Peng Xinwei observes that if viewed through modern eyes, China's pre-modern currency didn't have a system to speak of, but by relaxing standards somewhat, "each of these historical measures, no matter how chaotic or unreasonable, can be considered a system."

Setting aside the varying assertions of historical fact (for instance, the reasons for the Ming dynasty's attitude toward maritime trade and its passive fiscal policies), so-called dependent monetary policy had very different connotations in the past than it does today.

Is monetary sovereignty really so important? Does silver or the silver dollar involve externalizing monetary sovereignty or even greater potential perils? Viewed rationally, currency is a competitive game, and countries can't avoid affecting each other; it's very difficult for an independent monetary policy to exist in the real world, and so-called independence actually refers more to the independence of the central bank from the government mechanism. In the paper currency era, printing paper money had almost no cost, but in the precious metals era, gold and silver were themselves a commodity, and they became popular as the result of trade. The inflow and outflow of precious metals ultimately has a tipping point (like Hume's Price-Specie Flow Mechanism): "It seems a maxim almost self-evident, that the prices of every thing depend on the proportion between commodities and money, and that any considerable alteration on either has the same effect, either of heightening or lowering the price. Encrease the commodities, they become cheaper; encrease the money, they rise in their value. As, on the other hand, a diminution of the former, and that of the latter, have contrary tendencies."[123]

It cannot be denied that economic development is a process of economic monetization. The emergence of silver undoubtedly accelerated China's economic vitality in the Ming and Qing, triggering a series of economic consequences. On the surface, silver looks like the primer, but it all began with the backward political system.

Another concept, so-called monetary system dependency, in the precious metals era essentially resulted from the production of silver not keeping up with economic demand. As mentioned before, currency sovereignty was not a serious problem in the precious metals era; after all, the conceptions of many sovereign currencies and even nation-states actually derive from a subsequent theoretical framework. First of all, even though the comparative prices of silver and gold differ in various countries, they are themselves also commodities and don't materialize out of nowhere. The amount of silver may involve the distribution of wealth, but it is essentially a trade problem. Of course, the Chinese economy was forced to pay the price of unrest created by money's relative value, but other countries have also encountered similar difficulties. Second, national currencies in the sovereign sense are also a product of recent history and weren't acquired through competition; this is a point we must engrave in our memories when discussing currency sovereignty. Finally, even in the paper currency era, if a small country chooses to give up its power to choose its monetary policies and instead chooses the currency of another country (such as the United States), the effect is not easily judged as positive or negative. It may pay the price of losing the initiative when facing a crisis, but it also prevents that country from abusing its sovereign credit; after all, the credit of the U.S. central bank is better than that of the central banks of most countries. Therefore, monetary sovereignty really only has practical significance with the rise of a nation-state and its fiduciary currency. Although the concept of currency sovereignty seems self-evident today, it only came to be widely accepted by the various countries of the world in the twentieth century.

Placed in the historical setting, the so-called thinness or lack of Chinese currency sovereignty was a common failing of the precious metals era, and also a feature of the backwardness of China's currency system. China's former disorderly currency system looks like a paradise of free competition to today's proponents of denationalized currency, but for commerce it created a pure hell of troublesome and trivial exchange rates that had not improved even in the Republican era. Arthur N. Young, who spent many years as a foreign consultant to the Nationalist government, appraised China's monetary system by saying that China had "unquestionably the worst currency to be found in any important country."[124] Young went to China with a financial planning commission in the 1920s, and continued serving as financial advisor to the Nationalist government until 1947.

The popularity of foreign silver dollars therefore had much to do with the inadequately competitive native silver tael. Foreign silver dollars provided a good choice for the public, so what's wrong with that? Compared with the decentralization of minting privileges in European history, it created competition between currencies and financial innovation, and also restricted the ability of state rulers to expropriate the wealth of the general population through undervalued currency. The use of national financial security as a pretext for obstructing public welfare is actually not exceptional, in ancient times or in the present—a fact that deserves further consideration.

The basic reason for the popularity of silver and foreign silver dollars, apart from a weak sovereign currency mentality or the government's financial impotence, included the factor of China's backward minting technology (high minting costs were originally the main reason for the existence of private coin minting). In the absence of a sovereign currency mentality or even a sovereign state mentality, it is a luxury to talk of sovereign currency, and even more illusory to blame it for the stagnation and backwardness of China's development in the Ming and Qing dynasties. Silver was a crucial thread, and it led to many changes in Ming and Qing society, but the basic reason was this fossilized system's slow response to a changing world. It wasn't as if there weren't attempts at a sovereign currency; we can see examples in the Ming and Qing. But a central government without credit issuing a fiduciary currency can only bring about the ruin of empire.

The Sino-Japanese War of 1894–1895: The Divergent Fate of the Gold Standard in China and Japan

The Opium Wars undeniably scarred China, but the greatest blow came from the Sino-Japanese War of 1894–1895. After this war, the fates of China and Japan moved in diametrically opposite directions. One result was that the gold standard took root in Japan, while China merely brushed past it.

There are different narratives about this war even today, and many historical details provide food for thought. One train of thought is that this was a local war for China, but a long-planned, all-out war for Japan, and Japan's confrontation of China under its whole-nation system. Its outcome sent the two countries in different directions and also caused China enormous damage, especially as an attack from a neighboring country. The Sino-Japanese War's final balance of power has been appraised this way in the West: "From beginning to end, the Sino-Japanese War had been an unmitigated disaster. In the peace negotiations, China's most effective bargaining point was not the remaining strength of her military and naval forces, but rather Japanese guilt over the wounding of [Li Hongzhang] by a Japanese fanatic."[125]

The Treaty of Shimonoseki (1895) stipulated that China pay reparations of 200 million taels of silver. At that time the Qing government's fiscal revenues were only around 70 million taels, and Japan's fiscal revenues were only 80 million Japanese yen. Former Japanese minister of foreign affairs Inoue Kaoru said with no little delight: "Before these reparations, Japan's financial ministry never expected to have hundreds of millions of yen. Its entire revenues were only 80 million Japanese yen. So when we thought about having 350 million yen pouring in, the government and citizens all immediately enjoyed a sense of incomparable wealth."[126] The reparations from the Sino-Japanese War gave Japan enormous space to maneuver. Its national budget instantly doubled in scale compared to before the war, reaching 152.5 million yen, and the proportion of GNP for local government expenditure also doubled. This was enormous wealth that tremendously nurtured the rise of Japan. One of its most important effects was to serve as a reserve fund for adopting a gold standard, while the rise of financial conglomerates (*zaibatsu*) such as Mitsui paved Japan's road to capitalism.

Even before the Sino-Japanese War, the Japanese government realized the importance of finance to the development of the state and had repeatedly studied and discussed a currency system. The government in the early years of the Meiji Restoration was not in a good financial state; the official currency encountered repeated devaluations, and a plan to adopt the gold standard was declared a failure. One of the main problems with the gold standard was the inadequate supply of reserve funds. China's "compensation" to Japan of 200 million taels of silver (with a later addition of 30 million taels for "ransom of the Liaodong Peninsula"), which converted into 364.86 million yen, allowed Japan to finally adopt the gold standard in 1897.

Why did Japan take the direction of a gold standard while China did not? First, China's heavy reliance on silver discouraged a shift to the gold standard. While Chinese tend to harp on monetary sovereignty, what should be discussed is the issue of the monetary system versus the state system. Japan was the main Asian country that enjoyed monetary sovereignty while also successfully shifting to the gold standard, but Japan's monetary sovereignty was reflected not only in producing its own silver, but also in minting its own currency.

Japan's situation was a little different from China's. *Economic History of Japan: 1600–2000* states that during the Shogunate Period, Japan had a triple currency system—that is, gold, silver, and copper cash were all in general use. Japan's geographical disparity resulted in gold always having a certain status. Typically, western Japan had more silver-rich mountains, so during the Edo period, people in the Kansai region used silver, while in eastern Japan, gold-rich mountains were more common, so people in the Kanto region used gold. In earliest times, silver was widely used as weighed currency, but denominated currencies were repeatedly issued during the Shogunate Period. The name of Tokyo's famous Ginza commercial district, which means "silver seat," originated in the Edo period because there had always been silver currency mints there. The placename counterpart is Kinza—"gold seat." At that time Japan used the gold currency unit *shu* to issue its silver currency. (Japanese gold currency was denominated in *ryo, bu,* and *shu.* A *ryo,* based on the Chinese tael, was around fifteen grams, one *ryo* was equal to four *bu,* one *bu* was equal to four *shu.*) This more convenient denominated currency gradually replaced the original weighted currency, and gold and silver currencies were integrated using the same units of *ryo, bu,* and *shu.* Soon after the fall of the shogunates, by the second year of the Meiji era (1869), weighed gold and silver coins composed only 2.7 percent of Japan's currency. Japan then converted to the gold standard, avoiding the conversion of one system of measurement into another as in China, and allowing Japan's smooth transition into its yen system. In comparison, the West was using coins centuries before the Common

Era; Japan's coins came 2,000 years later, while China didn't began issuing machine-minted coins until the Qing dynasty was at the point of collapse, hundreds of years later than Japan.

Second, Japan's conversion to the gold standard wasn't completed until the end of the nineteenth century. Here it is necessary to mention one outstanding individual who prevailed over dissent to actively reform the system, Prime Minister Matsukata Masayoshi. Matsukata, who was from a samurai family, led Japan's financial administration for more than twenty years starting in 1881. A major decline in international silver prices at the end of the nineteenth century indirectly spurred the flourishing of Japan's exports and the rise of its industries. Observing that India, as a British colony, had adopted the gold standard in 1893, Matsukata overrode internal divisions to force through conversion to a modern currency system based on the gold standard. Japan also carried out a series of reforms. The first was the drafting of banking regulations in 1882, which stipulated that only the central Bank of Japan was authorized to issue paper currency, and the second was the use of reparations from the Sino-Japanese War to adopt the gold standard in 1897.

At that time, the gold standard was a world trend. Adopting the gold standard allowed Japan to control the upsurge in investment among the Japanese while also gaining international endorsement of the Japanese yen, which facilitated international investment in Japan. Even more important, the gold standard not only enabled Japan to engage in business after the Sino-Japanese War, but also allowed Japan to join the international monetary system dominated by England, which became a prerequisite for Japan and England to join forces in the Russo-Japanese War.

Finally, an examination of Chinese and Japanese currency from the political angle also produces different scenarios. As everyone knows, an optimal monetary and financial system is of major significance to a country's industrial takeoff, and in terms of monetary systems, China and Japan had a twenty-year time gap: Japan minted its "dragon dollar" in 1870, while Guangdong minted China's first "dragon dollar" in 1887. The Japanese yen was born in 1871, when Japan made its first unsuccessful attempt to adopt the gold standard. The Bank of Japan was established in 1882, and China began producing machine-minted coins that same year. The Imperial Bank of China was established in 1897, and the Great Qing Government Bank (Daqing Bank) in 1905.

Twenty years are a flash in the pan of history, but are of crucial importance in an era of dramatic change. Falling twenty years behind caused China to miss the time window for the gold standard, which meant missing a historic opportunity. The gold standard and fiduciary currency became mainstream practice all over the world in the late nineteenth century. China also wanted to join this historical tide, but domestic disputes and wrangles over the distribution of benefit slowed the process down every step of the way. The systemic backwardness of the late Qing discouraged a unilateral push toward monetary or financial reforms, and prevented turning back what Aleksandr Solzhenitsyn termed the Red Wheel of history.

The Sino-Japanese War thrust the empire deeper into its nightmare and triggered a series of political disasters. As Yun Yuding commented at the end of the Qing: "Military defeat in 1894, regime change in 1898, the attempted deposing and replacing of the Guangxu Emperor in 1899, the Boxer Rebellion in 1900, although different in name were in fact mutually engendering events that should be regarded as a ten-year political situation." In economic terms, in the midst of change China continued to rely on silver, and changes to silver in the international market had even more direct effects on China. The intensity of these changes triggered economic and political convulsions that weren't sorted out until the 1930s.

In retrospect, Japan managed to climb aboard the express train of that era and establish the monetary foundation for its subsequent industrial revolution and economic takeoff. The majority of the reparations paid by China went toward Japan's military expenses and allowed the untrammeled development of Japan's military prowess, foreshadowing the militarism to come. In the words of Japan's prime minister in the 1950s, Ishibashi Tanzan: "When we launched the Sino-Japanese War, not a single person opposed the war, a source of regret to this day. Likewise, on the eve of the Russo-Japanese War, there was inadequate argument against launching the war, and this is truly regrettable." Ishibashi is considered a representative figure of the "Small Japan" policy, but his liberalism was incompatible with the fanatical "Great Japan" policy that engulfed everything at that time.

China's and Japan's Different Traditions during the Edo Period

After a temporary divergence in the seventeenth century, the currencies and national fates of China and Japan converged once more in the nineteenth century. How did they start so close together—with the popularity of China's Ming and Qing copper coins in East Asia and its embrace of silver—and then end up so far apart, with Japan minting its own silver yen and then those yen flowing into China? The answer may require tracking Japan and China's different traditions during the Edo period.

China and Japan are separated by only 110 nautical miles,[127] enough to keep them apart, but also close enough for them to learn from each other. The two cultures had enormous differences, as described by this Republican-era observer: "China and Japan diverge in surface area and population by a multiple of ten, but diverge in culture by a multiple of thousands."[128] Japan was the Orient in the eyes of the world, but an outlier in the eyes of Asians, including themselves. In terms of geography, Japan lies east of the Asian continent and west of the Pacific Ocean, with all of its borders within Asian waters; Japan's environment is both closed and open, and apart from 1853, when the American naval fleet under Commodore Matthew Perry opened Japan's closed door, it was able to withstand repeated invasion attempts, including by Mongolian armored cavalry and then by England and Russia. This is why Japan was always able to accept foreign culture but also to close its door and absorb this culture independently.

Nagasaki was Japan's main door to the outside world during the Edo period. At that time, Japan's main trade was with China and Holland. Japan's trade with Holland has attracted considerable interest because of subsequent Westernization, but its trade with China also had distinctive qualities and even more widespread effect; it's only that as the increasingly modernizing Japan became distanced from China, its past trade with China became wittingly or unwittingly overlooked. The Japanese always say that Nagasaki's foreign flavor was in fact a Chinese flavor, and many Edo-period customs were deeply influenced by China. Furthermore, in the early Meiji period, Japan's study of European and

American works benefited from the depth and pervasiveness of Chinese studies in its intellectual class: "It would have been impossible for European and American culture to be introduced without the foundation of Chinese studies."[129]

History is a piece of wind-battered paper, with misreadings and obstructions everywhere. Apart from widespread Sino-Japanese trade, China also had a significant effect on Japan's modernization, even if only as a negative example.

Japan paid close attention to what was happening in China, and Japan's profound sense of crisis in China's experience in the Opium Wars made an "unconscious contribution" to Japan's modernization. In 1838, on the eve of the Opium War, a member of one of the Tokugawa shogunate's "three great houses," Tokugawa Nariaki, made a startling prophesy: "Japan will be the first target of the West's attack; China is too large, and the Ryukyu Archipelago and Korea are too small to attract the notice of the gunboats."

Japan drew lessons from China's experience, both positive and negative, from the Tang to the Qing; as the saying goes: "Drawing China's invisible threads to weave a splendid brocade for Japan." China's defeat in the Opium War in 1840 shocked the shogunate, and when the four powerful gunboats under the command of American commodore Matthew Perry appeared in 1853, the shogunate surrendered and opened its doors at Shimoda and Hakodate. The subsequent Unequal Treaties triggered resentment that led to the shogunate's political bankruptcy and the arrival of the Meiji Restoration.

The Opium Wars occurred in China rather than Japan, and this gave Japan time and led the shogunate to change its attitude toward overseas visitors even before the "black ship incident." But China did not have this time window, and the 1840 Opium War not only became a symbolic incident in Chinese history, but also changed Asian history. When the Japanese shogunate received news of the Opium War from Dutch boat captains, the fact that Tokugawa Nariaki's prophecy had been wrong did not dispel Japan's sense of crisis, but rather triggered even more discussion as a harbinger of things to come.

We know that many modern Chinese terms came from Japanese, for example, *quanwei* (authority), *quanyi* (rights and interests), *zhuyi* (doctrine), *geming* (revolution), and so on, but the modern exchanges between China and Japan were not one-way. A notable example is Wei Yuan's *Illustrated Treatise on the Maritime Kingdoms*. Chinese history books quote its famous saying "Learn the barbarians' skills to restrain the barbarians," but have otherwise ignored it, while in Japan this book initiated a great deal of discussion. For example, the late Edo scholar Sakuma Shōzan referred to Wei Yuan as a "comrade from another country," and drew salutary lessons from China's experiences in deciding that Japan had to step into "the top ranks of the world's powerful nations": "In today's world, we have learned from China that if we don't include the five continents and the greater economy, we will not be able to cope." This was not unrelated to the 1885 work "Escape from Asia" by Fukuzawa Yukichi.[130]

According to research by the Japanese historian Osamu Ōba, *Illustrated Treatise on the Maritime Kingdoms* was first introduced to Japan in 1851 in a batch of just three copies; because it involved content on the Western world it was initially regarded as a banned book. Shipping records for books can provide a glimpse of how the situation changed over time. The record for the first batch states, "This item has content banned by imperial decree." Eventually demand increased: "By the Edo its price was 100 times higher, and it became a book in urgent demand by the emperor." The *Illustrated Treatise* was reprinted in more than twenty editions over the next two years.

Osamu Ōba believes this transformation reflected "the different understanding of the situation between policy-makers and their subordinates." It is worth noting that another work by Wei Yuan, *A Military History of the Sacred Dynasty,* was introduced to Japan in 1844 and was also favorably received. Masuda Wataru's posthumously published *The Eastern Movement of Western Learning and Conditions in China* states that *A Military History of the Sacred Dynasty* "greatly influenced" Japanese thinking. Furthermore, a book that described the resistance of people in Zhapu during the Opium War (*Collective Chant of Zhapu*) became lost in China, but appeared in Japan in a copied block-print edition. This shows how closely Japan observed China before the First Opium War, out of self-interest, but also sympathy. This sympathy could not be sustained, however, and Chinese indulgence in opium led Japan to adopt a more contemptuous attitude and even anticipate taking a share of the spoils.

At the same time that it fell into the silver trap, China encountered the Opium Wars and the Taiping Heavenly Kingdom movement, while Japan pushed forward with its Meiji Restoration. This created a shift in the relative strength of China and Japan that reached its climax in the Sino-Japanese War. Comparing the differing fates of the *Illustrated Treatise on the Maritime Kingdoms* in China and Japan, Liang Qichao observed: "In today's China it is put away on a high shelf and ignored. Yet, Japan's Sakuma Shōzan, Yoshida Shōin and Saigō Takamori were all stimulated by this book, and it played an indirect role in the real-life drama of the Sonnō jōi restoration."[131]

Wei Yuan is often regarded as the first Chinese to have "opened his eyes to the world." This is an exaggeration, but regarding Wei Yuan as merely a scholar or government advisor would be underestimating him. His *Military History of the Sacred Dynasty* shows that he understood money better than most of his contemporaries. Wei Yuan demonstrates the hard struggles of China's intellectuals during an era of change, and the circulation of his ideas mirrors the changes in China and Japan.

If the war between China and Japan at the end of the sixteenth century is interpreted as the resentment of a fringe civilization toward a core civilization, by the end of the nineteenth century, the difference between Japan and China was that between a superior and an inferior civilization. In the eleventh year of the Guangxu era (1885), which was the eighteenth year of the Meiji era, Enlightenment thinker Fukuzawa Yukichi described the situation in this way: "The spread of civilization is like the measles. The current measles epidemic in Tokyo spread from Nagasaki in the west toward the east, expanding with the warm spring climate. Much as we may loathe the harm this epidemic causes, is there a feasible method to guard against it? I do not in fact know of such a method. The intense force of a purely harmful epidemic is such, not to mention that of civilization, which brings with it even greater harm and benefit. Not only can we not obstruct civilization, but we should do our best to help its spread and allow our people to bathe in the atmosphere of civilization as soon as possible; this is the wise course."[132] Ultimately, the elites of Meiji-era Japan decided on the three great objectives of "industrial vitalization, constitutional government and withstanding external enemies," and succeeded in all of them. The classic success of the cotton textile industry established the foundation for Japanese industry.

Japan's Edo period was the last period of feudal rule. It has often been described as a closed country at that time, but there was no Iron Curtain—while closed off, Japan also sought to develop all kinds of trade. The Edo period's influence on Japanese society was similar to that of the Middle Ages in Europe; it is often regarded ambivalently and as a focus of controversy, but more recent appraisals do not see the "closed off" Edo period as a dark and undeveloped time, but rather as a politically stable era of expansion and vitality.[133] Grain yield ("actual volume") during the entire Edo period increased 240 percent. People had more and better-quality clothing, transitioning from the linen and burlap of the past to cotton by the end of the seventeenth century, and then to increasingly popular silk products. The Edo period's enhancement of agricultural output, increase in trade, and development of the printing industry can be regarded as foreshadowing the industrialized society that was to come.[134] Without the transition of the Edo period, how could the Meiji Restoration have arrived?

Going a step further, compared with the West's external assault bringing the opening of Japan's ports, some explanations also hold that Japan, before opening its ports, was a "closed country that was smashed open." For example, Japanese historian Shisō Hattori maintains that at the end of the Shogunate Period, Japan was already in a "strictly workshop handicraft stage," and believes this is "the single rational way" to explain the domestic and diplomatic relations of the late Shogunate Period. In this respect Japan was unable to discard feudal society, while on the other hand this became the "critical moment" for surmounting a semicolonial crisis like China's.[135]

After comparing it with the unified China of the seventeenth to nineteenth centuries, Japan should also be compared with the rest of the world. In fact, Japan's nineteenth-century constitution was modeled on Prussia's, and given Japan's subsequent history, China has typically compared Japan with Germany when making international comparisons. Japan itself, however, has tended to boast of being the England of Asia as the Asian country that industrialized earliest.

In fact, the political structure of Japan's shogunate era had some commonality with Europe. Historian Samuel E. Finer regarded Japan as being the closest to Europe by some measures.[136]

On the surface, the Tokugawa shogunate occupied one-fourth of the country's land, with the leaders of nearly 100 vassal states submitting to it, but each vassal state had considerable political and economic freedom. For example, the Tsushima domain (or local feudal regime) went so far as to forge a state document apologizing for Toyotomi Hideyoshi's invasion of Korea in order to reestablish trade with Korea in the seventeenth century. The various domains also issued their own paper currencies in order to resolve money shortages. The earliest such record is for the Fukui domain in 1661. The issuance of currency in different regions triggered currency competition and the creation of credit, and even the preconditions for subsequent reforms to securitize currency. At that time, Japanese society was divided into four classes: samurai, farmers, workers, and merchants. The samurai were warriors, and although farmers had no freedom of movement and were regarded as bound to the land, they ranked second among the classes because of the importance of agriculture to the feudal states. Most agricultural production was by small clans, and in years when taxes were adequate, farmers enjoyed a measure of autonomy. The emperor was the nominal ruler, but the generals or *kanpaku* were the country's actual rulers, and their various major and minor vassals were effectively the feudal lords of their own land.

In this way Japan's political structure was in fact very similar to Europe's feudal lord system. Of course, beneath this superficial resemblance was an essential difference, which was the noncontractual nature of Japanese rule. It is worth noting that rebellion was relatively uncommon during the decline of the shogunates; in most cases, Japanese-style feudal relations were only vertical, with no parallel-rank relations. Local feudal lords had no real privileges vis-à-vis the central rulers, much less was there the potential for the emergence of anything like the Court of Marchers, which settled disputes between the king and feudal lords; any attempt to rise above one's station exacted an enormous price. For this reason, Japanese-style rule had a "police state" legal system, but no opportunity to foster the rule of law. Loyalty was always toward the individual, while the overall system was actually extremely fragile. This meant that the systemic setup under the Tokugawa shogunate was riddled with distrust and would not give rise to a genuine leading civilization. Of course, these longstanding factors also laid a certain transformational foundation for Japan's Meiji Restoration, while possibly causing Japan to pay a price in its modernization process.

Sino-Japanese trade flourished at one point, typically in the form of Chinese goods exchanged for Japanese silver. Japanese silver streamed into China from the Ming dynasty onward, but trade between the two countries had already been interrupted by the time Toyotomi Hideyoshi dispatched troops to Korea in 1592, and the shogunate also gradually put controls on trade from the end of the seventeenth century onward out of concern over the outflow of precious metals. The early Qing government in the seventeenth century issued a "maritime border removal decree" that forcibly evacuated towns and villages on the southeastern coast in an attempt to "eliminate the illicit trade on which [Ming loyalist Zheng Chenggong] had built an economically prosperous and, for the [Qing] at least, militarily dangerous maritime empire that stretched from Nagasaki to Southeast Asia."[137] At that time, the Zheng clan had accumulated a large amount of silver from trade with Japan, of which a considerable amount had flowed into China. The policy eventually forced the surrender of Zheng and his allies in their last stronghold, Taiwan, but at the expense of trade.

The story of silk and silver, like the national fates of China and Japan, started a new chapter after the Opium Wars, and the tide reversed. Chinese silk, tea, and other products were very popular in Japan and in the world marketplace, but most of these products did not have unique core competitive strength, and the advantage quickly disappeared as Japan emulated and overtook China's trade. In the typical example of raw silk, Japan was able to find substitutes for Chinese products on its home ground while also acquiring substitute products through alternative trade channels such as the Dutch and the Zheng clan. Imitating China in trade, Japanese raw silk began usurping the status of Chinese silk on the international market. In 1880, Chinese silk exports were five times those of Japan, but by 1935, Japan's silk exports were six times those of China.[138] Taiwanese scholar Lin Man-Houng sees the Opium

Wars as the watershed, with the trend becoming especially apparent from 1850 to 1880. China, with its influx of silver, contented itself with its existing technology and gave no thought to forging ahead, while Japan sought to squeeze into the market through a major effort to elevate its technology. The ultimate result was Japanese silk of "superior quality" to Chinese silk.[139]

The Sino-Japanese War of 1894–1895 looks like a major bifurcation in the national fates of China and Japan, but their fates had already been written much earlier. God has no ill intentions, but historical logic is a succession of close links. Perhaps it was the Edo period's turbulent undercurrent that caused China's and Japan's fates to converge in the "seventeenth-century crisis" and then to take separate roads in the nineteenth century. If the "seventeenth-century crisis" was more a natural crisis of dynastic change, the crisis that occurred in the nineteenth century was a modernist decisive moment. The dividing line between China and Japan in the nineteenth century was not only in their different monetary systems, but even more in the divergent pace of their modernization. As Japan began its modernization, war between China and Japan became inevitable; Fukuzawa Yukichi even referred to the Sino-Japanese War as a war between "civilization and barbarism."

History always knocks twice, first as comedy and then possibly as tragedy. Comparing China and Japan always provides food for thought. When the former Celestial Empire suzerain state became a barbaric land in the eyes of its neighboring country, change was inevitable. The process of modernization was mutually provoked and backfed, and China welcomed in another era of "self-strengthening."

From Pound Loss to Currency Reform

In the age of paper currency, China was constantly wary of inflation, and during the commodity currency era, monetary tightening was the norm. Dynasties that lacked paper currency typically suffered money famines, as in this record: "In recent years, public and private and the upper and lower classes all suffer from the lack of money. Goods cannot be obtained, and the people feel hard-pressed, calling it a money famine."[140] For China, silver was so important that it could be called the lifeblood of the economy. The silver supply long relied on imports from abroad, while currency actually circulated more among the general populace and less within the central government, which could be considered to have no monetary policy. Rising and declining external supply caused many changes during the late Qing. That is why the silver–copper cash exchange ratio is a crucial context for understanding social change in the late Ching; the chaos of war, "revival," and even the reforms of the late Qing were all critically related to silver.

Looking back at the bumper years of the Daoguang era, intense fluctuations in the silver–copper cash exchange ratio caused Chinese society to suffer instability; both money famines and silver famines seriously affected the empire's political stability, with famine and surplus both bringing their own hardships. At that time someone wrote: "The list of banned exports includes copper cash, rice, millet, and beans. It has caused yesterday's silver famine and today's copper cash famine, both of which bring suffering."[141]

That is why the idea of monetary reform sprang up in the late Qing. What started this train of thought? The late Qing's monetary system reform had internal and external reasons, but all involved diplomatic negotiations. External factors lay in overseas commercial and political forces giving rise to hopes that China would unify its currency, for the sake of their own convenience and benefit. For example, the Sino-British Treaty of 1902 (the Mackay Treaty) specifically referred to a national currency and touched on rectifying the tax system, standardizing measurements, and trademark protection, among other progressive content. Sir Robert Hart, who for many years served as an inspector general for China's Imperial Maritime Custom Service, remarked that if the great powers had completely accepted the treaty, and if China had executed it in full, it would have resulted in improvements.[142]

A domestic factor also related to convenience. For example, in reparation payments, pound loss (a loss suffered in the exchange rate) became routine, and foreign silver dollars also affected China's seigniorage (coin tax). In the most extreme example, after the Treaty of Nanking was signed in 1842, the Qing government paid England reparations of 21 million silver dollars. Because of problems with the silver content of Chinese silver dollars and tael silver, China ultimately paid the reparations in Mexican silver dollars at a conversion equivalent to some 14.7 million silver taels.

With the trend at that time of gold being costly and silver being devalued, and with major countries using the gold standard, the British pound sterling became the effective international settlement currency. China, settling its accounts in silver, routinely lost out to the pound's surging exchange rate. Liang Qichao deeply resented the pound losses and felt that because China didn't use the gold standard, "as a country using silver dealing with countries using gold, when we receive repayment of debts the price of silver rises, and when we hand over a debt payment the price of silver drops. Thus we are bled dry by so-called pound loss."[143]

Pound loss reflected not only the divergent fates of gold and silver in the nineteenth century, but also the financial gulf between China and the outside world. When New World silver poured into Europe in the seventeenth and eighteenth centuries, although most European countries had adopted a bimetal standard, gold coins were much more popular. By the mid-nineteenth century, when the basic trend was declining silver prices and rising gold prices, China went in the opposite direction and became the world's main exporter of gold and importer of silver. Gold experienced a favorable trade balance for twenty-seven of the forty years from 1889 to 1929, while silver had a favorable trade balance for only fourteen years and suffered a trade deficit for twenty-five years; gold's gross trade surplus was 96,760,217 taels, while foreign silver dollars suffered a trade deficit of 627,177,427 taels.[144]

The fate of silver coins in Europe was inseparable from Gresham's Law that "bad money drives out good." Widespread freedom to mint coins was also an important factor. Under a fixed gold–silver exchange rate, when the market exchange rate differed from the statutory exchange rate, the currency that had a higher market exchange rate than the statutory exchange rate (good money) would gradually decrease, and the currency with a market exchange rate lower than the statutory exchange rate (bad money) would steadily increase. For example, silver's market price was higher than its actual value, which meant that silver was overpriced and also that gold was underpriced, so people would melt gold coins and spend silver coins. The ultimate result was that the number of gold coins in the market steadily decreased.[145]

The Great Qing Empire's stagnation was not going to keep the outside world from moving forward. Finance evolved with the advancement of the Industrial Revolution. The discovery of silver mines in the New World made the shortcomings of bimetallism increasingly apparent. Silver became devalued, and the varying exchange ratios between the two metals routinely led to reminting and further price imbalance. For European countries, silver coins were typically where the trouble began, and the instability of currency values triggered economic fluctuations and caused heavy losses. In these countries, the importance of silver gradually dropped, and it headed toward "demonetization."

In 1717, the British pound sterling set its value against gold, and about 100 years later, in 1816, England promulgated its Coinage Act and issued gold currency, stipulating that silver currency would remain a fractional currency. As Europe advanced full steam into the Industrial Revolution in the nineteenth century, most European countries began adopting the gold standard.

The gold standard didn't mean using gold in business transactions. Although gold served as the value core in international trade, what people preferred to use was not cold metallic gold but rather the pound sterling with its stable exchange rate. Gold was already so standard before World War I that people recalling those peaceful prewar decades have the illusion of a golden era. At that time the international currency system basically used gold as international reserve capital, and the pound sterling served as the system for settling accounts. The pound became even more frequently used as the link between the currencies of various countries and gold; this was related to the status of the British economy at that time, as well as to the firm value of the pound sterling, and was also inseparable from the Bank of England's excellent operations and London's outstanding performance as an international financial center. For this reason, the system was referred to as the Sterling Exchange Standard System.

A stable gold standard established England's success, but upheavals in the silver standard tormented China. Whether one accepts the traditional viewpoint that China fell behind Western Europe after the Industrial Revolution, or goes along with Kenneth Pomeranz of the California School, who believes that the Great Divergence between East and West became most evident in the nineteenth century, there is no denying the backwardness of China in the early twentieth century. This was a comprehensive backwardness, from finance to economy, and the pound loss was just a minor footnote in its derailment from the international currency structure.

The Great Upsurge in Monetary Reform

As mentioned above, the Qing government mainly used silver in its expenditure. The government used silver for 80 percent of its payments and provisioning for the military, and encouraged and rewarded the use of silver among the general public, but small private-sector transactions still mainly used copper cash. On the other hand, the increasing importance of silver in China made the late Qing terrain very disadvantageous. By the Tongzhi period, most major countries had adopted the gold standard, and the emerging trend of expensive gold and cheap silver meant that China, as a trading nation, experienced a gradually devaluing currency, increasing trade deficits, an outflow of gold, year after year of pound losses, and chaos in its currency system. To make matters worse, fiscal chaos sparked a series of crises, especially after reparations to the invading Eight-Power Allied Forces in 1900 had to be converted into gold currency. A stable exchange rate became a matter of vital urgency, and the late Qing regime, facing the changing situation of its final years, was forced to make an effort to reform the monetary system.

The earlier narrative shows that the late Qing government had no concept of monetary policy or monetary sovereignty, and that the private-sector currency system was a mess. In the words of Republican-era economist Zhao Lanping, "Throughout the ages, our country had currency but no currency system."

There is no construction without destruction. Like so many "revival" efforts, systemic reform became a focus of discussion among late Qing elites, and reform of the currency system became a fad that divided opinion into multiple schools of thought. The brightest minds of that era chimed in, with leading thinker Liang Qichao referring to "the currency issue as financial lifeblood" and "delayed promulgation of the monetary system affecting the life and death of the nation."[146] While in Japan,

Liang had become fascinated with currency reform, seeing it as a means of saving China from extinction. This foreshadowed his subsequent appointment to key positions in finance and economics in the Beiyang government: "Since living in the east, I have wrung my hands in anguish over our country's affairs. Sorting out the monetary system and creating an efficient financial system are of top priority in saving China from collapse. Finance is a mainspring, the effective operation of which will drive the national economy and the people's livelihood." Liang Qichao's influence cannot be overestimated; he took part in many major discussions in order to keep up with the pressing economic and financial issues of the day, and eventually served as director general of the Tianjin Mint under the Republican government and later as minister of finance. He was the Isaac Newton of China.

"Currency law" became a popular term. *The Book of Han: Food and Money* states: "The Venerable Jiang established a currency law for the nine government departments of the Zhou: a square inch of gold weighing half a kilogram; a round coin with a square hole weighing one grain [*zhu*]; a bolt of cloth two feet two inches wide and four yards in length." Establishment and reform of the currency system corresponded to changes and stimuluses in the world as China began considering what kind of currency system could link it to the world.

The stands taken on monetary reform could be divided into several types. Most people endorsed a gold standard, which conformed to the world trend and would alleviate the silver crisis. Peng Xinwei has verified that people began proposing a gold standard starting in the Xianfeng period (1851–1861). A key advocate was the prefect of Shuntianfu, Hu Yufen, who during the 1895 Self-Strengthening Movement proposed minting gold, silver, and copper coins and establishing a Great Qing Government Bank (Daqing Bank) to issue paper currency.[147] A late Qing circuit intendant, Liu Shiyan, submitted *Simple Words on Coinage* in 1903, in which he also advocated a gold standard with silver and copper coins as supplementary currency, and the establishment of a national bank to issue paper currency.[148]

A Chinese envoy to Russia, Hu Weide, expressed this basic rationale in a petition to the emperor:

If China had its own national currency in the twenty-ninth year of the Guangxu era, it would rank with other nations, and would not have to worry about exchange. China [should have] gold, silver and copper coins, with a certain number of copper coins worth one silver coin, and a certain number of silver coins worth one gold coin. The ratios would be set and people would become familiar with their size, uniform in all places, far and near, used in official and private dealings without discounting, of uniform standard and easy to verify. This would constrain and repress the wrongful acts of fatuous officials and unscrupulous merchants to the benefit of the people's livelihood and the national economy. Therefore, it would be trusted in-country and overseas. In China's trade with the West, it would only be necessary to calculate normal fluctuations in the price of goods without accounting for damaging fluctuations in silver prices. Profit would be easily known and trade would flourish and accumulate; it would be beneficial in all respects.[149]

The second standpoint was to establish a gold-exchange standard, with the intention of using silver prices to establish gold prices. This was the stand taken by the inspector general of the Imperial Maritime Custom Service, Sir Robert Hart; Dutch economist G. Vissering; and others. According to Jin Guobao's *China's Currency System Problems*, Hart's plan required a new currency treasury standard, with the exchange price between silver and gold permanently fixed, and all new coins set at "eight taels to one English gold pound." Apart from minting privileges being centralized, Hart called for "the central government to establish a mint under its own control," where people could freely mint coins in accordance with the British model. Existing provincial mints would be closed down to ensure the uniformity of weight and fineness. "It was in fact a bimetal gold exchange and silver standard." All of this was an effort to first establish the weight of the gold currency and the statutory exchange ratio between gold and silver, and then gradually transition into a gold exchange standard.[150]

Also worth mentioning is a similar proposal by Jeremiah W. Jenks, a member of the International Exchange Commission established by the U.S. Congress in 1903. In his "A Detailed Discussion of China's New Dollar Laws" and "An Annotated Explanation of China's New Dollar Laws," he advocated a gold currency unit equivalent to one tael of silver, the minting of which could be requested by the people, along with the minting of silver coins at a gold–silver exchange ratio of 1:32. The Qing government would establish credit offices in London and elsewhere to buy and sell gold bills of exchange to maintain this exchange ratio. His most controversial recommendation was to have a foreign national serve as controller of the currency.[151]

A multitude of other plans also came up in the course of discussion, for example, recommending a bimetal gold and silver standard, or a silver standard operating in parallel with a gold-exchange standard. Cabinet minister Wang Daxie, who once served as ambassador to England, proposed several ways to use gold currency—for example, raising the value of the silver dollar and adjusting the gold–silver exchange ratio, or issuing gold currency to absorb the silver in the marketplace, and then redeeming the gold currency on demand with silver.[152] The ultimate objective of these plans was usually to establish a gold standard, or what could be called a virtual gold-exchange standard.

Why Silver Triumphed Once Again

In 1905, silver emerged triumphant once again as the Qing government decided to temporarily make the silver tael the standard hard currency. Gold was the world trend at that time, with major countries adopting the gold standard; Japan settled on a gold standard in 1897, and the United States also implemented a gold-standard system in 1900. So why did the silver standard ultimately triumph in the Qing dynasty's currency reforms? Judging by subsequent events, the 1904 "Jenks plan" was not only the first systematic plan in modern monetary history but may also have brought China the closest it would ever come to adopting a gold standard.

Two of the most virulent opponents of the Jenks plan were Liu Shiyan and Zhang Zhidong. As is usually the case in conceptual disputes, one reason for people being wrong was ignorance, and the other reason was personal interest. Peng Xinwei's judgment is that on the topic of currency, both the government and the public were completely out of their depth and didn't study the matter sufficiently; the reasons for opposing the various plans didn't really hold water, and even the proposers of the plans, apart from foreign experts, were all laymen. The foreign experts always encountered the harshest rebuttal simply because of their foreign status.[153] Furthermore, the pressure of "pound loss" also lessened over time.

As foreigners observed at the time, the Qing dynasty's fiscal administration and currency were extremely chaotic; the government looked unified, but in fact each level of local government enjoyed a great deal of authority and freedom. People who consider China a big, unified totalitarian country routinely overlook the capabilities and the role of local government; the asymmetry between control of money on the one hand and duties and responsibilities on the other inevitably causes local officials to scheme for access to money.

In terms of reform, strengthening central fiscal administration required centralizing financial authority and unifying the currency. Especially after the blow of the Sino-Japanese War of 1894–1895, when the price of silver dropped precipitously and China had to make payments in gold, suffering unbearable pound loss in the process, the Qing government was motivated to undertake currency reform, and foreign countries enthusiastically joined in out of self-interest. *The Cambridge History of China: The Late Ch'ing* observes that currency reform would have been hard to implement without foreign cooperation: "The Ch'ing government, together with the Mexican government which was still on the silver standard, asked the United States to cooperate on friendly terms in an effort to establish stable relations between the currencies of countries on the gold standard and those on silver."[154] The Jenks plan was therefore bound to have countries locking horns behind it, with each side reacting according to its own interests; Germany and France agreed with it, while England and Russia opposed it.

Zhang Zhidong was a key opponent of the Jenks plan, and he wielded genuine power in the Qing government at that time; in fact, he dominated the late Qing monetary reforms. Zhang believed that foreign countries used the gold standard because their high prices and high cost of living made the use of gold more convenient.

> This is not the case for China. Our people are poor and our goods are cheap. Laborers are paid meagerly, and the mass of people eat so little that their daily expenses can be calculated in copper cash ... Throughout China, silver and copper are still used together, and the area using copper is ten times as large as that using silver. The national expenditure is calculated in silver, while daily living expenses are calculated in copper cash. Foreigners consider China a nation that uses silver, but it is actually a country that uses copper. It is different in foreign countries, where goods are costly and people are wealthy, and the use of gold is advantageous. Given China's current situation, if the use of gold coins was desired, there would not be enough gold to mint them, nor would it be appropriate.[155]

Zhang Zhidong's main objections hinged on two aspects: The first revolved around principle; he felt that the gold standard was inappropriate for China because China used copper cash and seldom used gold; the decrease in silver prices was good for exports, and the 1:32 exchange ratio was also unreasonable. The second objection was emotional; in terms of nationalism, a foreign plan constituted foreign interference: "Perhaps foreigners are enticing us with material gain with the intention of curtailing our rights and cutting off our sources of profit, for instance, by engaging a foreigner to manage our finances."

It also did not escape notice that most of the countries adopting the gold-exchange system at that time were colonies, and the Jenks plan also called for foreigners to manage the currency reforms. Ultimately the plan was cold-shouldered. Jenks's monetary reform plan, although ultimately aborted, provides a glimpse of the difficulties of currency reform in the late Qing and even in contemporary China. In economic terms, it is a question of encouraging compatibility, and especially the need to consider vested interest groups. Why did Zhang Zhidong oppose the gold standard so strongly? The reasons he listed did not really stand up; it was mainly a matter of interests and benefit.

As mentioned earlier, foreign silver dollars poured in during the nineteenth century because the elegance and stable content of the machine-minted coins made them popular; coins from the Spanish real to the Mexican eagle all led the field for a time.

Fujian tried using machines to mint coins in 1885, but the idea of minting large numbers of domestic silver coins by machine originated with Zhang Zhidong: the machine-produced silver coin called the "dragon dollar" because it was stamped with a dragon. It was because of the spread of foreign coins that Zhang Zhidong, who at that time was governor general of Guangdong and Guangxi, called for minting a domestic dollar in 1887, which resulted in silver coins being minted in the Guangdong Silver Dollar Office for the first time in 1889.

This shows that vested interests remained the top priority for reformist bureaucrats such as Zhang Zhidong. Liang Qichao was always very concerned about monetary reform, and in his assessment of the various plans, he noted that "the real fight is over who is in control of the reform," which hit the nail on the head. Liang criticized the lack of professional knowledge apparent in Zhang Zhidong's writings: "I see that the *Shanghai Times* carried Hubei Governor Mr. Zhang's disparagement of the Jenks plan. On the issue of jurisdiction, I sympathize, but in discussing the flaws of the plan, he doesn't touch on economic principles and uses a lot of layman's language."[156]

Here it seems necessary to provide some details about the association between these two men. Liang Qichao and Zhang Zhidong were old acquaintances. Liang had paid his respects to Zhang many years before, and Zhang "abandoned other guests to receive him," indicating that Liang was in Zhang's good graces. Liang appraised Zhang as "one of the great and virtuous persons of our age," and even regarded himself as Zhang's pupil: "I seek him out to understand Western thought, and perceive its deep origins; I seek him out for comprehensive Chinese learning, made intensive and succinct." But their paths ultimately diverged, especially as Zhang Zhidong's waffling over the Hundred Days' Reform (1898) came under criticism. While joining in this criticism, Liang Qichao emphasized, "It is not my place to rake up Wenxiang's faults,[157] but his words are being used against the truth . . . Wenxiang's words are said to represent the views of the majority of people in China, even today. This is absurd, but it prevents good law from being implemented. There is nothing that can be done about it."[158]

In the chess game of political interests, the silver standard ultimately triumphed, and arguments over whether to use the dollar or the tael as a unit began right after that. Zhang Zhidong, Yuan Shikai, and other provincial governors advocated using the silver tael, while those who supported the silver *yuan* were mainly the Board of Revenue and Chinese and foreign merchants. History is seldom ruled by "the way things should be," and circumstances generally favor those with actual power. This time Zhang Zhidong triumphed again; in 1905, the Qing government adopted a hard currency using the silver tael as its standard, and a central mint was established in Tianjin to produce the one-tael silver coin as its main currency. The Hubu (Board of Revenue) Bank was established at the same time.

Karma came around four years later as the main supporters of the silver tael faded from the picture; for example, Zhang Zhidong died in 1909. The situation then shifted in favor of proponents of the silver dollar. In the second year of the Xuantong period (1910), the Qing government promulgated its Coinage Regulations, which stipulated a "temporary silver standard." This is considered China's earliest silver-standard regulation. The government was exclusively empowered to mint currency, and the national monetary unit was the dollar, or *yuan,* weighing 0.72 treasury ounces, with a fineness of 900 parts per thousand and a pure silver content of 0.648 treasury ounces.

Yet, Kang Youwei's 1910 book *Saving the Nation with Gold Currency* voiced this lament: "Is it not ludicrous that an ancient nation with 5,000 years of civilization and 400 million people could perish merely because of silver declining and gold rising?" The year after the Coinage Regulations were issued, the Qing dynasty diplomat Zhang Yintang also declared his persistent fealty to the gold standard: "In a situation of trade wars with foreign countries it is by no means appropriate to hesitate, while examination of the domestic economy cannot be hasty. In deliberating between the two, we must declare a currency system aiming for the gold standard and remint the legal tender, urging the people to prepare. After two or three years we can watch for an opportune moment, and implementing the gold standard will be very easy."[159]

The silver issue was never satisfactorily resolved during the Qing dynasty, and repeated discussion ultimately melted into history's lament. The main reasons that China never made progress on the currency issue can be glimpsed in the process described above. Even if the gold standard was a policy that conformed to historical trends, it was never pushed by a competent political authority, and interest groups could not be budged.

Currency reform dominated the Qing government's fading years as a last resort for national salvation, but right until the dynasty formally ended in 1911, the hoped-for unified currency never materialized. Consequently, the reform received little praise: "The new silver dollar was merely added to the old system, serving only to increase the confusion, which continued to the end of the dynasty."[160] It even led to the dollar-versus-tael dispute continuing for another quarter of a century.

Ultimately, the late Qing currency reforms didn't change the path taken by the dynasty or China, and this may have been predetermined from the outset; after all, systemic evolution transcends the scope of financial capacity. It was still a stride forward toward modernization, and the nationwide debate led to modern concepts such as currency reform and monetary sovereignty invisibly establishing roots. Financial reforms triggered by social conditions routinely need one or two generations of effort to be realized; the logic is the same, from England to China, even when their routes are different.

The Republican Era
Farewell Silver, Hello Inflation

I still remember that I had thirty or forty dollars in notes issued by the two banks [Bank of China and Bank of Communications] at the time, but I had suddenly become a pauper, almost to the point of having to forgo food, and I was more than a bit panicked. The frame of mind of the Russian rich who held paper rubles at the time of the revolution was no doubt quite similar, or at most just a bit more intense. So I could only resort to making inquiries—could banknotes be converted to silver at a discount? I was told there was no market. Fortunately, a covert market eventually developed, with bills going for just over 60 percent of their face value. I was delighted and immediately sold half of my paper money right then. Later the rate went up to 70 percent, which made me even more delighted, and I converted all my banknotes to silver, which weighed heavily in my pocket, as if representing the full weight of my existence. Had it been normal times, if a money changer shorted me even a penny, I would have found it absolutely unacceptable.

But just as I stuffed a bag of silver in my pocket and began feeling a weighty comfort and delight, another thought suddenly dawned on me: how easily we become slaves, and once it happens, we are even utterly delighted by it.

Lu Xun (1881–1936), "Jottings under Lamplight"

Gatsby was overwhelmingly aware of the youth and mystery that wealth imprisons and preserves, of the freshness of many clothes, and

of Daisy, gleaming like silver, safe and proud above the hot struggles
of the poor.

F. Scott Fitzgerald (1896–1940), The Great Gatsby

No Banks without States and No States without Banks.

Charles W. Calomiris and Stephen H. Haber, Fragile by Design

Foreign Banks Come to China

After the Manchu Emperor abdicated, the Beiyang period began.
The most important thing that the Beiyang government did during its
currency reform was promulgating the Coinage Regulations in 1913,
which formally stipulated that the currency unit would be the silver
yuan weighing 0.72 treasury ounces and with a silver content of 89 percent; this was the "Yuan Shikai dollar," known as "Big-head Yuan."
Although there were many controversies during Yuan's rule, in terms of
monetary history, the Yuan dollar was probably the most successful self-
produced currency in China's recent history. According to the memoirs
of the Republican-era writer Chen Cunren,[1] "Every silver dollar is made
of 0.72 treasury ounces of silver," with the Mexican eagle dollar setting
the standard for quality.

Let's review the currency reform of the early Beiyang period. In
February 1912, Yuan Shikai succeeded Sun Yat-sen as provisional president of the Republic of China, and the next fifteen years of rule by the
Beiyang government is called the Beiyang period.[2] Although the Beiyang period lasted only fifteen years and has been criticized for its tangled warlord battles, it can actually be considered a relatively peaceful
and worry-free time. Journalistic censorship was lifted and the economy
became quite marketized; China's economy made progress during this
time, and modern finance made its start.

The Qing dynasty fiscal system had generally continued the Ming
dynasty system. Imperial expenses were separate from state finance,
public funds were assigned to the state exchequer, and each province
had a provincial treasury. As China faced increasing external assaults,
the government needed to borrow money, but China had no banks in

the modern sense, so this obliged the government to rely on foreign banks. This eventually spurred the halting launch of China's banking industry. The establishment of the Imperial Bank of China (IBC) in 1897 brought China its first commercial bank and ended the financial era dominated by foreign banks and local private banks. Its founder Sheng Xuanhuai's slogan was "Without the establishment of Chinese banks as a matter of urgency, the vitality of Chinese commerce will be controlled by foreigners." The IBC, as Sheng proposed it, was a national bank authorized to issue treasury capital as paper notes and enjoyed official patronage, entrusted with taking in and issuing money like banks in England and France, and operating outside of the Board of Revenue.[3]

By the time the Qing dynasty collapsed, twenty Chinese-invested banks had been established; most did not last. During the Beiyang period, 313 new banks were established, with a total capitalization of more than 200 million *yuan*.[4] China's banking industry took off during the Beiyang period, the most outstanding banks being the Bank of China and the Bank of Communications. In the thirty-first year of the Guangxu period (1905), the Hubu Bank (Board of Revenue Bank) was established in Beijing's Legation Quarter as China's earliest state bank. It later changed its name to Daqing (Great Qing) Bank. The bank's objective was "to aggregate the flow of wealth and currency." The Daqing Bank was reorganized in 1912 into the Bank of China. The Bank of Communications was created by the Qing government's Ministry of Posts and Communications in 1907 as a bank jointly operated by the government and private merchants. These two banks both enjoyed the privilege of handling government bonds, and also took on the management of state finance.

The government's weak fiscal administration meant that financial institutions had a lot of say. Customs tariffs and salt tax constituted the main reserves for repayment of foreign debt. Added to its enormous military expenses, the Beiyang government took on a great deal of debt, relying on foreign banks as well as the domestic Bank of China and Bank of Communications.

The chaos of war and the government's repeated acts of bad faith, as in the "Beijing bank note panic" detailed below, caused numerous banks to declare bankruptcy during the Beiyang period and incited many state-owned banks to shift toward commerce during the late

Beiyang period. From 1912 to 1923, 161 new banks were established, but 115 banks closed down. The most prominent of the new banks were the "three southern banks" (Shanghai Commercial and Savings Bank, Zhejiang Industrial Bank, National Commercial Bank) and the "four northern banks" (Kincheng Bank, Yien Yieh Commercial Bank, China and South Sea Bank, Continental Bank).

At this point, foreign-invested banks, Chinese-invested banks, and local private banks formed a tripartite and mutually complementary balance of power. Foreign banks had the absolute advantage when it came to international remittances. They first entered China in the last years of the Qing dynasty with the establishment of the Oriental Bank, but this bank was not very large-scale. A foreign bank's capabilities were always inseparable from its host country's influence in China. British banks were considered the best, with the Hongkong and Shanghai Banking Corporation (HSBC) serving as a special case. Established in Hong Kong in 1865, HSBC is even today referred to there as a "foreign hong,"[5] but on the mainland it was more often regarded as a British bank. In fact, HSBC was not only deeply rooted in Hong Kong, but owed its growth and development to the favorable circumstances there. Its name highlights HSBC's roots in China but even more its glorious past in Shanghai. At that time, Shanghai was not only China's biggest city, but also a treaty port that radiated enormous vitality to the Yangtze Delta and northern China. When HSBC was formally established in Hong Kong, the population of Shanghai was 650,000, while the population of Hong Kong was only 115,000. One month later, the bank opened a branch in Shanghai in one of the Bund's signature buildings, known today as the Shanghai Pu Fa Building.

Shanghai was gradually becoming a financial center of the Far East, and the first foreign bank, the Oriental Bank, also established its first branch in Shanghai, while HSBC's focus on Shanghai goes without saying. Republican Shanghai's financial status is almost forgotten today, but at that time not only foreign banks but also Chinese-invested banks (Central Bank, Bank of China, Bank of Communications, and other important Chinese financial institutions) also chose to locate their headquarters in Shanghai. Republican history would have been much less colorful without those "Jiangzhe (Jiangsu-Zhejiang) bankers."

The history of China's modernization is closely tied to the Opium Wars and the customs, postal service, banking, and other modern institutions that followed in their wake. Twenty-three years after the Treaty of Nanking was signed, in 1865, America's Civil War effectively ended with the Confederates' surrender at Appomattox, and HSBC was established in Hong Kong that same year. Seven years later, HSBC was considered the most important "listed company" in China. The year after HSBC was founded, Hong Kong already had eleven foreign banks, and Shanghai had ten.

Late Qing borrowing and lending and the 450 million taels in reparations under the 1901 Boxer Protocol[6] were mortgaged with customs tariffs, salt tax, and provincial transit duty. The Boxer Protocol stipulated that all indemnity payments would be transacted in Shanghai, with nine foreign banks initially charged with receiving and holding the payments, including HSBC and Crédit Agricole Corporate and Investment Bank. Later HSBC, the Deutsch-Asiatische Bank, and the Russo-Chinese Bank served as trustees for customs duty, which reverted to HSBC after World War I. At a time when China had mostly only local private banks, foreign banks saw opportunities. HSBC maintained a cooperative relationship with the Qing government in the reparation payment arrangements, and continued to be responsible for custody of customs revenue until 1929.

HSBC's Shanghai branch continued to exist even after 1949 (when the People's Republic of China was founded) and put great effort into its business; it was one of the "old four" foreign-invested banks that remained in China after 1949. When the World Trade Organization's five-year extension on the banking industry reached its deadline in 2007 and China lifted its restrictions on the registration of foreign banks, HSBC became the first of the "old four" to be granted permission, and it chose Shanghai for its place of registration.

The Rise and Fall of China's Local Private Banks in the Twentieth Century

The role that China's local private banks played in the early twentieth century is nearly unimaginable now. *The Cambridge History of China: Late Ch'ing* points out, "Apart from the important role of modern foreign banks in financing international trade, the pre-1911 banking system of China was almost entirely limited to transfer banks of the Shansi bank type [*piaohao*] and to local 'native banks' [*qianzhuang*]."[7]

As before, the whys and wherefores lay in the shortcomings of China's fiscal administration. Given the weak tradition of central fiscal administration and the politics of inaction, a string of foreign debt, sundry military expenditures, and traditionally quota-based central tax revenues, "the share of the potential fiscal resources of the country which the central government could control was largely inelastic. It had no chance to increase revenue from the growth of foreign trade, because tariff rates could not be changed without the unanimous consent of the treaty powers, and it had only limited ability to manipulate the salt gabelle and various minor taxes."[8]

The local private banks flourished during this transitional period. The main reason, of course, was China's chaotic currency system; converting the various weights and measures would have been unthinkable without the local private banks. In the market space for exchanging various currencies, the local private banks controlled traditional services such as *yangli* (the conversion of foreign silver dollars to the Shanghai standard dollar[9]) and *yinchai* (the interest paid among the local private banks for short-term loans of silver taels), and this was the main reason that the local private banks existed. The local private banks initially maintained a separate turf from the foreign banks, but the introduction of modern Chinese banks established a tripartite balance of power among the three. It wasn't until the elimination of the silver tael and conversion to the silver dollar in the 1930s that banks gradually began to replace the local private banks, as will be detailed later.

The service orientation of the local private banks made them partial to commerce and tied them to many industrial and commercial entities. At this stage of China's economic development, the local private banks cooperated with Chinese and foreign banks by acting as proxies for depositing and drawing bank notes, and banks also accepted their promissory notes (*zhuangpiao*). At the outset, a large local private bank actually had higher status than a new-style bank.

Generally speaking, the local private banks prospered because of the flourishing of capital, and especially of the urban economy. The local private banks experienced repeated ups and downs. In the final years of the late Qing, many local private banks closed down, mainly due to the 1883 speculation crisis, but then reopened, numbering 115 in 1908. They then went into decline again under the assault of the 1910 "rubber stock crisis," but when the economy subsequently stabilized, the local private banks revived again.

The resurgence of local private banks climaxed in the 1920s. Yeh-Chien Wang's research has determined that the total assets of local private banks and Chinese banks in 1925 (including capital, reserve funds, bank deposits, and paper currency issuance quotas) was 202 million and 207 million in Chinese dollars (C$), respectively, making them almost evenly matched. In terms of profit, we can look at the first twenty-five years of the twentieth century. The local private banks performed well, and profit margins actually reached 59 percent in 1912. By 1926, the number of local private banks had risen again to more than eighty, and their total assets and average capital increased nearly four times over historical levels while maintaining profit margins of 25 percent.

Once the Nationalist government settled in Nanjing, the 1930s can be considered the beginning of the end for the local private banks; by 1936 only forty-eight remained. One reason was the elimination of the silver tael and conversion to the silver dollar; the legal tender system altered the professional foundation of the local private banks. Another reason was related at least in part to the Nationalist government's support for modern banks; government financing increasingly relied on the new-style banks rather than local private banks. Taking the years 1927 to 1935 as an example, all local private banks together carried C$26.975 million in government debt, while bank loans reached more than C$1 billion. The local private banks enjoyed a temporary revival at the last stage of the Sino-Japanese War, when Shanghai's isolation and a wave of speculation brought their number to more than 200. When the Sino-Japanese War ended, however, the local private banks faded from view (see Table 5-1).

As a counterpoint to the flourishing of the local private banks in the first twenty-five years of the twentieth century, we should add the story of the money-exchange shops. The local private banks offered multiple services, but they focused on exchange. The rise of the money-exchange

Table 5-1. Data on Shanghai's Local Private Banks (1858–1936)

	1858	1903	1912	1926	1936
Number of banks	70 (at peak)	82	28	87	48
Total capital (*yuan*)	1,145,000	4,592,000	1,488,000	18,757,000	1,800,000
Average capital (*yuan*)	16,000 (at lowest)	56,000	53,000	216,000	375,000
Total profit (*yuan*)	—	2,149,000	884,000	4,530,000 (1925)	63,000
Average profit (*yuan*)	—	26,000	32,000	54,000 (1925)	13,000
Average profit rate (profit/ capital) as percentage	—	46%	59%	27% (1925)	3.5%

Source: Zhang Zhongli, 1987, *Selected Treatises on China's Modern Economic History*

shops in Shanxi after the Ming dynasty ended is a major focal point in the history of finance. The specific time period is believed to be the Daoguang era in the early nineteenth century. The old model of the late Qing still existed, and *The Travels of Lao Can*[10] includes descriptions of the money-exchange shops that show their convenience: "When Lao Can went there the next day, he thought of the 1,000 taels of silver placed in his residence and had no peace of mind. He therefore went to an exchange shop called Sunrise Prosperity located on the main street in front of the court, and he remitted 800 taels back to his southern hometown, Tuzhou, while keeping more than 100 taels of silver money to himself." At that time, Sunrise Prosperity operated on a notable scale under the slogan

"One money order can remit throughout the country." Shanxi merchants were once the richest in China, and one of the reasons was the money-exchange shops, of which there were three main groups, based on the locations of their headquarters in Qi County, Pingyao, and Taigu. The family of the prominent Republican-era banker H. H. Kung came from Taigu. According to the *Qing Anthology of Petty Matters,* large money-exchange shops operated on a scale of 6 million to 7 million taels of silver, and even small ones handled 500,000 to 600,000 taels.

Monetary changes, fluctuations in the exchange ratio between silver and copper cash, as well as speculative trading and other factors caused the money-exchange shops to suffer many setbacks at the end of the Qing. Repeated runs on the establishments greatly affected their business, and the rise of state-run banks and foreign banks caused a major contraction in the government deposit services the money-exchange shops once provided. They ultimately began shutting down, and the certificates they issued "for the most part could not be redeemed."[11] The sense of crisis created a public panic: "People feared that the vouchers would become scrap paper and demanded payment from the local private banks. They flocked from near and far for ten days. The larger local private banks were able to draw from one to make up the deficits in another, but the smaller establishments were unable to manage."[12]

During the turbulent Beiyang period, Shanghai had already become a global financial center hosting not only many financial institutions but also many financial functions. Scholar Du Xuncheng believes that in modern times China experienced both free market and monopoly models of financial systems, which have fundamentally different functions and characteristics. He holds that China's pre-1927 system can be categorized as the free market type; although it advanced slowly, it had a fine-grained market orientation and a strong innovative quality. In comparison, the monopoly-style finance system advances rapidly and vigorously, but with only formalistic transformation. Under a free market system, finance and economy have a parallel relationship, but under a monopolistic system, the economy relies on finance, and finance is controlled by the government, so the financial markets lack spontaneous creativity.[13]

The period from the Beiyang government to the Nationalist government was a gradually deepening process from freedom to monopoly.

From the government's perspective, monopoly facilitates centralization of power and wartime response; from the financial perspective, centralization can also reduce transaction costs. But the problem with monopolies lies in their inability to make the government "keep its hands off." For that reason, the transition from freedom to monopoly superficially ends chaos and confusion, but in fact it lays the groundwork for excessive issuance of currency, inflation, and other malpractices.

The Bank of China and the "Beijing Bank Note Panic"

Just as for England, paper currency was an unavoidable step for China to take on the march toward a modern currency system. It was a very tough step, however, and the "Beijing bank note panic" was its first test.

In this case, "bank notes" mainly refers to exchange certificates issued by banks and circulating in Beijing. In May 1916, Yuan Shikai declared a moratorium on redeeming the notes issued by the Bank of China and the Bank of Communications for silver. The bank notes of that time originated in the same way as the paper currency of most countries of the world; they were in fact exchange notes, meaning that the bank had issued them to the customer in exchange for silver dollars, and if the customer took the exchange certificate to the bank, the bank would have to give the customer silver dollars in exchange. That was only way the public could be persuaded to accept bank notes and the bank could have credit. History had evolved for 1,000 years since the Northern Song paper-currency experiment, and now paper had returned to China once again; but this time, the operating mechanism and the competitive environment were both very different, and the outcome and contrast are thought-provoking.

The Beiyang government's crisis broke out before Yuan Shikai proclaimed himself emperor. It had become unable to centralize power and the country had become carved up by warlords. This created a situation in which the various provinces withheld the funds they would normally have passed to the central government, leaving the government unequal to dealing with either domestic or foreign affairs challenges. Left with such scanty revenues, the government "had to rely on borrowing for almost every expense in its budget."[14] The Beiyang government's inability to transmit its decrees also limited its sphere of influence, and it teetered on the brink of bankruptcy. At that time customs duty and salt tax were controlled by foreign countries; customs duty was mainly used to repay domestic and foreign debt, while salt tax was dammed up at the local level. Beijing's fiscal situation at that time has been referred to as "medieval." The 1925 budget had an outlay of 310 million *yuan*, but when Wellington Koo (Gu Weijun) became minister of finance the next year, he reported that actual receipts and payments averaged only about C$1 million monthly, of which about half was from loans.[15] Financial deficiency further weakened central authority, followed by even greater financial decline in a vicious circle.

Under the circumstances, the government-run Bank of China and Bank of Communications also suffered second thoughts from their clientele. Both banks had enjoyed excellent credit in the early years of the Republican era, and the bank notes they were authorized to issue were very popular. At that time Lu Xun recorded:

> There was a time in 1912 or 1913 when the credit-worthiness of the banknotes of a number of national banks in Beijing was growing by the day; it can truly be said to have been soaring by the day. I've heard that even country folk who had always been obsessed with silver realized that banknotes were not only convenient but reliable and were thus quite happy to accept them and keep them in circulation. Those who were somewhat more discerning—not necessarily those of the "special intellectual class"—had long since stopped carrying around heavy and burdensome silver coins and enduring the unnecessary nuisance it entailed. In retrospect, aside from those who had a particular love of silver or collected it as a hobby, almost everyone used banknotes, and mostly notes issued by Chinese banks at that.[16]

If taking for granted that silver was inconvenient and therefore had gradually retreated from the historical stage, the reader might underestimate the government's peril. These bank notes issued by banks were not national currency, and their vitality was maintained by institutional credit. The Bank of China and the Bank of Communications could be considered state banks, whether from orientation or actual function at that time. The Bank of China's previous incarnation was the Daqing Bank, which enjoyed privileges such as acting as agent for the state treasury, collecting and repaying public debt, issuing bank notes, and minting and issuing national currency. The Bank of Communications, established by the Qing government's Ministry of Posts and Communications in the thirty-third year of the Guangxu era (1907), had been authorized at that time to issue paper currency and pay government bonds and issue bank notes, and was also granted administrative authority over the ministry's funding for steamship lines, railways, and telegraph and postal facilities. As a result, both banks were obliged to take on a great deal of the responsibility for advancing money to the Beiyang government, and this laid the groundwork for lurking peril.

At the outset, the Beiyang government placed its hopes in government bonds and in 1914 established a "Government Bond Bureau," which issued bonds three times in two years. Yet as the market's confidence in Yuan Shikai's negotiable securities became depressed, the amount of funding raised declined, and the government's fiscal administration had to rely on advances of money from the banks. Statistics show that the Bank of China loaned more than C$52 million to the Beijing government in 1916, and the Bank of Communications advanced more than C$38 million. This enormous sum of advance capital was not an endless stream and could only be topped up by recklessly issuing bank notes. With reserve funds inadequate, silver and copper cash regained favor in the market. This created a vicious circle in which Beijing-issued bank notes, including those of the Bank of China and the Bank of Communications, began to lose value the more they were issued, and the banks faced the risk of bank runs.

Nineteen-sixteen was a year of twists and turns, and the political situation tended toward chaos: First Yuan Shikai was forced to abolish his monarchy, and Duan Qirui[17] took up the post of prime minister; then the southwestern provinces began declaring independence one after another, and the fragile Beiyang government faced an even greater dilemma. Given the lack of supervision and fiscal discipline, the government's debts were ultimately borne by the banks. Forced by circumstances, the Bank of China and the Bank of Communications fell into the trap of excessively issuing paper currency, threatening the credit they had established with such great difficulty. Facing an unmanageable hole in the fiscal dike, Yuan Shikai's advisor, Liang Shiyi, who had long controlled the Bank of Communications, conspired with Duan Qirui's trusted subordinate, Xu Shizheng, to issue unconvertible paper currency. Inevitably, news leaked out and triggered a bank run, starting in Beijing and Tianjin and then gradually spreading and growing in intensity.

The plan to refuse redemption of bank notes was a desperate but futile move, since issuing too many bank notes meant they couldn't be cashed at any rate: "In terms of domestic and foreign debt, there was already no alternative; if they continued to issue banknotes to meet various military and government expenses, it was certain to lead to savings withdrawals and bank runs, and the banks might have to close down, with the situation becoming uncontrollable."[18] According to calculations by Li Sihao, the Beiyang government's minister of finance, the Bank of China and the Bank of Communications issued bank notes totaling more than C$70 million, of which the Bank of Communications issued C$36.83 million but had only C$20 million in cash reserves. Apart from commercial loans of around C$20 million, loans to the government totaled around C$40 million. Of course, the number of bank notes issued in this case cannot be compared to the subsequent *fabi* and *jinyuan-quan*. These bank notes were not legal tender; silver was still being used as the main currency and reserves, and inflation cannot rise very much under a metal currency, which is another reason why the Beiyang government schemed to issue unconvertible paper currency. Unfortunately, under the conditions at that time, the excessive quota of bank notes combined with various rumors was enough to destabilize the market and undermine public confidence.

With no means of balancing its accounts, the Beiyang government handed down an order in the name of the State Council in May 1916, before the new finance minister, Sun Baoqi, could take office. The Bank of China and the Bank of Communications were to halt cash redemption of bank notes and payment of cash from savings accounts. The "bank note moratorium order" stated:

It is observed that when various countries are in pressing financial situations, cash redemption of paper currency issued by state banks is temporarily suspended and cash withdrawals are forbidden in order to maintain capital and preserve cash; all sectors save capital and revolve funds. This is a good method with universal benefit and should be imitated. The Ministry of Finance and Ministry of Posts and Communications hereby order the Bank of China and Bank of Communications, as of today, to temporarily suspend cash redemption of bank notes issued by the two banks and cash withdrawals from savings deposits. After the overall situation has been settled, a State Council order will be issued for cash redemption at fixed intervals. The two banks are entrusted with sealing up all reserve cash on deposit for safekeeping.

As soon as the order was issued, it in fact revealed the government's intention to default on its loans. The banks were already in dire straits and the market was in chaos; the value of paper currency decreased the more it was issued. Lu Xun recorded the proceedings in detail:

In the same year that Yuan Shikai decided to become emperor, Cai E fled Beijing for Yunnan to start an insurrection. One of the aftereffects was that both the Bank of Communications and the Bank of China ceased to exchange their bank notes for silver. Although the banks stopped honoring them, the government still had the authority to force merchants to continue using the bills; but the merchants had their own way of circumventing this: they didn't say they wouldn't accept them, but said instead that they couldn't make change. I don't know how it worked if you tried to buy things with notes denominated in the tens or hundreds, but who would actually be willing to pay a whole dollar for a pen or a pack of cigarettes? Not only would you be unwilling, you wouldn't have had that many dollar bills to begin with. If you tried to exchange them for copper coins, even at a reduced rate, the merchants would say they had no copper coins. Then how

could you expect friends or relatives to have money when
you went to ask them for a loan? At that point, you would
be willing to lower your standards, ignore patriotism, and
ask for notes issued by foreign banks. But foreign bank notes
at the time were equivalent to silver, so if you asked for a
loan of such notes, it was the same as lending you actual
silver.

This incident clearly had a serious effect on the credit of the newly established Chinese banking industry. Lu Xu's record shows that the independence of foreign banks in fact guaranteed the reliability of their bank
notes. A few days later, the Beijing and Tianjin branches of the Bank of
China and the Bank of Communications all ceased redeeming bank
notes. Anticipation of currency devaluation intensified, with the result
that everyone began dumping paper currency and scrambling to buy
goods, and the market devolved into chaos and panic.

The bank run started in the north, so it was called the "Beijing
bank note panic." Lu Xun could finally only sell off the bank notes in his
possession at a discount:

I still remember that I had thirty or forty dollars in notes issued by the two banks [Bank of China and Bank of Commu-
nications] at the time, but I had suddenly become a pauper,
almost to the point of having to forgo food, and I was more
than a bit panicked. The frame of mind of the Russian rich
who held paper rubles at the time of the revolution was no
doubt quite similar, or at most just a bit more intense. So I
could only resort to making inquiries—could bank notes be
converted to silver at a discount? I was told there was no
market. Fortunately, a covert market eventually developed,
with bills going for just over 60 percent of their face value. I
was delighted and immediately sold half of my paper money
right then. Later the rate went up to 70 percent, which made
me even more delighted, and I converted all my bank notes
to silver, which weighed heavily in my pocket, as if representing the full weight of my existence. Had it been normal times,

if a money changer shorted me even a penny, I would have
found it absolutely unacceptable.

This veritable plunder terrified the populace and thrust the financial
market into upheaval. In May 1916, in China's financial center, Shanghai,
the Bank of China's Shanghai branches all received the order to suspend
cashing bank notes.

At that time, however, Shanghai was home to a man who subsequently became one of the leading lights of the banking world: Zhang
Gongquan (also known as Zhang Jia-ao).[19] After studying in Tokyo,
Zhang joined the Bank of China at the age of twenty-five, and from then
on his life became closely bound to China's financial history and even its
history overall; the actions of Yuan Shikai, Sun Yat-sen, Chiang Kai-shek,
and others in modern Chinese history brought about major turning
points in Zhang Gongquan's life.

Back in 1916, when Zhang Gongquan and the general manager
of the Bank of China's Shanghai branch, Song Hanzhang, received the
moratorium order, they saw that rumor had become reality, and their
first response was "absolute panic"; they had a profound sense of being
buried alive with the Bank of China's credit. If they executed this
order, China's banks would lose all credit and hope of recovery, and
it would be difficult for the financial industry to ever again shake off
the shackles of foreign banks. The two of them conferred and decided
to defend the bank's independence. After examining and calculating
the bank's cash and asset situation, they made an astonishing decision,
which was to categorically refuse to execute the order in hopes of
gaining the public's understanding and support: "It was hoped that the
bank's rejecting the government's illegal control would be sufficient
to defend China's financial life." After thinking things out, the two of
them sent a reply cable to the Beiyang government, saying, "In order to
fulfill our responsibility to bank note bearers, no matter how difficult the
environment we find ourselves in, we will do our utmost and pay out
cash reserves to the last *yuan* before we will execute the moratorium on
payments."

Refusing to execute the order didn't mean there was no cost to stub-
born and categorical resistance. Zhang Gongquan and Song Hanzhang's

first worry was that the Beijing government would relieve them of their posts because of their defiance, and that once they were sacked, the bank would go adrift with no one at the helm. They therefore drew on the laws of the International Concession and instructed the bank's private shareholders to sue them personally; once a case was filed, they would not be allowed to vacate their positions or be dismissed until a court rendered a verdict.

Zhang Gongquan recalls that this was to prevent the bank run and to resist the Yuan government with the support of shareholders. A leading business figure, Zhang Jian, helped them establish a new stockholders' federation to take charge of business. Zhang Gongquan was elected chairman of the federation, with Ye Kuichu as vice-chairman and Qian Xinzhi as secretary general. The newspapers published an announcement stating that the bank's Shanghai branch was continuing business as usual and declared to the outside world: "None of the country's key branches is as important as Shanghai's. Shanghai is the country's financial hub and creates an image overseas. We therefore believe that in order to save the Bank of China, we must start with the Shanghai branch. This was borne out during the collapse of the Daqing Bank in 1911; fortunately a stockholders' federation was established in Shanghai and did its utmost to preserve the Shanghai branch, and because of that the Shanghai branch was saved."[20]

After retaining its management structure, the Shanghai branch still needed to prove that it had the financial strength to deal with the impending bank run. A bank run is the nightmare of all banks, and more frightening yet is that this nightmare often becomes a reality; not even an established central bank such as the Bank of England could avoid this experience. Zhang Gongquan observed the bank run for several days, and the fear lingered even years later when he recalled it.

Zhang Gongquan left his home for the bank at eight o'clock in the morning on May 12; he saw crowds of people while still three blocks away. Squeezing his way to the bank entrance, he discovered that at least 2,000 people were running on the bank: "Vying to be first, they crashed against the door and clambered up windows, as if they didn't care whether they lived or died." Many as they were, these unfortunate people weren't demanding a great deal of money. Zhang Gongquan noticed that they were holding only handfuls of one-*yuan* or five-*yuan* notes, or deposit receipts for 200 or 300 *yuan*.

The bank run continued on May 13 with about as many people as the day before. In order to calm public sentiment, the Shanghai branch extended its Saturday hours from the normal half a day to all day. This reduced the size of the crowd by 400. The bank also remained open for business on Sunday, when it was usually closed, and as a result, not even 100 people gathered to run on the bank. At this point, Zhang Gongquan was finally able to breathe a sigh of relief and wrote, "The storm has subsided." But even he didn't have a full grasp of the situation. The bank run he'd witnessed on May 13 had depleted the Shanghai branch's cash, and it was by no means certain that it could continue that way; the branch would need help from foreign banks.

Although dealing with the crisis to the best of its ability, days of bank runs had brought the Shanghai branch close to collapse. When all is said and done, a bank run is a process of comparative trust; in a market stampede, no one knows when a bank run will pass, and indeed, it is when the crisis begins to abate that the pressure is greatest: "The Shanghai branch had cash reserves of more than C$2 million, but more than C$1.6 million was withdrawn during the bank run, and business account withdrawals also reached C$1 million."[21] The help of foreign banks was therefore critical. On May 15, Manager Song Hanzhang visited HSBC and the Yokohama Specie Bank and asked for help. Several foreign banks agreed to help the Shanghai branch "as much as necessary" and loaned it a total of C$2 million to cover its overdraft.

At that time the credit of foreign banks was excellent, so their bank notes enjoyed even greater popularity; their silver dollar reserves were plentiful, so the Shanghai branch could not help but draw on their support. The foreign banks, for their part, also needed the market to stabilize. HSBC, the most powerful foreign bank at that time, defended the stability of the market by taking on one-fifth of the loan at C$400,000. It also decided on that day to "make a morning withdrawal from the storehouse" at the Russo-Chinese Bank Building (funds usually left the storehouse in the afternoon, so a morning withdrawal was considered early) to help the Shanghai branch. In fact, the Shanghai branch never ended up using that money, but soon after the news reached the market, the bank run evaporated.

Of course, as the participants recall, although Song Hanzhang had an excellent reputation among the foreign banks, he didn't rely on trust alone during the negotiations, and offered the deeds to the bank building and its storehouse and property along the Suzhou River as a pledge. Although there were also appeals to help the Bank of Communications, its reputation was not as strong as the Bank of China's, so the attitude of the foreign banks was also different.

By May 19, the panic was over, and Zhang Gongquan recorded the results of the battle:

> The credit of Shanghai's Bank of China bank notes became increasingly evident from then on. The Nanjing and Hankou branches, observing the appropriateness of the suitability of the Shanghai branch's measures, obtained the cooperation of local government departments, and they paid out cash on the bank notes they issued and on their savings deposits as normal. The effect was such that Zhejiang, Anhui, and Jiangxi provinces made full use of the bank notes issued by the Bank of China in those places.

In economic terms, the Shanghai branch had already won; it was literally a case of "money in the bank." As the bank added hours and staff, the bank run subsided. Economics was only one aspect, however; at this point, support was offered from all sides. On May 16, the Beijing missions of various countries sent telegrams agreeing to help the Shanghai branch, but Zhang Gongquan said that the bank run had ended and the Shanghai branch no longer needed outside help.

Although the bank didn't need outside help financially by then, the political implications of foreign aid were very clear and won the bank some leeway in subsequently pursuing accountability. The Shanghai branch's response also influenced many people. Institutions and individuals who had originally maintained a neutral and equivocal attitude also explicitly supported the Shanghai branch. For example, the Shanghai General Chamber of Commerce stated in the Shanghai newspaper

Shen Bao, "We have examined the Bank of China's reserves and have found them sufficient, not only for honoring the bank notes they have issued, but also for paying out savings deposits when they come due. The Shanghai branch's reliability and trustworthiness have been proven. As long as its cash-backed bank notes continue to circulate in the market, it will remain financially solvent. The Shanghai branch has maintained its credit with full cash reserves and cash redemption, and the various business establishments are accepting its bank notes as before." Li Sihao recalls that by the time Duan Qirui took over the government after Yuan Shikai died on June 6, 1916, Duan had become much more relaxed about the Shanghai branch's defiance of the moratorium order. He acknowledged that the order was an emergency tactic, and that given the Shanghai branch's deep ties with foreign merchants in the International Concession, "it would have had difficulty suspending cash payments."

After Yuan Shikai's death, the overall situation became settled, and the controversy caused by the moratorium order also implied that the Shanghai branch had completely triumphed. As for the originator of the disastrous "moratorium order," Liang Shiyi, after Yuan Shikai's death the new president, Li Yuanhong, issued a warrant for his arrest, and he fled overseas. Once calm was restored, he managed to stage a comeback; he returned to the Bank of Communications and revitalized it with the support of loans from an international consortium—such were the boisterous political affairs of Republican era.

The run on the Beijing bank notes was replayed in 1921. The Bank of China and the Bank of Communications managed to sort out their financial situations in several stages amid the chaos of war from 1916 to 1923. In the process, the Bank of China lived up to its reputation as China's leading bank. In 1926, the bank took in savings deposits totaling C$328.48 million and issued C$137.42 million in bank notes, composing 35.1 percent of the total savings deposits and 60 percent of the bank notes issued by the top twenty-five Chinese banks.

While developed under the campaign strategy of Zhang Gongquan and others, part of this success also relied on the larger political and economic backdrop of that time.

First of all, it must be acknowledged that the weakness of the Beiyang government prevented it from being too overbearing with its moratorium order. The Beiyang period was in fact quite temperate. That is why the moratorium on cash payouts was not very rigorously enforced, and the south was able to express its dissent toward the Beiyang government's methods: "The action announced by the Beijing government will cause a devaluation of the bank notes of the Bank of China and Bank of Communications and create panic in the independent provincial economies, allowing Beijing to mop up the cash to issue military payroll." This atmosphere also gave Zhang Gongquan and others some leeway to defy the order. This was in fact a manifestation of "the southeast's self-preservation" in the financial sector under decentralized power. Even if it brought the potential for later score-settling, the resistance and mediation of all sectors eventually deescalated the crisis.

Second, this looked like a victory for Zhang Gongquan, but in fact it was a victory for the Jiangzhe tycoons, industrialists, and merchants, as well as a victory for the market. Zhang Gongquan relied on the power of his stockholders and the commercial and industrial sector. He depended on Zhang Jian and on the National Commercial Bank trustee Jiang Yizhi, the Zhejiang Industrial Bank general manager Li Ming, the Shanghai Commercial and Savings Bank general manager K. P. Chen (Chen Guangfu), and others, and drew on the power of his stockholders to proclaim to the entire country, "None of the country's key branches is as important as Shanghai's. Shanghai is the country's financial hub and creates an image overseas. We therefore believe that in order to save the Bank of China, we must start with the Shanghai branch. The Bank of China Shanghai has decided at its stockholder meeting to carry on to the best of its ability, and any losses suffered by enterprises in the various industries will be negotiated with the government by the Federation of Stockholders."

In other words, this victory relied on the formidable reputations of the Bank of China's stockholders. This was also a major characteristic of the Beiyang period, because the Beiyang government was so financially vulnerable that its shareholdings in the bank were meager, giving private stockholders the majority shareholding and considerable authority. Stockholders were no longer mostly merchant-officials as in the late Qing, but rather were from the private-sector business world. The government owned most of the stock in the Bank of China in 1915, but the proportion of privately owned stock increased from then on, from 17.01 percent to 59.29 percent in 1917, and then to 72.64 percent in 1921, and surged to 97.47 percent in 1923. According to the memoirs of Feng Gengguang, who once served as president of the Bank of China, the bank's leaders, whatever their temperaments, all wanted the bank to be well run, and recognized that maintaining the bank's relative independence in a changing political situation required maximizing the rights and interests of private stockholders and diluting the power of government stockholders: "The Beiyang government's Ministry of Finance was always in need of money and often took out loans using its Bank of China shares as collateral. We convinced them to sell their stock to commercial banks. On the eve of the Northern Expedition [1926], the amount of government-owned stock was minute, only around C$50,000."[22]

Finally, the status of the Bank of China's Shanghai branch executives cannot go without mention. At that time, the headquarters of both the Bank of China and the Bank of Communications were in Beijing, but their Shanghai branches carried a great deal of weight, not only because of Shanghai's central status as a financial center, but even more because the Shanghai branches held half of the cash reserves of both banks. According to Zhang Gongquan's memoirs, "At that time, the bank notes issued by the Bank of China and the Bank of Communications were valued at more than C$70 million, and their cash reserves were C$23 million. The Bank of China had reserves of 3.5 million taels and C$4.88 million in silver dollars, and the Bank of Communications had reserves of 6 million taels and C$5.4 million in silver dollars. Half of these cash reserves were held by the Shanghai branches of both banks."

The Bank of Communication's history was different from that of the Bank of China. The Beiyang government greatly facilitated the Bank of Communications becoming a state bank, and Yuan Shikai's trusted lieutenant, Liang Shiyi, started out as the bank's deputy director and ultimately rose to president. Although the Bank of Communications from the outset had banking relationships with the steamship, railway, post office, and telegraph sectors, years of advance payments and suboptimal management led to total losses of at least 2.8 million taels: "Business was stagnant to the point of being nearly unsustainable." Liang Shiyi sought Yuan Shikai's support to expand the power of the Bank of Communications, and he remained in control after the Bank of Communications became a state bank authority, but the bank's management was never as good as the Bank of China's. Shanghai's *Sin Wan Pao* published a "special communique from Beijing" that stated:

> Before the headquarters of the Bank of China and Bank of Communications stopped cashing bank notes, and before the State Council moratorium was issued, cables were sent to each branch soliciting their views. The Bank of Communications branches offered no opinions, but the Bank of China's branches all disagreed and even used the words, "The Bank of Communications can commit suicide if it likes, but the Bank of China will not die along with it. We would rather suffer punishment than resign ourselves to that fate."

In the national context, regional differences meant that execution of the cash-out moratorium varied in strength and pace in different places. Most regions complied, so the determined resistance by the Bank of China's Shanghai branch was unique. The Shanghai branch had a special status. After the 1911 Revolution broke out, banks suspended business and settled accounts, but the Daqing Bank had private stockholders as well as government-held stock. Through the mediation of private stockholders, the provisional Nanjing government agreed to the reorganization of the Daqing Bank as the Bank of China, which starting doing business in Shanghai in 1912 (at the original address of the Daqing Bank). Only in the next year was the headquarters relocated to Beijing. The bank set its capital at C$60 million, split evenly between the government and private stockholders. This shows the status that the Bank of China's Shanghai branch enjoyed within and outside of the bank.

As for the Shanghai branch of the Bank of Communications, its top managers were transport and communications officials who never served in their postings for long and were unfamiliar with the commercial and banking worlds; foreign banks also regarded it differently. As a result, the Bank of Communications was obliged to comply with the moratorium. The outcome for the Bank of Communications' Shanghai branch was therefore different from that of the Bank of China's Shanghai branch; it didn't resume business until a year later, and its headquarters nearly closed down.

Surviving this crisis made Zhang Gongquan famous throughout the banking world, and he was widely commended in political and media circles. Eventually Liang Qichao invited him to serve as vice-president of the Bank of China, where he spent years rectifying the Beijing bank note problem in Beijing and Tianjin. This established the foundation for him subsequently to represent the Jiangzhe tycoons in expressing support for Chiang Kai-shek.

The successful resistance to the cash-out moratorium was not only due to Zhang Gongquan's individual effort. According to well-informed individuals, Zhang was active in social communications and had many ties with Jiangzhe bankers, political figures, and journalists, and his experience in government gave him competence in dealing with the outside world. Within the profession, however, Song Hanzhang had genuine influence and also enjoyed the trust of the foreign banking community. The Shanghai branch's assistant manager at that time, Mr. Hu, had status in the old-style private local banks, and because of his mediation in the market transactions, Shanghai's local private banks treated the Bank of China as a colleague rather than an ordinary client. The fact that these three men "each had their strengths and shone more brightly in each other's company" made it easier for the Bank of China to stand firm during the bank note panic.

Although Song Hanzhang is mentioned less frequently than Zhang Gongquan, his contribution to the Bank of China was immense; he served the bank even longer, and with better qualifications and experience. He was with the Bank of China during the Qing dynasty, the Beiyang period, and under the Nationalist government. Zhang Gongquan appraised Song Hanzhang as "silent and taciturn, but benefiting from many associates and having the virtues of self-sufficiency, simplicity, industriousness, and conscientiousness. He showed caring concern for public property and drew a clear distinction between public and private interests." Song Hanzhang subsequently served as general manager of the Bank of China, and in 1946 served on the Four Banks Joint Business Office.[23] When H. H. Kung (Kong Xiangxi) resigned as chairman of the board of the Bank of China in 1948, the nearly eighty-year-old Song

Hanzhang was appointed his successor with the objective of preserving the bank's independence. In 1949, Song resigned and went to Brazil, and he died in Hong Kong in 1968 at the age of ninety-six. Apart from his resistance to the Beiyang government's moratorium, Song Hanzhang refused a demand for funding by warlord Chen Qimei and Chiang Kai-shek; he has even been referred to as the spiritual leader of the Bank of China. As for Mr. Hu, Zhang Gongquan said his familiarity with the history and professional services of the local private banks made him especially valuable in discussions of market conditions.

During the resistance to the cash-out moratorium, the Bank of China's Federation of Stockholders stated in its cable to the State Council, the Ministry of Finance, and the bank's Beijing headquarters:

> The State Council's moratorium on cash redemption of bank notes of the Bank of China and Bank of Communications is tantamount to declaring the government bankrupt. Shutting down the banks will directly or indirectly devastate our compatriots, destroy the country's vitality, and eliminate all financial credit from this day forward. The Bank of China's Shanghai stockholders passed a resolution and notified its managers to continue redeeming bank notes as usual, and not to comply with the State Council decree. Supported from all sides, the Bank of China will continue its orderly operations in ardent hopes of preserving the country's vitality and extending a lifeline to the people.

Subsequent developments largely met the bankers' expectations. Although the political situation was in flux, the Bank of China developed as rapidly as ever. Its total deposits were C$140 million at the end of 1917 and C$380 million at the end of 1928; the total value of bank notes issued was C$70 million at the end of 1917 and C$170 million at the end of 1928. That was more than half of the C$290 million in bank notes issued by all of China's banks at the end of 1928. The current accounts and fixed-term deposits of the country's various banks totaled C$980 million, of which the Bank of China's deposits made up 40 percent. The Bank of China's status was not only outstanding within China, but was even higher than the official Central Bank in Shanghai and other places. "At the end of 1934, the bank's savings deposits totaled C$500 million, and its various loans totaled C$400 million, both of which were double those of the Central Bank. It issued a total of C$200 million in bank notes, more than triple the amount issued by the Central Bank."[24]

The Beijing bank note panic and the resistance to the cash-out moratorium not only reflected the brevity of the golden era for China's banking industry and bankers, but also offered a subtle lesson: When the government enjoys no credit, the people will always prefer precious metal currencies such as silver. The existence of precious metal currencies naturally restrains inflation of paper currency; otherwise, the uncontrolled issuance of paper currency inevitably causes inflation and triggers financial turmoil. Unfortunately, this lesson was not absorbed by the subsequent Nationalist government. After silver withdrew from the historical stage, the effect of paper currency was magnified over and over again as the Nationalist government galloped down the road of inflation to extinction.

The Advantageous Terrain for "Eliminating the Silver Tael and Converting to the Silver Dollar"

Before the cavalry can be sent out, rations and supplies have to be arranged. Given that finance was the lifeblood of the state economy, military battles were also currency battles, and silver played a key role in the upheavals of the Republican era.

China's traditional currency unit was the tael, but there were many different scales for weighing physical silver; there were reportedly more than 100 during the Beiyang period. Virtual or value silver currencies (*xuyin*) came in an even greater variety of forms; so-called *wenyin* (fine silver shaped like a horse's hoof) was an "imaginary standard silver" with a silver content of 93.5347 percent, and the values of other categories of silver were calculated against the value of *wenyin*; for example, Shanghai's "98 standard dollar" meant that it had 98 percent of the silver content of the *wenyin*. The Tianjin dollar was likewise standardized at 99.2 percent.[25]

Chaos breeds opportunity, and after the Qing, the collision of traditional economy and modern transformation gave birth to a modern financial system. In modern times, China ostensibly adopted the silver standard, but in reality it always used a dual coinage system of "silver for large sums and copper cash for small sums." As foreign silver dollars and self-minted silver dollars began circulating, currency values became extremely complicated. Yan Hanzhong, a professor at Shanghai University of Finance and Economics, believes that from the late Qing to the Republican era, China's monetary situation was more chaotic than at any other point in its history, to the point that China could be considered to have no standard currency. As the Beiyang government acknowledged in 1914, "China's greatest ill today is its lack of a currency standard."[26] At the same time, this was the period when the changes were greatest and the reform most thorough.[27]

Although Yuan Shikai issued Coinage Regulations, they were largely ineffective in China. There was subsequent discussion of a gold standard, but the silver dollar and silver tael continued to be used together in the market just as before, and the government itself often used both. After Yuan Shikai died, there was no one to forcefully push forward unification of the currency system. The ununified currency system created massive inconvenience, but the chaos of war and personal interests kept silver circulating in various forms as before. The scholarly community had long called for reform; for example, economist Ma Yinchu began calling for changing "bad money" from the 1920s onward: "If we want China to be strong, China's industry must develop; if we want China's industry to flourish, we must improve the currency system. In other words, if China's currency system isn't improved, the new situation for China's industry will not prosper; if China's industry doesn't flourish, China has no hope of prospering."

The Beiyang government also planned to take advantage of the favorable situation to eliminate the tael and convert to the silver dollar, but because central power was weak and the country was carved up by warlords, coupled with lack of enthusiasm in financial circles, the plans ultimately came to nothing. Opposition in the financial industry mainly came from the local private banks and foreign banks, both for the sake of their own interests. The main business of the local private banks was exchanging silver and copper cash. Since existing loans, salt tax, and customs duty were all calculated in silver taels, conversion between silver taels and silver dollars always depended on the exchange rates provided by banks, and the different regulations in different places resulting in complex calculations that created a threshold; this situation created a great deal of business for foreign banks and local private banks. Banker Zi Yaohua recalls that foreign exchange rates were set by the foreign-invested HSBC based on the silver tael, and the bank used this advantage to profit from forex transactions.[28]

The Nationalist government gained a favorable climate and topographical advantage for pushing forward monetary reform. First of all, it had the political foundation of unification and the strengthening of centralized government power. After the Nationalist government was established in 1927, even before nominal unification was completed it set about reforming the currency system. In the "Outline for Arranging Fiscal Administration" tabled at the National Financial Conference held in July 1928, the government emphasized the importance of currency reform:

> The currency system controls the pivot of fiscal administration and is most relevant to the national economy. The maladies of China's currency system are longstanding and fundamental and require complying with the president's currency reform plan and resolutely implementing it step by step. At present we should plan in two stages. The first is to implement a centralized paper currency, remove the old currency, and convert to a new currency issued by authorized state banks; each region should establish branches and exchange offices of the state banks for purposes of centralization. The second step is to adopt a gold-exchange standard. A silver-currency standard is not the world trend, but a gold standard is beyond the capacity of our country's wealth. Most appropriate for the present circumstances is to first eliminate the silver tael and convert to the silver dollar and establish a silver standard; the second step is to adopt a gold-exchange standard. We will start by establishing international exchange banks with outstanding credit to implement the standard.

China's history ten years before the War of Resistance against Japan (1937–1945) broke out was in fact the birth of a modern country out of nothing. This was accompanied by the strengthening of centralized power, especially in fiscal administration. In 1929, T. V. Soong (Song Ziwen) stated that the government was only able to control the finances of four provinces—Jiangsu, Zhejiang, Anhui, and Jiangxi—and that only Jiangsu and Zhejiang handed over a substantial portion of their revenues. As the Nationalist government stabilized its power, it began carrying out its plan of financial unification, and the first step was to control the banks.

At that time the main targets were the two banks with the best credit, the Bank of China and the Bank of Communications, both of which were forced to reorganize and add government shareholdings in the late 1920s. The Bank of China had to add 5 million government-owned shares to its capital stock of C$25 million, and the Bank of Communications headquarters was moved to Shanghai, where 2 million government-owned shares were added to its capital stock of C$12 million.

The Bank of China's private stockholders were very powerful at the end of the Beiyang era, while the government had little say and was constantly selling off its shares, with only C$50,000 left on the eve of the Northern Expedition (1926). Under the governance of Zhang Gongquan and the others, the Bank of China was becoming a first-rate commercial enterprise and already ranked at the top among domestic banks in terms of actual strength. As the central government's power increased and the financial system underwent reform, however, the Bank of China inevitably experienced an increase in government influence and a retreat of private-sector influence. The Bank of China's headquarters was moved from Beijing to Shanghai in 1928, and C$4.95 million in government bonds was added to its original C$50,000, for a total of C$5 million, or one-fifth of its total stock. The Ministry of Finance also appointed three directors and one member to the supervisory board.

In terms of China's domestic situation, 1927–1937 was a period of rare stability and peace that fostered an economic Indian summer. The period from when the Nationalist government established its capital in Nanjing on April 18, 1927, until it relocated to Chongqing on November 20, 1937, is considered a "golden decade."

The American general Albert Coady Wedemeyer, who had a profound but critical understanding of China, appraised these ten years highly in a speech to the United States Congress in the 1950s: "There was a period 1927–37 . . . known in China as the golden decade . . . it was during that period that China enjoyed improved communications, a stabilized economy, and even objective foreigners, Americans who lived there for years, will tell you that Chiang Kai-shek was building schools and helping his people during that period."[29]

The elimination of the silver tael and conversion to the silver dollar were also supported by the political situation at the time. The major international episode of the 1920s and 1930s, the Great Depression, changed the face of the world and had a hidden but significant effect on China's monetary system.

After World War I, even more countries switched to the gold standard and silver prices began dropping. When countries abandoned the gold standard after the Great Depression, gold and silver prices plummeted. London silver prices fell from 61.95 pence per ounce in 1920 to 25 pence per ounce in 1928, and then to 2.5 pence per ounce in 1931.[30] The Great Depression was catastrophic in most parts of the world, and it also had a major effect on China.

At that time, China was the world's only major country using the silver standard, and falling silver prices profoundly affected China, both positively and negatively. In terms of repayment of debt and foreign exchange, this change was detrimental to China, prompting the suggestion to change the silver standard. But in terms of exports, this development worked in China's favor. Milton Friedman believes that China's silver standard effectively gave China a floating exchange rate. The result was that China's exports decreased less than its imports did after the Great Depression, and China enjoyed a balance-of-payments surplus in 1930 and 1931. The Chinese government's economic advisor at that time, Arthur N. Young, believed that the Great Depression didn't begin in China until 1932. Friedman believes that China's international balance-of-payments surplus reflected net imports of gold and silver, and this judgment is consistent with China's circumstances at the time. Silver dollars streamed into Shanghai in 1932, to the point of oversupply, reaching a total of C$54.66 million (see Table 5-2).[31]

Table 5-2. Customs Statistics on China's Silver Imports and Exports,
1928 to September 1933 (in Customs Taels)

Year	Amount imported	Amount exported	Surplus
1928	111,662	5,267	+106,395
1929	121,430	15,605	+105,826
1930	102,560	35,554	+67,006
1931	75,888	30,443	+45,445
1932	62,255	69,601	−7,346
1933 (Jan.–Sept.)	64,336	85,845	−21,509

Source: Dai Jianbing, 2005, *Silver and the Modern Chinese Economy (1890–1933)*

By 1933, the Ministry of Finance calculated that the amount of silver dollars in circulation totaled C$1.4 billion; adding C$200 million in reserve funds made a grand total of C$1.6 billion. Comparatively speaking, the amount of silver *ding* (ingots) in circulation was calculated at 153 million Shanghai taels (around C$200 million). There was only C$600 million in silver dollars in the entire country in 1928.

The drop in the price of silver created the perfect conditions for eliminating the silver tael and converting to the silver dollar. Like most people at that time, Zi Yaohua experienced the era of using silver dollars and also the gradual retreat of silver from the historical stage. As someone long embroiled in the gold and silver issue, Zi Yaohua sighed, "Normally no one pays any attention to the problem of silver prices, but in one leap it has become the issue that everyone in the country is talking about." In a book on this subject that he published in 1930, Zi Yaohua held that the high price of gold and low price of silver affected the country's wellbeing and the people's livelihood in a way that would be impossible to remedy without a comprehensive plan. Coming up with such a plan would require comprehensive research on silver's status in the economy as a commodity and as currency. A commodity was "the objective of a commercial transaction," while a currency was "a medium of exchange with the capacity to circulate." "Silver qualifies as both a commodity and a currency. Therefore, if we wish to study all issues relating to silver, we are obliged to start with observation of both."[32]

Regarding falling silver prices, the Bank of China's president at the time, Zhang Gongquan, recalled: "From 1928 to 1931, the average price of a silver dollar was 0.73 treasury ounces in Shanghai standard dollars. In 1932 it dropped to 0.6995 treasury ounces. The silver dollar's purchasing power dropped, while the price of goods rose, the people cried out in protest, and everyone hoped to eliminate the tael and convert to the dollar as soon as possible ... Once the conversion took place, the value only increased and did not decrease."[33] Zhang Gongquan pointed out, however, that foreign banks and some local private banks worried that the conversion would trigger the excessive issuance of paper currency and that there wouldn't be enough silver dollars to meet demand. The Bank of China publicly stated that paper currency would be issued under public monitoring and that the stockpile of silver dollars was adequate. The Bank of Communications and the Central Bank followed suit, and in that way the elimination of the tael and conversion to the dollar proceeded smoothly.

Finally, apart from conditions being right, social harmony also played a role. Originally only the modern banks pushed for elimination of the tael and conversion to the dollar, while foreign banks and local private banks opposed it. By the 1930s, the situation had changed. The Great Depression brought economic panic, but China entered its "golden decade" and drew attention as an economic bright spot. If foreign banks hoped to develop further in China, a unified currency was the only logical course. It is because of this, according to Zi Yaohua's recollections, that foreign banks changed from opposition to endorsement of the plan to scrap the tael and convert to the dollar.

Economic change is the foundation of changes in financial policies, and the long-debated plan to eliminate the tael and convert to the dollar was finally put on the agenda. After Minister of Finance T. V. Soong emphasized that China's extremely chaotic monetary system had to be put in order in 1928, a series of resolutions was passed relating to elimination of the tael and conversion to the dollar. The Nationalist government issued a formal directive to implement the conversion in 1933, and from then on China's currency system was officially based on the silver dollar or *yuan*.

On March 8, 1933, the Nationalist government promulgated the "Silver Standard Currency Minting Ordinance," which stipulated that the currency unit of the silver standard was the *yuan* at a set weight of 26.697 grams, and would be issued as the unified silver currency of the entire country. The face of the silver currency was engraved with the bust of Sun Yat-sen and the obverse engraved with a junk, and it was referred to as the "Sun dollar."

The significance of this advancement has always been underestimated. Compared with the subsequent leap of legal tender from silver to paper, it would seem that the conversion from the tael to the dollar was not that great. In fact, without this conversion, it would have been impossible to talk of legal tender reform. It was a small step in China's currency system, but a great leap in Chinese history. More than 2,000 years after the king of Lydia minted gold and silver currency, China finally bade farewell to the tael and began its own coin-minting era with the *yuan*. The conversion to the dollar meant that the backward silver tael system had finally retreated from the historical stage, and this greatly facilitated the integration of the national market. Soon afterward, the once flourishing Chinese local private banks further declined with the elimination of the silver tael and gradually became extinct.

The *Fabi* Resulting from the Silver Purchase Act

The Great Depression changed the logic of the world, but silver diverted China from the world mainstream. At the very beginning, major countries all used the gold standard, while China's use of the silver standard allowed it to prosper under the exchange-rate devaluation.

International silver prices dropped by more than half from 1928 to 1932. As China replaced India as the world's greatest consumer of silver, its silver prices remained higher than in the rest of the world, and silver began pouring into China. This exacerbated the international trade imbalance; the price of imports rose and repayment of foreign debt increased, but at the same time all kinds of floating capital flowed into Shanghai, property prices in the International Concessions also began to rise, foreign and domestic capital both bought in on a large scale, and banking institutions busily speculated on property. Property prices in Shanghai's International Concessions reached a historic peak, and high property prices led to massive subletting, with the emergence of a "seventy-two tenant" phenomenon.

China was a debtor nation, and sinking silver prices caused the government to suffer financial losses. The Chinese government repeatedly protested about this. Minister of Finance T. V. Soong spoke to U.S. president Franklin Roosevelt in May 1933, asking the United States to stabilize silver prices. He also appealed for stabilization of silver prices at an international currency economy conference in London in June. On July 22, he signed an international silver pact to control the amount of silver sold by various countries.

In 1933, just as China was replacing the tael with the *yuan,* the world changed again. After the Great Depression, the gold standard that had once prevailed throughout the world became "golden fetters." Whoever abandoned the gold standard first enjoyed economic recovery first, while the drop in silver prices became even more of a trend. The United States abandoned the gold standard in April 1933, and the U.S. dollar became greatly devalued. Great Britain, Japan, and other countries had already abandoned the gold standard in 1931.

In a move that affected China even more than the United States abandoning the gold standard, President Franklin Roosevelt signed the Silver Purchase Act on June 19, 1934. The price of silver had dropped steadily up until then, from US$0.58 per ounce in 1928 to US$0.25 in 1932. After the act was passed, the price of silver rose steadily in 1935, and even soared to more than US$0.80 per ounce, reaching US$0.81 on April 27 that year.

Although the American silver industry involved fewer than 3,000 people in 1929, its political influence was enormous, covering seven western states. Under pressure from the silver industry, Roosevelt empowered the secretary of the Treasury to purchase silver on the domestic and overseas markets until the market price of silver reached US$1.29 per ounce, or until the monetary value of silver stock held by the Treasury reached one-third of the monetary value of the gold stock.[34] The tabling of this act was entirely political; its objective was to raise the price of silver, but its result was to subsidize the domestic silver industry. Silver production increased from 33 million ounces in 1934 to 70 million ounces in 1940.

This sudden move caused depressed international silver prices to rise dramatically, but it created a major predicament for countries reliant on silver, especially China, where it triggered deflation. Deflation was fatal to economies after the Great Depression. Many factories were shuttered, and one-fifth of Shanghai's local private banks closed down within a few months. On the other hand, as the price of silver surged on the international market, the purchasing power of silver increased and the silver that had been flowing into China began to flow out; even a 10 percent export duty that Chinese Customs imposed in 1934 failed to change the trend. The typical estimate is that after the Silver Purchase Act was signed, moving silver from Shanghai to London yielded a profit of 15 percent. This led to rampant smuggling, but even without taking smuggling into account, the amount of silver exported was shocking. According to data in *China's Foreign Trade and Industrial Development (1840–1948)*,[35] China's net exports of silver were valued at C$257 million in 1934, five times higher than its previous highest export level. The vast majority was exported in the four months after the Silver Act was signed, a silver version of today's capital flight.

China had converted from the tael to the *yuan* only a short time before this. With silver prices suddenly surging, China experienced a silver outflow crisis similar to that at the end of the Qing, and Shanghai, which had been reaping the benefits of its golden period under the Nationalist government, also fell into decline. The classic manifestation of the outflow of silver was a slump in property prices: "In former days Shanghai market conditions flourished, and property prices and rents became more expensive than anywhere else in the country, and also gradually rivaled international prices. The market is depressed, and industry and commerce are burdened with enormous rents; how can anyone win? The effect has been plummeting property prices, the proliferation of empty units on the market, and property developers falling into ruin."[36]

From Shanghai to the rest of the country, factories began shutting down, local private banks closed, and bank runs occurred. In March 1935, Chiang Kai-shek recorded in his diary: "Finances are in shambles and the economy declines by the day. It is very worrying."[37]

The Silver Purchase Act's economic consequences were not unanticipated, and the China Banking Guild had expressed its opposition during initial discussion of the act, but politics is always driven by po-litical logic; Roosevelt replied that the problem was "China's business and not ours; that they could stop the outflow of silver if they so desired and that it was not up to us to alter our policy merely because the Chi-nese were unable to protect themselves."[38] History always repeats itself, and America's silver policy is like today's Federal Reserve policies; for-eign countries can grumble as much as they like, but American policies are based on America's domestic needs, and the United States has no time to take account of the chaos created overseas by the overflow effect of its policies.

At that time, someone observed that when the free market had not yet declined and the international gold standard had not yet collapsed, the laissez-faire attitude that the Chinese government took toward silver prices was above reproach, but it should have reacted when the situation changed. Some also lamented China's negligent management of currency:

> China, which cannot control the future of the silver market, has been seized under duress by New York speculators and Washington congressmen. The fate of 400 million Chinese heeds the decision of a small number of Americans. The en-tire country's assets have gradually diminished and people's living standards have sunk to an extent too dreadful to con-template. The majority lack food and clothing; they are mal-nourished and on the brink of death, or have become bandits. The entire nation is on the verge of destruction. What respon-sibility is the government taking for this?[39]

Meanwhile, Japan had invaded Manchuria in China's northeast in the Mukden Incident of September 1931, and its forces were infiltrating northern China and other places with the intention of making northern China "autonomous." Zi Yaohua traveled to northern China during this troubled time and sensed Japan's strong influence. The Shanghai Com-mercial and Savings Bank that he led was considering establishing a branch in the northeast, but was not able to do so until the end of the War of Resistance against Japan in the 1930s.

Under the influence of the U.S. Silver Purchase Act, capital flowed out of China, bringing economic panic along with deflation. On top of that, Japan was waiting for its opportunity to pounce, so China was encountering a severe economic crisis along with the threat of war. Systemic inertia made incursion by the state and retreat by the private sector all but inevitable. The effort to consolidate central power lent enormous impetus to monetary reform and brought an end to the golden age enjoyed by China's nascent modern banking industry.

Although the state-owned Central Bank had been established for a long time by then, it had much less actual power than the Bank of China or the Bank of Communications. Those two banks had long histories, and the market had more faith in them than in the Central Bank, which had been established in 1924. The Central Bank, the Bank of China, and the Bank of Communications had combined assets of C$1.879 billion in 1934, of which C$478 million (25.44 percent) belonged to the Central Bank, C$976 million (51.94 percent) to the Bank of China, and $C425 million (22.52 percent) to the Bank of Communications. The Bank of China likewise controlled more than half of the total stock issued, while the Central Bank controlled less than the Bank of Communications.

Zhang Gongquan lamented that with the Bank of China controlling one-fourth of total deposits and one-third of total stock issued in 1935, "it has attracted the government's attention, and needless to say the Central Bank is envious." Chiang Kai-shek's plan unfolded in two directions. One was to increase the government's shareholdings by seizing stock in the Bank of China, the Bank of Communications, and other commercial banks with good credit. The other was to control the right to issue currency as well as personnel matters. Even Zhang Gongquan, who had created the Bank of China legend, was forced out in 1935 and replaced by T. V. Soong as chairman of the board.

Chiang Kai-shek held discussions with H. H. Kung and T. V. Soong in Wuhan in mid-March 1935, and decided to increase the issue of government bonds by C$100 million, to pull out C$20 million for government-owned stock in the Bank of China and C$10 million for the Bank of Communications, and to put T. V. Soong in charge of China's banking industry.[40] Soon after that, Chiang Kai-shek sent H. H. Kung a cable from

Sichuan framing the reorganization of the Bank of China and the Bank of Communications as a means of saving the economy and the state, and outlined a plan to control finance and currency: "The state and society are on the brink of bankruptcy. The crux of the malady is that the financial and currency system and issuing of currency cannot be unified ... The only way for our country and people to survive the present crisis, whether in the government or in society, is to make the three banks absolutely obey the orders of the central government and cooperate thoroughly."[41]

In accordance with the steps Chiang Kai-shek outlined, the Ministry of Finance planned at the end of March 1935 to add 25 million shares to the C$25 million in shares the government already held in the Bank of China. This immediately raised objections from the bank's board of directors, and eventually the two sides compromised by increasing the government's shareholding by C$15 million.[42] In this way the shares were owned half by the government and half by the private sector. T. V. Soong became chairman of the board of the Bank of China, and the bank's control shifted from the general manager to the chairman of the board. Song Hanzhang became the bank's general manager, and Zhang Gongquan, who had served the bank for so many years, was forced to resign at the end of March.

As during the Beijing bank note crisis twenty years earlier, the response from the Bank of Communications to its reorganization was muted. An additional C$12 million in shares increased the government's stake to 55 percent of the bank's total capital, while the leadership level remained the same. After reorganizing the Bank of China and the Bank of Communications, reorganizing the Central Bank was even less complicated, and everything went according to plan. In April 1935, the Nationalist government used an indirect rescue of industry and commerce as a rationale to issue C$100 million in government bonds to replenish the capital of the Central Bank, the Bank of China, and the Bank of Communications; C$30 million was used to replenish the Central Bank's reserves.

Once everything was prepared, currency reform was all but certain. In summer 1935, the Kuomintang's top leaders gathered at Lushan. Arthur Young, who served as a financial consultant in China for many years, emphasized that the objective of this meeting was to decide the direction of monetary reforms, and the formal implementation was carried out in extreme secrecy.[43] The fate of Chinese finance was thus set in 1935. The original plan was to adopt the gold standard after converting from the tael to the dollar, but with other countries abandoning the gold standard after the Great Depression, China followed the trend by making a direct leap into paper currency.

Eighteen months after the Silver Purchase Act, in 1935, the vice-minister of finance, Hsu Kan (Xu Kan), formulated the *fabi* (legal tender) policy. The Ministry of Finance Currency Reform Order, issued on November 3, explained the reason for reform of the currency system: "Our country uses silver as currency, and the violent fluctuation in silver prices has had immense repercussions, the most evident being the domestic phenomenon of deflation. This has caused the depression of industry, commerce, and all trades, and a steady outflow of capital, an unfavorable international balance of payments, steady decline in the national economy, and a plethora of other negative conditions."

Apart from designating the *fabi*, the reform withdrew the authority to issue currency from all but the Central Bank, the Bank of China, and the Bank of Communications, and the government subsequently took controlling shareholdings in the Bank of China and the Bank of Communications. "First, as of November 4 this year, the bank notes issued by the Central Bank, the Bank of China, and the Bank of Communications are prescribed as legal tender [*fabi*] . . . Fourth, all silver-standard currency, silver dollars, raw silver, or other types of silver held by establishments, shops, and other public and private institutions or individuals must be handed over to the Currency Reserve Board or its designated banks for exchange into *fabi* starting on November 4 . . ."

The *fabi* was born in the midst of crisis, and finance became a key chess piece in an era of domestic and international chaos. Undeniably, it was economic crisis and even political survival that gave the central government an opportunity to concentrate control over the financial sector. Internationally, supporting China became the shared interest of Great Britain, the United States, and other countries, and this support by foreign governments, especially Britain and America, was of tremendous significance to the emergence of the *fabi*. The British financial consultant Frederick Leith-Ross was instrumental in issuing the *fabi*, and the

British government fully supported the currency reforms, demanding the compliance of British enterprises, companies, and banks in China.

On November 4, the British envoy to China, Sir Alexander Cadogan, relayed a decree by the king of England in response to the Chinese government's order. The decree stated that any British subject or entity attempting to evade China's currency law would be subject to a maximum sentence of three months in prison or hard labor and a fine of up to 50 pounds. British-owned banks were authorized not to issue payment in silver in any form.[44] HSBC, Chartered Bank, and other influential British banks eventually handed over their stores of cash and silver to the Bank of China, comprising the majority of the C$26 million in payments by Shanghai's foreign banks.

As for China's top trading partner, the United States, the U.S. envoy to China quietly urged American banks to hand over their silver to the Central Bank and no longer use silver dollars. Even so, the American government's attitude was somewhat ambivalent. China's currency reform had been hatched by a British financial advisor and China's top financial officials, H. H. Kung and T. V. Soong, but the United States had caused the silver turmoil in the first place, and the birth of the *fabi* was inevitably seen as a victory for Britain. The United States retaliated by suspending its purchase of silver on the London market.

In March 1936, through the mediation of banker K. P. Chen, the Nationalist government finally reached an agreement with U.S. Treasury secretary Henry Morgenthau, who had always been on good terms with President Franklin Roosevelt. The American government acknowledged that China's currency reforms favored U.S. interests in the Far East, and in May 1935 the U.S. government agreed to purchase 50 million ounces of silver from China. This tied China's *fabi* to both the British pound and the U.S. dollar and gave China's international allies an even greater stake in its success. The mutual ties in a currency system are in fact an affirmation of a community of interests.

The legal tender issue also involved monetary sovereignty and international manipulation; subsequent reports indicate that the United States, Japan, and Great Britain all hoped to peg China's currency to their currencies, and China strove to mediate among the three in hopes of securing support as well as an independent say. The process involved a chess game of economic say-so and financial negotiating ability. The United States was initially not very willing to help, and China opposed the dominance of any single foreign country, while also striving not to offend any side. The final outcome was relatively advantageous to China, while Great Britain and the United States also gained something.[45]

The Nationalist government mainly drew on its British financial consultant to gain international support. Frederick Leith-Ross did not spend much time in China, and the main part of the plan was actually drafted by the Nationalist government, with a substantial contribution from the American Arthur Young. This version of events is verified by banker K. P. Chen, Eduard Kann, and others. K. P. Chen was one of the Republic of China's top bankers and a close associate of H. H. Kung and others. He and his banking colleagues felt that "Yongzi [H. H. Kung's courtesy name] couldn't handle it," and as a result, Kung "kept his mouth shut while soliciting opinions"[46] and complied with Arthur Young's recommendation of a reform plan that did not involve a deficit. Not everyone in the overseas community was happy with the *fabi*, Japan being notably disappointed. K. P. Chen stated bluntly that Japan had nothing good to say about the new currency system and in fact tried to sabotage it. Japan had always hoped that the West would acknowledge its special interest in China as Japanese investment in China (especially in the northeast) had rapidly increased, reaching US$1.412 billion in 1930. As soon as the *fabi* reform was announced, the Japanese military pronounced it an "open challenge" to Japan, and even used it as a pretext to insist that northeastern tax revenues of more than 50 million in silver dollars could not be sent south. The subsequent War of Resistance against Japan launched a further war between China's *fabi* and the Japanese *yen*. The Marco Polo Bridge incident occurred the day before H.H. Kung and Henry Morgenthau agreed on a second purchase of silver in 1937.[47]

From replacing the tael with the *yuan* to launching the *fabi*, this was a new era with many tortuous complications. As a financial professional, Zi Yaohua saw differences between adopting the *yuan* and *fabi* reform, but he regarded the *fabi* reform as also "quite successful." Although conversion from the tael to the *yuan* unified the currency unit and imposed a monopoly on minting currency, the issuance of bank notes was still dispersed among numerous private banks, and fractional currencies still circulated in the market. With the issue of the *fabi,* the Nationalist government completely banned use of the silver dollar and hard fractional currencies, and the monopolized issuance of currency gave the *fabi* genuine legal tender status.

The history of finance has shown that the greatest profit from seigniorage (coin tax) comes from fractional currency, while paper currency is practically free of cost. Unifying the currency was in fact invaluable to the Nationalist government in establishing a monetary foundation for the subsequent War of Resistance against Japan and burying the hidden peril of subsequent inflation. In a time of domestic turmoil and foreign invasion, unifying the currency opened a new chapter in China's financial history. Although the *fabi* was blamed for rampant inflation following the Japanese invasion, this was in fact because it took on the burden of military expenditure. Its achievements and errors must be left to the judgment of subsequent generations.

The launch of the *fabi* was the beginning of a financial reshuffle, and the unified currency pulled China into a phase of monopolistic finance, the groundwork for which had been laid even before the *fabi* came into being. With its forcibly imposed controlling stakes, the Nationalist government basically controlled the Central Bank, the Bank of China, and the Bank of Communications, the total capital of which exceeded the total of all other Chinese banks by 40 percent, and savings deposits by nearly 60 percent. The comparative power of state banks and private banks began to shift. Furthermore, for commercial banks such as the Shanghai Commercial and Savings Bank headed by Zi Yaohua, the emergence of the *fabi* meant the loss of currency-issuing privileges. Zi Yaohua said that at that time it was common for banks to help each other by issuing "secret mark certificates." Commercial banks that didn't have bank note–issuing privileges could obtain certificates from banks that did have these privileges, which were marked with a mutually agreed stamp, and this gave a larger number of commercial banks de facto currency-issuing privileges. After the *fabi* was issued, the overall profits of the banking industry declined, the money market tightened, and business hit a low ebb.[48]

From then on, China had its own legal tender notes, the *yuan,* also called the *fabi.* The *fabi* was an enormous leap for China's currency system, not only in the shift from silver to paper, but even more in the shift from metal currency to fiduciary money, which essentially presaged the shift from a traditional economy to a credit economy. It looked as if the curtain had finally fallen on silver's multiple entanglements with China, from the silver tael to the silver dollar, and from the chaotic bimetal system to the combined use of silver and copper cash.

Inflation's Finale and Revelation

The birth of the *fabi* looked like a temporary close to silver's centuries of entanglement in China's financial history, and Chinese finance went from relative freedom into a stage of increasing control. History doesn't always travel in a straight line, however, and is full of repetitions and reversals; silver didn't retreat from the historical stage in one step, but the *fabi*, like other paper currencies throughout Chinese history, passed from stability to light inflation and then into inextricably rampant inflation, ultimately resulting in the emergence of a new gold-backed currency, the *jinyuanquan*. Privately held silver and gold forex once again became the target of government plundering, creating the greatest panic in China's financial history.

The transition from the silver standard to the *fabi* was in itself a double-edged sword. It reduced transaction costs on the commodities market and put an end to China's chaotic and backward currency structure, but also extended the scope of the Nationalist government's power at this stage. Currency reform deprived many banks of the right to issue currency, and their minting equipment was confiscated; the local private banks, already under supervision and management because of poor operations, came under further control. Economist Ma Yinchu credited the *fabi* with "effectively launching a new epoch in China's currency system," while also expressing concern about the potential for inflation: "This new currency system, since it does not allow cash conversion, is not inflationary in itself, but it creates the fundamental conditions for inflation. Whether the government will engage in inflationary measures on the basis of these fundamental conditions will require observing its actual performance from now on."[49] Who could know? In this way history is foretold over and over again.

The *fabi* ended the previous chaos of using both silver and copper cash, and also created conditions that facilitated the government extending its reach in efforts to unify China both geographically and monetarily. The Nationalist government spent ten years improving the financial system, but the Japanese invasion changed everything. The *fabi* was introduced, finance came under centralized control, and financial markets shifted toward government dominance. At the same time, the logic of war was as ruthless as ever; the fall of the northeast into enemy hands was a serious blow to revenues from customs duty, salt tax, and commodities tax, and the Nationalist government's newly restored fiscal administration became unsustainable. The *fabi* initially enjoyed the support of England and the United States and remained relatively stable in the early stage of the War of Resistance against Japan, but the Nationalist government, falling into deficit, soon resorted to printing money. As the financial deficit reached a peak of 86.9 percent, the printing of *fabi* became a lifeline for sustaining the war effort. Even so, the rate of printing money could not keep up with plunging fiscal revenues, and as military expenses soared, the *fabi* inevitably slid into the abyss of inflation. The basic reason for the collapse of the *fabi* differed little from historical precedent; as before, it involved the overlap of military defeat and financial crisis. The Nationalist government's effort to buy time with its currency ultimately failed (see Table 5-3).

What were the successes and failures of the *fabi*? Different people assess it differently. For example, Milton Friedman says that the U.S. Silver Purchase Act changed Chinese history by pushing China toward a paper currency standard that resulted in hyperinflation and subversive change:

> Government expenditure soared skyward to meet the cost of suppressing the Japanese invasion, and later to finance the civil war against the Communists . . . No doubt government expenditures would have soared even if the United States had not driven up the price of silver, and China would sooner or later have left the silver standard and gone on a paper standard. But the U.S. action assured that the paper standard and inflation came sooner, not later. Chiang's position was

directly weakened by the loss of the silver reserves that could have financed at least the initial expansion of government spending, thereby postponing the need to engage in inflationary monetary creation. He was weakened indirectly by the severely disturbed economic conditions to which the U.S. action contributed and which undermined popular support for the Nationalist regime.[50]

Its subsequent hyperinflation has caused Chinese historians to assess the *fabi* poorly. But it can also be evaluated from another perspective.

First of all, for a virtually premodern major country to transition from a gold standard to a fiduciary currency is a massive leap in terms of financial reform. In fact, the logic of China's monetary system made implementing a paper currency just a matter of time; China had been seriously discussing abandoning the silver standard since at least early 1928, and the Silver Purchase Act merely accelerated this step. Furthermore, inflationary pressure on the *fabi* came from both within and without; the crux was the need to finance military affairs rather than the currency system itself. That is why the real issue was never the paper

Table 5-3. Fiscal Revenues, 1937–1945

Year	Budgeted expenditure (C$ millions)	Actual expenditure (C$ millions)	Fiscal revenue (C$ millions)	Fiscal deficit (C$ millions)	Percentage deficit / expenditure
1937	1,001	2,091	815	1,276	61.0%
1938	856	1,169	315	845	73.1%
1939	1,706	2,797	740	2,057	73.5%
1940	2,488	5,288	1,325	3,963	74.9%
1941	4,610	10,003	1,310	8,693	86.9%
1943	36,236	58,816	20,403	38,413	65.3%
1944	79,501	171,689	38,503	133,186	77.6%
1945	263,844	2,348,058	1,241,389	1,106,696	47.1%

Source: Zhang Gongquan, 1986, *History of Inflation in China*

standard versus a metal standard, but rather the possibility of effectively restraining the government's economic power, and whether the degree of inflation caused by war would exceed what people could bear.

In fact, the emergence of the *fabi* not only unified China's multitude of currencies and consolidated China's national power, it also became a form of resistance to Japan and its puppet currency. The *fabi* in fact played a major role in the War of Resistance against Japan; the Japanese have even held the view that if China had not undertaken currency reform in 1937, it might not have been able to sustain its resistance for so long and might have been defeated and overthrown early on, or even sued for peace under humiliating circumstances, and history would have been rewritten.[51]

Second, *fabi* reform followed the aforementioned centralized type of financial control. Chiang Kai-shek was already planning a similar approach to other sectors, and finance was always just a supplement to political and military measures. This may look like a personal leadership style, but in fact it was determined by political patterns.

During the Northern Expedition, Chiang Kai-shek gained considerable support from the Shanghainese banking community, especially the so-called Jiangzhe tycoons. This phrase first appeared in Japanese newspapers: "The success of the revolutionary army's Northern Expedition benefited from the support of the Jiang[su-]Zhe[jiang] tycoons." Japanese scholars devoted considerable study to this phenomenon in the 1920s and 1930s, identifying leading bankers and industrialists from Jiangsu and Zhejiang provinces such as Zhang Jingjiang, Yu Qiaqing, Li Ming, Zhang Gongquan, Qian Xinzhi, and K. P. Chen. Chiang Kai-shek obtained considerable help from Jiangzhe bankers in covering military expenses, but Chiang didn't like being beholden to others, while the bankers also bristled under the government "treating banks like the national treasury," resulting in a growing rift between the financial and government cliques.

Zhang Gongquan, for example, contributed a great deal to Chiang's Northern Expedition, both economically and diplomatically. Chiang was initially very deferential to him, and even attended the funeral of Zhang's mother in April 1927, but by September 1928 the two were at odds. Fearing that Chiang would strong-arm him into serving as minister of finance,

Zhang avoided going to Nanjing, and Chiang angrily ordered Zhang's arrest. [Politician] Huang Fu and [leading businessman] Yu Qiaqing were finally able to smooth things over, but without resolving the crux of the matter. Zhang Gongquan had hoped that the newly established Central Bank would share the heavy responsibilities of China's other leading banks and allow the Bank of China, which he had single-handedly created, to avoid becoming the government's fundraising apparatus. What happened instead was that the government forced Zhang out of the Bank of China after the Central Bank was established.

An even more important factor was the general situation, which with the haze of war fast approaching involved controlling not only the military but also the banks. Chiang Kai-shek's thinking is revealed in a famous encrypted telegram he sent to H. H. Kung in 1935:

> The state and society are both on the verge of bankruptcy. The crux is in the inability to unify the financial and currency systems and the issuance of currency, in particular the outmoded traditions and policies of Bank of China and Bank of Communications, which suck the blood and marrow of the country and the people and ignore the state and society. If not categorically addressed, there will be no hope for the revolution, and the life of our nation will be cut off by these two banks. This is in fact an even greater sabotage of the revolution than the carving up of the country by warlords. Today the country is in crisis, and for the sake of the government and society, we must make the three banks absolutely obey the orders of the central government and thoroughly cooperate in order to allow our country and our people to survive. Please convey to President Lin and to Mssrs Wang, Sun, Yu, Ju and Dai that they should stand firm and persist to the end in order to save our critically imperiled party and country. I hear Bank of China general manager Mr. Zhang Gongquan intends to resign. In my opinion he should immediately resolve to separate himself from Bank of China and accept some other government appointment or serve as vice-president of the Central Bank. It would be most fortunate if he could focus

his efforts on developing the Central Bank and facilitating the country's unification, satisfying the needs of both the public and private sectors.[52]

For Chiang Kai-shek, war meant the need for financial support, either finagled or seized. It was a matter of seizing the opportunity, even if gangster methods were required, and kidnapping and murder were by no means rare back then. The approach of the Nanjing government and Shanghai capitalists has been described in this way:

> Coercion was seldom used, but it was always a potentiality. Whenever the need arose, as with the bond reorganizations of 1932 and 1936, Tu Yueh-sheng [Du Yuesheng] and Chang Hsiao-lin [Zhang Xiaolin][53] gave their support to Chiang. As the decade wore on, Nanking gained control of business and banking organizations, seized the banking industry, and usurped the leadership of the commercial and industrial sectors. These later events, however, have not been so widely reported as the April 1927 coup.[54]

It was previously believed that the Jiangzhe tycoons shared a battle line with the Nationalist government. In fact, they were becoming increasingly distanced from each other by the end of the 1920s, and had become completely estranged by the last years of the Nationalist period in the 1940s. During a crackdown on economic crimes in 1948, Chiang Ching-kuo threatened to arrest bankers Li Ming, Zhou Zuomin, and others,[55] but that was just a highlight of the rupture, and another case of the Nationalist government crushing dissent and turning potential allies into opponents. When Chinese capital encounters autocratic power, the result is always lamentable. K. P. Chen, known as the "Chinese Morgan," expressed disgust in his journal at the expression "Jiangzhe tycoon," and Zhang Gongquan said this group could not be compared with Japanese tycoons: "In fact the power these people wielded could not compare with Japan's Mitsui, Yasuda and other such clans; how could they claim to be tycoons? It all depended on individual status and public confidence. With the Chinese populace longing for orderly governance after long chaos, people let the circumstances guide their actions."[56]

The Nationalist government and the capitalists had a delicate relationship: sometimes brothers, sometimes strangers, sometimes adversaries, and after a brief honeymoon period, the status of master and servant was set. The Kuomintang regime resisted serving any class or any clique, perhaps due to its premodern genealogy, and also because the changing times made autocracy difficult to turn back. Scholar Lloyd E. Eastman concludes that the Kuomintang only served its founders, and its regime seldom demonstrated any governing capacity, relying almost entirely on its military and out of touch with society: "Groups and individuals—for example, some capitalists, some landlords, and some student and patriotic groups—did on occasion mount sufficient pressure to influence the formation or implementation of specific policies. There existed, however, no regular and institutionalized means by which to bring these pressures to bear upon the government."[57]

The Kuomintang was essentially fragmented and disjointed in its governance of China, and the lack of an intermediate foundation meant increasingly centralized power surrounded by a country disintegrating among separatist warlords. The actions and even protests of various political entities, whether Jiangzhe tycoons or students or small businessmen, did influence the country's leaders, but not essentially. In fact, any bureaucratic system exists to maintain rule, and if it does nothing but expand, it leaves no room for nonestablishment groups and civil society to survive. Ultimately it self-inflates, recycles, and destroys itself: Leaders swallow up political parties, and political parties swallow up society. The Nationalist government had neither the open-mindedness to embrace interest groups, nor the dictatorial power to destroy them. Already preoccupied with its own affairs as it strove to modernize itself, the regime treated interest groups with inconsistency and mutual exploitation. The financial sector was no exception.

Finance is the lifeblood of the economy, and economic policies are derived from political will. The state seizing everything means destroying everything, and heedlessly seizing all economic lifelines inevitably moves toward heedless sacrifice—even if in the name of saving the nation from domestic turmoil and foreign attack. In terms of finance, this means that bringing China's finances under control required pushing forward the "four banks, two bureaus and one treasury." The "four banks" referred to the Central Bank, the Bank of China, the Bank of Communications, and the Farmers Bank of China. The "two bureaus" were the Central Trust Bureau and the Postal Savings and Remittance Bureau, and the "one treasury" was the Central Cooperative Treasury.

To this end, the Nationalist government established the Central Bank, which formally opened in Shanghai on November 1, 1928, with T. V. Soong as president and its headquarters in Shanghai. At the same time the government began controlling the overall financial situation, using currency reform and the financial crisis as a rationale to swallow up stock in private banks and local private banks. For example, two of the "four banks," the Bank of China and the Bank of Communications, originally enjoyed great prestige and strong independence, but the Nationalist government effectively gained control of both banks by moving their headquarters to Shanghai, reorganizing them, withdrawing privileges, increasing government shareholdings, and changing personnel. That turned these two commercial banks into state banks. Zhang Gongquan and other executives were forced out, and the Bank of China began taking orders from Chiang Kai-shek, T. V. Soong, and others.

Thus the curtain fell on the market-dominated Beiyang era. The Jiangzhe tycoons—once considered the main backers of Chiang Kai-shek's political moves, and once China's most hopeful bankers, such as K. P. Chen, Qian Xinzhi, and Zhang Gongquan—gradually became government vassals. Zhang Gongquan and the others could only bemoan their own fates and sigh over the country's uncertain economic and political future. "All good things must come to an end, and why should the beautiful bouquet one grasps be placed only in one's own home? . . . My one regret is that I hoped, after the Republic was established, that the power of the Bank of China would assist the government in establishing an excellent Preparatory Central Bank while also preserving a strong currency, and also create a division of labor and cooperation among public and private financial institutions as well as a financial system that could develop the economy, and a capital-rich domestic financial market that could earn the firm trust of foreign capital and catch up with the economic prosperity of Japan and Germany. Most regrettably, this desire has come to naught."⁵⁸

Behind the changes in the financial market was another of Chinese history's cycles of order and disorder. An excessively weak government had difficulty building the country and expanding the market; an excessively strong government lacking systemic constraints ultimately smothered the market. This weakness or strength was not in the government's ruling capability, but rather the demarcation of its power boundaries. A powerful government that is tempted to kill the goose that lays the golden egg by smothering the market will have difficulty solving its own problems. Likewise, the Nationalist government endlessly wracked its brains over economic problems, but after gaining control of the commercial banks, it was unable to shake off its financial deficit and instead slid into an even darker abyss. Changes in the situation of silver provide a glimpse of the successes and failures of China's economy over the generations. The intermediate forces between politics and capital were always disadvantaged and even deficient. Capital was either destroyed for lack of political protection or suffocated in obtaining political protection. The success or failure of commerce, and especially finance, is always closely bound to politics, but without the development of intermediate forces, commerce is excessively constrained and politics is ultimately also thwarted.

Put in today's context, the Republic's financial predicament is by no means unfamiliar; this is the corrupt personal rule that has plagued China for 1,000 years. The American scholar Francis Fukuyama believes that an orderly society requires a combination of three essential factors: the state itself, the rule of law, and accountability in government, combined in a stable balance.⁵⁹ Unfortunately, in times of chaos this apparently simple "political sandwich," subjected to the dispersal of power internally and the encirclement of enemies externally, not only created the tragedy of financial deficit and currency devaluation in the Republic's last years, but ultimately veered into political tragedy.

Returning to the main thread of silver, the Central Bank should have been the ultimate and most important defense against inflation. Unfortunately, the Republican government's Central Bank was not actually a central bank in the modern sense, and for the most part was merely a counting-room cashier controlled by the government. Economic historian Du Xuncheng refers to it as a "freak of nature." From the time it was established in 1928, the Republic of China's Central Bank had many disadvantages; not only was its initial status no higher than that of the Bank of China, the Bank of Communications, and the Farmers Bank, but its currency-regulating methods were also hindered and it had no independence to speak of. The position of president was most of the time held concurrently by the minister of finance, for five years in the case of T. V. Soong, and then twelve years by H. H. Kung, and then for several more months by Yu Hung-chun (a.k.a. Yu Hongjun or O. K. Yui). It wasn't until June 1946 that the Central Bank had its first full-time president, Tsuyee Pei (Bei Zuyi), who came from the Bank of China and was the father of the great architect I. M. Pei.

Currency has externality. The *fabi*'s early success and the failure of the *jinyuanquan* both show that good money can exist, while bad money is doomed for withdrawal from circulation and may even cause the public to turn toward commodity currency. At the last stage of the *jinyuanquan,* the price of goods skyrocketed, but people had already abandoned the *jinyuanquan* and were using gold, silver, or U.S. dollars, or were even resorting to barter.

Finance is very important, but it can only demonstrate its effectiveness in a stable and orderly society. Throughout its history in mainland China, the Kuomintang regime never organized or mobilized in the deep hinterland, especially in the rural areas, and this huge vacuum resulted in the separation and encirclement of the cities. When the cities ultimately lost their military and economic advantage, the Nationalist government's defeat became inevitable. This in fact was the fate predestined for its fragile system from the outset.

Beginning with the influx of foreign silver and ending with real gold and genuine silver, this is the cycle of China's silver centuries. It encompassed the rise and fall of numerous dynasties and the hard effort of many outstanding individuals, all of it reverberating through history. The historical cycle includes countless cosmic questions awaiting answers. The answer is silver, as well as human greed, and more than that, major systemic failure.

Afterword

This is not the book I meant to write, and its final form is in fact very different from what I originally envisaged.

Yet, of all of my books, it is the one on which I've expended the most effort and attention. In the nearly four years from when I first picked up my pen until I wrote these words, I abandoned the book at certain points until summoning the courage to take it up again.

This book started out to some extent as a continuation of *The Money Printers*, but structurally it is clearly larger and more complex. The main topic of *The Money Printers* was the history of the central bank and financial crises, including the Bank of England. While comparing the Asian and Western banking systems, I discovered that the great divergence between the two economies had also given rise to a great divergence in the currency and financial systems. Put simply, medieval Europe used a combination of gold and silver coins while China's Song, Yuan, and Ming dynasties were carrying out various experiments with paper currency; that was an enormous difference. On the opposite side of the globe, great geographical discoveries brought precious metals from the Americas. Although Europeans initially dreamed of finding "El Dorado," the amount and influence of silver far surpassed those of gold.

In this way, silver flowed into Europe, and in the course of trade China also absorbed the world's silver and accomplished its own silver monetization. From then on, the West and Asia developed in nearly opposite directions. The discovery of large amounts of silver caused price revolutions in Europe, and excessive amounts of silver sent bimetallism on a downslide; most countries abandoned bimetallism for the gold standard and ultimately developed modern banking and paper currency systems. But for China, it was the beginning of a long, mysterious obsession with the white precious metal, silver.

I was fascinated by the kaleidoscopic image projected by this historical prism. Historians tend to focus more on dynastic change, while economic historians compare GDPs; neither group has paid enough attention to currency. That's hardly strange; even now, macroeconomists typically regard money as a veil over the real economy. The history of finance therefore still contains many lacunae, and I sometimes felt that I could not simply criticize the market dominance of books on currency wars or conspiracy theories (and even simply opposing currency wars), because neither economists nor historians pay much attention to the history of finance.

Curiosity has always been my natural instinct and the motivation for my reading and writing. I was very curious about the subject of silver and the Asian and Western currency systems, curious about the differences between them, about the mechanisms and dynamic principles beyond what is superficially apparent, and about the results and the latent effects. This book therefore begins with the legend of silver, recording its past and present in China, from remote antiquity to the twentieth century, in an effort to provide a monetary history of China with a global perspective. Following the fossil record layer after layer, this book's length and the time it consumed exceeded my expectations, and became an interrogation of the tortuous history of imperial finance, economy, and politics.

How could I track down the historical truth about silver and China's monetary history? I initially intended to carry out quantitative calculations by comparing various sources, for example, calculating the amount of silver that flowed into China. In the process, however, I discovered that such works already existed, some possibly path-breaking and some merely expendable supplementary information. Establishing a numerical benchmark might serve as a shortcut into a certain domain, but it wasn't my preferred method. In my view, the fascination of historical research is in exploring complexity and the logic behind ambiguities. In the end I chose the method I excel at, which is sorting historical threads in search of an overall political-economic logic and an even better explanation.

Economics is more of a methodology, with its own succinct, ruthless logic, while history is different; its genuine majesty and dignity don't require much deduction or strained interpretation. In recent years there has been repeated criticism of Chinese people's loss of faith. Setting aside whether these criticisms are correct or biased, I often have the vague feeling that history is in fact the collective religion of the Chinese; solving so many of today's problems requires going back to former times.

Everyone has their own learning method, and that's what writing is for me. I've often joked that if I don't understand something, I'll write a book about it; so this book is my first foray into the domain of financial history. I used to publish one or two books per year, leading my friends to exclaim over my productivity whenever they saw me. This is actually a product of my occupational training, which demands rapid response to financial incidents, but another reason is accumulation; many of my past books could be traced back at least ten years. This book was different, however; the history of finance is a new frontier that has begun to interest me in recent years, and the additional effort demanded by the size and scope of the topic inevitably slowed down the writing process.

It is because of this that the duration of the writing process and the amount of work involved greatly exceeded my expectations; the greater the number of spheres it touched on, the more time was required, and the texts I read increased exponentially. An overabundance of material on a particular subject is a blessing but also a burden to a specialist in that sphere, and a modicum of ambition made me feel the oppressiveness of the demand for plentitude and complexity. One respected scholar of Chinese history exclaimed how listing his references had made it obvious how far his efforts had strayed. When I read this sentence I knew what he meant; the interdisciplinary history of finance is also like that. The enormous time span and vast scope of this book required too much supplemental information, and the books and articles listed here are only a part. Yet, as always, too much unfinished reading stretches out before me as extension points of future interest. I sometimes think that if I read all the books I want and need to read, I might end up bleeding from both eyes, and also, that if I'd known from the start that this book would require so much of me, I might not have had the courage to begin.

Economists pay attention to opportunity costs, and the greatest cost in human life is time; life is short, so we should spend our time on only the best things. Whenever I thought about spending nearly four years on a single book that differed from existing scholarly treatises and popular reading matter, I had to consider whether it was actually meaningful or whether my work had any genuine added value. Midway through, I even wondered if I'd be able to finish it, and I stopped and started several times—the difficulty was not only the intrusion into my work and everyday life; sometimes just thinking of how the topic was expanding was enough to make me lose confidence. Fortunately, the grandness and fascination of the topic itself always summoned me back to my desk.

The history of finance is a road that few people have taken, and many of those only because they veered off on the wrong path. But when fortunate enough to encounter an interesting topic, I hope to imbue it with a new understanding. Taking the long view, all human effort is just the ashes of time, but in the end, I choose to believe in the value of this effort; after all, obsession is one of the impetuses that moves human life forward.

This book dissects finance and economics and touches on fiscal administration, military affairs, politics, diplomacy, and other spheres, leading me into many unfamiliar domains. I pay tribute to the scholars in these domains, and I beg the reader's forgiveness for any errors and omissions in these fortuitous encounters. Along the way I obtained direct and indirect assistance from various teachers and friends. Teacher Wei Sen, Mr. Liu Haiying, and others gave me a great deal of support from the time I began writing, and provided me with many valuable opinions during repeated readings of the book. Cai Menghan, Wei Zhou, Zhao Peng, Zhi An, and others did not hesitate to provide many valuable opinions at the last juncture before publication. Jiang Yongjun, Zhu Lijun, Sun Qi, and other editors at CITIC Press Group gave me enormous encouragement before *Empire of Silver* was finished and spared no effort in correcting many deficiencies during the publication process. Their effort saved me from many rudimentary errors. I am deeply grateful and thank them here once again.

What I've written up to now may sound like a lot of complaining, but that's not the whole story. After completing this book, I spent several months revising it at night after work. It was at this time, knocking out words under lamplight deep into the Shanghai night, with the occasional flash of car lights outside the window and the faint tooting of a ferry on the distant river, that I gained the sense of a sculpture taking shape, or the agitation of bursting from a cocoon, or a rush of almost inconceivable thoughts and feelings—and this feeling was more sweet than sour. It was like what one Japanese novelist said about making sweet snacks during the hard labor of writing a book: "People who have read my books and eaten my desserts have sampled the hardship and joy of my work."

This is how it ends. Perhaps it is like the patterns of behavioral economics: Our judgment of whether a memory is happy or not is decided less by the process than by how it ended.

Next time I should try writing a novel, or perhaps make a box of chocolate.

Further Reading

This book attempts a new perspective in reexamining the economic history of China, and the history of China generally, at certain turning points in monetary history. As the Indian-British writer V. S. Naipaul said, "Men need history; it helps them to have an idea of who they are. But history, like sanctity, can reside in the heart; it is enough that there is something there."[1]

This is an interdisciplinary work, and I drew aid from many primary sources, including classics such as *History of the Tang Dynasty, History of the Song Dynasty, History of the Yuan Dynasty,* and *History of the Ming Dynasty,* as well as the writings of our forebears, and articles from publications of the Republican and Nationalist eras such as *Shen Bao, Dagong Bao, Bankers Weekly,* and *Bankers Monthly.* My further reflection and research drew aid from many secondary sources.

"Give a man a fish and you feed him for a day; teach a man to fish and you feed him for a lifetime." I would here like to recommend some scholars who take a variety of approaches, in hopes that readers will go on to read their works and better understand our past and future, as well as to pay tribute to them as providers of material or sources of thought for my book. Modern people read not only to enhance knowledge, but also as an interesting form of consumption. During my college years, I joined with others in publishing a literary magazine called *Readings,* and today I use my public platform, *Xu Jin Economist* (WeChat ID: econhomo), as a book club to regularly share readings and recommended booklists on economics. There are many others who also hope that readers can find the most outstanding and valuable reading materials among the numerous choices on offer. Reading can be lonely, but sharing books makes reading even more enjoyable.

I feel that works by these experts, even if somewhat academic, make excellent further reading. Searching under their names will lead down a rabbit hole of further readings, but specific book titles can be found in the Bibliography.

History

Hosea Ballou Morse, Frederick W. Mote, John King Fairbank, Fernand Braudel, Peter Bol, Takeshi Hamashita, David Graeber, Miyazawa Tomoyuki, Guo Tingyi, Qi Xia

Economic History

Angus Maddison, David S. Landes, Katō Shigeshi, Ma Yinchu, Quan Han, Niall Ferguson, Li Bozhong, Yeh-Chien Wang

History of Finance

Zhang Gongquan, Peng Xinwei, Wan Zhiying, Jean Rivoire, Charles P. Kindleberger, William N. Goetzmann, K. Geert Rouwenhorst, Hong Jiaguan, Du Xuncheng, Kuroda Akinobu, Felix Martin

Silver

Qian Jiang, William S. Atwell, Lai Jiancheng, Lin Man-houng, Wan Ming, Shi Junzhi, Dai Jianbing

Politics

Max Weber, Samuel E. Finer, Francis Fukuyama, Charles Tilly

Economics

Douglass North, Milton Friedman, Jesús Huerta de Soto, Daron Acemoglu, James A. Robinson

History of Finance

Zhou Bodi, Ray Huang, Liang Fangzhong, Jia Shiyi, Iwai Shigeki, Wang Shengduo

There's an old saying: "It takes a village to raise a child." My writing likewise relied on the help of countless predecessors and contemporaries. I cannot thank them individually here, but would like to especially thank Wei Sen, Zhu Jiaming, Ma Debin, and Liu Haiying for their endlessly patient corrections and assistance. I have no way to express the depth of my gratitude, but only hope to meet the expectations of these teachers and friends in my writing from now on.

Chronology

B.C.E.

11th century	The first currency appears in China. The use of cowries as a means of payment already existed before this. The casting of bronze cowries is said to have begun in the 14th century B.C.E.
7th century	The first coins appear in the Mediterranean with the minting of coins in Libya, in Asia Minor.
6th century	The silver drachma appears in Greece, and Persia produces a gold coin called the daric. The first private bank emerges in Greece.
524	King Jing of Zhou mints large coins.
4th century	The Macedonians unify Greek and Persian currency; Plato and Aristotle create the first theory of money; the first public banks appear in Greece.
269	Rome's first mint begins operating on the Capitoline Hill.
221	China's first emperor, Qing Shihuang, unifies China's coinage, divided between gold and bronze cash. Gold is the higher-value currency, using the *yi* as a standard unit; bronze cash is the lesser currency, with "half-ounce" stamped on it, and is therefore called the half-ouncer.
206	The Western Han is established. The first Han emperor declares Qin coins too heavy and hard to use and allows the people to mint coins (this right is later retracted). The catty becomes the standard unit for gold, and the half-ouncer is reduced in weight.
119	Emperor Wu of Han issues "white metal" and hide money. The *Book of Han Food and Commodities* states, "A square foot of white deer hide is valued at 400,000 [cash]." There are also three "white metal" coins of

| | various values, as well as bronze coins such as the five-grainer. Illegal minting becomes a capital offense. |
| 118 | The half-ouncer is abolished. The five-grainer is minted with a round shape and a square hole in the middle and stamped with the words "five grains." The "grain" was an ancient unit of weight equal to 1/25 of one tael. The five-grainer becomes China's longest-circulating coin. |

C.E.

6	The Western Han official Wang Mang usurps the throne, and the next year he reforms the monetary system by minting a gold-engraved knife, gold-inlaid knife, and "large spring" coin. Further currency reforms are carried out subsequently.
227	Persia's Sasanian Empire mints gold and silver coins.
3rd century	The Roman Empire's hard currency famine causes deflation, and prices surge.
301	Diocletian issues his Edict on Maximum Prices.
312	Constantine reforms the Roman Empire's coinage with the minting of a new gold coin and silver coin.
325	The Council of Nicaea bans clergy from charging interest on loans.
338	During the Xiankang era of the Eastern Jin dynasty, Li Shou is named king in Chengdu and renames his dynasty the Han. He mints Hanxing cash to mark the beginning of his dynasty, China's first dated cash.
6th century	The Eastern Roman emperor Justinian sets interest rates at 3.6% to 12%.
612	Emperor Gaozu of Tang abolishes the five-grainer and mints the "inaugural circulating treasure." From now on, coins are not named by weight.
7th century	The Arabs begin minting the gold dinar.
708	The Japanese mint the *wadō-kaihō* in the first year of the Wadō era under the order of Empress Genmei. The bronze coin is round with a square hole in the center.
755–768	France launches the minting of coins in medieval Europe with the silver denier.
781	Emperor Charlemagne reforms the currency system, setting a silver standard based on a pound of silver equal to 20 sous or 240 deniers.
789	Emperor Charlemagne extends the ban on charging interest on loans to the secular realm.
960	Song emperor Taizu mints the Song Original Circulating Treasure.
968	The Kingdom of Liao mints the Baoning Circulating Treasure.
980	In the fifth year of the Northern Song's Taiping Xingguo era, silver is permitted for the payment of taxes.

995	The Northern Song mints the Zhidao Circulating Treasure. Chengdu merchants use *jiaozi* as a medium of exchange in the market, heralding the emergence of paper currency.
970	Vietnam's Minister Dinh mints the *Thái Bình Hưng Bảo*.
996	Korea mints the Qianyuan Heavy Treasure iron and copper coins.
1023	The *jiaozi* exchange note authority is established in Sichuan.
1024	The Yizhou government issues the first official *jiaozi* in denominations from one string to ten strings.
1066	The currency system that originated with Charlemagne is formally adopted in England with the Norman Conquest. One English pound is divided into 20 shillings or 240 pence.
11th century	The Arabs mint forged dinars that subsequently become silver coins, then copper alloy coins, and finally copper coins.
1105	The *jiaozi* is changed into *qianyin* coin vouchers. Circulation is extended to Jingdong, Jingxi, Huainan, and the capital region. The amount of *qianyin* issued increases twenty times over the amount issued in the Tiansheng period. Tin alloy coins are minted.
1107	The Sichuan *jiaozi* authority is renamed the *qianyin* authority.
1137	The Southern Song general Wu issues *huizi* (silver account notes) in Hechi. This is China's earliest adoption of a silver standard.
1149	The Western Xia mints the Tiansheng Original Treasure.
1151	The Jin issues *jiaochao* exchange certificates.
1160	The Board of Revenue issues southeastern *huizi*.
1168	The Southern Song reforms the issuance of *huizi* by setting a maximum value limit of 10 million strings.
1180	The year of issue is stamped on the obverse of Southern Song coins. England mints the silver penny.
1189	The Jin abolishes expiration dates on its paper currency and allows *jiaochao* to circulate indefinitely.
1227	In Mongol-controlled territory, Heshi prints *Zhi huizi* in Bozhou.
1233	The Jin issues Taixing Treasure Account in Caizhou. "Taixing" is the last-year designation for the Jin dynasty, and the Taixing Treasure Account is the last coin minted by the Jin dynasty, which soon afterward is overthrown by the joint forces of the Mongols, Southern Song, and Northern Song and is extinguished in 1234.
1236	The Mongol khan Ögedei issues *jiaochao*.
1240	Within Mongol-controlled territory, Liu Su issues "mulberry currency" in Xingzhou.
1251	The paper currencies of the northern regions are not exchangeable; the Yuan dynasty decides on a dual system of silver and certificates (*chao*).

1252	Florence mints the Christian West's first gold coin, the florin (3.6 grams), initially equivalent to one lira.
1260	The Southern Song mints the Jingding Original Treasure. The Yuan issues *zhongtong* certificates and withdraws the local certificates circulating in the northern regions.
1262	Venice issues Monte Vecchio bonds.
1263	The Southern Song's Jia Sidao proposes the public fields law and the next year issues gold-, silver-, and copper-cash-denominated *guanzi* currency. The seventeenth term of *huizi* is abolished.
1266	France's King Louis IX imitates Arab coinage by minting a silver coin called the *gros tournois*.
1276	The Southern Song capital Lin'an falls to the Mongols; the Yuan dynasty rules the region south of the Yangtze and uses *zhongtong* certificates to recall the Southern Song paper currency. Boyan mints the Silver Original Treasure.
1279	In the Battle of Yamen against the invading Mongol Yuan dynasty, Prime Minister Lu Xiufu jumps into the sea while carrying the boy emperor Zhao Bing. Both drown, and the Southern Song falls.
1285	Lu Shirong proposes a plan to rectify paper currency. The Zhiyuan Circulating Treasure is minted. Venice mints a gold coin called the ducat.
1287	Yuan emperor Shizu issues Zhiyuan certificates.
1292	Guanghui Treasury pawnshops are established with a capital of 5,000 *ding* (ingots) in certificates.
1294	Persia's Ilkhan state circulates paper currency imitating China's.
1295	The Yuan dynasty mints Yuanzhen Circulating Treasure and Original Treasure; Japan circulates paper currency.
1309	Yuan emperor Wuzong reforms the currency system, issues *Zhida yinchao* (silver certificates), and mints Great Yuan Circulating Treasure and Zhida Circulating Treasure.
1311	Yuan emperor Renzong withdraws the Zhida silver certificates and abolishes the Zhida coins.
1350	The Yuan government reforms the paper-currency system a final time, issuing *Zhizheng jiaochao* (exchange certificates) printed with the words "Zhongtong Original Treasure exchange certificates," and mints Zhizheng Circulating Treasure.
1360	France mints the franc, a gold coin weighing 3.88 grams. The franc is initially worth one Tours pound.
12th–14th centuries	Italian merchants and banks flourish. The trade fare in France's Champagne region becomes famous throughout Western Europe, and the Knights Templar compete with the active commercial and banking sectors.

1361	Zhu Yuanzhang (later Emperor Hongwu) mints the Dazhong Circulating Treasure.
1368	In the first year of his reign, Ming emperor Hongwu mints the Hongwu Circulating Treasure and proclaims the related coinage system.
1375	The Great Ming Treasure certificates are issued, and the Treasure Source Bureau stops minting coins.
1397	The Treasure Source Bureau again stops minting coins. The use of gold and silver is banned.
1421	The Ming dynasty moves its capital to Beijing in the nineteenth year of the Yongle era.
1436	During the Ming dynasty's Yingzong era, treasure certificates are devalued and the ban on silver is relaxed; "gold flower silver" is used to pay land tax.
1465	An order is issued to pay commercial taxes half in coin and half in certificates.
1472	Italy's Monte dei Paschi di Siena Bank is established.
1497	The Spanish for the first time use imported New World silver to mint a coin—the peso, worth eight Spanish reales (25.9 grams).
1519	A 35-gram silver coin is minted in the silver-mining town of Joachimsthal in the kingdom of Bohemia. The Joachimsthaler, usually called the Thaler, is equal in value to the gold florin.
1531	The world's first financial exchange, the bourse of Antwerp, is established.
1535	The Spanish mint their first silver coin in the Americas, the piastre, valued at eight reales in silver currency (24.4 grams). This coin was known as a Mexican dollar because of its similarity to the German Thaler.
1537	The Spanish for the first time use imported New World gold to mint coins, the escudo (3.10 grams) and the two-escudo, also known as the pistole (6.20 grams).
1539	Italy establishes the Monte di Pietà bank, which becomes part of Banco Nazionale di Napoli in 1794.
1545	The Potosi silver mine is discovered in Bolivia, and from 1560 onward, silver coins replace gold coins flowing from the Americas into Europe.
1557	The Portuguese take possession of Macau.
1570	The Ming dynasty mints the Longqing Circulating Treasure. The Spanish invade Luzon, and foreign silver begins flowing into China.
1572	In the sixth year of the Longqing era, Emperor Zaizi dies; ten-year-old Zhu Yijun ascends the throne and is named the Wanli Emperor the next year, reigning for forty-eight years. Zhang Juzheng becomes

grand secretary, and in the ninth year of the Wanli era promulgates the "Single Whip tax law." Silver becomes monetized, and a "Wanli restoration" emerges, followed by avid mining.

15th–16th centuries
: Major private banks emerge (owned by the Medici, Strozzi, and other families in Italy, by the Fugger family in Germany, and by France's Jacques Coeur and England's Thomas Gresham). Public banks revive during the Renaissance. Banking centers form in Bruges, Antwerp, and Lyon. Pawnshops flourish.

1601
: Japan's *kinza, ginza,* and *doza* currency guilds are established. The Keicho Tsūhō coin is issued in 1606, and China's Yongle coins are banned in 1608.

1609
: The Netherlands establishes the Amsterdamsche Wisselbank, also known as the Bank of Amsterdam. Its name is changed to Netherlandsche Bank in 1814, and it ceases operations in 1819.

1616
: The Manchus mint Tianming cash.

1621
: In the first year of the Ming dynasty's Tianqi era, large and small coins called Taichang Circulating Treasure and Tianqi Circulating Treasure are minted. Wang Xiangqian requests the minting of three denominations of large coins.

1625
: Japan begins minting the *kan'ei* coin, with large numbers minted in 1636, gradually replacing Chinese coins.

1637
: The British East India Company arrives in China.

1640
: The Bank of Amsterdam issues transferable certificates of deposit. England's King Charles I confiscates all of the gold and silver held in the Tower of London.

1643
: The Ming dynasty mints the Chongzhen ten-cash coin. Jiang Chen proposes issuing paper currency.

1644
: Qing emperor Shizu mints the Shunzhi Circulating Treasure in Beijing. The Prince of Fu mints the Hongguang Circulating Treasure in Nanjing. Li Zicheng mints the Yongchang Circulating Treasure in Xian. Zhang Xianzhong mints the Dashun Circulating Treasure in Chengdu.

1651
: In the eighth year of the Shunzhi era, a paper currency called *chaoguan* (string certificates) is issued. Shunzhi coins are increased in weight to 0.125 ounces. Japan mints the Yongle Circulating Treasure to aid Ming loyalist Zheng Chenggong's resistance against the Qing.

1656
: Johan Palmstruch establishes Stockholms Banco in Stockholm and begins issuing paper currency in 1661. The bank was reorganized in 1666 and eventually replaced by Sveriges Riksbank.

1666
: England's freedom to mint and its seigniorage tax come to an end.

1680
: Gold mines are discovered in Minas Gerais, Brazil.

1694	The Bank of England is established in London.
1706	Japan makes its currency lighter, and its *kanˈei tsūhō* begin flowing into China.
1715	A disciplinary court is established in France, which levies heavy taxes on bankers and financiers engaged in illegal accumulation of wealth.
1717	Sir Isaac Newton sets the price of gold at 3 pounds 17 shillings 10.5 pence per troy ounce. From then on, the pound is set at 111 grams of silver, equivalent to 7.32 grams of gold.
1717–1720	France adopts John Law's financial and monetary system. In 1717 the Mississippi Company is set up for speculation in French colonies in North America. The company suffers a run on its paper notes in 1720 and is dissolved in 1721.
1720	Guangzhou merchants organize a guild called the Cohong, and foreign silver dollars begin flowing into China in large quantities.
1724	The Bourse de Paris is established.
1727	The Royal Bank of Scotland is established.
1737	Beijing establishes ten official cash offices (*guanqianju*) to stabilize prices.
1747	Belgium's Nagelmackers Bank is established.
1755	Switzerland's Bank Leu is established; it is bought out by Crédit Suisse in 1990.
1774	England stops using silver coins as currency.
1700s	The American colonies used an array of separate currencies, but after the American War of Independence breaks out in 1775, the Continental Congress begins issuing Continental currency.
1776	Adam Smith publishes *The Wealth of Nations*.
1789	The French Revolution breaks out. France issues a paper currency called *assignats,* which becomes worthless by 1797.
1791	Bank of the United States is established.
1792	The United States sets the U.S. dollar at 24.06 grams of silver or 1.6038 grams of gold.
1794	The United States begins minting silver dollars.
1800	Banque de France is established, and later sets the franc at 45 grams of silver or 2.9033 grams of gold.
1806	Bank of Calcutta is established. It later becomes part of State Bank of India.
1808	Banco do Brasil is established.
1812	City Bank of New York is established.
1814	Guangdong establishes Ao Maritime Customs Silver House.

1816   England adopts the gold standard. The British pound's value is set
            against gold based on the 1717 evaluation. France's Caisse des Dépôts
            et Consignations is established.

1817   Canada's Bank of Montreal is established; Australia's Bank of New
            South Wales is established.

1822   Banco de la Nación Argentina is established.

1823   Mexico begins minting the "eagle dollar." British utopian socialist
            Robert Owen issues labor vouchers.

1824   Holland's Algemene Bank Nederland is established.

1826   British law permits creating a bank through the issuing of stock (joint
            stock banks).

1830   In the tenth year of the Daoguang era, a memorial is issued on new
            regulations for arranging the bankruptcy of coin shops. After this,
            China experiences decades of silver famine.

1840–1856   The First Opium War breaks out in 1840. England usually calls the
            First Opium War a trade war, and it is regarded as the beginning of
            China's modern history. The Qing government loses the war and
            signs the Treaty of Nanking with England, which requires it to pay
            restitution of 21 million silver dollars, cede Hong Kong to England,
            and open the ports of Canton (Guangzhou), Xiamen, Fuzhou, Ningbo,
            and Shanghai for commerce and trade. The Second Opium War breaks
            out in 1856.

1848   The British-owned Oriental Bank Corporation opens a branch in
            Canton.

1848–1850   The French franc circulates at a forcibly imposed market price.
            Banque de France's currency-issuing privileges are extended to
            neighboring countries. France establishes more than sixty discount
            banks. Banque de France is granted a nationwide monopoly on
            issuing currency.

1850   Franz Hermann Schulze-Delitzsch establishes the world's first credit
            union in Germany.

1852   Crédit Mobilier and Crédit Foncier de France are established in
            France.

1853   Bank runs occur in Beijing. The Xianfeng 10-cash coin is minted.
            Beijing establishes three official silver and cash houses. Provinces are
            ordered to set up official cash offices. Board of Revenue official bills
            (*guanpiao*) and Xianfeng certificates are issued. The Taiping Heavenly
            Kingdom mints Taiping Kingdom Sagely Treasure in Nanjing and
            other places.
            In the same year, the United States, although not yet on the gold
            standard, reduces the currency functions of silver.

1854	100-cash, 500-cash, and 1,000-cash large coins are minted. Treasure certificates are later used to redeem the large coins. England's Mercantile Bank of India, London, and China and the Commercial Bank of India open branches in Shanghai.
1855	Iron coins and lead coins are minted.
1856	Several Shanghai silver houses use steel molds to mint Xianfeng "silver cakes." The Small Sword Society mints Taiping Circulating Treasure sun and moon coins in Shanghai.
1857	Beijing merchants boycott the market and refuse to use large iron coins. The Treasure *Su* Office uses iron molds to mint Xiantong Circulating Treasure silver coins. England's Chartered Bank of India, Australia, and China (Chartered Bank) opens a branch in Shanghai.
1861–1865	The Civil War occurs in the United States. Large amounts of paper currency are issued (the term "inflation" comes into common use in the United States at this time). The U.S. dollar is forcibly circulated in the market until 1879.
1862	Official bills (*guanpiao*) cease to circulate. The Tongzhi Circulating Treasure is minted.
1863	The United States establishes a number of national banks, which begin competing with state-franchised banks.
1864	Rashidin mints coins inscribed with Arabic in Kulja, Xinjiang.
1865	Through a treaty establishing the Latin Monetary Union, France, Italy, Belgium, and Switzerland pledge their loyalty to the gold–silver bimetal standard while at the same time reducing the currency functions of silver. Belgium establishes a savings and retirement bank. The Hongkong and Shanghai Banking Corporation (HSBC) opens in Hong Kong, and then establishes branches in Shanghai, London, and other cities.
1866	Hong Kong mints silver dollars.
1867	The first edition of Marx's *Das Kapital* is published. In the same year, the late Qing statesman and military leader Zuo Zongtang borrows money from Hangzhou merchant Hu Xueyan and others to fund his army's westward march in what is considered a precedent for the Chinese government taking on external debt.
1868	Japan's Meiji Empire establishes a new government, after which it issues a paper currency called State Council Notes (*dajokan-satsu*).
1870	The Franco-Prussian War begins. The next year, the Treaty of Frankfurt requires France to pay 5 billion francs in restitution to Germany. The franc is forcibly circulated in the market until 1878. In the same year, Japan mints its Dragon Foreign Dollar.

1871	The Japanese yen is born. Japan makes an unsuccessful attempt to adopt the gold standard.
1873	Germany adopts the gold standard. The United States mints a Trade Silver Dollar.
1878	The countries of the Latin Monetary Union temporarily suspend the minting of silver coinage and adopt a de facto gold standard.
1882	Jilin tests the minting of the Changping silver coin, the first machine-minted coin in China. In the same year, the Bank of Japan is established.
1887	Guangdong mints the Dragon Foreign Dollar.
1894	The Sino-Japanese War breaks out.
1895	The Treaty of Shimonoseki (known as the Treaty of Bakan in China) ends the Sino-Japanese War. In the same year, the Russo-Chinese Daosheng Bank is established and issues paper money and Silver Original Treasure coins. England issues a silver dollar for circulation in the Far East. Because it bears a standing figure of the goddess Britannia holding a trident, the Chinese call it the Stick Foreign Dollar.
1897	The Imperial Bank of China is established and issues paper currency. Japan's Yokohama Specie Bank establishes a branch in Shanghai.
1900	The United States adopts the gold standard.
1905	The Board of Revenue establishes a silver and cash coin mint in Tianjin. The Great Qing Board of Revenue (Hubu) Bank is established.
1907	The Xinjiang Machine Office mints the Supply Gold coin. The Bank of Communications is established. The government requests opinions from provincial governors on the appropriate unit for a silver coin.
1908	The Great Qing Board of Revenue Bank is renamed the Great Qing Bank and issues the Great Qing Bank Regulations.
1909	The Xuantong Circulating Treasure is minted. A coinage investigation office is established.
1910	The Monetary System Regulations are promulgated, and the silver standard is implemented.
1911	China has twenty-six money-exchange shops (piaohao), which establish 459 branch offices in eighty cities throughout China. In the same year, the Xinhai Revolution breaks out. Sun Yat-sen issues Republic of China Gold Certificates to raise funds in San Francisco.
1912	The Qing Emperor abdicates, and Sun Yat-sen becomes provisional president in Nanjing. The government of the Republic of China is established. The Nanjing mint produces a commemorative coin with

the bust of Sun Yat-sen engraved on it. Daqing Bank branches throughout China change their name to Bank of China, continuing to serve as the state bank and issue exchange certificates.

1913   The United States establishes the Federal Reserve System.

1914   The Beiyang government issues the Coinage Regulations. The "Yuan [Shikai]-head dollar" is issued throughout the country. The Bank of Territorial Development and the Ministry of Finance Market Stabilization Currency Bureau begin operations and issue silver yuan notes (*yin yuan piao*) and copper coin notes (*tong yuan piao*).

1914–1918   World War I. Widespread bans are imposed on the export of silver, and paper currency is forcibly circulated in the market.

1915   The Beiyang government promulgates the Paper Currency Ban Regulations in order to address the rampantly excessive issuance of paper currency by various provinces and banks, but they are ineffective.

1916   Yuan Shikai restores the empire. The government expenditure is enormous and empties the Treasury. Bank of China and Bank of Communications stop redeeming bank notes for cash in Beijing, Tianjin, and other places, creating the "Beijing bank note panic." The Shanghai branch of Bank of China refuses to comply with the cash payout moratorium.

1917–1923   The price of goods soars uncontrollably in Russia, Austria, and Germany (the term "inflation," long in use in the United States, now becomes popular parlance in Europe).

1919–1922   Several commercial banks open for business, including Frontier Bank, Tah Chung Bank, Rural Commercial Bank, China and South Sea Bank, Bank of Mongolia and Tibet, Kangyo Bank, and National Industrial Bank, and they begin issuing bank exchange certificates.

1921   The Central Bank of Russia is established in the Soviet Union.

1922   The Genoa Conference advocates returning to a new form of the gold standard.

1924   Sun Yat-sen establishes the Central Bank in Guangzhou and issues silver dollar exchange certificates. Austria, Germany, and the Soviet Union (theoretically) reinstate the gold standard.

1925   Great Britain reinstates the gold standard based on the prewar exchange parity.

1928   France reinstates the gold standard based on one-fifth of the prewar exchange parity.

1927   The Nationalist government imitates the inaugural *yuan* of the Republic, minting a silver coin with the bust of Sun Yat-sen engraved on it.

1928   The Nationalist government establishes the Central Bank in Shanghai in November, and issues silver dollars and multiple paper currencies.

1929   Black Thursday occurs at the New York Stock Exchange on October 24.

1930   The Bank for International Settlements is established in Basel.

1931   Stock prices in banks all over the world plunge. Austria, Germany, and England abandon the gold standard.

1932   The Nationalist government's Central Bank issues Customs Gold Certificates (*guanjinquan*); the government of the enemy-occupied northeast organizes the Central Bank of Manchou and issues paper currency.

1933   The Nationalist government's Finance Ministry issues an order to eliminate the silver tael and convert to the silver dollar, stipulating that all private and public payments and transactions must use silver coins and can no longer use silver taels. In Shanghai, payments originally specified in silver taels are to be paid in silver coins at a rate of 0.715 treasury ounces per dollar. Outside of Shanghai, the conversion to the dollar begins on April 5 at a rate of 0.715 treasure ounces per dollar. Those in possession of silver taels can have them minted into coins at the Central Mint, or can exchange them for silver dollars at the Central Bank, Bank of China, or Bank of Communications. The first silver *yuan* is engraved with the bust of Sun Yat-sen on its face, and with two junks on its obverse. The Farmers Bank of Henan, Hubei, Anhui, and Gansu is established in Hankou and begins issuing paper currency. In the same year, the Chinese Soviet Republic Bank is established in Ruijin, and begins issuing paper currency in July.
           Also in this year, the Glass-Steagall Act in the United States strictly differentiates between commercial banks and investment banks. The United States implements a gold embargo that continues until 1974.

1934   The U.S. dollar suffers devaluation, and the price of gold soars to US$35 per ounce. The United States establishes the Export-Import Bank. In June, the United States passes the Silver Purchase Act, empowering the Department of the Treasury to buy silver on the market in the United States and overseas until the price of silver reaches US$1.29 per ounce or until the value of the Treasury Department's silver reserves reaches one-third of the value of its gold reserve. The Silver Purchase Act has a massive impact on major countries that mainly use silver, such as China.

1935   The Nationalist government implements a legal tender (*fabi*) policy. On November 4, the Central Bank, Bank of China, and Bank of Communications are required to issue bank notes in *fabi*, and the circulation of silver is banned. A national fiduciary legal tender is issued to replace the silver *yuan* under the silver standard.

1936	John Maynard Keynes publishes his book *The General Theory of Employment, Interest and Money.* France abandons the gold standard.
1939–1945	World War II. Comprehensive controls on foreign exchange.
1941	Nanjing's Wang Jingwei government establishes the Central Reserve Bank and issues reserve certificates.
1942	The Nationalist government decides to centralize the currency-issuing privileges of the Bank of China, Farmers Bank, and Bank of Communications in the Central Bank.
1944	The Bretton Woods Agreement is signed, establishing the International Monetary Fund and the International Bank for Reconstruction and Development.
1948	The Nationalist government carries out further currency reform. On August 18 it replaces the *fabi* with the *jinyuanquan* and compels exchange of gold, silver, and foreign currency for *jinyuanquan.*
	Also in that year, the Federal Republic of Germany reforms its currency and the Deutsche Mark is born.
1949	The Nationalist government loses its war with the Chinese Communist Party and issues "silver *yuan* certificates." In the same year, the People's Republic of China is established.
1950	The European Payments Union is established to handle payment in various European currencies.
1957	Germany establishes Deutsche Bundesbank.
1976	The International Monetary Fund changes its articles of agreement and abandons fixed exchange rates; gold is demonetized.

This chronology of major events in the monetary and financial systems in China and abroad was compiled from the research of Jean Rivoire, Charles P. Kindleberger, Peng Xinwei, and Yang Duanliu, as well as related material in Wikipedia.

Notes

Epigraphs

Keynes epigraph: John Maynard Keynes, 1919, *The Economic Consequences of the Peace*. Keynes attributes this statement to Lenin (translator's note [hereafter TN]).

Peng epigraph: Peng Xinwei, 1994, *A Monetary History of China*, trans. Edward H. Kaplan, Preface, p. xxii (TN).

North epigraph: "Douglass C. North," in Roger W. Spencer and David A. Macpherson (eds.), 2014, *Lives of the Laureates: Twenty-Three Nobel Economists*, sixth edition, pp. 162, 163.

Introduction

Mitchell epigraph: Quoted in Charles P. Kindleberger, 1984, *A Financial History of Western Europe*, p. 1.

1. Gaoxin Shi, also known as Emperor Ku, is a legendary emperor believed to have ruled from around 2436 to 2366 B.C.E. (TN).

2. Yu of Xia was a legendary emperor who established the Xia, the first dynasty in traditional Chinese history, around 2070 B.C.E. (TN).

3. Sima Qian, 2012, *Records of the Historian*, "Treatise on the Balanced Standard."

4. The Spring and Autumn period lasted from 771 to 476 or 403 B.C.E. (depending on the authority). The Warring States period lasted from 481 or 403 to 221 B.C.E. (TN).

5. 907–960 C.E.

6. Ban Gu, 111 C.E., *The Book of Han*, "Treatise on Food and Commodities."

7. The translator of Peng Xinwei's *A Monetary History of China*, Edward H. Kaplan, translates this term as "original treasure," noting that the Chinese character *yuan*

is the same for the Yuan dynasty and for the word meaning "original." The term assumed a new meaning in later generations. See Peng Xinwei, 1994, op. cit., p. 473 (TN).

8. For pictures and classifications of Chinese tael silver, see Zhejiang Provincial Museum (ed.), 2015, *The Historical Course of Silver—From Silver Taels to Silver Dollars*.

9. The rebellion, which continued from 755 to 763, devastated the Tang dynasty (TN).

10. Huang Zongxi, 1993, *Waiting for the Dawn: A Plan for the Prince*, trans. William Theodore de Bary, p. 152.

11. Kang Youwei (1858–1927) was a prominent Confucian scholar and leader of the Hundred Days' Reform of 1898 (TN).

12. Plato, *The Republic*, Book 3.

13. There are some who believe that the Tang dynasty's use of "flying money" (*feiqian*) for remittances had the characteristics of paper currency, but it is generally believed that the Song dynasty's *jiaozi* and *huizi* were more influential.

14. Quan Hansheng, 1966, *The Ming Dynasty's Silver Classifications and Silver Production Quotas*; see also Liang Fangzhong, 1989, *Collected Essays on Economic History*.

15. Quan Hansheng, 1966, op. cit.

16. Kindleberger, 1984, op. cit., p. 26 (TN).

17. Friedrich Engels, "Decay of Feudalism and Rise of Nation States," in *The Peasant War in Germany*, Marxists Internet Archive, https://www.marxists.org/archive/marx/works/1850/peasant-war-germany/ (TN).

18. Earl J. Hamilton, 1934, *American Treasure and the Price Revolution in Spain, 1501–1650* (TN).

19. Adam Smith, 1776, *The Wealth of Nations*, Chap. 5, "Of the Real and Nominal Price of Commodities, or of Their Price in Labour, and Their Price in Money."

20. Yan Zhongping, 1981, "Silver Flowed into the Philippines and Silver Flowed into China," *Modern Historical Studies*, Vol. 1.

21. Cited in Quan Hansheng, 1969, "The Importation of American Silver to China in the Ming and Qing Dynasties," in *Commentaries on Chinese Economic History*, Vol. 1, pp. 435–439.

22. Quan Hansheng, 1957, "The Relationship between American Silver and Chinese Commodity Price Revolution in the Eighteenth Century," in *Commentaries on Chinese Economic History*, Vol. 1, pp. 475–508; Quan Hansheng, 1969, op. cit.; etc.

23. Andre Gunder Frank, 1998, *ReOrient: Global Economy in the Asian Age*, p. 143.

24. Ibid., Map 3.1, p. 148.

25. Ibid., pp. 142–149.

26. Calculations of silver differ not only in approach, but also in weights and measures. Some scholars calculate in tons and some in taels. Kamiki Tetsuo's research originally calculated in kilograms. Here all figures have been converted into taels. For Liu Guanglin's calculations, see Liu Guanglin, 2011, "Research in Ming Dynasty Currency Issues."

27. David S. Landes, 1999, *The Wealth and Poverty of Nations: Why Some Are So Rich and Some So Poor*, p. 165.

28. Dai Jianbing, 2005, *Silver and the Modern Chinese Economy.*

29. Frederic S. Mishkin, "Globalization—A Force for Good?," Weissman Center Distinguished Lecture Series, Baruch College, City University of New York, October 12, 2006.

30. Naitō Konan, "A Summary of Tang and Song Worldviews," in Naitō, 1992, *Selected Works by Japanese Scholars Researching Chinese History,* Vol. 1. [Naitō argued that the social, political, demographic, and economic changes that occurred between the mid-Tang dynasty and the early Song represented the transition between the medieval and early modern periods of Chinese history (TN).]

31. See Francis Fukuyama, 2012, *The Origins of Political Order: From Prehuman Times to the French Revolution;* and 2015, *Political Order and Political Decay: From the Industrial Revolution to the Globalization of Democracy.*

32. Zhou Bodi, 1981, *The History of China's Financial Administration;* Ray Huang, 1975, *Taxation and Governmental Finance in Sixteenth-Century Ming China;* etc.

33. Ray Huang, 1996, *China: A Macro History,* p. 222.

34. A term coined by scholar Qin Hui, referring to the tax reforms of the Ming dynasty political theorist Huang Zongxi to describe how the Chinese government's efforts to reduce taxation only result in even higher taxes (TN).

35. Iwai Shigeki, 2011, *Research on the History of China's Modern Fiscal Administration.*

36. Smith, 1776, op. cit., Chap. 7, "On Colonies," Part 2, "Causes of Prosperity of New Colonies."

37. Daron Acemoglu and James A. Robinson, 2012, *Why Nations Fail: The Origins of Power, Prosperity, and Poverty.*

38. Ibid., pp. 191ff.

39. Niall Ferguson, 2001, *The Cash Nexus: Money and Power in the Modern World, 1700–2000.*

40. This embedded relationship originated in the wars in Western Europe; the British king was obliged to take on debt, and the establishment of the Bank of England hastened the emergence of a powerful treasury bill market, while a competent taxation system ensured the realization of the government's rights and interests, and the existence of Parliament ensured the boundaries of political power.

41. The Westernization or Self-Strengthening Movement from 1861 to 1895 was a set of institutional reforms initiated following the devastating Opium Wars, the ravages of the Taiping rebellion, and other domestic and international events (TN).

42. Karl Marx, 1867, *Das Kapital,* Vol. 1, Chap. 31, "Genesis of the Industrial Capitalist" (TN).

43. Frederick Engels, 1884, *Origins of the Family, Private Property, and the State,* Chap. 9, "Barbarism and Civilization," trans. Alick West with revisions at https://www .marxists.org/archive/marx/works/1884/origin-family/ch09.htm.

44. "The key problem is to find out why that sector of society of the past, which I would not hesitate to call capitalist, should have lived as if in a bell jar, cut off from the rest; why was it not able to expand and conquer the whole of society? . . . [Why was it

that] a significant rate of capital formation was possible only in certain sectors and not in the whole market economy of the time?" Fernand Braudel, 1982, *Civilization and Capitalism, 15th–18th Century,* Vol. 2: *The Wheels of Commerce,* trans. Siân Reynolds, p. 248.

45. Kato Shigeshi, 1959, *Outline of Chinese Economic History.*

46. Ma Duanlin, 2006a, *Wenxian Tongkou,* Vol. 23.

47. Regarding the differences between the feudal land systems of the East and West, see Ma Keyao, 1991, "A Comparative Study of Chinese and West-European Feudal Institutions."

48. 1985, *Research Materials in China's Modern Economic History,* Vol. 4, p. 111.

49. Hernando De Soto, 2005, *The Mystery of Capital: Why Capitalism Triumphs in the West and Fails Everywhere Else,* pp. 51–59.

50. Kato Shigeshi, 2006, *Research in Tang and Song Dynasty Gold and Silver: Centered on the Function of Gold and Silver Currency.*

51. Mancur Olson, 2000, *Power and Prosperity: Outgrowing Communist and Capitalist Dictatorships* (TN).

52. J. Bradford DeLong, 2000, "The Shape of Twentieth Century Economic History," National Bureau of Economic Research Paper No. 7569, https://www.nber.org/papers/w7569 (TN).

53. *A Financial History of Western Europe,* p. 1, quoting Wesley C. Mitchell, 1944, "The Role of Money in Economic History."

54. The Needham Question, which will be explained in detail later in the book, asks why modern science developed in Europe rather than China or India (TN).

55. Niall Ferguson, 2009, *The Ascent of Money: A Financial History of the World.*

56. Zheng Guanying, 2008, *Warnings to a Prosperous Age.*

57. Also known by the Chinese pinyin spelling of his name as Rong Hong, 1828–1912 (TN).

58. Hong Renxuan (1822–1864) was a distant relation of Taiping founder Hong Xiuquan (TN).

59. See Yung Wing's biographies, memoirs, and other materials.

60. Creative destruction, sometimes known as Schumpeter's gale, is a theory of economic innovation and the business cycle that is usually associated with the Austrian economist Joseph Schumpeter, who derived it from the work of Karl Marx (TN).

ONE The Divergent Fate of Silver in the East and the West

Erya epigraph: *Erya* is the earliest dictionary of ancient China, compiled between the Warring States and Western Han periods.

1. Marx quoted Gladstone in *A Critique of Political Economy,* so many people erroneously attribute the quote to Marx.

2. John Kenneth Galbraith, 1975, *Money: Whence It Came, Where It Went,* p. 5 (TN).

3. Norman O. Brown, 1961, *Life against Death: The Psychoanalytical Meaning of History,* p. 246.

4. These quotes come from *Dongguan Hanji: Ma Yuan* and *The Book of Han: Xuzhuan*, respectively (TN).

5. Felix Martin, 2015, *Money: The Unauthorized Biography—From Coinage to Cryptocurrencies*, pp. 3–14.

6. Milton Friedman, 1994, *Money Mischief: Episodes in Monetary History*, p. 7.

7. Qian Mu, 2013, *The Economic History of China*.

8. Qian Jiaju and Guo Yangang, 1986, *A Historical Outline of Chinese Currency*.

9. The first comprehensive Chinese character dictionary, compiled by Xu Shen in 121 C.E. (TN).

10. Adam Smith, 1776, *The Wealth of Nations*, Book 1, Chap. 4, "Of the Origin and Use of Money" (TN).

11. Ibid.

12. Caroline Humphrey, "Barter and Economic Disintegration," *Man*, Vol. 20, No. 1 (March 1985), pp. 48–72 (TN).

13. David Graeber, 2010, *Debt*.

14. Marcel Mauss, 1950, *The Gift: The Form and Reason for Exchange in Archaic Societies*.

15. Karl Marx, 1859, *A Contribution to the Critique of Political Economy*, Chap. 2, "Money or Simple Circulation, 4: The Precious Metals," trans. S. W. Ryazanskaya, https://www.marxists.org/archive/marx/works/1859/critique-pol-economy/ch02_1 .htm (TN).

16. The Holy Bible, Matthew 22:21 (TN).

17. Quoted in Kabir Sehgal, 2015, *Coined: The Rich Life of Money and How Its History Has Shaped Us*, p. 105.

18. Andre Gunder Frank, 1998, *ReOrient: Global Economy in the Asian Age*, p. 55.

19. Marx, 1859, op. cit.

20. Sima Qian, 2012, *Records of the Historian: Pingzhun Shu*.

21. Wang Mang usurped the throne to found the Xin dynasty, which lasted from 9 to 23 C.E. and marked the separation between the Western and Eastern Han dynasties (TN).

22. The 5-*zhu* coin weighed 1/24th of a tael (TN).

23. Chang'an was the capital of China during the Han and Tang dynasties (TN).

24. Qian Mu, 2013, *The Economic History of China*.

25. Kato Shigeshi, 2006, *Research in Tang and Song Dynasty Gold and Silver: Centered on the Function of Gold and Silver Currency*.

26. Qian Mu, 2013, op. cit.

27. Ibid. The Jiao-Guang region at that time covered what is now Guangdong, Guangxi, and northern Vietnam (TN).

28. Peng Xinwei, 1994, op. cit., pp. 278, 471 (TN).

29. Lin Manhoung, 2001, *China Upside Down: Currency, Society, and Ideologies, 1808–1856*.

30. Herodotus, *Histories*, 1:94.

31. Jean Rivoire, 1984, *Histoire de la banque*; and Kabir Sehgal, 2015, op. cit., p. 109.

32. Barry Eichengreen, 1996, *Globalizing Capital: A History of the International Monetary System*, p. 6.

33. Charles Montagu, after being appointed chancellor of the Exchequer in 1694, appointed Newton to the post of warden of the Royal Mint in 1696 (TN).

34. Barry Eichengreen, 1996, op. cit., pp. 3–4 (TN).

35. The troy ounce is the calculation unit normally used for trading gold in the international gold market.

36. Charles Kindleberger, 1984, *A Financial History of Western Europe*, p. 57.

37. Ibid., p. 25.

38. "Letter of Columbus on the Fourth Voyage," American Journeys Collection, Wisconsin Historical Society, http://www.americanjourneys.org/pdf/AJ-068.pdf, p. 412 (TN).

39. Marx, 1859, op. cit., "Theories of the Medium of Circulation and of Money" (TN).

40. Milton Friedman, 1962, *Capitalism and Freedom*, p. 40.

41. "Gold die-hards" refers to gold investors who are so convinced of gold's prospects that even when the price of gold drops, they would rather hold it for several years without making money than let gold slip out of their hands.

42. Friedman, 1962, op. cit., p. 41.

43. Ibid., p. 42.

44. Ibid., p. 40.

45. Ibid.

46. Mazin Sidahmed, "Ramen Is Displacing Tobacco as Most Popular US Prison Currency, Study Finds," *The Guardian*, August 22, 2016, http://www.theguardian.com/us-news/2016/aug/22/ramen-prison-currency-study.

47. Steven Cheung, 2014, *Economic Explanation*, Vol. 4: *The Choice of Institutional Arrangements*.

48. Friedman, 1962, op. cit., p. 40 (TN).

49. Adam Smith, 1776, *The Wealth of Nations*, Book 4, Chap. 3, Part 1, "Digression Concerning Banks of Deposit, Particularly Concerning That of Amsterdam."

50. Ibid.

51. Ibid.

TWO   The Song and Yuan Dynasties

Epigraph: A *mo*, originally a string of 100 copper cash, later became a measure of money popular in the Song dynasty, expressed as up to 100 cash.

1. English edition, 1939, trans. John D. Sinclair (TN).

2. Qian Mu, 2013, *The Economic History of China*.

3. Ibid.

4. The Guanlong Group, based in the northwest, was one of the regional aristocratic groups (TN).

5. 1031–1095, Song dynasty scientist and official (TN).

6. Shiba Yoshinobu, 2012, *Research on the Economic History of Southern China in the Song Dynasty*.

7. Zhu Ruixi, 1983, *Research on Song Dynasty Society.*

8. Ge Jinfang, 1991, *Economic Research and Analysis of the Song, Liao, Xia, and Jin Dynasties.*

9. A *min* represented a string of 1,000 cash. It was sometimes interchangeable with *guan* (TN).

10. Zeng Xiongsheng, 2014, *A Comprehensive Agricultural History of China.* [A *min* was a string of 1,000 bronze cash (TN).]

11. Xu Song, 1957, *Compiled Social Record of the Song: Food and Money,* p. 42.

12. S. A. M Adshead, 1988, *China in World History.*

13. Wang Mingqing, 1961, *Waving the Duster,* Vol. 1.

14. Su Che, or Su Zhe (1039–1112), was a politician and essayist (TN).

15. Su Zhe, 1987, *Luan City Collection Number 3,* Vol. 8.

16. 1150–1223, a neo-Confucian scholar (TN).

17. Ye Shi, 1961, *Shui Xin's Anthology,* Vol. 2.

18. Jia Qihong, 2015, "Research into Certain Problems of Song Dynasty Military Logistics."

19. Traditionally, a catty weighed 16 taels (*liang*), the Chinese ounce. In modern times, a catty is equivalent to half a kilogram (TN).

20. The name once given to the region of China south of the Yangtze River (TN).

21. Ma Duanlin, 2006b, *Wenxian Tongkou: Currency.*

22. Li You, 1935, *Song Dynasty Facts,* Vol. 16.

23. Takahashi Hiromi, 2010, *Historical Research on Currency in the Song, Jin, and Yuan Dynasties: The Formation of the Yuan Dynasty's Monetary Policies.*

24. Tuo Tuo et al., 1985, *History of the Song: Food and Money.*

25. Emperor Renzong, 1023–1031 (TN).

26. Ma Duanlin, 2006b, op. cit. [See also Peng Xinwei, op. cit., p. 409 (TN).]

27. Marking the end of the Northern Song, the Jingkang Incident took place in 1127 when the forces of the Jurchen-led Jin dynasty besieged and sacked Bianjing (present-day Kaifeng), the capital of the Song dynasty, and captured Emperor Qinzong along with other members of the imperial family and court (TN).

28. In office 1101–1125 (TN).

29. Anonymous, proofread by Li Zhiliang, *Complete History of the Song,* Vol. 23 (Yuan).

30. A prefecture in northwest Guangxi (TN).

31. Wei Jing (Song Dynasty), *Houle Ji,* Vol. 15, "Notification on Fuzhou Rishang Imperial Temple Banknote Disaster," quoted in Wang Shengduo (ed.), 2004, *Compiled Materials on the Monetary History of the Two Song Dynasties.*

32. Zhou Bodi, 1981, *Financial History of China.*

33. Zhang Ruyu, 1992, *Critical Compilation of a Multitude of Books.*

34. This meant accepting a string that contained fewer coins than one string (*guan*) was officially designated to contain. This could be seen as a monetary innovation that ameliorated the effect of currency famines.

35. This policy allowed people to evade compulsory labor service (corvee) through payment of a cash fee (TN).

36. Qi Xia, 2009a, *Complete Works*, Vol. 4.

37. Takahashi Hiromi, 2010, op. cit.

38. Miyazawa Tomoyuki, 1998, *Song China's State and Economy*, p. 498, quoted in Richard von Glahn, 2016, *The Economic History of China*, p. 235 (TN).

39. Gao Congming, 1999, *Research on Song Dynasty Currency and Currency Circulation*, pp. 311–312, quoted in von Glahn, 2016, op. cit., p. 235 (TN).

40. Zhu Jiaming, 2012, *From Freedom to Monopoly: Two Thousand Years of Chinese Monetary Economy*, Vols. 1 and 2.

41. 1968, *Research into the Commercial History of the Song Dynasty*; English edition, 1970, *Commerce and Society in Sung China*, trans. Mark Elvin (TN).

42. Wan Zhiying and Zhou Xinghui, 1990, *Innovations in Research on Song Dynasty Monetary History*, Song History Research Collection, p. 90.

43. Wang Shengduo, 2016, *History of the Song, Full Text*, Vol. 23, Part 1.

44. Yue Fei was a general during the Southern Song dynasty who was executed in 1142 on false charges of treason. Emperor Xiaozong posthumously pardoned and honored him in 1169. Yue Fei has become a folk hero in China and is considered a paragon of loyalty (TN).

45. See Tuo Tuo et al., 1985, *History of the Song: Food and Commodities*; Anonymous, 2007, *Imperial Ordinances of the First Two Reign Periods of the Southern Song*, Vol. 54; Hong Mai, 2005, *Rongzhai Sanbi*, Vol. 14; etc.

46. Deng Guangmin, 1957, *Xin Jiaxuan's Collected Poetry and Essays: On Using Huizi*.

47. See Richard von Glahn, 1996, *Fountain of Fortune: Money and Monetary Policy in China, 1000–1700*, p. 43 (TN).

48. Yang Wanli, 2005, *Cheng Zhai Collection*, Vol. 30.

49. Huang Zongxi, 1993, *Waiting for the Dawn: A Plan for the Prince*, trans. William Theodore de Bary, p. 157.

50. See Table 7.5, p. 263, in von Glahn, 2016, op. cit.

51. The *liaozhiju* was a bureau established to print money (TN).

52. Zhou Bodi, 1981, *Financial History of China*.

53. A measure of about 10 liters (TN).

54. Fang Hui, 1981, *Tongjiang Collection*, Vol. 6.

55. Peng Xinwei, 1994, *A Monetary History of China*, p. 425.

56. S. A. M. Adshead, 2000, *China in World History*, third edition, p. xii (TN).

57. Xiao Hongying (ed.), 2008, *Inventions in the Printing Arts: Origin and Development, Biographies, Influence*.

58. That is, in the Republican era, as will be described later in the book (TN).

59. Song Lian, 1976, *History of the Yuan: Biography of Zhang Rong*.

60. Kato Shigeshi, 2006, *Research in Tang and Song Dynasty Gold and Silver: Centered on the Function of Gold and Silver Currency*.

61. 1900, *The Journey of William of Rubruck to the Eastern Parts of the World, 1253–55, as Narrated by Himself, with Two Accounts of the Earlier Journey of John of Pian de Carpine*, translated from the Latin and edited with an introduction by William Woodville Rockhill.

62. Jonathan Spence, 1999, *The Chan's Great Continent: China in Western Minds*, p. 2. Spence believes that Rubruck, although he never reached Chinese soil, made use of his 1253 journey to the Mongol capital of Karakorum, on China's northwestern border, to record the living conditions of the many Chinese living there. For instance, it seemed that in "Cathay" there was a city with "walls of silver and battlements of gold," and that the "Catians" Rubruck met were the people known to the Romans as "Seres" or "Silk People," "because the finest silk came from their domains."

63. Ibid., p. 1.

64. Apart from the words in parenthesis, translated from the Chinese, this quote is drawn from 1993, *Excerpt from the Book of Ser Marco Polo: The Venetian Concerning Kingdoms and Marvels of the East*, Vol. 1, trans. and ed. Colonel Sir Henry Yule, Book 2, Part 1, Chap. 24.

65. Ibid. (TN).

66. Ibid. (TN).

67. Ibid. (TN).

68. Ibid. (TN).

69. Ibid. (TN).

70. Gu Yanwu, 1985, *Notes on the Daily Accumulation of Knowledge* (*Rizhilu*).

71. Song Lian, 1976, op. cit. [See also Peng Xinwei, 1994, op. cit., pp. 514–515 (TN).]

72. Gordon Tullock, 1957, "Paper Money—A Cycle in Cathay," *The Economic History Review*, Vol. 9, No. 3, p. 394.

73. Milton Friedman, 1962, *Capitalism and Freedom*, p. 39.

74. Richard von Glahn, "The Origins of Paper Money in China," in William N. Goetzmann and K. Geert Rouwenhorst, 2005, *The Origins of Value*, p. 66 (TN).

75. Ibid. (TN).

76. Ibid. (TN).

77. Tullock, 1957, op. cit., p. 406.

78. David Hume, 1752, "Of Money" (TN).

79. Ibid. (TN).

80. Milton Friedman, 1962, op. cit., "The Control of Money," p. 41 (TN).

81. Tuo Tuo et al., 1985, *History of the Song: Food and Money* (TN).

82. A measure equal to one hectoliter. The Chinese term, which refers to the amount of rice that can be carried on a shoulder pole, is Romanized variously as *shi*, *dan*, or *tam* (TN).

83. *History of the Song*, 1345, Vol. 126.

84. Tuo Tuo et al., 1985, *History of the Song: Food and Money*, "Agricultural Fields."

85. Emperor Renzong of Song, the fourth emperor of the Song dynasty, reigned from 1022 to his death in 1063 and was the Song's longest-reigning emperor (TN).

86. 1223–1275, a Yuan official sent by Kublai Khan (TN).

87. The "Southerners" referred to the people within the borders of the Southern Song, who were regarded as the fourth class of people in the Yuan dynasty.

88. Zhou Zuoren, 2011, *In My Own Garden*.

89. Song Lian, 1976, op. cit.

90. Luciano Pezzolo, "Bonds and Government Debt in Italian City-States, 1250–1650," in Goetzmann and Rouwenhorst, 2005, op. cit. (TN).

THREE The Ming Dynasty

Lanling Xiaoxiaosheng epigraph: Lanling Xiaoxiaosheng (Ming), *The Golden Lotus*; English edition, 2011, trans. Clement Egerton and Shu Qingchun (Lao She), Vol. 1, Chap. 3, p. 77 (TN).

"Lamentation" epigraph: Meaning, it is the repayment of life lent by God.

1. Kenneth Pommeranz, 2000, *The Great Divergence: China, Europe, and the Making of the Modern World Economy*, pp. 36, 219–225 (TN).

2. Lin Xinfeng, 2010, "On the Transformation during the Transitional Period from the Yuan to the Ming," *Gudai wenming* (Ancient Civilization), No. 4 (TN).

3. The *lijia* system was a form of grassroots organization in the Ming dynasty. Every 110 households were counted as one *li* or village, and heads of the ten households possessing the most grain served as village heads (*lizhang*), while the heads of the other 100 households were called headmen (*jiashou*). The ten *lizhang* rotated serving one-year terms, and each year one *lizhang* would lead ten *jiashou* in serving corvee, and was responsible for "managing the matters of the *li*."

4. The Tumu Crisis, also called the Crisis of Tumu Fortress or Battle of Tumu, was a frontier conflict between the Oirat tribes of Mongols and the Chinese Ming dynasty, which led to the capture of the Ming emperor Yingzong on September 1, 1449, and the defeat of an army of 500,000 men by a much smaller force (TN).

5. 1528–1588, a military leader famous for combating invading Japanese pirates in the mid-1500s (TN).

6. Frederick W. Mote, 1992, *The Cambridge History of the Ming Dynasty*.

7. Zhang Tingyu, 1974, *History of the Ming: Food and Money*, "Money."

8. Ibid.

9. Ibid.

10. A *li* was equivalent to about 0.05 grams (TN).

11. Zhang Tingyu, 1974, op. cit.

12. Peng Xinwei, 2007, *A Monetary History of China*, pp. 578–579.

13. 1739, *History of the Ming: Biography of Jiang Dejing* (TN).

14. Gordon Tullock, 1957, "Paper Money—A Cycle in Cathay," *The Economic History Review*, Vol. 9, No. 3, p. 405 (TN).

15. Zhang Tingyu, 1974, *History of the Ming: Food and Money*.

16. Liang Fangzhong, 1936, "The Single Whip Tax System," *Collected Papers on China's Modern Economic History*, Vol. 4, No. 1.

17. Wei Yuan, 1984, *A Military History of the Sacred Dynasty*.

18. Zhao Yi, 2008, *Twenty-Two Historical Jottings*.

19. Xie Zhaozhi, 2012, *Wu Za Zhu*, Vol. 12, p. 226.

20. *History of the Ming*, Vol. 205: *Biography of Zhu Wan* (TN).

21. Henry Kissinger, 2014, *World Order*, p. 18.

22. John King Fairbank, 1976, *The United States and China,* fourth edition, p. 151.

23. Wei Yuan, 1984, *A Military History of the Sacred Dynasty* (TN).

24. Kato, Shigeshi, 2006, *Research in Tang and Song Dynasty Gold and Silver: Centered on the Function of Gold and Silver Currency.*

25. Andre Gunder Frank, 1998, *ReOrient: Global Economy in the Asian Age,* p. 115 (TN).

26. James Bromley Eames, 1974, *The English in China,* pp. 62–63.

27. William S. Atwell, 1982, "International Bullion Flows and the Chinese Economy Circa 1530–1650," p. 74.

28. Ward Barrett, "World Bullion Flows, 1450–1800,' "in James D. Tracy (ed.), 1990, *The Rise of Merchant Empires: Long-Distance Trade in the Early Modern World,* 1350–1750, Chap. 7, pp. 224–254.

29. Wan Ming, 2005, "Issues and Research on Changes in Late Ming Society."

30. Andre Gunder Frank, 1998, op. cit., p. 147.

31. Ibid., p. 55.

32. William S. Atwell, 1986, "Some Observations on the 'Seventeenth-Century Crisis' in China and Japan," *The Journal of Asian Studies,* Vol. 45, No. 2, p. 224.

33. Gefei (Liu Yong), 2014, *Heron Hidden in Snow.*

34. Shao Wankuan and Zhang Guochao, 2007, *The Golden Lotus Cookbook.*

35. David Hume, 1752, "Of Money," in Hume, 2007, *Writings on Economics,* ed. Eugene Rotwein, with a new introduction by Margaret Schabas, p. 37.

36. Werner Sombart, 1976, *Luxury and Capitalism,* p. 171.

37. Ibid., p. 57.

38. Ibid., p. 62. [Here Sombart is quoting L. S. Mercie, *Tableau de Paris* (TN).]

39. Ibid., p. 55.

40. Ibid., p. 50. [Here Sombart is quoting Petrarch (TN).]

41. Ibid., pp. 42, 43.

42. *The Golden Lotus,* Vol. 2, Chap. 93, p. 557.

43. Fernand Braudel, 1992, *Civilization and Capitalism, 15th–18th Century,* Vol. 3: *The Perspective of the World,* trans. Siân Reynolds, p. 157 (TN).

44. See Ray Huang, 2015, *Capitalism and the 21st Century* (in Chinese) (TN).

45. Lance Davis and Douglass C. North, 1971, *Institutional Change and American Economic Growth,* Chap. 1, p. 10.

46. Werner Sombart, 2005, *History of the Modern European Economic System* (Chinese edition).

47. Referring to Ray Huang's *1578: A Year of No Significance: The Ming Dynasty in Decline* and Valerie Hansen's *The Open Empire: A History of China to 1600* (TN).

48. Valerie Hansen, 2000, *The Open Empire: A History of China to 1600.*

49. Peng Xinwei, 1994, op. cit., p. 607.

50. Adam Smith, 1776, *The Wealth of Nations,* Vol. 1, Chap. 11, "Digression Concerning the Variations in the Value of Silver during the Course of the Four Last Centuries."

51. Frederic Wakeman, 1985, *The Great Enterprise: The Manchu Reconstruction of Imperial Order in Seventeenth-Century China,* Introduction, pp. 2–3.

52. Ibid.

53. Eric Hobsbawm, 1954, "The Crisis of the Seventeenth Century," *Past and Present,* Vol. 5, Issue 1, pp. 33–53 (TN).

54. Pierre Vilar, quoted in Immanuel Wallerstein, 1980, *The Modern World-System II: Mercantilism and the Consolidation of the European World-Economy, 1600–1750* (2001 edition), p. 19.

55. Ge Jianxiong, 2008, *Unity and Division.*

56. Henry Kissinger, 2011, *On China,* Chap. 1.

57. Pierre Chaunu, 1966, *Les Philippines et le Pacifique des Ibériques (XVIe, XVIIe, XVIIIe siècles),* p. 267, cited in footnote in Wakeman, 1985, op. cit., pp. 4–5 (TN).

58. Han Yuhai, 2010, *Who Has Written History for 500 Years?*

59. Fernand Braudel, 1984, op. cit., p. 490 (TN).

60. William S. Atwell, 1986, "Some Observations on the 'Seventeenth-Century Crisis' in China and Japan," op. cit., p. 227.

61. Ibid., p. 229.

62. Wakeman, 1985, op. cit., p. 10.

63. Gang Feng was the pen name Hai Rui used, meaning "firm mountain" (TN).

64. Wakeman, 1985, op. cit., p. 9 (TN).

65. Huang Zongxi, 1993, *Waiting for the Dawn: A Plan for the Prince,* trans. William Theodore De Bary, p. 154 (TN).

66. Wang Fuzi, 2013 (1865), *Comments on Reading the Tongjian* (TN).

67. John Kenneth Galbraith, 1975, *Money: Whence It Came, Where It Went,* p. 15 (TN).

68. Research on this aspect by Earl J. Hamilton of the Chicago School has influenced many subsequent scholars.

69. Gu Yanwu (1613–82), *Advantages and Disadvantages of Administrative Units Within the Realm,* Vol. 26: *Fujian* (TN).

70. Joao Rodrigues, 1973, *This Island of Japan,* trans. and ed. Michael Cooper, p. 78, quoted in Atwell, 1986, op. cit., p. 224.

71. Head of the Daijō-kan during and after the Nara period (TN).

72. Peng Xinwei, 1994, *A Monetary History of China.*

73. This is as opposed to hammering blank coins between two dies, or casting coins from dies (TN).

74. In 1523 (the second year of the Ming Jiajing reign), a brawl occurred between trade representatives of Japan's Ōuchi and the Hosokawa daimyō clans in the Chinese city of Ningbo, Zhejiang Province. The Ōuchi representatives pillaged and harmed local residents, causing massive damage.

75. Angus Maddison, 2003, *The World Economy: A Millennial Perspective,* p. 71, http://piketty.pse.ens.fr/files/Maddison2001Data.pdf. [The three heroes of the warring states refer to Oda Nobunaga, Toyotomi Hideyoshi, and Tokugawa Ieyasu (TN).]

76. See, for example, Cesare Polenghi, 2003, "Hideyoshi and Korea: The Reasons, the Chronicle and the Consequences of the Japanese Invasion, 1592–1598," in The Samurai Archives, https://www.samurai-archives.com/hak.html (TN).

77. Donald N. Clark, "Sino-Korean Tributary Relations under the Ming," in Denis Twitchett and Frederick W. Mote, 1998, *The Cambridge History of China*, Vol. 8: *The Ming Dynasty, 1368–1644, Part 2*, p. 298 (TN).

78. Atwell, 1986, op. cit., pp. 235, 236 (TN).

79. Ibid., p. 236 (TN).

FOUR The Late Qing

1. Qian Jiaju and Guo Yangang, 1986, *Outline of China's Monetary History*.

2. Zhang Tingyu et al., 2000, *Qing Dynasty Documents: Currency*.

3. Hosea Ballou Morse, 1910–1918, *The International Relations of the Chinese Empire*, Vol. 1: *The Period of Conflict, 1834–1860*, Chap. 2, "Taxation in China," pp. 28–29.

4. People's Bank of China Central Branch Advisers Office Financial History Document Group, 1986, *Material on China's Modern Monetary History*, Vol. 1, p. 91 (TN).

5. Huang Jianhui, 2002, *History of Money-Exchange Shops in Shanxi*.

6. Shi Junzhi, 2012, *General History of China's Monetary System*.

7. Zhang Jiaxiang, 1925, *History of the Chinese Currency System*.

8. Morse, 1910–1918, Vol. 1, op. cit., p. 29.

9. Liu Ping, 2010, *Foreigners' Experience of Late Qing Finance*.

10. Morse, 1910–1918, op. cit., p. 29.

11. Lanling Xiaoxiaosheng (Ming), *The Golden Lotus*; English edition, 2011, trans. Clement Egerton and Shu Qingchun (Lao She), Vol. 2, Chap. 87, p. 372.

12. Morse, 1910–1918, op. cit., p. 29.

13. Ray Huang, *1587: A Year of No Significance: The Ming Dynasty in Decline*; Preface to Chinese edition, 1997.

14. Yeh-Chien Wang, 1974, *Land Taxation in Imperial China, 1750–1911*.

15. Huang, 1997, op. cit., Preface to Chinese edition.

16. Huang Zongxi, 1993, *Waiting for the Dawn: A Plan for the Prince*, "Land System (Part 3)," trans. William Theodore de Bary, p. 134.

17. Qin Hui, 2005, "Tax Reform by Aggregation and Huang Zongxi's Law," in "Tax and Fee Reform, Village Autonomy, and Central and Local Finance," trans. Ma Jisen, *The Chinese Economy*, Vol. 38, No. 6, p. 5.

18. Iwai Shigeki, 2001, *Research on the History of China's Modern Fiscal Administration*.

19. Qin Hui, 2005, op. cit., pp. 6–7.

20. Iwai Shigeki, 2001, op. cit.

21. Zhonghua shuju (ed.), 2008, *Veritable Records of the Qing*.

22. Dwight H. Perkins, 1969, *Agricultural Development in China, 1368–1968*.

23. Morse, 1910–1918, op. cit., pp. 25–26.

24. Ibid., pp. 27, 26.

25. "Monstres à détruire," a pamphlet distributed during the French Revolution, Association pour l'histoire de l'administration des douanes, *L'administration des douanes*

en France sous la révolution, p. 12, quoted in Hironori Asakura, 2003, *World History of the Customs and Tariffs*, World Customs Organization.

26. Jiang Tingfu, 2001, *Modern History of China*, Chap. 2 (TN).

27. Shen Shixing (ed.), 1989, *Collected Statutes of the Ming Dynasty*Zhonghua shuju; Fan Shuzhi, 2006, *Sixteen Talks on National History*.

28. *Wang Zhi* 36, adapted from the James Legge translation.

29. See Fan Shuzhi, 2015, *The Great Change in the Late Ming* (TN).

30. Paul M. Evans, 1988, *John Fairbank and the American Understanding of Modern China*, p. 167.

31. John King Fairbank, 1976, *The United States and China*, fourth edition, p. 147.

32. Ibid.

33. Jiang Tingfu, 2001, op. cit., Chap. 1.

34. Ibid.

35. Liang Tingnan, 2002, *Guangdong Customs Records*. [English translation of the emperor's edict from J. Mason Gentzler (ed.), 1977, *Changing China: Readings in the History of China from the Opium War to the Present* (TN).]

36. Takeshi Hamashita, 2008, *China, East Asia, and the Global Economy*, p. 18.

37. Ibid.

38. Ibid.

39. Fernand Braudel, 1992, *Civilization and Capitalism, 15th–18th Century*, Vol. 3: *The Perspective of the World*, p. 25.

40. Ge Zhaoguang, 2014, *Imagined Alien Land—Reading Korean Joseon Dynasty Chinese-Language Swallow Journey Documents and Jottings*.

41. Takeshi Hamashita, 2009, *China, East Asia, and the Global Economy*, Chinese edition.

42. Andre Gunder Frank, 2008, *ReOrient: Global Economy in the Asian Age*, pp. 116–117.

43. Ibid., p. 115.

44. Morse, 1910–1918, op. cit., p. 50.

45. Ibid., p. 41.

46. Ibid., p. 46.

47. Ibid., p. 48.

48. Ibid., p. 49.

49. Ibid.

50. Jiang Tingfu, 2001, op. cit.

51. Morse, 1910–1918, op. cit., p. 75.

52. Ibid., p. 54 (TN).

53. Jiang Tingfu, 2001, op. cit.

54. Morse, 1910–1918, op. cit., p. 81.

55. Jiang Tingfu, 2001, op. cit.

56. Peter Auber, 1834, *China: An Outline of Its Government, Laws, and Policy*, p. 256, quoted in Morse, 1910–1918, op. cit., p. 56.

57. Samuel Wells Williams, 1848, *The Middle Kingdom: A Survey of the Geography, Government, Education, Social Life, Arts, Religion, etc. of the Chinese Empire and Its Inhabitants,* Vol. 2, p. 459, quoted in Morse, 1910–1918, op. cit., pp. 57–58.

58. Morse, 1910–1918, op. cit., p. 58.

59. Jiang Tingfu, 2001, op. cit.

60. Fairbank, 1976, *The United States and China,* fourth edition, p. 158.

61. Braudel, 1992, op. cit., p. 464.

62. Smith, 1776, op. cit., Book 1, Chap. 5.

63. Susan Mann Jones and Philip A. Kuhn, "Dynastic Decline and the Roots of Rebellion," in John K. Fairbank (ed.), 1978, *The Cambridge History of China,* Vol. 10: *The Late Ch'ing, Part 1,* p. 130.

64. 2008, *Veritable Records of the Qing.*

65. George L. Staunton, "Macartney's Embassy," ii, p. 496, in Morse, 1910–1918, op. cit., p. 175, fn.

66. The quote is by Lee Hsien Loong, prime minister of Singapore since 2004, interview with *Caixin,* February 16, 2014, http://news.nanyangpost.com/2014/02/PM-Lee-TPP.html (TN).

67. Takeshi Hamashita, 2009, *China, East Asia, and the Global Economy,* Chinese edition, p. 13.

68. Inoue Hiromasa, 2011, *Research into the History of the Qing Dynasty's Opium Policies.*

69. Ian Morris, 2010, *Why the West Rules—for Now,* pp. 7–8; Chinese edition, 2014.

70. See Nicolas Standaert and R. G. Tiedemann (eds.), 2010, *Handbook of Christianity in China,* Vol. 2, p. 358 (TN).

71. "Li Yuandu's Letter Summoning Shi Dahia to Surrender," in Luo Ergang, Xie Xingyao, and Peng Zeyi (eds.), 1992, *Minguo Congshu,* Vol. 4, p. 530.

72. Morris, 2010, op. cit., p. 7 (TN).

73. Patricia Buckley Ebrey, 1996, *The Cambridge Illustrated History of China,* p. 237.

74. See Dr. Edkins, *Historical Note,* quoted in Joshua Rowntree, 1906, *The Imperial Drug Trade: A Re-Statement of the Opium Question, in the Light of Recent Evidence and New Developments in the East,* p. 12 (TN).

75. Palace Museum, 1968, *Historical Documents of Qing Dynasty Diplomacy (Jiaqing Reign).*

76. Morse, 1910–1918, op. cit., p. 121.

77. See ibid., pp. 257–260.

78. Morris, 2010, op. cit., p. 8.

79. Morse, 1910–1918, op. cit., "Chronology," pp. xxxiv–xxxv.

80. Smith, 1776, op. cit., Book 1, Chap. 8, "Of the Wages of Labour."

81. Jonathan Spence, 1998, *The Chan's Great Continent: China in Western Minds,* p. 60.

82. Julia Lovell, 2015, *The Opium Wars: Drugs, Dreams and the Making of China*, p. 223.

83. 2008, *Veritable Records of the Qing*.

84. Official English translation of the Treaty of Nanking, Articles 4, 5, 6, signed August 29, 1842 (TN).

85. See Hong Jiaguan, 2008, *General Monetary History of China*, Vol. 4; Yan Zhongping, 1989, *Economic History of Modern China (1840–1894)*; etc.

86. Wang Qingyun, 1985 [1850], *Superfluous Records of the Imperial Court*, Vol. 5, *A Record of Silver and Cash Values*. Beijing: Guji chubanshe (TN).

87. Imperial Censor Liu Liangju (TN).

88. Bao Shichen, "Letter to Former Minister of War Xu Taichang," in *Four Books on Governing Suzhou*, Vol. 26 (1888) (TN).

89. Peng Zeyi, 1961, "China's Economy and Class Relations under the Fluctuating Silver and Copper Cash Values Ten Years after the Opium Wars," *Historical Research*, Vol. 6, pp. 40–68.

90. Ibid.

91. Morse, 1910–1918, op. cit., p. 202, fn.: "From 1818 to 1830 the known import of treasure (mainly by American ships) amounted to $60,000,000, and the known export (entirely by English ships to India) amounted in round figures to $40,000,000; from 1831 the tide turned, the import was reduced to small amounts, and the trade could be balanced only by increasing shipments of treasure."

92. Lin Man-houng, 2007, *China Upside Down: Currency, Society, and Ideologies, 1808–1856*.

93. Wei Yuan, 1984, *A Military History of the Sacred Dynasty*.

94. 2008, *Veritable Records of the Qing*, "Veritable Records of the Daoguang Court" (TN).

95. Lin Man-Houng, 2011, op. cit., p. 75.

96. Ibid., Introduction (TN).

97. Xu Guangqi or Hsü Kuang-ch'i (1562–1633), also known by his baptismal name Paul, was a Chinese scholar, politician, and writer who was a colleague and collaborator of the Italian Jesuits Matteo Ricci and Sabatino de Ursis (TN).

98. Zhu Weizheng, 2015, *Rereading Modern Chinese History*, pp. 21–22.

99. Angus Maddison, 2001, *The World Economy: A Millennial Perspective*, p. 263.

100. Douglass North, 1976, *The Rise of the Western World: A New Economic History*, p. 1.

101. Liu Haiying, 2014, *China's Enormous Debt*.

102. Heshen (1750–1799), of the Manchu Niohuru clan, was an official of the Qing dynasty who also owned pawnshops (TN).

103. See Peng Xinwei, 1994, op. cit., p. 674 (TN).

104. This book was a recollection of the Republican era by a doctor of traditional Chinese medicine in Shanghai, Chen Cunren, who was born at the end of the Qing dynasty and experienced many events. The book contains many interesting details.

105. William Edgar Geil, 1914, *A Yankee on the Yangtze*, p. 67.

106. Chester Holcombe, 1895, *The Real Chinaman,* pp. 331–332; Chinese edition, Liu Ping trans., 2010.

107. See, for example, Peng Xinwei, 1994, op. cit., pp. xxiii, xxiv, xxviii, xxix, 337, 344.

108. Qian Mu, 2013, *Economic History of China* (TN).

109. Zhang Huixin, 1994, *Historical Narrative of Chinese Currency.*

110. Chen Cunren, 2007, *Life in the Age of the Silver Dollar* (TN).

111. See Peng Xinwei, 1994, op. cit., p. 681 (TN).

112. These names were based on the figures stamped on the coins. See ibid., p. 672 (TN).

113. Jack Belden, 1970, *China Shakes the World,* p. 47; Chinese edition, 1980.

114. Qian Mu, 2013, op. cit.

115. Samuel Wells Williams, 1863, *The Chinese Commercial Guide, Containing Treaties, Tariffs, Regulations, Tables, etc., Useful in the Trade to China and Eastern Asia,* fifth edition, Chap. 5, Section 1, "Chinese Currency," p. 265.

116. Also known as Chang Chih-tung, 1837–1909 (TN).

117. See Peng Xinwei, 1994, op. cit., p. 684 (TN).

118. Liu Ping, 2011, "The Financial Industry of the Late Qing Dynasty in the Eyes of Foreigners," *The Chinese Banker,* No. 7.

119. Mrs. Archibald Little, 1899, *Intimate China: The Chinese as I Have Seen Them,* p. 133. [Alicia (Mrs. Archibald) Little was a writer and a British campaigner for women's rights who later campaigned against foot-binding in China (TN).]

120. Steven Cheung, 2014. *Economic Explanation,* Vol. 4: *The Choice of Institutional Arrangements,* Chap. 6, "Economic Adjustments and the Monetary System," Part 4, "Not Backing the Issue of Currency with Commodities Is the Reason for Debasement of Money."

121. Han Yuhai, 2010, op. cit.

122. Yeh Kuo-chun, 2012, *Return to the Glory of International Currency.*

123. Hume, 1752, op. cit.

124. Arthur N. Young, 1971, *China's Nation-Building Effort, 1927–1937: The Financial and Economic Record,* p. 163. [Young was quoting a report by Princeton economist Edwin Kemmerer (TN).]

125. John King Fairbank, *Cambridge History of China: The Late Ch'ing,* Part 2, Chap. 7, p. 405.

126. Ding Mingnan and Yu Shengwu, 1992, *Imperialist Aggression against China.*

127. One nautical mile equals 1.852 kilometers.

128. Jiang Boli and Dai Jitao, 2012, *On the Japanese and Japan.*

129. Osamu Ōba, 1997, *Secret Talks between Japan and China in the Edo Period.*

130. Fukuzawa Yukichi was a Japanese writer, teacher, translator, entrepreneur, and leader who founded Keio University and other institutions and was an early advocate for reform. The famous editorial "Datsu-A Ron," translated as "Escape from Asia," published anonymously in the newspaper *Jiji Shimpo* on March 16, 1885, is generally attributed to him (TN).

131. Sonnō jōi was a political philosophy in Japan and China that called for "revering the emperor and expelling the barbarians," which became a slogan in the movement to overthrow the Tokugawa shogunate (TN).

132. This quotes the editorial "Datsu-A Ron," attributed to Fukuzawa (TN).

133. My friend Cai Menghan, who has focused for a long time on the history of political thought, points out that Western academics have gradually revised their views of the Edo period since the late 1950s. A Japanese political historian, Masao Maruyama, also believes that the Edo period was a period of development of modern society, but with some reversals.

134. Kenichi Ohno, 2006, *From Edo to Heisei*.

135. Takeshi Hamashita, 2009, op. cit.

136. Samuel E. Finer, 1999, *The History of Government from the Earliest Times*.

137. Atwell, 1986, op. cit., p. 234.

138. Yan Zhongping, 2012, *Selected Statistical Data in China's Recent Economic History*.

139. Lin Man-huong, 2011, op. cit.; see also Lin's interview after being accepted into the Committee for Promotion of Ming-Qing Studies of Taiwan's Academia Sinica.

140. Tuo Tuo et al., 1985, *History of the Song Dynasty: Food and Commodities*.

141. Xia Xie, 1988, *Chronicle of China and the West: Opium Tax*.

142. Lu Hanchao, 2009, *A Man of Two Worlds: The Life of Sir Robert Hart, 1835–1911*.

143. Liang Qichao, 1989, *Collected Works from the Ice-Drinker's Studio*.

144. Dai Jianbing, 2005, *Silver and the Modern Chinese Economy (1890–1935)*.

145. Regarding the gold and silver standards, see Chap. 1 of this author's *The Money Printers*.

146. Liang Qichao, 1999, "Our Currency System and Financial Policies," in *Complete Works of Liang Qichao*, Vol. 5, p. 2731.

147. Peng Xinwei, 1994, op. cit., p. 797 (TN).

148. Ibid., p. 798 (TN).

149. The words "twenty-ninth year of the Guangxu era" were deleted from the original text; published in People's Bank of China Central Branch Advisers Office Financial History Document Group, 1964, *Material on China's Modern Monetary History*, Vol. 1: *Era of Qing Government Rule (1840–1911)*, p. 1223.

150. See also Peng Xinwei, 1994, op. cit., p. 798 (TN).

151. Qiu Fanzhen, 2005, *Jenks's Currency Reform Plan and the Late Qing Currency Issue*. [See also Peng Xinwei, 1994, op. cit., p. 799 (TN).]

152. See Peng Xinwei, 1994, op. cit., p. 799 (TN).

153. Ibid., pp. 799–801 (TN).

154. John K. Fairbank and Kwan-Ching Liu, 1980, *The Cambridge History of China*, Vol. 11: *The Late Ch'ing*, Part 2, p. 403.

155. Zhang Zhidong, 1904, "Memorial against an Empty Gold Standard," in *Complete Works of Zhang Wenxiang*, 63, Memorials. For more detailed content of the memorial, see Peng Xinwei, 1994, op. cit., pp. 499–501, fn. 15 (TN).

156. Liang Qichao, 1936, "China's Currency Problem," in *Collected Works from the Ice-Drinker's Studio*, Vol. 16, pp. 99, 124.

157. Wenxiang was Zhang Zhidong's honorary title.

158. Liang Qichao, 1999, *Complete Works of Liang Qichao*, Vol. 4, p. 1994.

159. Ye Shichang, 2003, *History of Chinese Monetary Theory*.

160. Chizo Ichiko, "Political and Institutional Reform, 1901–1911," in John K. Fairbank and Kwan-Ching Liu, 1980, op. cit., p. 405.

FIVE The Republican Era

Lu Xun epigraph: Lu Xun, 1925, "Jottings under Lamplight," trans. Theodore Huters, in Lu Xun, 2017, *Jottings under Lamplight*, ed. Eileen J. Cheng and Kirk A. Denton, p. 143 (TN).

1. Chen Cunren, 2007, *Life in the Age of the Silver Dollar;* this book vividly and accurately describes the sights and sounds of these times. It is even more unusual as a detailed record of the expenses of daily life in terms of how much is spent in bronze cash and silver, and has therefore always been an essential text for economic history aficionados. Chen's role was to analyze life in the silver-dollar era from the perspective of market life, and while his record is unusually lively, it is largely unconfirmable, a classic example being Zhang Taiyan and Chiang Kai-shek's experience in Hangzhou.

2. The government's name came from the Beiyang army, which dominated the country's politics with the rise of Yuan Shikai, a Qing dynasty general. After Yuan's death in 1916, the Beiyang army continued to dominate the government, but split into factions and competed for power in what was called the Warlord Era (TN).

3. Sheng Xuanhuai, *A Collection from Imperial Times*, Vol. 2 (TN).

4. Du Xuncheng, 2002, *General Financial History of China*, Vol. 3.

5. David Kynaston and Richard Roberts, 2015, *The Lion Wakes: A Modern History of HSBC*.

6. The Boxer Protocol was signed on September 7, 1901, between the Qing government and the Eight-Nation Alliance after China's defeat in the intervention to quell the Boxer Rebellion. Regarded as one of the Unequal Treaties, the protocol required the payment of 450 million taels of silver as indemnity to Russia, Germany, France, the United Kingdom, Japan, the United States, Italy, Belgium, Austria-Hungary, the Netherlands, Spain, Portugal, Sweden, and Norway (TN).

7. Albert Feuerwerker, "Economic Trends in the Late Ch'ing Empire, 1870–1911," in *The Cambridge History of China*, Vol. 11: *The Late Ch'ing*, Part 2, p. 59.

8. Ibid., pp. 63–64.

9. The standard dollar, or *guiyuan*, was the silver ounce standard dollar that Shanghai's mercantile world used to keep its accounts. Its fineness was set at 98 percent pure silver. See Peng Xinwei, 1994, *A Monetary History of China*, p. 669 (TN).

10. A book by Liu E, written in 1903–1904 and published in 1907, which thinly disguises the author's views as those of the physician-protagonist in describing the rise of the Boxers in the countryside, the decay of the Yellow River control system, and the hypocritical incompetence of the bureaucracy (TN).

11. People's Bank of China, Central Branch Advisers Office, Financial History Document Group, 1964, *Material on China's Modern Monetary History*, Vol. 1: *Era of Qing Government Rule (1840–1911)*, p. 139.

12. Xu Mei, "Chao li tiao lun, No. 5"; Sheng Kangji, *Texts on Dynastic Affairs, Continued*, Vol. 60: *Administration of Residency 32, Currency*, Vol. 2, p. 44.

13. Du Xuncheng, 2000, "A Comparison of China's Two Financial Systems in Modern Times," *China Social Sciences* (2000), No. 2, pp. 178–190.

14. Zhou Ziqi, "Report Presented to the President to Remedy the Financial Difficulty," in *Selected Literary and Historical Documents*, Vol. 2 (July 1990), p. 463.

15. Arthur N. Young, 1971, *China's Nation-Building Effort, 1927–1937: The Financial and Economic Record*, p. 5.

16. Lu Xun, 1925, op. cit.

17. 1865–1936, a Beiyang military leader in the 1920s and head of the Anhui clique (TN).

18. December 2001, *Compilation of Stored Shanghai Literary and Historical Materials: Economy and Finance*, Vol. 5, p. 2.

19. Zhang Jia'ao (Chang Kia-ngau), courtesy name Gongquan, was born in Jiading, Jiangsu Province, in 1889.

20. "Record of the Establishment of the Bank of China Stockholder's Federation," *Minguo Ribao*, May 13, 1916.

21. December 1991, *History of the Bank of China Shanghai Branch, 1912–1949*, p. 18.

22. Feng Gengguang, "My Time in the Bank of China," in Lin Hanfu (ed.), *Selected Literary and Historical Material*, Vol. 5 (TN).

23. The Four Banks Joint Business Office (*Silian zongchu*), the full name of which was "The Joint Business Office of the Central Bank, Bank of China, Bank of Communications and Farmers Bank of China," was established in Shanghai in July 1937. It became the most powerful financial organization in China during the War of Resistance against Japan. It was disbanded in October 1948 and its functions taken over by the Central Bank (TN).

24. See history of the Bank of China, memoirs, and other materials.

25. See Du Xuncheng, 2002, *General Financial History of China*, Vol. 3; Peng Xinwei, 2007, *A Monetary History of China*; etc.

26. Bank of China Headquarters Reference Room (ed.), 1986, *Historical Material on Republican Currency*, p. 91.

27. Yan Hongzhong, 2012, *China's Monetary and Financial System (1600–1949)*.

28. Zi Yaohua, 2005, *Footsteps of the Century*.

29. U.S. Congress, *Military Situation in the Far East: Hearings before the Committee on Armed Services and the Committee on Foreign Relations, United States Senate*, Testimony of Lt. Gen. Albert C. Wedemeyer, June 12, 1951, p. 2433.

30. Chinese Academy of Social Sciences Institute of Modern History, 2011, *History of the Republic of China*, Vol. 8.

31. Bank of China Economic Research Office, 1934, *National Banking Yearbook*. [Milton Friedman, 1994, *Money Mischief: Episodes in Monetary History*, p. 172 (TN).]

32. Zi Yaohua, 2005, op. cit.

33. Yao Songling, 2014, *Draft Chronology of Mr. Zhang Gongquan.*

34. Milton Friedman and Anna J. Schwartz, 1963, *Monetary History of the United States, 1867–1960*, p. 127, fn. 6 (TN).

35. Zheng Youkui et al., 1984, *China's Foreign Trade and Industrial Development (1840–1948).*

36. *Shen Bao* (Shanghai News), February 1935.

37. Pan Xiaoxia, 2102, *The Opportunity within Danger: The Reorganization of Bank of China and Bank of Communications in 1935.*

38. Warren I. Cohen, 1971, *America's Response to China: A History of Sino-American Relations*, p. 127.

39. 1994, *Compilation of Historical Archives of the Republic of China*, Vol. 5.

40. Wu Jingping, 1998, *Chronology of Song Ziwen's Political Career.*

41. 1991, *Compilation of Historical Materials of Bank of China*, Vol. 1.

42. See Hong Jiaguan, 2008, *General Financial History of China;* as well as the history of the Bank of China, etc. See also Wu Jingping, 2016, *The Modern Chinese Finance: Through the Lens of Cooperation and Competition between Politics and Business*, p. 318.

43. Arthur N. Young, 1971, *China's Nation-Building Effort, 1927–1937.*

44. Zhou Bodi, 1936, *The Silver Problem and China's Monetary Policies.*

45. Jonathan Kirschner, 1995, *Currency and Coercion: The Political Economy of International Monetary Power*, pp. 51–61; Chinese edition, 2013.

46. Chen Guangfu (K. P. Chen), 2002, *The Journals of Chen Guangfu.*

47. Kirschner, 1995, op. cit., p. 54. The Marco Polo Bridge Incident, also known as the Lugou Bridge Incident or Double-Seven Incident, was a conflict between China's National Revolutionary Army and the Imperial Japanese Army launched on July 7, 1937, which is widely considered the start of the Second Sino-Japanese War (TN).

48. Zi Yaohua, 2005, op. cit.

49. Wu Xiaofu, 1936, *Series on China's Currency Problems.*

50. Milton Friedman, 1994, op. cit., pp. 176–177.

51. See the Japanese NHK television documentary *War of the Yen.*

52. 1991, *Compilation of Historical Materials of Bank of China*, Vol. 1.

53. Tu Yueh-sheng and Chang Hsiao-lin were leaders of the Green Gang, a major organized crime group (TN).

54. Parks M. Coble, Jr., 1986, *The Shanghai Capitalists and the Nationalist Government, 1927–1937*, p. 265.

55. Chiang Ching-kuo, Chiang Kai-shek's son, was deputy chief of the Economic Supervisory Office in Shanghai. Chiang Ching-kuo had set special targets for the Zhejiang Industry Bank and Kincheng Banking Corporation, but he did not trust the bank holdings reported by Li Ming and Zhou Zuomin and placed Zhou under house arrest. See Ji Zhaojin, 2016, *A History of Modern Shanghai Banking: The Rise and Decline of China's Financial Capitalism* (TN).

56. See *Journals of Chen Guangfu, Draft Chronology of Mr. Zhang Gongquan*, Coble's *The Shanghai Capitalists and the Nationalist Government*, etc.

57. Lloyd E. Eastman, 2002, *Seeds of Destruction: Nationalist China in War and Revolution, 1937–1949*, p. 2.

58. Yao Songling, 2014, *Draft Chronology of Mr. Zhang Gongquan*.

59. Francis Fukuyama, 2011, *The Origins of Political Order* (TN).

Further Reading

1. V. S. Naipaul, 1987, *The Enigma of Arrival*.

Bibliography

Abu-Lughod, Janet. 1989. *Before European Hegemony: The World System, AD 1250–1350.* New York: Oxford University Press.

Acemoglu, Daron, Simon Johnson, and James Robinson. 2002. "Reversal of Fortune: Geography and Development in the Making of the Modern World Income Distribution." *Quarterly Journal of Economics* 2002:117.

Acemoglu, Daron, and James A. Robinson. 2012. *Why Nations Fail: The Origins of Power, Prosperity, and Poverty.* Crown Business. Chinese edition, trans. Li Zenggang. 2015. Hunan kexue jishu chubanshe.

Adshead, S. A. M. 2000. *China in World History.* 3rd edition. Basingstoke and New York: Palgrave. Chinese edition. 2009.

Akinobu, Kuroda. 2007. *World History of Monetary Systems.* Chinese edition, trans. He Ping. Beijing: Zhongguo renmin daxue chubanshe.

Anonymous (proofread by Li Zhiliang). 2005. *Complete History of the Song.* Vol. 23 (Yuan). Harbin: Heilongjiang renmin chubanshe.

———. 2007. *Imperial Ordinances of the First Two Reign Periods of the Southern Song.* Vol. 54. Beijing: Beijing tushuguan chubanshe.

Attwell, William S. 1977. "Notes on Silver, Foreign Trade, and the Late Ming Economy." *Journal of World History* 3(8):1–33.

———. 1982. "International Bullion Flows and the Chinese Economy, circa 1530–1650." *Past and Present* 95(1):68–90.

———. 1986. "Some Observations on the 'Seventeenth-Century Crisis' in China and Japan." *The Journal of Asian Studies* 45(2).

Bagehot, Walter. 1873. *Lombard Street: A Description of the Money Market.* Chinese edition, trans. Shen Guohua. 2008. Shanghai: Shanghai caijing daxue chubanshe.

Barrett, Ward. 1990. "World Bullion Flows, 1450–1800." In James D. Tracy, ed. 1990. *The Rise of Merchant Empires: Long-Distance Trade in the Early Modern World, 1350–1750.* Cambridge: Cambridge University Press.

Belden, Jack. 1970. *China Shakes the World*. Monthly Review Press. Chinese edition, trans. You Yingjue et al. 1980. Lhasa: Xizang renmin chubanshe.

Blair, E. H., and J. A. Robertson. 1903. *The Philippine Islands, 1493–1898*. Vol. 2. Cleveland: The Arthur H. Clark Co.

Bol, Peter. 1992. *This Culture of Ours: Intellectual Transitions in T'ang and Sung China*. Chinese edition, trans. Liu Ning. 2001. Nanjing: Jiangsu renmin chubanshe.

Braudel, Fernand. 1982. *Civilization and Capitalism, 15th–18th Century*. Vol. 2: *The Wheels of Commerce*. Trans. Siân Reynolds. New York: Harper & Row.

———. 1992. *Civilization and Capitalism, 15th–18th Century*. Vol. 3: *The Perspective of the World*. Trans. Siân Reynolds. Berkeley: University of California Press.

Brook, Timothy, and Bob Tadashi Wakabayashi. 2000. *Opium Regimes: China, Britain, and Japan, 1839–1952*. Chinese edition, trans. Hong Xia. 2009. Hefei: Huangshan shushe.

Brown, Norman O. 1961. *Life against Death: The Psychoanalytical Meaning of History*. New York: Vintage. Chinese edition, trans. Feng Chuan and Wu Houkai. 1994. Guiyang: Guizhou renmin chubanshe.

Calomiris, Charles W., and Stephen H. Haber. 2014. *Fragile by Design: The Political Origins of Banking Crises and Scarce Credit*. Princeton: Princeton University Press. Chinese edition, trans. Liao Min, Yang Dongning, and Zhou Yejing. 2015. Beijing: Zhongxin chubanshe.

Campbell, Colin, and Gordon Tullock. 1954. "Hyper-Inflation in China, 1937–1940." *Journal of Political Economy* 62(3):236–245.

Canizares-Esguerra, Jorge, and Erik R. Seeman. 2007. *The Atlantic in Global History, 1500–2000*. Upper Saddle River, NJ: Pearson Prentice Hall.

Chanda, Nayan. 2007. *Bound Together: How Traders, Preachers, Adventurers, and Warriors Shaped Globalization*. New Haven: Yale University Press.

Chen, Cunren. 2007. *Life in the Age of the Silver Dollar*. Guilin: Guangxi shifan daxue chubanshe.

Chen, Guangfu. 2002. *The Journals of Chen Guangfu*. Shanghai: Shanghaishi dang'anguan.

Cheung, Steven. 2014. *Economic Explanation*. Vol. 4: *The Choice of Institutional Arrangements*. Beijing: Zhongxin chubanshe.

Chinese Academy of Social Sciences Institute of Modern History. 2011. *History of the Republic of China*. Beijing: Zhonghua shuju.

———. 2013. *Youth Academic Forum of the Chinese Academy of Social Sciences Institute of Modern History*. Beijing: Shehui kexue wenxian chubanshe.

Chinese People's Bank and Chinese People's Bank Shanghai Branch historical documents collections.

Chinese Political Consultative Conference Historical Documents Committee. 1985. *Fabi, Jinyuanquan and the Gold Panic*. Beijing: Wenshi ziliao chubanshe.

Chown, John F. 1997. *A History of Money: From AD 800*. Chinese edition, trans. Li Guangqian. 2002. Beijing: Shangwu yinshuguan.

Clark, Hugh R. 2009. "Frontier Discourse and China's Maritime Frontier: China's Frontiers and the Encounter with the Sea through Early Imperial History." *Journal of World History* 20(1) (March).

Coase, Ronald, Armen Alchian, and Douglass North. 1994. *Property Rights and Systemic Change*. Chinese edition, trans. Liu Shouying. Shanghai: Shanghai renmin chubanshe.

Coble, Parks M., Jr. 1986. *The Shanghai Capitalists and the Nationalist Government, 1927–1937*. Cambridge: Harvard University Asia Center. Chinese edition, trans. Cai Jingyl. 198/. Tianjin: Nankai daxue chubanshe.

Cohen, Warren I. 1971. *America's Response to China*. 5th edition. 2010. Chinese edition, trans. Zhang Jinger. 1997. Shanghai: Fudan daxue chubanshe.

Compilation of Historical Archives of the Republic of China. Vol. 5. 1994.

Compilation of Historical Materials of Bank of China. Vol. 1. 1991.

Compilation of Stored Shanghai Literary and Historical Materials: Economy and Finance (5), Shanghai: Shanghai guji chubanshe. December 2001.

Dai, Jianbing. 2005. *Silver and the Modern Chinese Economy (1890–1935)*. Shanghai: Fudan daxue chubanshe.

Dai, Zhiqiang. 2013. *Collecting and Appreciating Currency*. Beijing: Yinshua gongye chubanshe.

Davis, Lance, and Douglass C. North. 1971. *Institutional Change and American Economic Growth*. Cambridge: Cambridge University Press. Chinese edition. 1994.

Deng, Guangmin. 1957. *Xin Jiaxuan's Collected Poetry and Essays: On Using Huizi*. Shanghai: Gudian wenxue chubanshe.

Ding, Mingnan, and Yu Shengwu. 1992. *Imperialist Aggression against China*. Beijing: Renmin chubanshe.

Du, Xuncheng. 2000. "A Comparison of China's Two Financial Systems in Modern Times." *China Social Sciences* 2000(2):178–190.

———. 2002. *General Financial History of China*. Vol. 3. Beijing: Zhongguo jinrong chubanshe.

Eames, James Bromley. 1974. *The English in China*. London: Curzon Press.

Eastman, Lloyd E. 2002. *Seeds of Destruction: Nationalist China in War and Revolution, 1937–1949*. Stanford: Stanford University Press.

Ebrey, Patricia Buckley. 1996. *The Cambridge Illustrated History of China*. Cambridge: Cambridge University Press. Chinese edition, trans. Zhao Shiyu, Zhao Shiling, and Zhang Hongyan. 2002. Jin'an: Shandong huabao chubanshe.

Eichengreen, Barry. 1996. *Globalizing Capital: A History of the International Monetary System*. Princeton: Princeton University Press. Chinese edition. 2009.

Elvin, Mark. 1973. *The Pattern of the Chinese Past*. Stanford: Stanford University Press.

Evans, Paul M. 1988. *John Fairbank and the American Understanding of Modern China*. Oxford: Basil Blackwell.

Fairbank, John King. 1976. *The United States and China*. 4th edition. Cambridge: Harvard University Press. Chinese edition. 1999.

Fan, Shuzhi. 2003. *History of the Late Ming*. Shanghai: Fudan danxue chubanshe.

———. 2006. *Sixteen Talks on National History*. Beijing: Zhonghua shuju.

Fang, Hui. 1981. *Tongjiang Collection*. Vol. 6. Beijing: Shangwu yinshuju.

Faure, David. 2002. "The Sprouts of Chinese Capitalism." *Research in China's Economic History* 2002(1).

Ferguson, Niall. 2001. *The Cash Nexus: Money and Power in the Modern World, 1700–2000.* New York: Basic Books. Chinese edition, trans. Tang Yinghua. 2012. Beijing: Zhongxin chubanshe.

———. 2003. "Empire: How Britain Made the Modern World." *African Business* 288:62.

———. 2006. *The War of the World: Twentieth-Century Conflict and the Descent of the West.* New York: Penguin. Chinese edition, trans. Yu Chunlan. 2015. Guangzhou: Guangdong renmin chubanshe.

———. 2008. *The Ascent of Money: A Financial History of the World.* New York: Penguin. Chinese edition, trans. Gao Cheng. 2009. Beijing: Zhongxin chubanshe.

———. 2011. *Civilization: The West and the Rest.* New York: Penguin.

Finer, Samuel E. 1999. *The History of Government from the Earliest Times.* Chinese edition, trans. Wang Zhen and Ma Bailiang. 2014. Shanghai: Huadong shifan daxue chubanshe.

Flynn, Dennis O., and Arturo Giraldez. 1995. "Born with a 'Silver Spoon': The Origin of World Trade in 1571." *Journal of World History* 6(2):201–221.

Frank, Andre Gunder. 1998. *ReOrient: Global Economy in the Asian Age.* Berkeley: University of California Press.

Friedman, Milton. 1962. *Capitalism and Freedom.* Chicago: University of Chicago Press. Chinese edition. 2004. Beijing: Shangwu yinshuguan.

———. 1994. *Money Mischief: Episodes in Monetary History.* Chinese edition, trans. An Jia. 2006. Beijing: Shangwu yinshuguan.

Fu, Lecheng, and Duan Changguo. 2010. *Chinese History: Modern History.* Beijing: Jiuzhou chubanshe.

Fu, Lecheng, and Jiang Gongtao. 2010. *Chinese History: History of the Ming and Qing.* Beijing: Jiuzhou chubanshe.

Fu, Yiling. 1956. *Merchants and Commercial Capital in the Ming and Qing Periods.* Beijing: Renmin chubanshe.

———. 1988. "China's Traditional Society: A Diverse Construction." *Research in Chinese Socio-Economic History* 1988(3).

Fukuyama, Francis. 2011. *The Origins of Political Order.* New York: Farrar, Straus and Giroux. Chinese edition, trans. Mao Junjia. 2012. Guilin: Guangxi shifan daxue chubanshe.

———. 2014. *Political Order and Political Decay: From the Industrial Revolution to the Globalization of Democracy.* New York: Farrar, Straus and Giroux. Chinese edition, trans. Mao Junjia. 2015. Guilin: Guangxi shifan daxue chubanshe.

Galbraith, John Kenneth. 1975. *Money: Whence It Came, Where It Went.* Boston: Houghton Mifflin.

Gao, Congming. 1995. "The Characteristics of Currency Circulation in the Song Dynasty." *Research in Chinese Economic History* 1995(3).

———. 1996. "On the Discrepancy between Southern Song Financial Revenues and Northern Song Annual Revenues." *Hebei Journal* 1996(1).

———. 1997. "The Relationship between the Northern Song Central and Local Fiscal Administration from the Perspective of 'Additional Taxes.'" *Research in Chinese Economic History* 1997(4).

——. 2000. *Research on Song Dynasty Currency and Currency Circulation.* Baoding: Hebei daxue chubanshe.

——. 2011. "On the Main Reasons for the Kuomintang's Failure on the Mainland." *History Teaching: Secondary School Edition.*

Ge, Jianxiong. 2008. *Unity and Division.* Beijing: Zhonghua shuju.

Ge, Jinfang. 1991. *Economic Research and Analysis of the Song, Liao, Xia and Jin Dynasties.* Wuhan: Wuhan chubanshe.

Ge, Zhaoguang. 2014. *Imagined Alien Land—Reading Korean Joseon Dynasty Chinese-Language Swallow Journey Documents and Jottings.* Beijing: Zhonghua shuju.

Gefei (Liu Yong). 2014. *Heron Hidden in Snow.* Nanjing: Yilin chubanshe.

Geil, William Edgar. 1914. *A Yankee on the Yangtze.* London: Hodder and Stoughton. Chinese edition, trans. Liu Ping. 2010.

Glahn, Richard von. 1996. *Fountain of Fortune: Money and Monetary Policy in China, 1000–1700.* Berkeley: University of California Press.

Goetzmann, William N., and K. Geert Rouwenhorst. 2005. *The Origins of Value.* Oxford: Oxford University Press. Chinese edition, trans. Wang Ning and Wang Wenyu. 2010. Shenyang: Wanjuan chuban gongsi.

Graeber, David. 2011. *Debt: The First 5000 Years.* New York: Melville House. Chinese edition, trans. Sun Tan and Dong Ziyun. 2012. Beijing: Zhongxin chubanshe.

Gu, Yanwu. 1985. *Notes on the Daily Accumulation of Knowledge (Rizhilu).* Shanghai: Guji chubanshe.

Guo, Tingyi. 1987. *Journal of Modern Chinese Historical Facts.* Beijing: Zhonghua shuju.

——. 1999. *Outline of Modern Chinese History.* Beijing: Shehui kexue wenxian chubanshe.

Hamilton, Earl J. 1934. *American Treasure and the Price Revolution in Spain, 1501–1650.* Cambridge: Harvard University Press.

Han, Yuhai. 2010. *Who Has Written History for 500 Years?* Beijing: Jiuzhou chubanshe.

Hansen, Valerie. 2000. *Open Empire: A History of China to 1600.* Revised edition. New York: W. W. Norton. Chinese edition. 2007.

Herodotus. *Histories.* Chinese edition. 1985.

History of the Republic of China. 2011. Vol. 8. Beijing: Zhonghua shuju.

Holcombe, Chester. 1895. *The Real Chinaman.* New York: Dodd, Mead & Co. Chinese edition, trans. Liu Ping. 2010.

Homer, Sidney, and Richard Sylla. 1963. *A History of Interest Rates.* New Brunswick: Rutgers University Press. 4th edition, 2005. Wiley Finance. Chinese edition, trans. Xiao Xinming and Cao Jianhai. 2010. Beijing: Zhongxin chubanshe.

Hong, Jiaguan. 2008. *General Financial History of China.* Vol. 4. Beijing: Zhongguo jinrong chubanshe.

Hong, Mai. 2005. *Rongzhai Sanbi.* Vol. 14. Beijing: Zhonghua shuju.

Horowitz, Richard. 2004. "International Law and State Transformation in China, Siam, and the Ottoman Empire during the Nineteenth Century." *Journal of World History* 15(4):445–486.

Huang, Jianhui. 2002. *History of Money-Exchange Shops in Shanxi.* Taiyuan: Shanxi jingji chubanshe.

Huang, Ray. 1975. *Taxation and Governmental Finance in Sixteenth-Century Ming China*. Cambridge Studies in Chinese History, Literature and Institutions. Cambridge: Cambridge University Press. Chinese edition. 2001. Shanghai: Shanghai sanlian chudian.

———. 1981. *1587: A Year of No Significance: The Ming Dynasty in Decline*. New Haven: Yale University Press.

———. 1996. *China: A Macro History*. M. E. Sharpe. Chinese edition. 2016. Beijing: Zhongxin chubanshe.

Huang, Zongxi. 2008. *Mingyi Daifang Lu* [A Plan Awaiting a True Prince]. English edition, trans. William Theodore de Bary. 1993. *Waiting for the Dawn: A Plan for the Prince*. New York: Columbia University Press.

———. 2000. *Small Farmer Economy and Social Change in Northern China*. Beijing: Zhonghua shuju.

Hume, David. 1752. "Of Money." In *Writings on Economics*. 2007. Piscataway, NJ: Transaction Publishers. Chinese edition, trans. Chen Wei. 1984. Shanghai: Shangwu yinshuguan.

Humphrey, Caroline. 1985. "Barter and Economic Disintegration." *Man* 20(1) (March 1985):48–72.

Inoue, Hiromasa. 2011. *Research into the History of the Qing Dynasty's Opium Policies*. Trans. Qiang Kang. Lhasa: Xizang renmin chubanshe.

Iwai, Shigeki. 2011. *Research on the History of China's Modern Fiscal Administration*. Beijing: Shehui kexue wenxian chubanshe.

Jia, Qihong. 2015. "Research into Certain Problems of Song Dynasty Military Logistics." Ph.D. thesis, Hebei University.

Jia, Shiyi. 1930. *National Debt and Finance*. Shanghai: Shangwu yinshuguan.

Jiang, Boli, and Dai Jitao. 2012. *On the Japanese and Japan*. Nanjing: Fenghuang chubanshe.

Jiang, Tingfu. 2001. *Modern History of China*. Shanghai: Shanghai guji chubanshe.

Kann, Eduard. 2006. *Illustrated Catalog of Chinese Coins*. Vol. 1: *Gold, Silver, Nickel and Aluminum*. New York: Ishi Press.

Kato, Shigeshi. 1959. *Outline of Chinese Economic History*. Chinese edition, trans. Wu Jie. Shanghai: Shangwu yinshuju.

———. 2006. *Research in Tang and Song Dynasty Gold and Silver: Centered on the Function of Gold and Silver Currency*. Beijing: Zhonghua shuju.

Kenichi, Ohno. 2006. *From Edo to Heisei*. Trans. Zang Xin et al. Beijing: Zhongxin chubanshe.

Kennedy, Paul. 1987. *The Rise and Fall of the Great Powers*. Chinese edition, trans. Liang Yuhua. 1990. Beijing: Shijie zhishi chubanshe.

Keynes, John Maynard. 1936. *The General Theory of Employment, Interest and Money*. New York: Macmillan.

Kikuchi, Hideaki. 2014. *The Late Qing Dynasty and Modern China*. Trans. Ma Xiaojian. Guilin: Guangxi shifan daxue chubanshe.

Kindleberger, Charles P. 1984. *A Financial History of Western Europe.* London: George Allen & Unwin. Chinese edition, trans. Xu Zijian, He Jianxiong, and Zhu Zhong. 2010. Beijing: Zhongguo jinrong chubanshe.

Kirschner, Jonathan. 1995. *Currency and Coercion: The Political Economy of International Monetary Power.* Princeton: Princeton University Press. Chinese edition, trans. Li Wei. 2013. Shanghai: Shanghai renmin chubanshe.

Kishimoto, Mio. 2010. *Commodity Prices and Economic Fluctuation in Qing Dynasty China.* Trans. Liu Dirui. Beijing: Shehui kexue wenxian chubanshe.

Kissinger, Henry. 2011. *On China.* New York: Penguin.

——. 2014. *World Order.* New York: Penguin.

Kozo, Yamamura, and Tetsuo Kamiki. 1983. "Silver Mines and Sung Coins—A Monetary History of Modern Japan in International Perspective." In J. F. Richards. 1983. *Precious Metals in the Late Medieval and Early Modern Worlds.* Carolina Academic Press.

Kynaston, David, and Richard Roberts. 2015. *The Lion Wakes: A Modern History of HSBC.* London: Profile Books. Chinese edition. 2015. Beijing: Zhongxin chubanshe.

Landes, David S. 1999. *The Wealth and Poverty of Nations: Why Some Are So Rich and Some So Poor.* New York: W. W. Norton.

Lanling, Xiaoxiaosheng. 2011. *The Golden Lotus.* Trans. Clement Egerton and Shu Qingchun (Lao She). Rutland: Tuttle.

"Li Yuandu's Letter Summoning Shi Dahia to Surrender." In Luo Ergang, Xie Xingyao, and Peng Zeyi (eds.). 1992. *Minguo Congshu.* Vol. 4. Shanghai shudian. P. 530.

Li, Bozhong. 1999. "The Formation of China's Whole-Country Market, 1500–1840." *Tsinghua University Journal* 1999(4):48–54.

Li, Hong. 2015. *Illustrated History of Finance.* Beijing: Zhongxin chubanshe.

Li, Lungsheng. 2004. "Further Exploration of Foreign Silver's Effects on China's Late Ming Economy." *Hong Kong Sociology Journal.*

——. 2005. "Estimates of Late Ming Silver Stores." *China Numismatics* 22(1):3–8.

Li, You. 1935. *Song Dynasty Facts.* Vol. 16. Shanghai: Shangwu yinshuguan.

Liang, Fangzhong. 1936. "The Single Whip Tax System." *Collected Papers on China's Modern Economic History* 4(1).

——. 1939. *Ming Dynasty International Trade and the Import and Export of Silver.* *Collected Papers on China's Socio-Economic History* 6(2).

——. 1957. *The Ming Dynasty Grain-Growing System.* Shanghai: Shanghai renmin chubanshe.

——. 1989. *Collected Essays on Economic History.* Beijing: Zhonghua shuju.

Liang, Jiabin. 1999. *Guangdong's Thirteen Hongs.* Guangzhou: Guangdong renmin chubanshe.

Liang, Qichao. 1936. "China's Currency Problem." In *Collected Works from the Ice-Drinker's Studio.* Vol. 16. Shanghai: Shangwu yinshuguan.

——. 1999. "Our Currency System and Financial Policies." In *Complete Works of Liang Qichao.* Vol. 5. Beijing: Beijing chubanshe.

———. 1999. *Complete Works of Liang Qichao.* Vol. 4. Beijing: Beijing chubanshe.

Liang, Tingnan. 2002. *Guangdong Customs Records.* Guangzhou: Guangdong renmin chubanshe.

Lin, Man-houng. 2006. *China Upside Down: Currency, Society, and Ideologies, 1808–1856.* Cambridge: Harvard University Press. Chinese edition. 2011. Taipei: Taida chuban zhongxin.

Lin, Tongfa. 2003. *China's Post-War Situation.* Taipei: Taiwan shangwu yinshuguan.

Little, Mrs. Archibald. 1899. *Intimate China: The Chinese as I Have Seen Them.* London: Hutchinson & Co.

Liu, Binglin. 1962. *Brief History of Modern China's Foreign Debt.* Shanghai: Sanlian shudian.

Liu, Haiying. 2014. *China's Enormous Debt.* Beijing: Zhongxin chubanshe.

Liu, Ping. 2010. "Foreigners' Experience of Late Qing Finance." *Banker.*

———. 2011. "The Financial Industry of the Late Qing Dynasty in the Eyes of Foreigners." *The Chinese Banker* 7.

Liu, William Guanglin. 2011. "Research in Ming Dynasty Currency Issues." *Chinese Economic History Studies* 1:72–83.

Lovell, Julia. 2015. *The Opium Wars: Drugs, Dreams and the Making of China.* New York: Abrams. Chinese edition, trans. Liu Yuebin. 2015. Xinxing chubanshe.

Lu, Hanchao. 2009. *A Man of Two Worlds: The Life of Sir Robert Hart, 1835–1911.*

Lu, Xun. 1925. "Jottings under Lamplight." Trans. Theodore Huters. In Lu Xun. 2017. *Jottings under Lamplight.* Ed. Eileen J. Cheng and Kirk A. Denton. Cambridge: Harvard University Press. Pp. 143–150.

Ma, Duanlin. 2006a. *Wenxian Tongkou,* Vol. 23. Beijing: Zhonghua shuju.

———. 2006b. *Wenxian Tongkou: Currency.* Beijing: Zhonghua shuju.

Ma, Keyao. 1991. "A Comparative Study of Chinese and West-European Feudal Institutions." *Journal of Peking University (Humanities and Social Sciences)* 1991(2).

Ma, Yinchu. 1999. *Complete Works.* Hangzhou: Zhejiang renmin chubanshe.

Maddison, Angus. 1998. *Chinese Economic Performance in the Long Run.* OECD, 1998.

———. 1999. *The World Economy.* Vol. 1: *A Millennial Perspective.* Foreign Affairs. Chinese edition. 2003.

———. 2003. *The World Economy: A Millennial Perspective.* OECD Publishing. http://piketty.pse.ens.fr/files/Maddison2001Data.pdf.

Martin, Felix. 2014. *Money: The Unauthorized Biography—From Coinage to Cryptocurrencies.* New York: Knopf. Chinese edition, trans. Deng Feng. 2015. Beijing: Zhongxin chubanshe.

Marx, Karl. *History of the Opium Trade.* Chinese edition. 1995. In *The Selected Works of Marx and Engels.* Vol. 1. 2nd edition. Beijing: Renmin chubanshe.

Mauss, Marcel. 1990 (1950). *The Gift: The Form and Reason for Exchange in Archaic Societies.* London: Routledge. Chinese edition. 2005.

Ministry of Finance Research Committee. 1935. *China's Silver Problem.*

Mio, Kishimoto. 2013. *Basic Problems in Ming and Qing Dynasty History.* Trans. Zhou Shaoquan and Luan Chengxian. Beijing: Shangwu yinshuguan.

Morris, Ian. 2010. *Why the West Rules—for Now.* New York: Farrar, Straus and Giroux. Chinese edition, trans. Qian Feng. 2014. Beijing: Zhongxin chubanshe.

Morse, Hosea Ballou. 1910–1918. *The International Relations of the Chinese Empire.* Vol. 1: *The Period of Conflict, 1834–1860.* London: Longmans, Green, and Co. Chinese edition, trans. Zhang Huiwen. 2006. Shanghai shudian chubanshe.

Mote, Frederick, and Denis Twitchett (eds.). 1998. *The Cambridge History of China: The Ming Dynasty.* Chinese edition. 1992. Beijing: Zhongguo shehui kexue chubanshe.

Mutsu, Munemitsu. 1963. *Record of Hardship.* Trans. Yi Sheshi. Beijing: Shangwu yinshuguan.

Naitō, Konan. 2004. *Selected Works on Chinese History.* Shehui kexue wenxian chubanshe.

———. 2009 (1992). "A Summary of Tang and Song Worldviews." In *Selected Works by Japanese Scholars Researching Chinese History.* Vol. 1. Beijing: Zhonghua shuju. Secondary School History Teaching Reference Materials.

North, Douglass. 1976. *The Rise of the Western World: A New Economic History.* Cambridge: Cambridge University Press. Chinese edition, trans. Li Yiping and Cai Lei. 2009. Beijing: Huaxia chubanshe.

———. 1981. *Structure and Change in Economic History.* New York: W. W. Norton.

Osamu, Ōba. 1997. *Secret Talks between Japan and China in the Edo Period.* Beijing: Zhonghua shuju.

Palace Museum. 1968. *Historical Documents of Qing Dynasty Diplomacy (Jiaqing Reign).*

Pan, Xiaoxia. 2012. *Zhongguo shehuike xueyuan jindaishi yanjiusuo qingnian xueshu luntan* [The Opportunity within Danger: The Reorganization of Bank of China and Bank of Communications in 1935]. 2012 edition published 2013.

Peng, Xinwei. 1994. *A Monetary History of China.* Trans. Edward H. Kaplan. Bellingham: Western Washington University. Chinese edition. 2007. Shanghai: Shanghai renmin chubanshe.

Peng, Zeyi. 1961. "China's Economy and Class Relations under the Fluctuating Silver and Bronze Cash Values Ten Years after the Opium Wars." *Historical Research* 6:40–68.

People's Bank of China Central Branch Advisers Office Financial History Document Group. 1964. *Material on China's Modern Monetary History.* Vol. 1: *Era of Qing Government Rule (1840–1911).* Beijing: Zhonghua shuju.

Perkins, Dwight H. 1969. *Agricultural Development in China, 1368–1968.* Chicago: Aldine.

Qi, Xia. 1999. "Song Taizhong and Defending the Interior and Vacating the Exterior." *Song History Research Commentaries.*

———. 2009a. *Complete Works.* Baoding: Hebei daxue chubanshe.

———. 2009b. *Economic History of the Song Dynasty.* Beijing: Zhonghua shuju.

Qian, Jiaju. 1984. *Historical Materials on the Public Debt of Old China.* Beijing: Zhonghua shuju.

Qian, Jiaju, and Guo Yangang. 1986. *Outline of China's Monetary History.* Shanghai: Shanghai renmin shubanshe.

———. 2014. *History of the Development of China's Currency.* Shanghai: Shanghai renmin chubanshe.

Qian, Jiang. 1988. "Investigation of the International Flow of Silver and Its Import into China in the 16th to 18th Centuries." *Nanyang Issues Research* 1988(2):84–94.

Qian, Mu. 1974. *Natural Science and Art.* Song History Research Collection. Vol. 7. Zhonghua: Congshu bianji weiyuanhui.

——. 2005. *Research Methods of Chinese History.* Beijing: Sanlian shudian.

——. 2012. *China's Political Gains and Losses over the Generations.* Beijing: Jiuzhou chubanshe.

——. 2013. *The Economic History of China.* Beijing: Beijing lianhe chuban gongsi.

Qin, Hui. 2005. "Tax Reform by Aggregation and Huang Zongxi's Law." In "Tax and Fee Reform, Village Autonomy, and Central and Local Finance." Trans. Ma Jisen. *The Chinese Economy* 38(6). Original Chinese version published in *Peasant China: Historical Reflections and Realistic Options.* 2003. Zhengzhou: Henan renmin chubanshe. Pp. 17–41.

Qiu, Fanzhen. 2005. "Jenks's Currency Reform Plan and the Late Qing Currency Issue." *Jindaishi Yanjiu* 3.

Quan, Hansheng. 1957. "The Relationship between American Silver and Chinese Commodity Price Revolution in the Eighteenth Century." In *Commentaries on Chinese Economic History.* 2012. Beijing: Zhonghua shuju. Pp. 475–508.

——. 1966. "The Ming Dynasty's Silver Classifications and Silver Production Quotas." *Xinya shuyuan xueshu niankan* 9:245–246.

——. 1967. "Changes in Silver's Purchasing Power in the Song and Ming and the Reasons for It." *Xinya xuabao.*

——. 1969. "The Importation of American Silver to China in the Ming and Qing Dynasties." *Journal of the Chinese Cultural Research Institute* 2(1):59–80.

——. 2011. *Quan Hansheng's Works on Economic History.* Zhonghua shuju.

Reid, Anthony. 1993. *Southeast Asia in the Age of Commence, 1450–1680.* New Haven: Yale University Press.

Rivoire, Jean. 1984. *Histoire de la banque.* Paris: Presses Universitaires de France. Chinese edition. 2001.

Rong, Hong. 2012. *Memoirs of Rong Hong.* Beijing: Dongfang chubanshe.

Rowntree, Joshua. 1906. *The Imperial Drug Trade: A Re-Statement of the Opium Question, in the Light of Recent Evidence and New Developments in the East.* London: Methuen. 2nd edition.

Schumpeter, Joseph A. 1934. *The Theory of Economic Development: An Inquiry into Profits, Capital, Credit, Interest and the Business Cycle.* Cambridge: Harvard University Press.

Sehgal, Kabir. 2015. *Coined: The Rich Life of Money and How Its History Has Shaped Us.* Chinese edition, trans. Luan Lifu. 2016. Beijing: Zhongxin chubanshe.

Shanghai People's Political Consultative Conference Historical Materials Committee. 2001. *Compilation of Shanghai Cultural and Historical Documents.* Shanghai: Guji chubanshe.

Shao, Wankuan, and Zhang Guochao. 2007. *The Golden Lotus Cookbook.* Ji'nan: Shangdong huabao chubanshe.

Shen, Shixing (ed.). 1989. *Collected Statutes of the Ming Dynasty.* Beijing: Zhonghua shuju.

Sheng, Kangji. *Texts on Dynastic Affairs, Continued.* Vol. 60. *Administration of Residency 32. Currency.* Vol. 2.

Shi, Junzhi. 2012. *General History of China's Monetary System.* Beijing: Zhongguo jinrong chubanshe.

Shiba, Yoshinobu. 2012. *Research on the Economic History of Southern China in the Song Dynasty.* Trans. He Zhongli. Nanjing: Jiangsu renmin chubanshe.

Shinobu, Seizaburo. 1980. *Diplomatic History of Japan.* Trans. Tianjin Academy of Social Sciences. Beijing: Shangwu yinshuguan.

Sima, Qian. 2012. *Records of the Historian: Pingzhun Shu.* Hunan: Yuelu shushe.

Smith, Adam. 1776. *An Enquiry into the Nature and Causes of the Wealth of Nations.* Chinese edition. 2014.

Sombart, Werner. 1976. *Luxury and Capitalism.* Ann Arbor: University of Michigan Press. Chinese edition, trans. Wang Yanping and Hou Xiaohe. 2005. Shanghai: Shiji chuban jituan.

Song, Lian. 1976. *History of the Yuan: Biography of Zhang Rong.* Daocaorenshuwu.com.

Soto, Hernando de. 2005. *The Mystery of Capital: Why Capitalism Triumphs in the West and Fails Everywhere Else.* New York: Basic Books. Chinese edition, trans. Wang Xiaodong. 2005. Nanjing: Jiangsu renmin chubanshe.

Spence, Jonathan. 1999. *The Chan's Great Continent: China in Western Minds.* New York: W. W. Norton. Chinese edition, trans. Yuan Shumei. 2013. Guilin: Guangxi shifan daxue chubanshe.

Stavrianos, Leften Stavros. 1970. *The World since 1500: A Global History.* Chinese edition, trans. Wu Xiangying and Liang Yimin. 1992. Shanghai: Shanghai shehui kexueyuan chubanshe.

Su, Zhe. 1987. *Luan City Collection Number 3*, Vol. 8(3). Shanghai: Shanghai guji chubanshe.

Takahashi, Hiromi. 2010. *Historical Research on Currency in the Song, Jin and Yuan Dynasties: The Formation of the Yuan Dynasty's Monetary Policies.* Shanghai: Shanghai renmin chubanshe.

Takeshi, Hamashita. 1999. *The International Turning Point of Modern China—The Tribute Trade System and the Modern Asian Economy.* Trans. Zhu Yingui and Ouyang Fei. Beijing: Zhongguo shehu kexue chubanshe.

———. 2006a. *The Resurgence of East Asia: From a Perspective of 500, 150 and 50 Years.* Trans. Ma Yuan. Beijing: Shehui kexue wenxian chubanshe.

———. 2006b. *Research in China's Modern Economy: The Customs Finance of the Late Qing and the Treaty Port Market.* Trans. Gao Shujuan and Sun Bin. Nanjing: Jiangsu renmin chubanshe.

———. 2008. *China, East Asia and the Global Economy.* New York: Routledge. Chinese edition, trans. Wang Yuru et al. 2009. Beijing: Shehui kexue wenxian chubanshe.

Tamagna, Frank M. 1942. *Banking and Finance in China.* New York: International Secretariat Institute of Pacific Relations Publications Office.

Taylor, Jay. 2009. *The Generalissimo: Chiang Kai-shek and the Struggle for Modern China.* Cambridge: Harvard University Press. Chinese edition, trans. Lin Tiangui. 2010. Beijing: Huawen chubanshe.

TePaske, John J. 1983. "New World Silver, Castile, and the Philippines, 1590–1800." In *Precious Metals in the Late Medieval and Early Modern Worlds.* Durham: Carolina Academic Press.

Tilly, Charles. 1990. *Coercion, Capital, and European States, AD 990–1990.* Chinese edition, trans. Wei Hongzhong. 2012. Shanghai: Shanghai renmin chubanshe.

Tomoyuki, Miyazawa. 1999. "On the Tang-Song Social Transformation." *Chinese History Research Trends* 1999(6).

Tullock, Gordon. 1957. "Paper Money—A Cycle in Cathay." *The Economic History Review* 9(3):394.

Tuo, Tuo, et al. 1985. *History of the Song: Food and Commodities*. In *Veritable Records of the Qing*. 2008. Beijing: Zhonghua shuju.

Ueda, Makoto. 2014. *The Ocean and Empire: The Ming and Qing Dynasties*. Trans. Gao Yingying. Guilin: Guangxi shifan daxue chubanshe.

Wakeman, Frederic. 1985. *The Great Enterprise: The Manchu Reconstruction of Imperial Order in Seventeenth-Century China*. Berkeley: University of California Press. Chinese edition, trans. Suzhen Chen and Bao Xiaoying. 2008. Nanjing: Jiangsu renmin chubanshe.

Wallerstein, Immanuel. 1980. *The Modern World-System II: Mercantilism and the Consolidation of the European World-Economy, 1600–1750*. New York: Academic Press.

Wan, Ming. 2003. "A Preliminary Examination of the Silverization of Money in the Ming Dynasty." *Research in Chinese Economic History*.

———. 2004. "The Silverization of Money in the Ming Dynasty: A New Perspective on China's Links with the World." *Hebei Journal*.

———. 2005. *Issues and Research on Changes in Late Ming Society*. Beijing: Shangwu yinshuju.

Wan, Zhiying, and Zhou Xinghui. 2012. *Innovations in Research on Song Dynasty Monetary History*. In *Song History Research Commentaries*. P. 90.

Wang, Fangzhong. 2014. *Chronology of China's Economic History, 1842–1949*. Beijing: Zhongguo renmin daxue chubanshe.

Wang, Mingqing. 1961. *Waving the Duster*. Vol. 1. Beijing: Zhonghua shuju.

Wang, Shengduo. 1995. *Financial History of the Two Songs*. Beijing: Zhonghua shuju.

———. 2003. *Monetary History of the Two Songs*. Beijing: Shehui kexue wenxian chubanshe.

———. 2004. *Compilation of Historical Documents on the Currency of the Two Songs*. Beijing: Zhonghua shuju.

———. 2016. *History of the Song*. Vol. 23, Part 1.

Wang, Wencheng. 2011. *Research on Silverization of Currency in the Song Dynasty*. Kunming: Yunnan daxue chubanshe.

Wang, Xin. 2010. "A Comparison of China's Trade Surpluses in the Ming and Qing and Today." *International Economic Review* 2010(1).

Wang, Yeh-Chien. 1974. *Land Taxation in Imperial China, 1750–1911*. Cambridge: Harvard University Press.

———. 1981. *The Evolution of China's Modern Currency and Banks (1644–1937)*. Taipei: Academia Sinica.

———. 2003. *Collected Essays on Qing Dynasty Economic History*. Vol. 1. Taipei: Taiwan daoxiang chubanshe.

———. 2008. *Qing Dynasty Land Tax*. Beijing: Renmin chubanshe.

Weber, Max. 1905. *The Protestant Ethic and the Spirit of Capitalism.* Chinese edition, trans. Yan Kewen. 2010. Shanghai: Shanghai renmin chubanshe.

———. 1922. *Economy and Society.* Chinese edition, trans. Yan Kewen. 2010. Shanghai: Shanghai renmin chubanshe.

Wei, Sen. 2006a. "From Hayek's Spontaneous-Expansion Order Theory Viewing Smith's Dynamic of Economic Growth and Braudel's Bell Jar." *Dongyua luncong.*

———. 2006b. "Smith's Dynamic and Braudel's Bell Jar—A Possible New Angle for Studying the Historical Reasons for the Modern Rise of the Western World and the Late Qing Empire's Corresponding Decline." *Social Science Frontline.*

Wei, Wen Pin. 1914. *The Currency Problem in China.* New York: Columbia University Press.

Wei, Yuan. 1984. *A Military History of the Sacred Dynasty.* Hunan: Yuelu shushe.

Wen, Hao. 2013. *Financial Tycoons of the Republic.* Zhongguo wenshi chubanshe.

Williams, Samuel Wells. 1863. *The Chinese Commercial Guide, Containing Treaties, Tariffs, Regulations, Tables, etc., Useful in the Trade to China and Eastern Asia.* 5th edition. Hong Kong: A. Shortrede & Co.

Wong, Roy Bin. 1998. *China Transformed: Historical Change and the Limits of European Experience.* NCROL. Chinese edition, trans. Li Bozhong and Lian Lingling. 1998. Nanjing: Jiangsu renmin chubanshe.

Wood, John H. 2008. *A History of Central Banking in Great Britain and the United States.* Cambridge: Cambridge University Press. Chinese edition, trans. Chen Xiaoshuang. 2011. Shanghai caijing daxue chubanshe.

Wu, Chengming. 1995. "Research in Economics Theory and Economic History." *Economic Research* 1995(4).

———. 2002. *Collected Works.* Beijing: Zhongguo shehui kexue chubanshe.

Wu, Jingping. 1998. *Chronology of Song Ziwen's Political Career.* Fuzhou: Fujian renmin chubanshe.

———. 2016. *The Modern Chinese Finance: Through the Lens of Cooperation and Competition between Politics and Business.* Shanghai: Shanghai yuandong chubanshe.

Wu, Xiaofu. 1936. *Series on China's Currency Problems.* Shanghai: Guangming shuju.

Wu, Xingyong. 2009. *The Secret Files of Gold.* Nanjing: Jiangsu renmin chubanshe.

Xia, Xie. 1988. *Chronicle of China and the West: Opium Tax.*

Xiao, Hongying (ed.). 2008. *Inventions in the Printing Arts: Origin and Development, Biographies, Influence.* Guiyang: Guizhou keji chubanshe.

Xie, Henai. 2008. *Daily Life in China on the Eve of the Mongolian Yuan Invasion.* Beijing: Beijing daxue chubanshe.

Xie, Zhaozhi. 2012. *Wu Za Zhu.* Vol. 12. Shanghai: Shanghai guji chubanshe.

Xu, Jin. 2015. *Keynes's China Gathering.* Shanghai: Shanghai sanlian chubanshe.

———. 2016. *The Money Printers.* Beijing: Zhongxin chubanshe.

Xu, Mei. "Chao li tiao lun, No. 5."

Xu, Song. 1957. *Compiled Social Record of the Song: Food and Commodities 42.*

Yamamoto, Sugumu. 2012. *Socio-Economic History of the Qing Dynasty.* Ji'nan: Shandong huabao chubanshe.

Yan, Hongzhong. 2011. *Currency Supply, Monetary Structure and China's Economic Trends: 1650–1936*. Beijing: Jinrong yanjiu.

———. 2012. *China's Monetary and Financial System (1600–1949)*. Beijing: Zhongguo renmin daxue chubanshe.

Yan, Zhongping. 1981. "Silver Flowed into the Philippines and Silver Flowed into China." *Modern Historical Studies* 1.

———. 1989. *Economic History of Modern China (1840–1894)*. Beijing: Beijing renmin chubanshe.

———. 2012. *Selected Statistical Data in China's Recent Economic History*. Beijing: Shehui kexue chubanshe.

Yang, Duanliu. 2007. *Historical Sketch of Qing Dynasty Currency and Finance*. Wuhan: Wuhan daxue chubanshe.

Yang, Peixin. 1985. *Inflation in Old China*. Beijing: Renmin chubanshe.

Yang, Wanli. 2005. *Cheng Zhai Collection*. Vol. 30. Digital reproduction: https://archive.org/stream/06074027.cn#mode/2up.

Yang, Yinpu. 1932. *Yang's Commentaries on Chinese Finance*. Shanghai: Liming shuju.

Yao, Songling. 2014. *Draft Chronology of Mr. Zhang Gongquan*. Beijing: Zhonghua shuju.

Ye, Shi. 1961. *Shui Xin's Anthology*. Vol. 2.

Ye, Shichang. 2003. *History of Chinese Monetary Theory*. Xiamen: Xiamen daxue chubanshe.

Yeh, Kuo-chun. 2012. "Return to the Glory of International Currency." *Taiwan Banker* 2012(3).

Yi, Luoyi. 2009. *The Seeds of Destruction*. Nanjing: Jiangsu renmin chubanshe.

Young, Arthur N. 1965. *China's Wartime Finance and Inflation, 1937–1945*. Cambridge: Harvard University Press.

———. 1971. *China's Nation-Building Effort, 1927–1937: The Financial and Economic Record*. Stanford: Hoover Institute. Chinese edition. 1981.

Yu, Ying-shih. 2005. "The Function and Significance of the Imperial Civil-Service Examination System in Chinese History." *Twentieth Century*. June 2005.

Zeng, Xiongsheng. 2014. *A Comprehensive Agricultural History of China*. Beijing: Zhongguo nongye chubanshe.

Zhang, Gongquan. 1986. *History of Inflation in China*. Beijing: Wenshi ziliao chubanshe.

Zhang, Guohui. 2003. *A General Financial History of China*. Vol. 2. Beijing: Zhongguo jinrong chubanshe.

Zhang, Huixin. 1994. *Historical Narrative of Chinese Currency*. Taipei: Taiyang.

Zhang, Jiaxiang. 1925. *History of the Chinese Currency System*. Minguo daxue chubanshe.

Zhang, Jungu. 2011. *Biography of Du Yuesheng*. Beijing: Zhongguo dabaike quanshu chubanshe.

Zhang, Naiqi. 1997. *Collected Writings*. Beijing: Huaxia chubanshe.

Zhang, Ruyu. 1992. *Critical Compilation of a Multitude of Books*. Beijing: Shumu wenxian chubanshe.

Zhang, Tingyu. 1974. *History of the Ming: Food and Commodities.* Beijing: Zhonghua shuju.

Zhang, Tingyu, et al. 2000. *Qing Dynasty Documents: Currency.* Beijing: Zhonghua shuju.

Zhang, Zhongli. 1987. *Selected Treatises on China's Modern Economic History.* Shanghai: Shanghai shehui kexueyuan chubanshe.

Zhao, Yi. 1984. *Twenty-Two Historical Jottings.* Beijing: Zhonghua shuju.

Zhejiang Provincial Museum (ed.). 2015. *The Historical Course of Silver—From Silver Taels to Silver Dollars.* Beijing: Wenwu chubanshe.

Zheng, Guanying. 2008. *Warnings to a Prosperous Age.* Shanghai: Shanghai guji chubanshe.

Zheng, Yijiao. 2012. *Southern Song Currency and War.* Baoding: Hebei daxue chubanshe.

Zheng, Youkui, and Cheng Linsun. 1984. *China's Foreign Trade and Industrial Development (1840–1948).* Shanghai: Shanghai shehui kexueyuan chubanshe.

Zhou Ziqi. 1990. "Report Presented to the President to Remedy the Financial Difficulty." In *Selected Literary and Historical Documents.* Vol. 2. July 1990. Beijing: Zhongguo wenshi chubanshe. P. 463.

Zhou, Bodi. 1936. *The Silver Problem and China's Monetary Policies.* Beijing: Zhonghua shuju.

———. 1981a. *Financial History of China.* Shanghai: Shanghai renmin chubanshe.

———. 1981b. *The History of China's Financial Administration.* Shanghai: Shanghai renmin chubanshe.

Zhou, Xueguang. 2014. "From 'Huang Zongxi's Law' to the Logic of Empire: The Historical Threads of China's National Governance Logic." *Open Era* 4.

Zhou, Zuoren. 2011. *In My Own Garden.* Beijing: Beijing shiyua wenyi chubanshe.

Zhu, Jiaming. 2012. *From Freedom to Monopoly: Two Thousand Years of Chinese Monetary Economy.* Vols. 1 and 2. Taipei: Yuanliu chuban shiye gufen youxian gongsi.

Zhu, Ruixi. 1983. *Research on Song Dynasty Society.* Zhengzhou: Zhongzhou shuhua she.

Zhu, Ruixi, et al. 1998. *A Living History of Song, Liao, Western Xia and Jin Society.* Beijing: Zhongguo shehui kexue chubanshe.

Zhu, Ruixi. 2010. *Rereading Modern History.* Shanghai: Zhongxi shuju.

Zhu, Weizheng. 2015. *Rereading Modern Chinese History.* Leiden: Brill.

Zi, Yaohua. 2005. *Footsteps of the Century: The Autobiography of a Modern Financier.* Changsha: Hunan wenyi chubanshe.

Zong, Zeya. 2012. *The Qing-Japanese War.* Shijie tushu chuban.

Index

Page numbers in *italics* refer to tables.